COMPUTERS, PATTERN, CHAOS AND BEAUTY

D1250492

COMPUTERS, PATTERN, CHAOS AND BEAUTY

GRAPHICS FROM AN UNSEEN WORLD

Clifford A. Pickover

ST. MARTIN'S PRESS
NEW YORK

COMPUTERS, PATTERN, CHAOS AND BEAUTY. Copyright © 1990 by Clifford A. Pickover. All rights reserved. Printed in the United States of America. No part of this book may be used or reproduced in any manner whatsoever without written permission except in the case of brief quotations embodied in critical articles or reviews. For information, address St. Martin's Press, 175 Fifth Avenue, New York, N.Y. 10010.

Library of Congress Cataloging-in-Publication Data

Pickover, Clifford A.
    Computers, pattern, chaos, and beauty/Clifford A. Pickover.

        p.   cm.
    Includes bibliographical references.
    ISBN 0-312-06179-X (pbk.)
    1. Computer graphics.   I. Title.
T385.P5   1990
006.6—dc20 89-70068 CIP

First Paperback Edition: September 1991
10 9 8 7 6 5 4 3 2 1

To Elahe

Preface

"We are in the position of a little child entering a huge library whose walls are covered to the ceiling with books in many different tongues ... The child does not understand the languages in which they are written. He notes a definite plan in the arrangement of books, a mysterious order which he does not comprehend, but only dimly suspects."   Albert Einstein

The Fisherman's Approach

Sometimes I consider myself a fisherman. Computer programs and ideas are the hooks, rods and reels. Computer pictures are the trophies and delicious meals. A fisherman does not always know what the waters will yield; however a fisherman may know where the fishing is good, where the waters are fertile, what type of bait to use. Often the specific catch is a surprise, and this is the enjoyment of the sport. There are no guarantees. There are often unexpected pleasures. Readers are urged to participate by dipping into unknown waters. Hopefully, readers will enjoy looking at the catches or dissecting them further to learn more about their internal structures.

Adventures in Computing

This book could be subtitled "Adventures in Computing." The reader is taken on a roller-coaster ride through various scientific and artistic realms. Note that the book is intended to be a catalog of the author's published works. The reader should be forewarned that some of the presented material involves sophisticated concepts (e.g. *Chapter 3: Fourier Transforms*) while other material (e.g. *Chapter 2: Hidden Worlds*) includes very basic information. Hopefully, readers can pick and chose from the smorgasbord of topics. Some areas of the work are touched upon to give the reader just a flavor of an application. Additional information is in the referenced publications. In order to encourage reader involvement, computational hints and recipes for producing many of the figures are provided. For many readers, seeing pseudocode will clarify the concepts in a way which mere words cannot.

The book is divided into three main sections. The first part of the book gives background information on computer graphics and the creative use of computers. The second part of the book describes various graphical methods for representing and detecting patterns in complicated data. The third part of the book illustrates simple techniques for visualizing graphically interesting manifestations of chaotic behavior. The Appendix contains some exercises and mathematical recreations for students, teachers, and other imaginative readers. At the end of each chapter is a short Reading List section which often contains historical background information to the topics presented. Some of the special symbols used in this book are listed within the Glossary entry *Symbol*. In order to give credit to the source publication where portions of the author's material first appeared, and also to help the reader locate the papers in the Reference section for more details, a compact citation often appears at the end of various book sections – for example, (Pick87e, *Computers and Graphics*).

Where possible the book is aimed to scientists, artists, laypeople, programmers and students. Thus, the book is not intended for *mathematicians* looking for deep, *mathematical* information. In the same spirit as Hunter and Madachy's book *Mathematical Diversions* (1968, Van Nostrand: New York), the present book combines old and new ideas – with emphasis on the fun that the true lover of recreational computer graphics finds in doing, rather than in reading about the doing! Some information is repeated so that each chapter contains sufficient background information, and the reader may therefore skip sections if desired. The symbols [and] are used to delimit material which the reader can skip upon a casual reading.

This book does not attempt to give a detailed historical background to the field of chaos and non-linear dynamics, even though the field of chaos and the mathematics of iteration has a rich history. The computer graphical experiments in this book only hint at the important past mathematical work of others from which I have received considerable inspiration. For background, the reader should consult the various books in the reference section, and in particular, the books of Gleick (Viking, 1987), Mandelbrot (Freeman, 1983), and Moon (Wiley, 1988).

Ivars Peterson (*Science News*, 1987, vol. 132) has the right idea. He notes that mathematicians have begun to enjoy and present bizarre mathematical patterns in new ways – ways sometimes dictated as much by a sense of aesthetics as by the needs of logic. Moreover, computer graphics allows non-mathematicians to experience some of the pleasure mathematicians take in their work and to better appreciate the complicated and interesting graphical behavior of certain simple formulas.

A poster displaying high-resolution images from this book is available from: Media Magic, PO Box 507, Nicasio, California 94946.

*"Truly the gods have not from the beginning
revealed all things to mortals, but by long seeking,
mortals make progress in discovery."*

Xenophanes of Colophon

Contents

PART III
PATTERN, SYMMETRY, BEAUTY

Part I

INTRODUCTION

Chapter 1

Computers and Creativity

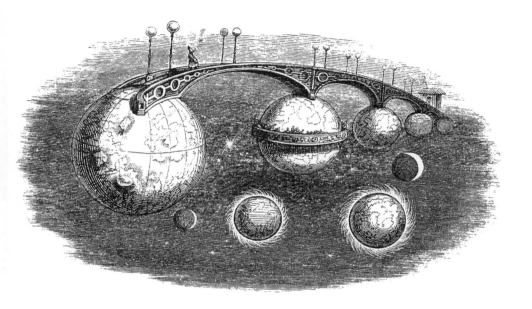

"The heavens call to you, and circle about you, displaying to you their eternal splendors, and your eye gazes only to earth."   Dante

Imagine a world with no shadows, no sun.

Imagine computing, with no mystery, no creativity, no human dreamer. The beauty and importance of computers lie mainly in their usefulness as a tool for reasoning, creating and discovering. Computers are one of our most important tools for reasoning beyond our own intuition. In order to show the eclectic nature of computer "territory," this book contains a collage of topics which have in common their highly visual nature, and each can be effectively explored using a computer.

Imagery is the heart of much of the work described in this book. To help understand what is around us, we need eyes to see it. Computers with graphics can be used to produce visual representations with a myriad of perspectives. These perspectives are demonstrated by the subjects presented in this book. The applications are varied and include fields as diverse as speech synthesis, molecular biology, mathematics, and art. Yet it is hoped that they all combine to illustrate the wonder in "lateral thinking" with computers (defined in Sect. 1.2 "Lateral Use of Computer Software Tools" on page 4).

1.1 Objectives

Where possible, the material is organized by subject area. The purpose of this book is:

1. to present several novel graphical ways of representing complicated data,
2. to show the role of the aesthetics in mathematics and to suggest how computer graphics gives an appreciation of the complexity and beauty underlying apparently simple processes,
3. to show, in general, the beauty, adventure and potential importance of creative thinking using computers,
4. to show how the computer can be used as an instrument for simulation and discovery.

1.2 Lateral Use of Computer Software Tools

"He calmly rode on, leaving it to his horse's discretion to go which way it pleased, firmly believing that in this consisted the very essence of adventures."   Cervantes, *Don Quixote*

"Lateral thinking" is a term discussed by writer/philosopher, Robert Pirsig (author of *Zen and the Art of Motorcycle Maintenance*). As he explains it, lateral thinking is reasoning in a direction not naturally pointed to by a scientific discipline. It is reasoning in a direction unexpected from the actual goal one is working toward (see also de Bono, 1975). In this book, the term "lateral thinking" is used in an extended way to indicate not only action motivated by unexpected results, but also the deliberate drift of thinking in new directions to discover what can be learned. It is also used to indicate the application of a single computer software tool to several unrelated fields.

Let's list a few examples of the lateral use of computer software tools. These examples will be discussed in greater detail later in the book. To give some personal history and examples: while creating analysis tools for speech synthesis research (Chapter 3), the author drifted laterally and examined their application to the study of the breathing motions of proteins. This naturally led to other biological molecules such as genes. In this application, the sequence of bases in a human bladder cancer gene is treated as if it were a speech waveform in order to gain a new perspective. These studies presented traditional graphics and analysis in new applications in an effort to visualize complex data.

This idea of novel ways for making complicated data understandable led to the application of Chernoff faces (cartoon faces whose facial coordinates depend on the input data). These faces can be applied to a range of sounds, mathematical equations, and genetic sequences. The faces rely on the feature-integration abilities of the human brain to condense a vast amount of data.

Does there exist an optimal representation for visual characterization and detection of significant information in data? This question, along with the face research, further stimulated my interest in the human visual system. Part of Chapter 4 discusses the use of a perceptual illusion, achieved with patterns of dots, to the characterization of subunit relationships in proteins. These patterns, called "Moire interference patterns," resemble galaxies and whirlpools. The interference patterns led to another question concerning vision and data characterization: Can symmetry operators, like the mirrors in a child's kaleidoscope, help us to understand data? To answer this question, another dot-based tool was developed; this representation is comprised of snowflake-like patterns of colored dots and is used to characterize sounds.

Intriguing even as an art form, these dot patterns may be a way of visually fingerprinting natural and synthetic sounds and of allowing researchers to detect patterns not easily captured with traditional analyses.

A short quote from Robert Pirsig can apply to the joy computer programmers, artists, and scientists often experience when experimenting on a computer:

> *"It's the sides of the mountain which sustain life, not the top. Here's where things grow."*

1.3 Reading List for Chapter 1

Two interesting books on the topics of creativity and lateral thinking are De Bono (1970) and Pirsig (1975).

Chapter 2
Hidden Worlds

"If we wish to understand the nature of the Universe we have an inner hidden advantage: we are ourselves little portions of the universe and so carry the answer within us."   Jacques Boivin, *The Heart Single Field Theory*

2.1 Digits, Symbols, Pictures

We live in a civilization where numbers play a role in virtually all facets of human endeavor. Even in our daily lives we encounter multidigit zip-codes, social security numbers, credit card numbers, and phone numbers. In many ways the requirements for ordinary living are a great deal more complicated than ever before. Digits...digits...digits.... It all seems so dry sometimes. And yet, when one gazes at a page in a scientific journal and sees a set of complicated-looking equations, such as those chosen from pages of scientific texts (Figure 2.1), a sense of satisfaction is generated: *the human mind, when aided by numbers and symbols, is capable of expressing and understanding concepts of great complexity.* Ever since "visionary" mathematical and physical relations trickled like rain onto the rooftop of 20th century man, we have begun to realize that some descriptions of nature lie beyond our traditional, unaided ways of thinking.

The *expression* of complicated relations and equations is one magnificent step – *insight* gained from these relations is another. Today, computers with graphics can be used to produce representations of data from a number of perspectives and to characterize natural phenomena with increasing clarity and usefulness. *"Mathematicians couldn't solve it until they could see it!"* a caption in a popular scientific magazine recently exclaimed when describing work done on curved mathematical surfaces (*Science Digest*, January, 1986, p. 49). In addition, cellular automata and fractals – classes of simple mathematical systems with exotic behavior – are beginning to show promise as models for a variety of physical processes (see "Genesis Equations" on page 104 and "Tesselation Automata Derived from a Single Defect" on page 295). Though the rules governing the creation of these systems are simple, the patterns they produce are complicated and some-

$$F(t, \omega) = \frac{1}{2\pi} \int_{-\infty}^{\infty} s^*(t - \tau/2) e^{-i\tau\omega} s(t + \tau/2) \, d\tau$$

$$N = 1 \;\; if \; (\exists k \in A) \ni \left[\left(\frac{F_k - L}{H - L} \right) \eta \geq j \;\; \cap \;\; \left(\frac{F_k - L}{H - L} \right) \eta \right]$$

$$\mathbf{n}_\alpha(\mathbf{x}) \cdot \left[\mathbf{D}_S^+(\mathbf{x}) - \mathbf{D}_S^-(\mathbf{x}) \right] = \Omega \tag{8}$$

$$\frac{\partial \phi(\mathbf{x})}{\partial n_+} = -2\pi\sigma(\mathbf{x}) + \int_S d^2x' \, \sigma(\mathbf{x}') \, \mathbf{n}(\mathbf{x}) \cdot \nabla \frac{1}{|\mathbf{x} - \mathbf{x}'|} \tag{B.4}$$

$$\phi_C(\mathbf{x}) \equiv \sum_i \frac{\varepsilon_{L(i)}}{\varepsilon_i} \int_{C_i} d^2x' \, G(\mathbf{x}, \mathbf{x}') \sigma_i(\mathbf{x}') \;, \tag{3}$$

$$\phi_S(\mathbf{x}) \equiv \sum_\alpha \frac{\varepsilon_{K(\alpha)}}{\varepsilon_0} \int_{S_\alpha} d^2x' \, G(\mathbf{x}, \mathbf{x}') \sigma_\alpha(\mathbf{x}') \;, \tag{4}$$

$$= -(\varepsilon_\alpha^+ - \varepsilon_\alpha^-) \sum_i \frac{\varepsilon_{L(i)}}{\varepsilon_i} \int_{C_i} d^2x' \, [\mathbf{n}_\alpha(\mathbf{x}) \cdot \nabla G(\mathbf{x}, \mathbf{x}')] \, \sigma_i(\mathbf{x}') \;.$$

Figure 2.1. *The symbols of mathematics.*

times seem almost random, like a turbulent fluid flow or the output of a cryptographic system.

Today, in almost all branches of the scientific world, computer graphics is helping to provide insight and to reveal hidden relationships in complicated systems. Figure 2.2 is just one example of the use of graphics to represent the behavior of mathematical functions. Notice the complexity of the behavior exhibited by the function used to create Figure 2.2 – behavior mathematicians could not fully appreciate before computers could display it.

Like computer models of a host of natural phenomena such as vortices, fluid flow, and other chaotic (irregular) systems, pictures such as these reveal an unpredictable, exciting and visually attractive universe.

2.2 Computers and Art

> *"Salvador Dali once exploded a bomb filled with nails against a copper plate, producing a striking but random pattern. Many other artists have also utilized explosives in their work, but the results have generally been unpredictable."* Febr. 1989, *Scientific American*

Not only can computers and graphics be used in counting and measuring, but they also are of enormous help in producing visual art (Figure 2.3). (See the

Figure 2.2. *Mathematics and beauty.* Appealing as an art form, this intricate diagram is called a Halley map, and it can be used to represent properties of numerical methods. The generating function is $z \to z^7 - 1$ (see "Numerical Approximation Methods" on page 275).

Reading List at the end of the chapter for more information on computer art.) The break between artistic and scientific pursuits is often apparent today. Whereas the earlier thinkers pursued science and art in the light of guiding principles such as harmony and proportion, today some hold the view that science stifles the artistic spirit. Nevertheless, the computer is capable of creating images of captivating beauty and power. Techniques such as animation, color and shading all help to create fantastic effects (Figure 2.4).

In much of the work in this book, beauty, science and art are intertwined, and – judging from the response from readers – this contributes to the fascination of these approaches for both scientists and laypeople. From an artistic standpoint, mathematical equations provide a vast and deep reservoir from which artists can draw. New algorithms ("recipes"), such as those outlined in this book, interact with such traditional elements as form, shading and color to produce futuristic images. The mathematical recipes function as the artist's assistant, quickly taking care of much of the repetitive and sometimes tedious detail. By becoming familiar with advanced computer graphics, the computer artist may change our perception of art.

2.3 Computer Graphics: Past and Present

"Computers are useless. They can only give you answers. "   Pablo Picasso

In the beginning of the modern computer age, computer graphics consisted of the multitude of Abe Lincolns, Mona Lisas, and Charlie Brown cartoons spewed forth from crude character line-printers in campuses and laboratories. Better hardware led to better images. In the 1970s we saw an increasing amount of computer animation, computer generated-commercials and films – and Pacman. Today, in science, computer graphics is used to reveal a variety of subtle patterns in nature and mathematics. The field of computer graphics is very important in: 1) revealing hidden correlations and unexpected relationships (and as an adjunct to numerical analysis), 2) simulating nature, and 3) providing a source of general scientific intuition. Naturally, these three uses overlap. Pseudo-color, animation, three-dimensional figures, and a variety of shading schemes are among the techniques used to reveal relations not easily visible in more traditional data representations.

2.4 Computers: Past and Present

Taking a step back: how long ago did computing really begin? Probably, the first calculating machine to help expand the mind of man was the abacus. The abacus is a manually operated storage device which aids a *human* calculator. It consists of beads and rods and originated in the Orient more than 5,000 years ago. Archeologists have since found geared calculators, dated back to 80 BC, in the sea off northwestern Crete. Since then, other primitive calculating machines have evolved, with a variety of esoteric sounding names, including: Napier's bones (consisting of sticks of bones or ivory), Pascal's arithmetic machine (utilizing a mechanical gear system), Leibniz' Stepped Reckoner, and Babbage's analytical engine (which used punched cards) (see Gardner, 1986, for more detail).

Continuing with more history: the Atanasoff-Berry computer, made in 1939, (Mackintosh, 1988), and the 1500 vacuum tube Colossus, were the first program-

Figure 2.3. *Complexity and simplicity.* This iteration map represents the complicated behavior of a simple function, $z \to z^2 + \mu$. (See "More Beauty from Complex Variables" on page 113 for more information on this plot).

mable electronic machines. The Colossus first ran in 1943 in order to break a German coding machine named Enigma. The first computer able to store programs was the Manchester University Mark I. It ran its first program in 1948. Later, the transistor and the integrated circuit enabled micro-miniaturization and led to the modern computer.

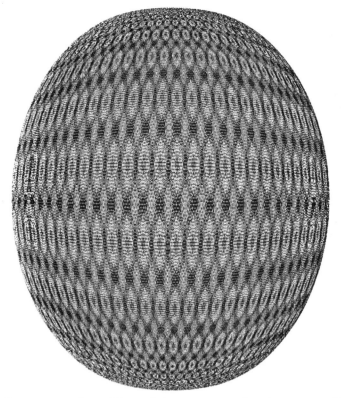

Figure 2.4. *Computers and art.* Many of the ornaments of modern man and his ancient cultures consist of symmetrical and repeating designs. Here, this tiled egg-shape is produced from a simple generating formula, $z_{xy} = \alpha(\sin x + \sin y)$ (see "Synthesizing Ornamental Textures" on page 227).

In 1988, one of the world's most powerful and fastest computers is the liquid-cooled Cray-2 produced by Cray Research. It performs 250 million floating point arithmetic operations per second − much more expensive than the abacus or Napier's bones, but also much faster!

2.5 The Human Brain vs. the Computer Brain

2.5.1 The Human Brain

While it's clear that the computer "brain" is vastly superior to man's brain in certain tasks, for perspective it is useful to mention some of the lesser known capacities of the human mind-machine.

The human brain weighs about three pounds and is made of roughly 10 billion neurons, each neuron receiving connections from perhaps 100 other

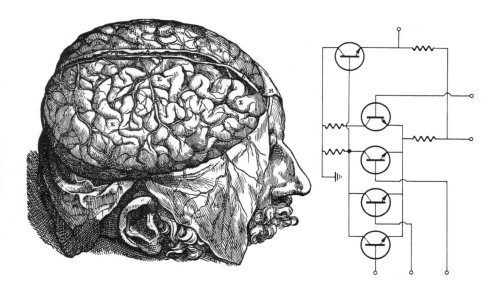

Figure 2.5. *The human brain and an electronic circuit.*

neurons and connecting to still 100 more (Figure 2.5). The web of interconnections is so complex that the whole cortex can be thought of as one entity of
integrated activity. Many neurobiologists believe that memory, learning, emo-
tions, creativity, imagination – all the unique elements of human character – will
ultimately be shown to reside in the precise patterns of synaptic interconnections
in the human brain. The importance of the brain's system of pathways has led
some scientists to hypothesize an *equation for consciousness* itself: $C = f_1(n)f_2(s)$
(Rose, 1976). Consciousness C is represented on the cellular level by a function of
neural cell number, n, and connectivity s. It has been shown that small systems of
neurons (i.e., under 10,000 neurons), such as those in simple invertebrates, are
capable of learning and memory. In 1987, computer models of neural networks

helped researchers begin to untangle the complexities of biological processes such as vision.[1]

2.5.2 Human Computers

We know that the human brain is capable of profound and important functions such as creativity and imagination, but often little is said of its computing and storage capabilities. In some instances, the human memory can be great. For example, in 1974, one individual recited 16,000 pages of Buddhist texts without error. Later, a 23-year old Indian man recited π from memory to 31,811 places in about 3 hours. (Note that in 1987 a NEC SX-2 supercomputer *calculated* π to more than 134 million digits. In 1989, the Chudnovsky brothers, two Columbia University mathematicians, computed over one billion digits of π using a Cray 2 and an IBM 3090-VF computer.)

As an example of computational capabilities of the human brain, Willem Klein in 1981 was able to extract the 13th root of a 100-digit number in about one minute. In addition, there are the autistic savants – people who can perform mental feats at a level far beyond the capacity of a normal person but whose overall IQ is very low.

2.6 New Applications of Calculating: A Sampling and Digression

In many branches of science, progress is enhanced by finding new ways to calculate and simulate. Among these fields are plasma physics, astrophysics, molecular biology, and geology. In music and speech, computers are making an impact. With the increasing availability and improvement of voice synthesis technology, singing synthesizers may herald the next revolution in music, much as did the electronic music synthesizers of the 1970s. Not only will computers be singing songs, but they will be writing the songs they sing (see "Singing Computers" on page 23).

In medicine, carefully designed computer programs and systems assist in making medical diagnoses. Psychiatrists at the Salt Lake City Veterans' Administration Hospital have been testing such systems to diagnose mental illness. A patient is first greeted by a human receptionist who takes him to a private room containing a computer terminal. A computer program then presents a battery of tests, and twenty minutes later a staff psychiatrist reviews the questions to make a final judgement about the person's condition. Diagnosis by computer programs has meant substantial savings in time and money for the patient, and, most importantly, computer diagnosis has proved to be remarkably accurate. The computer never tires, never is biased – and the impersonal relationship appears actually to help. Another medical use is in the hospital operating room which has become

---

[1] Some more brain trivia: Information theorist John von Neumann once estimated that the memories stored in the human brain during an average lifetime would amount to approximately 280 quintillion (2.8×10^{20}) bits, assuming nothing is ever forgotten.

increasingly colonized by "electronic nurses": computers that allow doctors to regulate operating-room lighting, adjust instruments, or even call "scalpel" with just the punch of a keyboard.

Advances in bioengineering allow, in some cases, the restoration of sight to the blind and hearing to the deaf. Computer-driven prostheses have been designed to take over the function of body organs such as bladders, blood vessels, testicles, and fallopian tubes. Perhaps one of the greatest advances in computers and medicine is the display and reconstruction of the interior of portions of the body (tomography). Magnetoencephalography and magnetocardiography now describe the subtle magnetic fields emanating from the brain and heart.

In short, computer calculations are now beginning to radically *change how scientists pursue and conceptualize problems*, and computer models open up entire new areas of exploration. In fact, of all the changes in scientific methodology, probably none is more important than the use of computers. The sheer amount of data generated by experiments is so large that comparisons and conclusions could not be made without computers. For example, massive DNA sequences have been uncovered – and only with the computer can hidden correlations be found within these bases in the genetic materials of organisms. Not unlike the search for extraterrestrial signals from space, scientists try to reconstruct "messages" and patterns in DNA strands, mathematical progressions, and a range of natural phenomena.

Educational areas vastly benefit from computerization. With appropriate software, university networks of personal workstations are facilitating remedial learning. Students are also using the computer as a tool for learning computational physics. The computer-assisted videodisc combines computer and video technique in an instructional tool which is changing the way chemistry, physics, and engineering is taught. Even Chaucer has become computerized; for example, a student studying Chaucer's *Canterburry Tales* can now display the original text side-by-side with notes on the meanings of individual words and a modern English translation.

The remarkable panoply of computer applications seems to be growing: computers play a role in the design of other computers, in video analysis systems, in protein structure determination and design, cryptographic systems, robotics, and molecular evolution studies. Computer-drawn 3-D structures of viruses, such as polio viruses, may lead us to new cures. Thunderstorm modelling today involves the simulation of the growth of a single cloud into storms that can produce tornadoes. Extensive earthquake-detecting systems consist of the interplay of computers, instrumentation, telemetry and data reduction. The search for extraterrestrial intelligence employs the automatic detection of interstellar signals and requires sophisticated computers. Flight-deck automation is changing the role of the human pilot. Computer information services offer biographies and high-resolution graphics of the FBI's most wanted fugitives (*Science Digest*, 1986, January, p. 15). Now some computers not only learn how to draw artistically in the style of famous artists, but actually improve with practice (Kluger, 1987). (Readers interested in computer programs which mimic the artwork of Miro should see Kirsh and Kirsh, 1988.)

Computer-aided design (CAD) is rendering the blueprint obsolete. CAD programs can allow on-screen tours inside buildings, and future systems will be able to simulate the flow of sunlight at various times of the day. Finally, just a week before this chapter was written, an article appeared which described the use of high-speed computers to create the perfect bowling ball! After seven years of research, a precisely weighted polyester ball has been created that is almost entirely free of minute wiggles and bounces that bedevil the average bowler.

2.7 One Final Word

"Au fond de l'Inconnu pour trouver du nouveau" (Into the depths of the Unknown in quest of something new)   Charles Baudelaire, in *Le Voyage*

If the properties we assign to the natural world are partly expressions of the way we think and our capacity for understanding, then the introduction of new tools such as the computer will *change* those properties. The computer, like a microscope, expands the range of our senses. The world made visible by the computer seems limitless.

2.8 Reading List for Chapter 2

Gardner (1986) gives additional information on one of the early computing machines mentioned in this chapter (Napier's bones). Mackintosh (1988) describes the early 1939 Atanasoff-Berry computer. For interesting speculative information on the brain, computers, and consciousness, see Rose (1976).

There has been a well-developed history of computer art since the 1960s. Some references to this work are given in "Reading List for Chapter 13" on page 238. Of particular interest is J. Reichardt's book *Cybernetic Serendipity: The Computer and the Arts* which contains a very stimulating collection of papers on the alliance of art and technology. J. Kluger's 1987 article in *Discover Magazine* presents some beautiful artwork from many contemporary computer artists such as Yoichiro Kawaguchi, Jennifer Bartlett, Larry Rivers, Harold Cohen, and Melvin Prueitt, just to name a few. The reader is also directed to the wonderful journal *Leonardo* (2030 Addison St, Suite 400 Berkeley, CA 94704) which is devoted to the interaction of the arts, sciences, and technology. The journal focuses on the visual arts and also addresses music, video, and performance.

The endpiece figure for this chapter is entitled "A Twilight Friend," and the computer graphic illustration is from a collection of the author's mathematically derived sculptures entitled *I Have Dreams at Night*. Only three trigonometric curves are used to shape the creature's body.

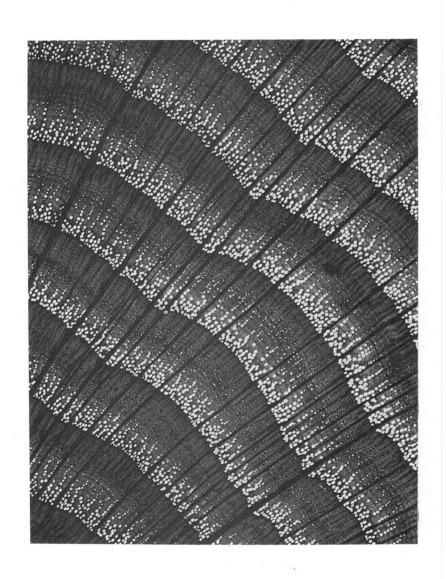

Part II

REPRESENTING NATURE

Chapter 3

Fourier Transforms
(The Prisms of Science)

"It is indeed a surprising and fortunate fact that nature can be expressed by relatively low-order mathematical functions."　　　　Rudolf Carnap

"Art, literature, and music create order. Science searches for order that already exists."　　　　Anonymous

We live in a world filled with a maze of aural and visual patterns. Later chapters deal with the characterization of patterns residing in infinitely complicated mathematical worlds. In this chapter we are interested in representing the many facets of nature, that is, in finding patterns in phenomena as diverse as animal vocalizations, music and the genetic sequences of cancer genes. To help characterize this cacophony of complicated data, we first review a famous mathematical technique called the Fourier transformation. Like a prism which separates white light passing through it into its rainbow-colored components, the Fourier transform give us an idea of the hidden components in complicated input. The varied topics in the following sections all have in common the fact that the Fourier transform was used as a tool for finding patterns.

3.1 Fourier Analysis: A Digression and Review

The advent of the personal computer simplifies explorations of the patterns in nature. Let us begin gradually, with the introduction of a simple sine wave. A sine wave is a mathematical function that has unique and important properties. Usually it is graphed as a wiggly curve that periodically rises and falls. Mathematically, the sine wave has two attributes: amplitude and frequency.[2] A sine wave can be represented by the equation $y(t) = A \sin(2\pi f t)$, where A is the amplitude or maximum displacement of a varying quantity from its average value. f is the frequency, which tells us about the number of peaks occurring per

---

[2] Technically, a sine wave has a third attribute, "phase," which describes how the sine wave is shifted in time. This attribute will be discussed in the following chapter.

second, and t represents time.[3] The higher the frequency, the more times the sine wave goes up and down each second. f is often expressed in cycles per second or *Hertz*. The sound heard from a loudspeaker producing air pressure varying sinusoidally in time is a "pure tone."

Generally speaking, a waveform can be represented as the sum of a group of sinusoids. To those who are knowledgeable in mathematics, this statement is equivalent to saying that one can represent a wave by a Fourier series. For example, a complicated wave can actually be constructed by summing three sine waves: $y(t) = 3 \sin(2\pi 100t) + 5 \sin(2\pi 500t) + 10 \sin(2\pi 1500t)$. This equation represents a Fourier series, named after the French mathematician Joseph Fourier (1768-1830). What Fourier showed is that the behavior of the most complicated wave-shape can be described in terms of sines and cosines. If we had some way to solve for the amplitudes of each frequency component, we could decompose a function into its sinusoidal components and find the amplitude of each component. In fact, solving for the amplitude(s) is relatively simple. The process is called a Fourier transformation, and simple pseudocode is included here for its computation.[4] Usually what is plotted is the energy, or *"power"*, at each frequency; power is calculated from the square of the amplitudes. In the previous equation, all A's are zero, except for three frequencies. A *power spectrum*, computed from the Fourier transform, is visually shouting at the viewer, "hey, your input has repeating features which occur at three different, prominent frequencies." The three peaks indicate three important periodicities: one with frequency 100, one with frequency 500, and another with frequency 1500. For more mathematical information on the power spectrum, see Koopmans (1974). Pseudocode 3.1 shows the necessary steps for power spectrum computation.

[The operation in the inner DO loop is essentially an averaging of the product of the analyzed signal and a sine and cosine of each examined frequency. The method in the pseudocode is more rigorously known as a *discrete Fourier transform* and it allows one to compute the energy of each sinusoidal component with frequency, f (Morgan, 1984).]

Of course, most phenomena of nature are not nearly as simple as in the previous waveform example (see speech waveform in next section). Figure 3.1 contrasts an example of a three-dimensional power spectrum for the waveform representing sounds of a speech synthesizer and a human saying the word "seventeen." The 3-D power spectrum is an assemblage of 2-D spectra (such as in the

---

[3] We often think of sinusoidal fluctuations solely in terms of "time," for example, the fluctuation of air pressure as a function of time. However "time" is just one common variable in which physical fluctuations are considered; another common variable would be "space," as in the sinusoidal variation of heat as a function of distance from a source.

[4] For readers seeking a more complete formulation, the Fourier transform $S(\omega)$ of the time waveform $s(t)$ is often expressed rigorously as: $S(\omega) = \int s(t)e^{-i\omega t}dt$. $\omega = 2\pi f$. See Koopmans (1974) for more details on theory.

```
ALGORITHM: How to create a power spectrum
VARIABLES:  TimeInterval - the time between data points (seconds)
            NPTS          - the number of original data points.
INPUT:   Input(t) - waveform as a function of time.
OUTPUT:  Power(f) - amount of energy at each
         frequency (Hz).
Notes:   The power spectrum is useful for detecting patterns in
  complicated waveforms. Simply plot Power(f) vs. f. Peaks
  should occur at prominent frequencies.
  Real(f) and Imag(f) are simply real-valued arrays which hold
  intermediate values needed in the computation. See referenced
  books for windowing techniques used to improve spectrum.
─────────────────────────────────────────────────────────────
twopi = 6.283; TimeInterval =  0.0001 (* sec. *)
MAXF = 1/(2*TimeInterval);          (* set the highest frequency *)
DO f = 1 to MAXF;              (* x-axis range is 1 to MAXF (Hz) *)
  real(f),image(f) = 0;            (* initialize for summation *)
  arg=twopi*f*TimeInterval;
  DO i = 1 to NPTS;                (* Loop over points in input *)
    real(f) = real(f) + input(i)*cos(arg*i);
    imag(f) = imag(f) + input(i)*sin(arg*i);
  END;
  (* compute power spectrum - amount of energy at each f *)
  Power(f) = real(f)**2 + imag(f)**2;
END;
```

Pseudocode 3.1. *How to create a power spectrum.*

simple sine wave example power spectra) stacked through time to help us see how the occurrence of different frequencies changes through time.[5]

In the next sections, a variety of applications will be presented in which the 3-D Fourier transform has been used to analyze and detect patterns in data. Though the applications are varied, the idea that binds them is the use of this standard analysis tool in new ways. After one has developed a tool for analysis in a specific area, it can sometimes be applied to totally unrelated fields. For example, in the following section, the synthesis of a singing chorus by computer is discussed. Here, a 3-D power spectrum was used to examine the frequency composition of the various vocal parts.

3.2 Singing Computers

Speech synthesizers are common; we hear talking toasters, microwave ovens, scales, toys, and cars. These may seem like unimportant applications, but as devices become more complex some will become unworkable without speech. As equipment manufacturers begin to add sensors to determine different conditions, hazard monitoring by visual means alone will become difficult and dangerous. New speech products are also aiding the blind (for an excellent review of speech

---

[5] The term "spectrogram" is often used in place of 3-D power spectrum. A 2-D spectrogram is similar to the 3-D frequency composition maps except that mountain height is represented by darkness on the graph.

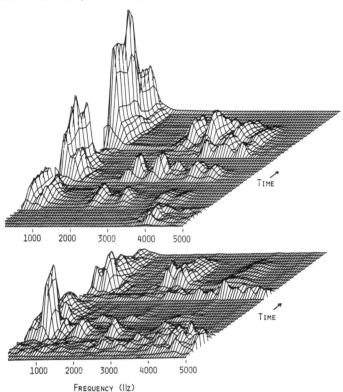

Figure 3.1. *Three-dimensional power spectrum for speech.* Graphs are computed for a synthesizer (top) and human (bottom) saying the word "seventeen." Time goes into the back of the page. The heights of the various maxima give an indication of how loud a particular frequency is. Frequency goes from 0 Hz (left) to 5000 Hz (right). By comparing the various mountain peaks, researchers are able to understand why a synthesizer does not always sound human.

synthesis, see Morgan (1984) and Witten (1982)). Most of these methods have one limitation – they have "canned" or recorded speech stored in their memory chips. Of greater interest are techniques for synthesizing a potentially unlimited variety of continuous speech utterances. With the method of synthesis discussed here, 11 parameters (Figure 3.2 shows these parameters in bubbles) are changed 100 times a second to control the output sound. (Using fewer than 11 parameters produced a less intelligible vocal output.) These parameters control such factors as how loudly vowels are spoken relative to consonants, and also the frequencies of *filters* which simulate various vocal tract resonances known as *formants*. As a useful analogy, think of a coffee filter which lets the coffee liquid go through but retains the coffee grounds. Similarly, an audio filter permits some frequencies to "go through," while stopping others. Filters consist of mathematical formulae which act somewhat like the tone knob on a hi-fi system – turning the knob, or

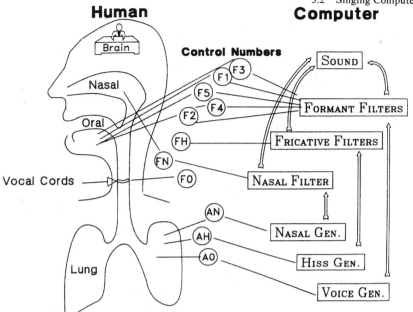

Figure 3.2. *How can computers sing?* In humans, the lungs act as a power supply forcing air through the vibrating vocal cords. In certain speech synthesizers, simple waveform generators substitute for the lungs. These are marked vowel, nasal, and fricative generators in the diagram. Filters shape the waveform further (taking the place of the changing vocal tract shape).

altering the filter equation, reshapes the frequency characteristics of the resulting sound. The reader may be interested in viewing pseudocode for producing a simple singing sound (Pseudocode 3.2). The code is presented here without a detailed explanation of all the variables. For more information on filter theory, see Witten (1982) and Morgan (1984). [For readers interested in more detail, the filter in the pseudocode produces a waveform with constant center frequency and bandwidth. Bandwidth controls the spread of frequencies. In synthetic singing, both bandwidth and band center vary slowly and smoothly, since they change as a result of motion of articulators (such as the tongue). The filter in the pseudocode is known as a second-order resonance filter.]

Speech production uses generating functions which simulate the air pressure waves produced by the lungs. These simple pressure waveforms are then shaped by filter functions in order to produce a more complicated speech-like signal. In other words, the generator functions simulate the pulses of air through the lungs and mouth. [For those already familiar with this field's terminology, the 11 control bytes which guide the synthesizer are: AN (nasal amplitude), FN (frequency of nasal resonance), F1, F2, F3, F4, F5 (frequencies of formants 1,2,3,4 and 5), A0 (voice amplitude), AH (hiss amplitude), FH (primary fricative frequency), F0 (fundamental frequency), and C0 (binary data, controlling: aspiration/frication, formant bandwidths (f1, f2, f3, f4, f5), and hiss modulation).

```
ALGORITHM: A FILTER TO PRODUCE A SINGING
WAVEFORM "M" (as in "mom")
```

```
INPUT:      freq - formant frequency of a singing sound
OUTPUT:     a waveform (amplitude vs. time)
VARIABLES: freq, bw
Notes:  If the waveform is converted to sound, it should sound
 like a steady state nasal sound. "Output(i)" must be initialized
 with a simple driving function such as a sine wave with f=120 Hz
 to simulate puffs of air through the vocal cords.
```

```
(*  center frequency of resonance (Hertz)    *)
freq = 260;         (* center frequency       *)
bw   = 100;         (* bandwidth of resonance  *)
npts = 1000;        (* number of waveform points *)
fs   = 10000        (* sample at 10,000 samples per sec    *)
t2pi=6.2831853/fs;
if gender = 'FEMALE' then freq = freq * 1.15;
y2n=0;y1n=0;
(*------ calculate filter coefficients ---------------*)
bb = exp(-bw*t2pi);
aa = 2.0 * exp(-(bw/2)*t2pi) * cos(freq*t2pi);
cc = 1 - aa + bb;
(*------- apply the filter to npts of data------------*)
do i = 1 to npts;
  output(i) = (cc*output(i))+(aa*y1n)-(bb*y2n);
  y2n = y1n;   y1n = output(i);
end;
```

Pseudocode 3.2. *A filter to produce a singing sound.*

This sequence of control data, after having been passed through the synthesizer and a digital-to-analog converter, results in speech output.]

A typical speech waveform (amplitude vs. time) looks like:

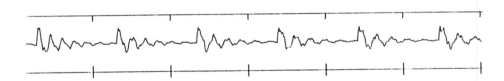

In order to establish the feasibility of using a synthetic speech system for producing a high-quality singing ensemble, the vocal parts of an excerpt of Handel's Hallelujah chorus were generated and mixed. The 3-D power spectrum (energy vs. frequency vs. time, discussed in the last section) was useful in analyzing and shaping the sounds (Figure 3.3). As suggested in the last section, one can look at the various spectral prominences and see the overall frequency composition and the relative loudness of vowels and consonants. One can also make comparisons with human speech. The spectrum from one of the synthetic voices is included so that the reader can visualize the complexity of the various mountain peaks representing the frequencies in the singing voice.

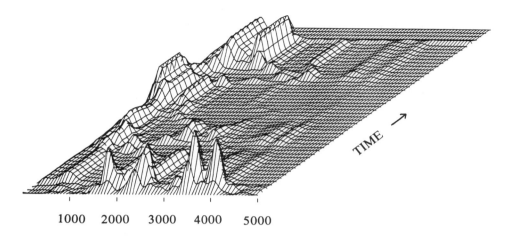

1000   2000   3000   4000   5000

FREQUENCY (HERZ)

Figure 3.3. *Computer chorus.* This three-dimensional map was used to analyze the synthetic singing of the Hallelujah chorus. In particular, this was computed for the synthetic bass singing voice: "Hal-le-lu-jah!" Again, loudness of the different frequencies is represented by height of the various hills.

The Hallelujah chorus is a piece from *The Messiah*, Handel's most successful and best-known oratorio, composed in the year 1741. The soprano, alto, tenor, and bass voices were each created separately and subsequently combined with a multi-track recorder. Short pieces introducing the work have appeared in popular magazines such as *Omni* (Rivlin, 1986) and business journals such as *Voice News* (Creitz, 1984). The most detailed report appears in *Computer Tech. Rev.* (see references). For more information on precisely how to generate the chorus, see these articles. Through this interesting exercise, it is apparent that with the increasing availability and improvement of voice synthesis technology, singing synthesizers may herald the next *revolution* in music, much as did the electronic music synthesizers of the 1970s.

Mormon Tabernacle Choir, watch out! Even the most proficient soprano or "basso profundo" is limited in the range, duration, and timbre of notes able to be generated due to the physical constraints of the vocal apparatus. The machine discussed here (Figure 3.2) has no such limits, and future composers will no doubt create songs which only synthesizers can sing. As stated earlier, not only will computers be singing songs, but they will be writing the songs they sing. In a preliminary exploration of this concept, programs were created which produce lyrics from lists containing 10 categories of English parts of speech (nouns, verbs, adjectives, etc.). Simple grammatical rules were used. Subsequently these lyrics were spoken by a commercially available voice synthesizer (Speech Plus PR2020 speech synthesizer) and mixed with several musical tracks. As strange as these songs sounded, they're just the first step. Using graphics, non-human, vowel-like sounds were constructed (by changing the vocal tract resonances), and it is clear that such novel near-human sounds can provide the musician with an entirely unexplored milieu within which to work. Perhaps similar speech systems will be developed for use by individuals dedicated to applying the resources of modern technology to the needs and problems of contemporary musical expression. (Pick88b, *Computer Tech. Rev.*)

3.3 Bach, Beethoven, The Beatles

In the last section, graphical representations of the 3-D Fourier transform were presented for synthetic and human speech sounds. Another useful application of the 3-D Fourier Transform is in the area of musical score representation. In this application the output spectrum is plotted as intensity vs. frequency vs. position in the melodic sequence of notes (explained below).

Various techniques of music visualization, music transcription, melody storage, and melody matching have been proposed (see Mitroo, 1979, and Dillon and Hunter, 1982). However, none of these methods has had as their primary focus the mathematical characterization of melody patterns using an interactive graphics system with a wide variety of controlling parameters. Spectra have been used to characterize instruments, voices, and large mixed musical ensembles (Cogan, 1984). In the work described in this section, a research system was developed which accepts as input a coded version of the musical score and subsequently computes digital spectrograms and topographic spectral distribution functions (another name for "power spectra") of melodic sequences.

While the power spectral analysis of instrument sounds, such as violins, has significantly advanced our understanding of psychoacoustics, it should be stressed that the methods presented in this section are sensitive to the periodicities in the melodic pitch sequence, and they do not have as an input a traditional acoustic sound source. The computer is not analyzing time waveforms as in the last section. Therefore, such parameters as loudness, attack, and timbre are not characterized. What is analyzed is something akin to the frequencies of the progression of hills and valleys of the musical score (which themselves represent fundamental frequencies of notes on a keyboard). The sounds are not analyzed.

Both the spectrogram and 3-D power spectrum present melodic sequence data in a way which allows patterns to be visually detected. As input, the ups and downs of a score were used (thereby producing an input resembling a picket fence). As output, 3-D maps were computed. A range of classical and contemporary pieces were tested. Duration-weighted mean and standard deviation of the input sequence of notes can be reported; for example, of the tested pieces, standard deviations ranged from a low of 49 Hertz for "Let the Sun Shine In" (from the rock opera "Hair") to a high of 371 Hertz for "Flight of the Bumblebee" (by Rimsky-Korsakoff). The resultant displays contain a rich variety of spectral features. The various mountain peaks indicate prominent periodicities and patterns in the musical score. The classical pieces tested appear

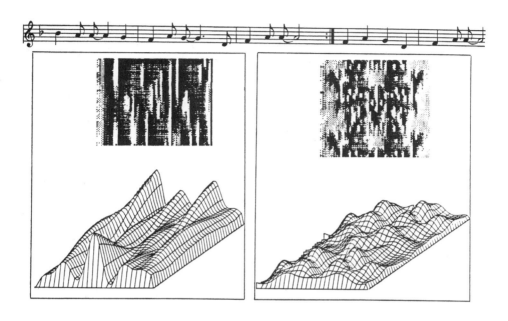

Figure 3.4. *Musical scores.* The hills and valleys of musical scores (top) can be analyzed with the same tool used in the previous figures. Top: spectrogram. Bottom: 3-D power spectrum. Here, the three-dimensional plots' axes are: intensity, frequency, and position in the melodic sequence of notes. Songs shown are *Cantata No. 96 Aria. Ach, ziehe die Seele mit Seilen der Liebe*, by J. S. Bach (left), and *The Entertainer (a Ragtime Two-Step)*, by Scott Joplin (right). High frequency patterns are shown towards the right of each of these "fingerprints."

to have a greater number of spectral prominences than do the more contemporary ones, and of the seven tested musical sequences, the Bach piece shows the greatest spectral amplitudes – followed closely by Chopin (Figure 3.4). Interestingly, the music of Frederic Chopin has been previously represented by a simple bar graph of the notes on the musical staff (by D. Hofstadter in *Scientific American*). His graph also suggests visually distinctive, regular patterns of the melodic sequence. In general, both Bach and Chopin (who revered Bach's music) were especially interested in the forms and patterns of music.

Many music researchers have yet to incorporate the power of the computer in their theorizing, and by far the most prevalent methods of computer analysis have involved the simple tallying of such features as "the number of C-sharps" in a composition (for a recent review of the research on music and artificial intelligence, see Roads (1985)). While there are theories to describe musical patterns and progressions, no current methods exist which truly distinguish compositions which will touch man's spirit from those which will not. However, it may be possible to use spectra, like those described here, as digital "fingerprints" for either certain historical musical eras or for certain composers, much as similar analyses are used in forensic voice identification and authentication.

Theories of musical quality are still primarily descriptive and do not allow one to create a new piece of extreme aesthetic interest. Those knowledgeable in noise theory will appreciate R. Voss's demonstration that melodies generated using $1/f^{\beta}$ noise generators produce progressions closest to "real" music when $\beta = 1$ (compared with $\beta = 0$ or $\beta = 2$).[6] However, none of the results would be judged as a sophisticated composition of a specific type of music. With the analysis routines presented here, we would certainly predict that a power spectrum with just one spectral peak corresponds to an input melody which is boring. Would it be possible to state that a certain number of peaks per unit time is most appealing for most people? This question remains unanswered. However, it may be possible to start with the 3-D map, isolate prominent spectral peaks, shift minor ones, and then inverse transform the spectra to create a new piece with characteristics of a particular author or musical era. (For more information on these topics, see Pick86b, *Computer Music J.*)

3.4 Breathing Proteins

This book's Introduction discusses the lateral use of computer software tools. The topics in this section and the previous section are good examples. The 3-D surface produced by a Fourier transform is used commonly in speech analysis. In this section, the same tools are used to study the "breathing motions" of proteins where the protein size-changes are represented as a waveform input to a Fourier transform.

As background, proteins are the structural building blocks of life and the catalysts for life's chemical reactions. Like all matter at room temperature, the protein molecules are continually vibrating due to thermal energy (M. Karplus has conducted extensive work in this area; see, for example, Karplus and McCammon (1979)). When large groups of atoms in the protein move in unison, this is sometimes referred to as "breathing" of the protein molecule. A complete description of a globular protein requires not only a static three-dimensional x-ray structure, but also an understanding of its flexibility and the role that structural fluctuations play in the protein's function. Two useful ways of describing the frequency composition of the breathing motions of globular proteins are the spectrogram and three-dimensional power spectrum, representations similar to those frequently used in the field of speech analysis (see sections "Fourier Analysis: A Digression and Review" on page 21 and "Singing Computers" on

---

[6] This method produces a pattern of numbers with greater correlations than totally random "white" noise.

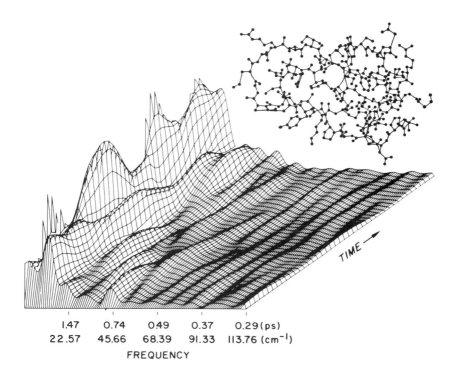

Figure 3.5. *Representing the motions of a breathing protein.* This three-dimensional map (bottom) computed from a Fourier transform gives an indication of the fluctuations in the shape of a small protein, bovine pancreatic trypsin inhibitor (top). 96 picoseconds (1 ps = 1×10^{-12} s) of data are represented in this plot.

page 23). In this section, we are most interested in low frequency vibrations of globular proteins which correspond to the collective oscillations of atoms from many different amino acids. Fluctuations in radii of gyration (R_g) (defined below) provide a sensitive way to characterize such concerted motions of proteins. One protein of interest is bovine pancreatic trypsin inhibior (BPTI), a small globular protein of molecular weight 6,500 daltons, consisting of one polypeptide chain with 58 amino acids and three disulfide bonds (Figure 3.5).

The radius of gyration of an object is an interesting physical measurement. It gives an idea of an object's spatial extent and shape (see Pseudocode 3.3).[7] R_g is

---

[7] Pseudocode for radius of gyration (R_g) determination is given since R_g is a measurement mentioned and used in other sections of the book. Note that Pseudocode 3.3 presents an R_g computation for a two-dimensional collection of points, and each point is assumed to have an equal weight.

```
ALGORITHM:   COMPUTE RADIUS OF GYRATION (RG)

INPUT: x(i), y(i)  - coordinates of collection of points
OUTPUT: Rg          - the radius of gyration
VARIABLES: Numpts  - number of points used
Notes:  The radius of gyration is a parameter useful for
  comparing the spatial extent of collections of points. Some
  readers may wish to compute the radius of gyration for a group of
  dots on a paper or for something more scientifically interesting.

sumx = 0; sumy = 0;  sumdist=0;
(* compute the 'center of gravity'*)
DO i = 1 to numpts;
    sumx=sumx+x(i); sumy=sumy+y(i);
END;
sumx = sumx/numpts; sumy = sumy/numpts;
(* compute distances from center  *)
DO i = 1 to numpts;
    dist=((x(i)-sumx)**2+(y(i)-sumy)**2);
    sumdist=sumdist+dist;
END;
Rg=sqrt(sumdist/numpts); (* compute radius of gyration *)
```

Pseudocode 3.3. *Compute radius of gyration.*

in the same units as the input, for example, inches or angstroms. For proteins, R_g changes with time. The radius of gyration of BPTI, derived from atomic coordinates, is given by:

$$R_g^2 = \left[\frac{\sum Z_i\, a_i^2}{\sum Z_i} \right] \tag{3.1}$$

where Z_i is the atomic number for atom i, increased by the number of attached hydrogen atoms. The sums are over all atoms. a_i is the distance of atom i from the electronic center of gravity. Equation (3.1) is described in detail in *Science* magazine.[8] The reader may be interested in computing R_g for a collection of dots. Figure 3.5 shows a stick-figure diagram of the protein where dots represent atoms.

A 3-D power spectrum computed for the R_g fluctuations (Figure 3.5) indicates that most of the power is below 1 picosecond, with a particularly prominent breathing mode centered at 3 picoseconds. Higher frequencies are evident to a lesser degree. The high ridge close to zero frequency may correspond to a slower radial oscillation or an infrequent process which is not observed long enough for adequate characterization in this conventional molecular dynamics simulation. Longer simulations would be required to determine the significance of such a

---

[8] Pickover, C. (1984) Spectrographic representations of globular protein breathing motions. *Science* 223: 181.

slower oscillation. There is experimental evidence for the existence of low frequency breathing vibrations in other proteins.

Since both the spectrogram and 3-D power spectrum present breathing motion data in a way which can easily be understood by the biophysicist, characterization of the dynamical richness of proteins is greatly facilitated. Why do we care about breathing motions? It has been hypothesized that the motions of globular proteins play an essential role in their function and may affect a number of important processes such as: binding of ligands, enzyme catalysis, hemoglobin cooperativity, immunoglobin action, electron transfer, and the assembly of supramolecular structures such as viruses. From the work described in this section and other studies, it is clear that a compact, rigid view of globular proteins is incomplete. In addition to the relatively fast processes including collisions between neighboring atoms and localized group vibrations, proteins may undergo somewhat regular low frequency breathing motions of varying complexity. These motions involve the collective motion of a large number of different atoms. The functional importance of such breathing modes, and protein motion in general, has begun to attract the interest of an increasing number of physical chemists as evidenced by the growing number of spectroscopic, kinetic, and theoretical studies of protein dynamics. (Much of the material in section 3.4 appeared in: Pick84a, *Science*. Related material on protein dynamics and conformation appears in: Pickover et al., 1979, *J. Biol. Chem.*; Pickover and Engelman, 1982, *Biopolymers*; McKay, Pickover, and Steitz, 1982, *J. Mol. Biol.*; Pickover and Engelman, 1982, *Biophys. J.*; Levinson, Pickover, and Richards, 1983, *J. Biol. Chem.*)

3.5 Cancer Genes (DNA Waveforms)

The 3-D Fourier transform representations may be applied to genetic sequences. In this work, the sequence of bases in a human bladder cancer gene is treated as if it were a speech waveform. As background, DNA contains the basic genetic information for all life on earth and is expressed in a four letter code: A, C, G and T (adenine, cytosine, guanine, and thymine). By associating each letter to a number we can treat the DNA sequence as a waveform, thereby opening up the whole array of speech analysis tools for molecular genetics.

The search for patterns in the sequence of bases in long DNA sequences is an active topic in molecular graphics. Periodicities and various patterns affect physical, chemical and biological properties of the DNA. An example of the output of a graphics system for an actual DNA sequence is presented in Figure 3.6. The calculation was performed for a 4000 base human bladder oncogene sequence. Oncogenes have been detected in tumors representative of each of the major forms of human cancer, and some have been shown to be able to induce malignant transformations in certain cell lines. This bladder carcinoma oncogene is derived from a sequence of similar structure present in the normal human genome (Reddy, 1983). Several prominent features can be seen on the map, and, interestingly, these features correspond to biologically important areas of the DNA sequence. The largest peak (1) occurring roughly between bases 590 and

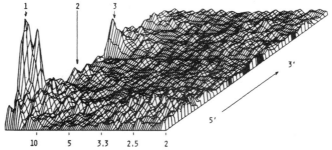

GGATCCCAGCCTTTCCCCAGCCCGTAGCCCCGGGACCTCCGCGGTGGGCG   50
GCGCCGCGCTGCCGGCGCAGGGAGGGCCTCTGGTGCACCGGCACCGCTGA   100

.

.

.

etc.

Figure 3.6. *A cancer gene.* Another three-dimensional map (amplitude vs. frequency vs. position in sequence) computed for the DNA sequence of a 4000 base human bladder cancer gene (bottom). The three peaks (1,2,3) are areas of biological interest. The spectrogram (inset), portrays position in sequence (ordinate) vs. frequency (abscissa). Amplitude is indicated by darkness on the plot.

900 corresponds with the sequence which, when deleted, drastically reduces the transforming activity of the oncogene, indicating the crucial role played by this non-coding sequence.

It may be possible to discover interesting periodicities in the DNA sequence by having the program produce many DNA maps by automatically iterating through a large number of different base-to-number assignments for input parameters (e.g. G=1, C=1, A=0, T=0; G=1, C=2, A=3, T=4 etc.). These assignments can be based on relative molecular weight, electrostatic potential, or other physical parameters. In this way, the program may suggest to the human analyst important features and parameters which would not even be considered otherwise. (More information can be found in Pick89, *Speculations in Science and Tech.*; Pick84b, *J. Mol. Graphics.*)

3.6 Reading List for Chapter 3

The history and theory of Fourier analysis has been extensively covered in the literature, and there have been many excellent books published on the practical use of Fourier transforms. For some general overviews, the reader should see Bendat and Piersol (1966), Koopmans (1974), MacDonald (1962), and Otnes and Enochson (1978). Readers wishing to explore the use of the 2-D Fourier transform for DNA pattern analysis should see Silverman and Linsker (1986).

There is also an extensive literature on speech science and computer synthesis of speech. For further information on human speech pathology see Borden and Harris (1983), and Ladefoged (1982). For information specific to the computer synthesis of speech, see Dixon and Maxey (1968), and Morgan (1984). For additional information on the visual representation of musical signals, see Cogan, R. (1984). A personal favorite on the subject of music and acoustics is: Pierce, J. (1983) *The Science of Musical Sound*. Scien. Amer. Library: New York. The reader may also consult *The Computer Music Journal* published by MIT Press.

The bibliography at the end of this book has additional references.

Chapter 4

Unusual Graphic Representations

"Who knows what secrets of nature lay buried in the terabytes of data being generated each day by physicists studying the results of numerical simulations or the image of a distant galaxy. Given the volume and complexity of scientific data, visualization in the physical sciences has become a necessity in the modern scientific world." Robert Wolff

In the last chapter, we saw some brief examples of how a Fourier transform could be used to capture patterns in data. The various mountain peaks indicated the frequency composition of data ranging from speech to breathing proteins. Unfortunately, the traditional techniques don't always distinguish potentially interesting features in input data. As an example, let's first consider speech. With the traditional Fourier representation, many perceptibly different sounds may give rise to only very subtle differences in the spectra. There has been past research which points out the limitations of the Fourier method in displaying acoustic features which are of importance in auditory perception. Such limitations naturally motivate the development of novel display techniques to help capture subtleties which may be difficult to see in the traditional displays.

This chapter includes several novel ways of displaying data which are applied to a range of fields including acoustics and genetics. Note that this chapter does not attempt to give a detailed historical background to the visual display of quantitative information. For background, the reader should consult the various books in the reference section, and in particular, the works of Tufte (*Graphics Press*, 1983), Wainer and Thissen (*Ann. Rev. Psychol.*, 1981), and Wolff (*Comput. in Sci.*, 1988) (all cited in "Recommended Reading" on page 349). Also note that some of the display methods devised by the author are new and speculative; however it is hoped that many of the methods presented here will stimulate other researchers to extend and further test these techniques in related fields in order to assess their usefulness.

4.1 Acoustics

From the dull, stentorian roar of a lion to the clanging of a cathedral bell, the remarkable range of audible sounds makes analysis exceedingly difficult. It is difficult to rigorously compare and characterize sounds by ear alone since the listening process is subject to the limitations and artifacts of both memory and perception. Also, there are individual variations in listeners' ability to localize and describe acoustic features. This problem is the primary motivation for graphic displays of speech. Some novel ways of graphically representing speech waveforms in order to capture information missing in the spectrogram will be discussed in the following sections; these include *phase-vectorgrams* displaying phase, frequency and amplitude in a cylindrical plot resembling a pipe cleaner, and *autocorrelation-faces* displaying speech in visually memorable ways for children.

The speech waveform is a complex entity which is difficult to manage, manipulate and characterize (see example waveform, "Singing Computers" on page 23). Simply recording the pressure variation over time in the acoustic signal generated by human speech produces a complicated waveform. The signal itself alternates between quasi-periodic vowel-like sounds, which often look something like smooth rippling ocean waves when plotted, and certain consonants "looking" much like plots of random noise. Scattered through the signal are rapidly occurring high-energy pops known as plosives interspersed by perceptually important silences. While traditional graphic analyses, such as the spectrogram (intensity vs. frequency vs. time), have been invaluable in showing the general frequency content of an input signal, sometimes it is difficult for users to see on the spectrogram differences which are perceptible to the ear. These difficulties motivate representations which can make subtle differences in input signals obvious to the human analyst. First, a review of data display methods in general.

4.2 New Ways of Displaying Data

The use of visual displays to present quantitative material has a long history. There are many examples in the chronicle of science where important phenomena have been detected using visual displays and have heralded the emergence of entire new fields of scientific endeavor.[9] The usefulness of a particular display is determined by the embodiment of desirable characteristics such as descriptive capacity, potential for comparison, aid in focussing attention, and versatility. New representations called iconic graphs are now being explored. In contrast to the most common graphs which are restricted to two or three dimensions, "icons" (or symbols) such as computer-generated faces are now sometimes used to represent multidimensional data. With icons, the data parameters are mapped into figures with n features, each feature varying in size or shape according to the point's

---

[9] Examples include the cloud, bubble, and spark chambers in physics, computer graphics of Julia Sets and other fractals in mathematics, and molecular graphics in drug design and structure-function assessment in biophysics.

coordinate in that dimension. Such figures capitalize on the feature-integration abilities of the human visual system. Icons will be described in more detail in following sections.

4.3 Snowflakes from Sound: Art and Science

Of the many displays of acoustical data developed, one of the most striking and colorful data-display techniques produces figures with the six-fold symmetry of a snowflake. The trick is to convert sound waves (or any data) into a collection of dots which are then reflected through mirror planes by a simple computer program. The resulting representation, a *symmetrized dot-pattern* (SDP), provides a stimulus in which local visual correlations are integrated to form a global percept. It can potentially be applied to the detection and characterization of significant features of any sampled data. The symmetry, color and redundancy of the dot-pattern is useful in the visual detection and memorization of patterns by the human analyst.[10] The 1986 *J. Acoust. Soc. Am.* paper describes a simple recipe for taking points on a speech amplitude-time waveform and computing the pattern.[11]

Figure 4.1 shows a symmetrized dot-pattern (SDP) for the "EE" sound of a human and a synthesizer producing the same vowel sound. Since SDPs can be considered, to a first approximation, merely a replotting of the time waveform, it could be suggested that one would do as well to "look" at the waveform to compare and contrast signals. However, as indicated by the superimposed input signals, waveform similarities can often obscure differences. Figure 4.2 shows some more SDP examples – three different occurrences of the sound "OO" as in "boot" spoken by three people. Despite sensitivity to speaker individualities, SDPs have a global similarity for all "OO's." SDPs may also help differentiate nasalized and nonnasalized sounds (Figure 4.3). In general, it is hoped that SDPs can supplement traditional analysis to make for faster detection and diagnosis of certain important features in data.

To implement a symmetrized dot-pattern on a personal computer, start with a digitized waveform. The waveform may represent sound where the jagged trace on a graph indicates how the sound's loudness changes through time. The data is mapped to a snowflake-like pattern by comparing the loudness of pairs of adjacent points and plotting the result on a polar coordinate graph (a graph that looks a little like a polar view of the earth, with the North Pole at the graph's center).

---

[10] Pilot tests indicate that people without formal training in phonetics or acoustics, and with no preparation, can recognize certain speech sounds represented by symmetrized dot-patterns (SDPs). In some cases people can also identify a particular speaker by looking at the speech-SDPs (see Pickover, C. (1986) On the use of computer generated symmetrized dot-patterns for the visual characterization of speech waveforms and other sampled data. *J. Acoust. Soc. Am.* 80(3): 955-960).

[11] Since most of the work with SDPs are in the field of speech, and since the plots vaguely resemble snowflakes, the representation has informally been called a "speech flake" (see color cover of *Science News*, 131, June 1987).

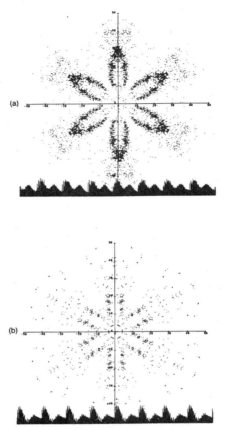

Figure 4.1. *Symmetrized dot-patterns for "EE" vowel sound.* Human-made "EE" sound (top) and a synthesized version of the same sound (bottom). Despite similar waveforms, symmetrized dot-patterns clearly show differences. (This figure and several others in this section appeared in *J. Acoust. Soc. Am.* (Pick86d).)

The points are then reflected, as though looking at them through a kaleidoscope (see Pseudocode 4.1). The correlations (relationships) between adjacent pairs of points determine the structure of the SDP.

The concentration in this section is focused on human speech sounds, but the SDP can also be applied to handwriting, and musical and animal sounds. To give the reader an indication of the variety of patterns sound can produce, Figure 4.4 shows symmetrized dot patterns computed from animal vocalizations. Of the animal vocalizations cataloged, dolphin-SDP were most similar to human-SDPs. Since dolphins have a developed and complex acoustic repertoire for communication and echolocation, SDPs may be of use in the visual characterization of their vocalizations. See (Pick86d, *J. Acoust. Soc. Am.*) for the use of the SDP to assess frequency content and waveform variability, and for the various pros and cons of the SDP approach for representing waveforms. See Pseudocode 4.1 for

Figure 4.2. *Family similarities for different speakers*. These SDPs were computed from three individuals ((a), (b), and (c)) for three different occurrences of the sound "OO" as in "boot." Despite sensitivity to speaker individualities, SDPs have a global similarity for all "OO's."

SDP color options, which make SDPs more useful in detecting data features (and more interesting from an artistic standpoint).

The use of this data display in representing cardiac sounds is discussed in the next section.

4.4 Medicine: Cardiology and SDPs

Symmetrized dot-patterns may have applications in representing heart sounds. Nearly a million Americans die each year of cardiovascular disease, according to the American Heart Association. The traditional diagnostic methods for cardiac disease – listening with a stethoscope (auscultation), examination of graphic records of the audible sounds (phonocardiography), or electrocardiogram (ECG) analysis – have been used for years by physicians and other medical personnel to

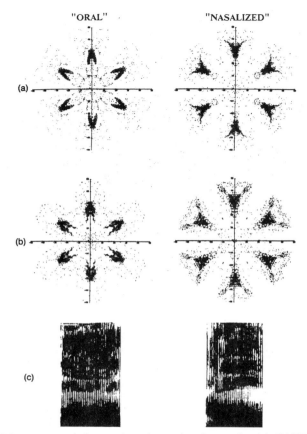

"ORAL"   "NASALIZED"

(a)

(b)

(c)

Figure 4.3. *SDPs computed for oral and nasalized sounds.* (a) "AH" and nasalized "AH" produced by a male speaker (as in the first vowel sound in "father" and "mom," respectively). (b) "AH" and nasalized "AH" produced by a female speaker. (c) Spectrograms for "AH" and nasalized "AH." SDPs can make the differences obvious, even for inexperienced users of SDPs. For comparisons of these patterns before and after symmetrization, see (Pick86d, *J. Acoust. Soc. Am.*).

detect abnormalities of the heart. The symmetrized dot-pattern display mentioned in the previous section can be used to represent normal and pathological heart sounds (mild mitral stenosis, and mitral regurgitation). Figure 4.5 shows example SDPs for cardiac sounds.

Unlike the ECG which measures electrical activity of the heart, the SDP described here uses acoustic input. The symmetrized dot-pattern (SDP) characterizes waveforms using patterns of dots and requires very limited computational time as prerequisite. Previous studies in texture discrimination and pattern recognition have shown that symmetry elements can make features more obvious to the human observer, and for this reason the SDPs have a high degree of induced symmetry (and redundancy) in order to aid the human analyst in recognizing and

```
ALGORITHM: How to create a Symmetrized Dot-Pattern
INPUT:        W(t) a waveform with npts sample points
OUTPUT:       snowflake-like SDP
VARIABLES: npts is the number of data points.
 angle controls the symmetry angle of the dot pattern.
 lag determines the time relationship between points.
Notes: Try changing the angle, top and lag parameters to optimize
 these values for finding features of interest in the data.

top = 50;                 (* scaling upper bound *)
(* find low and high values in data *)
hi=1.0 e-10; lo=1.0 e10;
do i = 1 to npts;
 if W(i) > hi then hi = W(i);
 if W(i) < low then low = W(i);
end;
do i = 1 to npts;  (* rescale data to range: 0 - top *)
 W(i) = (W(i)-low)*top/(hi-low);
end;
call set('POLAR'); (* place graphics in polar mode *)
call axis(-top,top,0,360); (* set up axes in r and theta    *)
angle=60;                  (* choose a symmetry angle        *)
lag= 1;                    (* choose a lag                   *)
do j = 1 to npts-lag;
 (* Color dots                           *)
 if W(j+lag)-W(j) >= 0 then Color(Red) else Color(Green);
 do i = 1 to 360 by angle;
  PlotDot(W(j),i+W(j+lag)); (* place dot at (r, theta)       *)
  PlotDot(W(j),i-W(j+lag));
 end;
end;
```

Pseudocode 4.1. *How to create a symmetrized dot-pattern ("speech flake").*

remembering patterns. In Figure 4.5, the SDP marked "normal" was computed from a normal heart beat. Another SDP represents the sounds from a patient with mild mitral stenosis. Mitral stenosis is an abnormal narrowing of the mitral valve usually resulting from a disease such as rheumatic fever, and obstructing the free flow of blood from left atrium to left ventricle. Figure 4.5 also shows an SDP computed from a patient with mitral regurgitation, the abnormal back-flow of blood into the left atrium. Prior work in speech (last section) has suggested that the SDP functions somewhat like an autocorrelator and is also sensitive to general frequency content and waveform variability. The higher frequency noise charac-terizing the back-flow segment in mitral regurgitation gives rise to the character-istic "fuzzy" pattern in the SDP in Figure 4.5. An intermediate amplitude region in mitral stenosis gives rise to the dark "flying v" formations. These SDPs were computed for samples of about one-half second duration; however, other time-lengths were tried, including the capturing of several heart beats per frame, with essentially identical results. Also, when studying different segments in time, essentially the same SDP was generated.

The several demonstrations included in this section indicate that SDPs can make differences obvious even to inexperienced persons. Unlike SDPs, the tradi-tional cardiac displays are not the same as pictures, since pictures have numerous

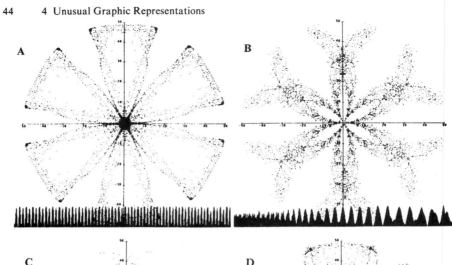

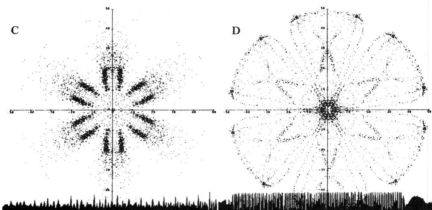

Figure 4.4. *Animal vocalizations.* SDP are sensitive to frequency variations. This set shows the differences evident in the sounds of (clockwise, starting at upper left) a rooster, a dolphin, a frog and a cat.

visual features that can be readily identified, labeled, remembered, and integrated into a coherent whole. The ease with which patterns can be recognized may have value in instances where feedback to the patient or other medical personnel is useful, particularly when a physician is unavailable. This recognition ease and SDP-sensitivity may also be useful for researchers and physicians when comparing and studying heart sounds. Obviously, more cardiac sounds and many subjects need to be studied to fully assess the extent of SDPs' usefulness. The specific visual correlates of acoustic-cardiac features which people use to distinguish one member of a cardiac class from another would provide an interesting avenue of future research. (Pick89, *Leonardo*.)

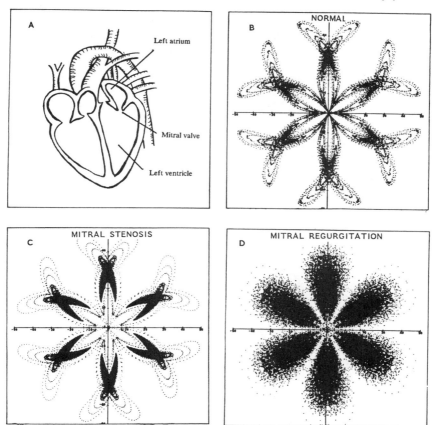

Figure 4.5. *Heart sounds.* A normal heart sound can be contrasted with cardiac sounds associated with various pathological conditions.

4.5 Another Dot-Display Used in Molecular Biophysics

Sections 4.3 and 4.4 showed how symmetrized dot-patters can represent data. Another example of a display used for data characterization at a more fundamental level of perception than the SDP is the random dot-display. This type of pattern was first researched in detail by Leon Glass in 1969 while studying visual perception. These patterns, also called random-dot moire patterns, are potentially useful in the global characterization of conformational changes occurring in biomolecules. As background, if a pattern of random dots is superimposed on itself and rotated by a small angle, concentric circles are perceived about the point of rotation. If the angle of rotation is increased, the perceived circles gradually disappear until a totally unstructured dot display is seen. This effect demonstrates the ability of the human visual system to detect local autocorrelations and may suggest a physiological basis of form perception in higher animals (Glass, 1969). Figure 4.6 shows an example of a dot interference pattern. The pattern is

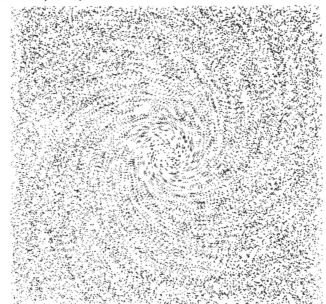

Figure 4.6. *Random dot-patterns.* Random dot-display produced by superimposing a figure containing 10,000 random dots upon itself and subsequent rotation by three degrees and uniform expansion by a factor of 1.1. Note: if the rotation is much larger, the eye looses the ability to perceive the spiral patterns.

comprised of a set of ten thousand random dots which was superimposed on itself and subsequently rotated and uniformly expanded. Though the pattern was calculated by computer, similar patterns can easily be generated using sprinkled ink and transparencies.

As an example of lateral use of computer software tools ("Lateral Use of Computer Software Tools" on page 4), the "Glass patterns" can be applied to a problem in biophysics. By placing random dots on a graphics representation of a protein molecule before and after rotation, the center of rotation can easily be found (just as we can easily perceive the center in Figure 4.6). There are sometimes crystal structures of two forms of a biomolecule related by a conformational change. Often it is desirable to ascertain an equivalent axis of rotation relating two structures in conformational space regardless of the fact that the actual transformation between the starting and ending form of the molecule may have involved many small intermediate rotational and translational components. (To learn more about how to use these techniques to visually capture motions in proteins and advantages over brute-force numerical methods, see Pick84, *J. Mol. Graph.*)

```
ALGORITHM: How to Create a Moire Dot-Pattern
Variables:
NumDots = the number of dots (e.g. 10,000)
Angle   = the rotation angle (e.g. 1 degree)
sf      = scale factor        (e.g. 1.1)
Notes:  The display area is assumed to go from 0 to 100. Random
 numbers are generated on the interval (0,1). The reader may
 experiment by gradually increasing the angle until the eye can no
 longer detect correlations.

DO i = 1 to NumDots;
  GenRand(randx); GenRand(randy);   (* Generate random numbers *)
  randx=randx*100; randy=randy*100;
  PrintDot(randx,randy);
  (* Rotate and Scale; Center is at (50,50) *)
  randxx =sf*((randx-50)*cosd(angle)+(randy-50)*sind(angle)) + 50;
  randy  =sf*((randy-50)*cosd(angle)-(randx-50)*sind(angle)) + 50;
  randx  = randxx;
  PrintDot(randx,randy);   (* Print superimposed pattern *)
END;
```

Pseudocode 4.2. *How to create a Moire dot-pattern.*

4.6 Autocorrelation Cartoon-Faces for Speech

"The most exotic journey would not be to see a thousand different places, but to see a single place through a thousand person's eyes."

Presented in this section is a rather unorthodox computer graphics characterization of sound and DNA sequences using computer generated cartoon faces. As background, computer graphics has become increasingly useful in the representation and interpretation of multidimensional data with complex relationships. Pseudo-color, animation, three-dimensional figures, and a variety of shading schemes are among the techniques used to reveal relationships not easily visible from simple correlations based on two-dimensional linear theories.

Showing correlations between two or three variables is easy: simply plot a two-dimensional or three-dimensional graph. But what if one is trying to present four or five or even ten different variables at once? The face method of representing multivariate data was first presented in 1973 by Chernoff, a Harvard statistician. Using gradations of various facial features, such as the degree of eyebrow slant or pupil size, a single face can convey the value of many different variables at the same time (Figure 4.7). Such faces have been shown to be more reliable and more memorable than other tested icons (or symbols), and allow the human analyst to grasp many of the essential regularities and irregularities in the data. In general, n data parameters are mapped into a figure with n features, each feature varying in size or shape according to the point's coordinate in that dimension. The data sample variables are mapped to facial characteristics; thus, each multivariate observation is visualized as a computer-drawn face. This aspect of the graphical point displays capitalizes on the feature integration abilities of the human visual system and is particularly useful for higher levels of cognitive proc-

5 5 5 5 5 5 5 5 5 5   **6 5 5 5 5 5 5 5 5 5**   **7 5 5 5 5 5 5 5 5 5**

Figure 4.7. *Cartoon faces and data analysis.* These cartoon faces can be used to represent the values of as many as 10 variables, each variable corresponding to a facial feature. Here only one facial feature, horizontal eye length, is changed. Other facial coordinates are set to a constant middle-position.

essing. Figure 4.8 shows the range of faces produced when random numbers ("white noise") are mapped to facial coordinates.

For speech applications, an autocorrelation analysis coupled to computer generated cartoon faces can be used to represent speech sounds. The autocorrelation of a signal $x(n)$ with lag k is defined as

$$\phi(k) = \sum_{n=-\infty}^{\infty} x(n)\, x(n + k). \tag{4.1}$$

The autocorrelation function for data describes the general dependance of the values of the data at one time on its values at another time. On a computer an autocorrelation function for a finite window in time can be implemented as shown in Pseudocode 4.3. For more on autocorrelation theory, see Bendat and Piersol (1968) and Witten (1982). In 1985, I devised the "autocorrelation-face" where 10 facial parameters are computed from the first 10 points of the autocorrelation function of a 50 ms sample of the speech sound. This process is described in more detail in the *J. Educ. Tech. Syst.*

In this and the following applications, ten facial parameters, $F(1, 2, 3, 4, 5, 6, 7, 8, 9, 10)$ are used, and each facial characteristic has ten settings, $S(1, 2, 3, 4, 5, 6, 7, 8, 9, 10)$, providing for 10 billion possible different faces. The controlled features are: head eccentricity, eye eccentricity, pupil size, eyebrow slant, nose size, mouth shape, eye spacing, eye size, mouth length, and degree of mouth opening. Head eccentricity, for example, controls how elongated the head is in either the horizontal or vertical direction. The mouth is constructed using parabolic interpolation routines, and the other features are derived from circles, lines, and ellipses. Pseudocode B.3 (in Appendix B) gives details on the computer generation of

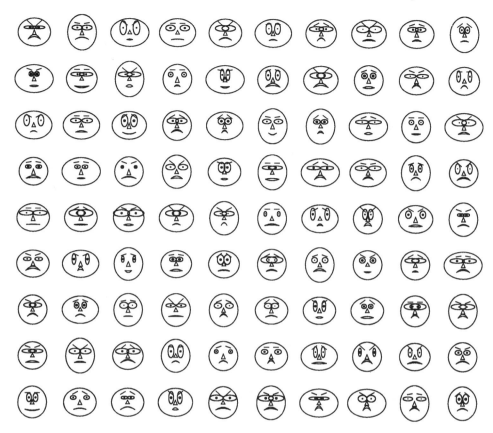

Figure 4.8. *The diversity of computer-generated faces.* The settings for each of the ten facial parameters were computed using a random number generator.

faces. Figure 4.9 shows some examples computed from human speech.[12] The resultant speech-faces could provide useful biofeedback targets for helping deaf and severely hearing-impaired individuals to modify their vocalizations in selective ways – especially since they may provide simple and memorable features to which children could relate. The traditional speech spectrogram displays are not the same as pictures, since pictures have numerous visual features that can be readily identified, labeled, and integrated into a coherent whole. To compare SDPs (previous section) and faces: note that unlike faces, SDPs do not elicit an emotional reaction. Emotion does confer a mnemonic advantage for the faces, but

---

[12] Various tests were done to assess whether people can differentiate sounds by looking at the faces. Test subjects were given sets of cards to sort into nine different categories of sound. The average percent correct for classification into 9 separate groups was 89 % ± 8%, with 3 perfect scores. (See Pickover, C. (1985) On the educational uses of computer-generated cartoon faces. *J. Educ. Tech. Syst.* 13: 185-198.)

```
ALGORITHM: Autocorrelation Function

Variables: npts = the number of data points
           Input = array of samples from a digitized waveform.
           Auto = autocorrelation function
Notes:  If the input data is a function of time then the
  autocorrelation function is also a function of time.

auto(*) = 0; (* initialize array *)
do p = 0 to npts-1;
  do q = 1 to npts - p;
   auto(p) = auto(p) + input(q)*input(q+p);
  end;
  (* correction factor *)
  auto(p) = auto(p)* (1/(npts-p));
end;
```

Pseudocode 4.3. *Autocorrelation function.*

can sometimes obscure the association, e.g. a smiling face representing cancer statistics. (Pick85a, *J. Educ. Tech. Syst.*)

4.7 Cartoon Faces in Education

A number of recreational and educational uses for the faces are suggested in the following sections. As background, research has demonstrated the potential value that visualization and iconic systems play in learning and instruction. Popular educational software for home computers is becoming available (e.g., the "FaceMaker" by Spinnaker (see references)) which allows children to create faces from sets of eyes, ears, and noses. Programs such as these help children become comfortable with computer fundamentals such as menus and cursors. The computer-drawn faces presented in the current section have particular value in that they are created under parametric control and can provide immediate visual feedback to the user. In addition, any face can easily be regenerated at a later time from its control-data.

4.7.1 Cognitive Association of Coordinates with Facial Features

There have been several studies in the literature which have explored the child's ability to organize and represent body location information. Here, a simple face-drawing system was developed where children can type numbers at the terminal keyboard and immediately view the results on an adjacent graphics screen. For example, faces were constructed from the control-data entered by Lisa, a 6-year-old girl with no prior experience with computers. One face in particular was her favorite, because she found the shape of the mouth amusing. She worked on the figure for several minutes, developing the mouth to her specifications, and

Figure 4.9. *Faces from sound.* Cartoon faces can be used to characterize speech sounds. The top row represents the fricative sound "s"; the second, "sh"; the third, "z"; and the fourth, "v." Sounds were repeated three times. For vowel and nasal sounds, see *J. Educ. Tech. Syst.* See **Appendix B** for pseudocode for face generation.

subsequently she recorded the final control-data on a piece of paper. This indicated that she understood the concept of number-to-face parameter mapping.

4.7.2 Target-Pictures for Children

The faces may also serve as target-pictures for children to draw. [For background information on the differential cue utilization by children in pattern copying, the development of drawing rules by children, and "tadpole drawing" (body representations where the legs and arms are attached to the head), see Taylor and Bacharach (1981).] Since the computer faces are created from control-data, the resultant faces can easily be regenerated at a later time, or altered slightly, in order to test hand-eye coordination and development. Figure 4.10 includes four computer-drawn faces and children's attempts to reproduce them. The drawing

Figure 4.10. *Target faces.* Drawings made by children in an attempt to reproduce the four computer-drawn targets at top. From top to bottom, the ages of the children were 6 , 6, 8, and 10.

task can be made much more difficult if the child is asked to view the face first and then required to draw it as well as possible from memory. Computer software, and hardware such as digitization tablets, make an analytic comparison between computer- and child-generated faces easy. Simple parameters such as center of gravity, and radius of gyration ("Breathing Proteins" on page 30) can be computed to characterize the drawings in an objective way.

For years psychologists have tried to determine when infants first realize how the features of the human face are naturally arranged and when an infant's ability to perceive facial expressions begins. Computer-generated faces might be ideal for the study of infant's perception of natural and distorted arrangements of a schematic face. In the study of Maurer and Barrera (1981), it was shown that 2-month-old infants show a preference for a natural arrangement of facial features on a cartoon face, as opposed to scrambled features. Though their cartoon faces were not computer-generated, computers could be used in the placement

Figure 4.11. *Which two are the same?* The faces can be used to illustrate the concept of similarity, sameness, and difference. Since the facial parameters are accurately controlled, the degree of difficulty of the task can be specified.

(random or otherwise) of the facial features on the head, giving the researcher rigorous control of the resultant expressions.

4.7.3 Learning by Means of Analogy

The faces can be used to illustrate the concept of similarity, sameness, and difference. Since the facial parameters are accurately controlled, the degree of difficulty of the task can be specified (Figure 4.11). Possible tasks include: Which two are the same? and Which one is different? The faces can be used to explore memory abilities: initially, one face is shown, then erased, and the user can subsequently be asked to choose the face from a small group, somewhat like picking from a police line-up.

4.8 Educational Aid for the Presentation of Statistical Concepts

The faces may be suitable as visual supplements in the presentation of statistical concepts, particularly distribution theory, to individuals inexperienced in mathematics and with no prior knowledge of the methods of statistical evaluation. In this work, faces were used to illustrate the concept of white noise (totally random distribution) such as that shown in Figure 4.8, in contrast to Gaussian noise (normal error distribution) (Figure 4.12), theories usually not introduced to indi-

Figure 4.12. *Faces produced by Gaussian noise.*

viduals prior to the high-school level due to the mathematical complexity of the subject matter. For the case of white noise, one hundred faces were generated, each facial characteristic having a setting determined from a random number generator. In the case of the Gaussian noise, the facial settings S_i are given by:

$$S_i = \sum_{j=1}^{N} \frac{\delta_j}{N} \tag{4.2}$$

where δ_j are random numbers, and N is 5 for weakly Gaussian noise or 20 for strongly Gaussian noise. i signifies the facial parameter used (from 1 to 10). Gaussian random noise was mapped to facial parameters (notice the faces have a more "middle of the road" look). For very young students, the faces could be used, in addition to standard techniques, for visualizing simpler concepts such as the mean, median, mode, and other measures of central tendency. For additional information, see Glossary entry *Gaussian white noise*. (Pick84e, *Computers and Graph.*)

4.9 Commercial and Military Air Traffic Control

One may speculate about potentially useful applications of the computer-drawn faces in the cockpit of airplanes. The growing complexity of aircraft controls and readouts are making aircraft almost too complex to fly. The faces can accommodate analog or digital input from a multitude of readouts, each facial parameter receiving input from one or more gauges. Deviations in the controls from their expected values would give rise to excursions of the facial parameters from their middle settings. While it is true that the more standard concept of having a gauge blink or beep when a parameter has gone beyond a critical value is valuable, the faces would be especially useful in alerting the pilot of conditions where several readings are not themselves at critical stages, but where the combined effect may be dangerous.

4.10 Faces and Cancer Genes

Face icons can be used to detect irregularities in DNA sequences. The deviation of the DNA statistical properties from their expected (random) value causes deviations of the facial parameters from their middle positions. The number of possible DNA characteristics that can be visualized by this method is large. (For further reading see: Pick89, *Speculations in Science and Tech.*; Pick84b, *J. Mol. Graph.*)

4.11 Back to Acoustics: Phase Vectorgrams

In this section, we return to a discussion of graphics for representing sounds. Here the "phase vectorgram" representation is presented, developed with colleagues in 1985.

Until recently it had been believed that the perceived sound of an audio signal could be completely characterized by its power spectrum (energy vs. frequency). As suggested in "Fourier Analysis: A Digression and Review" on page 21, a sine wave is characterized by amplitude (or extreme height), its period (the time between one peak and the next) and its phase (the position of the sine wave in time). Recent psychoacoustic experiments have revealed that phase relations between the sinusoidal components in signals can be perceived – yet they are not represented on spectrograms. This suggests that there is a more appropriate domain than that of the power spectrum in which to process signals. The phase information normally discarded via transformation to the domain of the power spectrum must be reconsidered. Unfortunately, the short-term phase of a dynamic signal is difficult to quantify and plot. [These difficulties are overcome in an analysis using an autocorrelation-based pitch detector, followed by discrete Fourier transform, and normalization of the plot to the phase of the fundamental frequency (ϕ_1) :

$$\phi_i = \phi_i - k\phi_1 \tag{4.3}$$

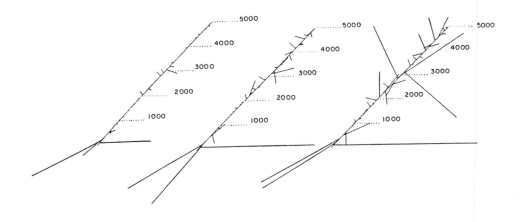

Figure 4.13. *Phase vectorgram.* Harmonics of a vowel sound are plotted as "bristles" emanating from a central axis, with an angle equal to the phase of each harmonic.

where k is the harmonic number and ϕ_1 is the phase of the fundamental. (These terms may be unfamiliar to some readers; see Otnes and Enochson (1978) for more information.) With knowledge of the fundamental frequency we can adjust the Fourier analysis so the reference point is synchronized to the fundamental period of the waveform, and the frequency sample points can be taken at more meaningful points corresponding to the harmonics of the fundamental.]

In the phase vectorgram (Figure 4.13) amplitude, frequency and phase are presented in a cylindrical plot resembling a pipe-cleaner or bottle-brush. Shown is a vectorgram for different regions in time for the human utterance "ee," as in "meet." Given the amplitudes for components k and the corrected phases (see Equation (4.3)), the "bristles" in the cylindrical plot may be drawn. The length of each bristle is determined by the gain at each frequency. Frequency extends from low frequency (0 Hz) to high frequency (5000 Hz) as the cylinder goes from front to back. Phase is represented by the angle the bristle makes with the central axis. Cylindrical plots are normalized so that all bristles may be accommodated in the same size graph. The cylindrical plot represents the phases more meaningfully than traditional two dimensional phase-vs.-frequency plots which typically have phase from -180 to +180 degrees on the ordinate and frequency on the abscissa — amplitude is not a factor in such plots. In our plots, the length of the bristle reflects the importance of that particular phase component since the bristle length is related to the amplitude. Low amplitude bristles due to noise or computational artifacts therefore do not obscure the plot. In addition, the cylindrical representation eliminates the need for "phase unwrapping" (Otnes and Enochson (1978)).

Generally, the cylindrical plot gives a clear indication of both phase and amplitude as a function of frequency. It may be of use in a variety of signal processing applications. Evidence of speaker-independent phase "signatures" for phonemes (the basic building blocks of speech) suggests the use of phase vectorgrams in speech recognition. (The phase vectorgram represents a collaboration between the author and M. Martin and M. Kubovy.)

4.12 Fractal Characterization of Speech Waveform Graphs

Presented in this section is an alternate way of characterizing speech. The methods use the concepts of fractal geometry set forth in B. Mandelbrot's book *The Fractal Geometry of Nature* (Mandelbrot (1983)). The beauty and complexity of fractal shapes in pure mathematics is discussed in Part III of this book.

4.12.1 Scale Invariance

Many objects and patterns in the natural world possess the quality of *"self-similarity"* – for a range of scales used to view the pattern, the magnified portion of the shape looks (qualitatively) like the original pattern. Such objects include mountains and coastlines, as well as several classes of patterns derived purely from mathematics. This scale invariance has been studied extensively by B. Mandelbrot, who coined the word "fractal" (in 1975) to describe such irregular shapes.

4.12.2 Fractal Characterization of Speech

A fractal object has a shape with increasingly detailed features revealed with increasing magnification, and examples include mountains and coastlines (this is explained in greater detail in the section on self-similarity). In contrast, the edge of a circle is not fractal since it is featureless upon increasing magnification (i.e., it becomes a straight line).

The fact that such complicated, and seemingly random, shapes of nature can be characterized by a single number, the "fractal dimension" D, motivates the test of fractal characterization in speech science. The speech waveform is a very irregularly shaped signal which can be treated as a coastline and studied using fractal mathematics. If speech waveforms can also be globally quantified and compared using a single number, a new way of understanding (and a new focus on) many problems in acoustics and phonetics might be provided.

In this work, the speech waveform in the time-range of ~ 2 seconds to ~ 10 milliseconds (ms) was studied, since this time scale represents the area in which important prosodic and phonetic events occur. Prosody includes a description of the "music" of speech (pitch, amplitude, timing and other "suprasegmental" features). Phonetics includes the study of the basic building blocks of speech such as phonemes, diphones, and coarticulation. The speech waveform is studied to determine whether its structure can be considered self-similar and whether a dimension (D) can be calculated. Synthetic and natural speech are also compared using this approach, and the effect of voice quality and nasality on D is determined. Graphic representations of speech and other natural phenomena are compared. The analyses and graphics are presented only for acoustic waveforms; however, these techniques can easily be applied to any data where one variable fluctuates through time or space. Past work by R. Voss in the global characterization of certain noise signals, and speech and music in a longer range of time (~ 10 seconds to several minutes), can be found in Clarke and Voss (1975). First, a classification of shapes and definition of terms used in this section are presented.

4.12.3 Classification of Shapes

4.12.3.1 Richardson's Coastlines and the Fractal Dimension

If one were to attempt to measure a coastline or the boundary of two nations, the value of the measurement would depend on the length of the measuring stick used. As the measuring stick decreased in length, the measurement would become sensitive to smaller and smaller bumps, and in fact the coastline's length would become infinite as the stick's length approached zero. Lewis Richardson was one of the first to quantify this phenomenon in an attempt to correlate the occurrence of wars with the shape of the boundary separating two or more nations (Richardson, (1960)). Mandelbrot built extensively upon Richardson's work and suggested that the relationship between the measuring-stick length (ε) and the apparent total length (L) of a coastline could be expressed by the parameter D, the fractal dimension. [An equivalent way to understand and calculate D is to study the relationship between the *number* of measuring sticks (N) and the length of the measuring stick (ε). For a smooth curve such as a circle, the relationship is:

$$N(\varepsilon) = \frac{c}{\varepsilon} \tag{4.4}$$

c is a constant. The number of sticks (N) needed to measure the circle's circumference increases as the length of the stick decreases. However for a fractal curve this relationship is altered slightly:

$$N(\varepsilon) = \frac{c}{\varepsilon^D} \tag{4.5}$$

If we multiply both sides of Equation (4.5) by ε the relation can be expressed in terms of the length of the measuring stick:

$$L(\varepsilon) = \frac{\varepsilon}{\varepsilon^D} \tag{4.6}$$

D corresponds somewhat to the traditional notion of dimension (a line is one-dimensional, a plane two-dimensional) except that D can be a fraction. Since a coastline is so convoluted (and has bumps upon bumps as it is magnified), it tends to fill space, and its dimension lies somewhere between a line and a plane. The fractal structure implies that repeated magnification of its graph reveals ever-finer levels of detail.] Fractals have many intriguing properties, such as being continuous everywhere but differentiable nowhere. Mandelbrot gives $D = 1.26$ for the coastline of Britain. For smooth lines, such as a circle, $D = 1$, and L quickly converges to the "true" circumference of a circle as ε decreases.

4.12.3.2 Self-similarity

If the features of an object (i.e., the general nature of its irregular bumpy structure) remains constant through successive magnifications, such as is the case for coastlines and mountains, the object is considered self-similar. This is the same as saying that the D calculated from the relationship between ε and N in Equation (4.5) remains constant for different ε. Researchers have *no problem with the idea that an object can be self-similar only in a certain range of length scales*. For practical purposes, D need only be constant for a suitably wide range of ε, a factor of 10 or more for example. Fractal objects need not be self-similar at all scales. Fractals need only show a certain amount of bumpiness with increasing magnification. However, researchers are most interested in self-similar fractals, and today the terms are often interchanged in the literature.

4.12.3.3 Types of Self-similarity: Definition of Terms

Figure 4.14 includes much of the self-similarity sub-classifications, as well as example patterns for some types. Self-similarity implies *scaling similarity* (i.e. the shapes are invariant under magnification). The edges of circles and lines are self-similar since they look the same at different magnification; however, they are smooth (and hence not fractal). They possess what is known as *standard scaling symmetry*. Objects with "bumpiness" but with scaling symmetry possess *non-standard scaling symmetry*. Certain mathematical constructs such as the Koch curve, which can be made by superimposing smaller and smaller triangles, have *exact scale invariance*. However, most objects are only *statistically scale invariant*, since they are only invariant in an average sense (magnifications of coastlines are qualitatively identical, not quantitatively). Recently, a host of statistically scale-invariant fractals derived from the iteration of complex functions has been described (*Julia sets*). Algorithms for the generation of these beautiful and complicated structures, as well as color computer graphics, are being studied, and their popularity is evidenced by the proliferating number of articles in the scientific and popular literature (see Part III of this book). As will be shown later, speech waveforms at sentence time scales can be classified as a statistically scale-invariant natural phenomenon.

4.12.4 Speech Fractal Dimension

4.12.4.1 Coastlines and Speech Compared

What do coastlines and speech time waveforms have in common, and how can they be visually and analytically compared? Figure 4.15 shows the coastline of England and a "speech-island" side-by-side to facilitate comparison. The speech island was computed by mapping the amplitude of the speech wave into radius

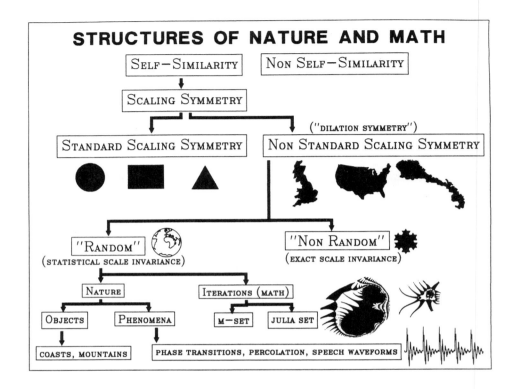

Figure 4.14. *Classification of the shapes of nature and math.* Self-similar structures, when magnified, look like the original shape. "Random" self-similar structures are self-similar only in the statistical sense so even though they don't repeat their pattern exactly, they clearly have the same look at different magnifications. Speech waveforms, at sentence time scales, are statistically self-similar.

and time into angle. For each sampled time point a line is drawn from zero radius to that point, thereby tending to fill the figure; this places a visual emphasis on the "texture" of the edge and facilitates visual comparison with other "closed-curve" natural objects (e.g., islands, clouds, leaves). This island comprises a sentence containing 2 seconds of speech (20,000 points at the digitization rate of 10,000 samples/second). Notice that both England and the speech graph have a highly convoluted surface, but that the speech looks much rougher. The fractal dimension D, in a sense, quantifies roughness, and is discussed in the following section.

A   B

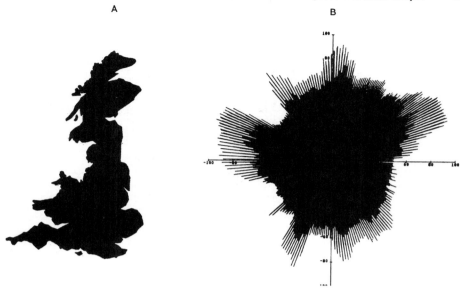

D = 1.26   D = 1.66

Figure 4.15. *Comparison between coastlines and speech waveforms.* Notice that the coast of England (A) and speech (B) have a highly convoluted surface, but speech looks somehow rougher. Mandelbrot's fractal dimension *D* quantifies the degree to which such irregular curves "fill space," and *D* = 1.26 for England's coast. For speech waveform graphs, *D* ~ 1.66 (here the amplitude trace is plotted in polar space with the middle filled in to focus visual attention on the "texture" of its edge and to facilitate comparison with other natural forms).

4.12.4.2 Speech-Wave Structure

If the waveforms were statistically self-similar, they could be characterized with just one number, *D*. Though the irregularity continues with each magnification, the degree of roughness seems to fluctuate slightly when looking at isolated magnifications. This does not invalidate the self-similarity judgement, since self-similarity applies only in the statistical sense and cannot be captured in just a few sample magnifications. In order to solve this problem, an approach like the one suggested by Equation (4.5) is used. The waveform graph is laid upon a grid (by computer), and the number of grid points (N) intersected is measured as a function of grid size, ε. Plots of log N vs. log ε are calculated; the slope determined by a least squares line fit to the data gives an estimate of $-D$ (Figure 4.16). This relationship gives the same information as the measuring stick relationships, but is easier for the computer to calculate. The log plot for different values of ε were computed for the utterance, "Nine men were hired to dig the ruins." "Self-similarity" was indicated by the remarkable straightness of the plotted line, and the slope indicated a fractional dimension *D* of 1.6 in the range studied (~ 2 s to ~ 10 ms). Note that technically, because the speech waveform's axes have different physical meanings, the term "self-affinity" might be used; in this section the term "self-similarity" is used in a general way to suggest the *scale invariance*

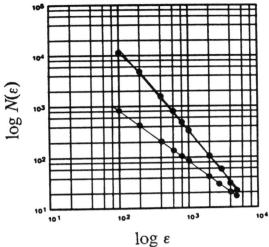

Figure 4.16. *Example speech graph.* A plot of log $N(\varepsilon)$ vs. log ε is shown for a male human speaker, superimposed with a plot for a digitized diagonal line ($D = 1$). The slope of these plots gives an estimate for the fractal dimension, D. The sentence plotted is: "Nine men were hired to dig the ruins." The ε axis is in units of the sampled data, so at 10,000 samples / second, "100" corresponds to 10 ms.

of a time-waveform when initially scaled to fit (graphically) in a square box. The D-computation is also based on the square-box scaling.

4.12.4.3 Numerical Evaluation

For Richardson's coastline measurements, published posthumously in 1960, a computer was not used, and the labor-intensive nature of his work is evident:

> "At first I tried to measure the frontiers by rolling a wheel of 1.8 centimeters diameter on maps; but there is often fine detail which the wheel cannot follow...considerable skill would be needed to guide the wheel...Much more definite measurements have been made by walking a pair of dividers along a map of the frontier..."

Note that as the measure gets smaller, measurement accuracies become critical. For example, in tracing a map boundary with a pair of dividers, the difficulty associated with accurately hitting the border line can greatly affect the measurement. A computer-based numerical approach helps to overcome this problem. Using the methods described above, D was computed for a variety of acoustic signals. For human speech, by averaging different sentence utterances for both male and female speakers of ~ 2 seconds in duration, $D = 1.66 \pm .05$ This remarkable invariance suggests that D is a characteristic parameter for speech (at least for the simple declarative English sentences studied). D seems to be unaffected by pitch (fundamental frequency), which is useful because it facilitates comparing different voices.

In humans, vocal stress is produced by increasing the subglottal air pressure via the lungs and is signaled by increased effort on the speaker's part and usually by increased intensity and pitch (overall intensity and pitch do not show up in the D calculation). One motivation for this work was the comparison of natural and synthetic speech with the goal of improving synthetic speech. For this work, synthetic speech was produced using a digital speech synthesizer (see Section 3.2). Interestingly, synthesized speech sentences gave a D very close to human speech ($D = 1.57 \pm .03$), suggesting that the global structure of the human and synthetic speech is very similar. However, when D for vocal stress was calculated just for vowels, D monotonically increased with increasing stress for humans (D climbed to ~ 1.88 over the range of stress studied) but decreased or stayed the same for the synthesizer, suggesting a problem with vocal stress modelling for this synthesizer.

In human speech, the fractal dimension for nasalized and non-nasalized vowels is significantly different, though unlike the case for vocal stress, the direction of change differs with the vowel (e.g. for the "ah" vowel sound in father, D decreases by a few tenths, but for "ee" vowel sound in meet, D increases).[13] In the synthesizer, no change in D is detected. Again, the fact that the D trend for human and synthetic speech differs suggests that the nasalization method employed is not sufficient to adequately simulate nasality in human speech.

4.12.5 Catalog of Other Acoustic Sounds

The diversity and range of D for speech and other natural sounds is not fully known at this time. D computations were made for animal sounds (of about 2 seconds duration) and are: dolphin, $D = 1.90$; cat, $D = 1.74$; angry cat, $D = 1.78$; and very angry cat, $D = 1.91$. Whispered human speech gave $D = 1.49$.

It should be noted that D gives information which spectrograms do not provide (see Pickover and Khorasani, 1986). A power spectral slope cannot be directly related to D because it omits phase information which describes the *arrangement* of bumps in the graph of an object. In fact, two objects with different Ds can have identical power spectra. For some educational demonstrations of this, see Pickover and Khorasani (1986e). A provocative area for future research would be to assess the extent to which D sensitivity to nasalization could be useful in providing feedback or diagnostic capabilities for certain speech pathologies where hyper/hyponasality can indicate anatomical or neurological difficulties in velar control or closure. Deaf speakers also produce inappropriate degrees of nasal resonance since they cannot hear the oral-nasal distinctions made by hearing speakers. (Pick86e and Khorasani, *Computers and Graph.*; Pick86f, *Computer Graph. Forum.*)

---

[13] The glossary has definitions for various speech terms.

4.13 A Monte Carlo Approach to Fractal Dimension

Unfortunately, large amounts of computer time are sometimes needed to accurately do self-similarity studies. It is possible to develop fast computer techniques for the characterization of self-similar shapes and signals based upon Monte Carlo methods. The algorithm is specifically designed for digitized input (e.g. pictures, acoustic waveforms, analytic functions) where the self-similarity is not obvious from visual inspection of just a few sample magnifications. Pickover (1986) has several visual aids for conceptualizing the Monte Carlo process (see reference above).

In brief, a Monte Carlo approach can be used for choosing grid points (as in the last section) which can speed the D computation considerably. The name "Monte Carlo" conveys the idea of chance or randomness inherent in a method. Monte Carlo calculations are often used in physics when modelling complex phenomena requiring an exorbitant number of terms and calculations if done explicitly, for example using only a percentage of the number of atoms in a molecule when simulating x-ray scattering phenomena. For fractals, instead of searching every grid square of a picture or graph at a particular value of ε, only a small random subset of grid squares is studied to represent the entire population of grid elements. This was tested for many speech sentence waveforms for different speakers, using different random numbers, and the Monte Carlo method gave D values very close to D determined by the explicit method. D was computed from the slope of a line fit by linear regression in plots of log $N(\varepsilon)$ *vs.* log ε. Normally intractable problems, such as the assessment of self-similarity for several minutes of speech, now become manageable. (Pick86f, *Computer Graph. Forum.*)

4.14 Other Speech Graphics, Wigner Distributions, FM Synthesis

Other interesting ways to display and synthesize speech are described in the above references which discuss, among other things, Wigner distributions and FM synthesis of speech sounds. I present some technical notes on these areas below, and the reader is directed to the published papers for a more detailed account. Readers not intimate with signal processing theory should skip the next section.

4.14.1 Wigner Distribution

The Wigner distribution, originally used in quantum statistical mechanics, can be used to create trivariate representations for speech signals which are similar to spectrograms. [In the past few years there has been considerable interest in a class of joint distributions which potentially offer a powerful technique for the study of signals. The unique feature of these distributions is that they satisfy the correct marginals,

$$\int_{-\infty}^{\infty} F(t, \omega) \, d\omega \;=\; |s(t)|^2 \tag{4.7}$$

$$\int_{-\infty}^{\infty} F(t, \omega) \, dt \;=\; |S(\omega)|^2 \tag{4.8}$$

where $F(t, \omega)$ is the joint distribution, $s(t)$ the signal, and $S(\omega)$ the spectrum:

$$S(\omega) = \frac{1}{\sqrt{(2\pi)}} \int_{-\infty}^{\infty} s(t) e^{-it\omega} \, dt \tag{4.9}$$

Furthermore the joint distribution is uniquely related to the signal $s(t)$:

$$s(t) \, s^*(t') = \frac{1}{2\pi} \int_{-\infty}^{\infty} \frac{F(t'', \omega)}{f_N(\theta, t - t')} \, e^{i\theta(t''-t+t'/2) + (t-t')\omega} dt'' \, d\omega \, d\theta \tag{4.10}$$

where the signal $s(t)$ is obtained by taking any convenient value for t' such as zero. The standard spectrogram does not posses either of these two properties. In particular, we studied bilinear distributions. All bilinear distributions can be obtained from

$$F(t, \omega) = \frac{1}{4\pi^2} \int_{-\infty}^{\infty} \int_{-\infty}^{\infty} \int_{-\infty}^{\infty} e^{-i\theta t - i\tau\omega + i\theta u} f(\theta, \tau) \tag{4.11}$$

$$\bullet \; s^*(u - \tau/2) \, s(u + \tau/2) du \, d\tau \, d\theta$$

and particular distributions are obtained by choosing different functions for the kernel $f(\theta, \tau)$ such that $f(0, \tau) = f(\theta, 0) = 1$. Using $f(\theta, \tau) = 1, \cos(\theta\tau/2), e^{i\theta|\tau|/2}$, one obtains the Wigner-Ville, the Margenau-Hill-Rihaczek, and the Page distributions respectively.] Our research compares several joint time-frequency distributions for speech (Cohen and Pickover, 1986c, *IEEE Int. Conf. on Circuits & Syst.*).

4.14.2 FM Synthesis of Speech

In 1985, the Yamaha Corporation offered the first commercial music synthesizer based on FM synthesis. FM synthesis involves the modulation of one pure sine wave with another; this produces a variety of complex and natural-sounding waveforms. In conventional music (and speech) synthesizers, basic input waveforms (such as sawtooth and rectangular) are filtered to create the final output sounds. In our research, we have applied the FM synthesis approach to speech sounds (Pick87d). See also Chowning (1973) for pioneering work in this field. Note that (Pick85f) describes a system called "TUSK" with 30 different displays for analyzing speech.

4.15 Molecular Genetics: DNA Vectorgram

4.15.1 Background

As we said in "Cancer Genes (DNA Waveforms)" on page 33, DNA contains the basic genetic information of all living cells. The sequences of bases of DNA (adenine, cytosine, guanine, and thymine – A,C,G, and T) may hold information concerning protein synthesis as well as a variety of regulatory signals. For example, specific AT-rich regions are thought to be codes for beginning transcription. Also, certain *specific* viral sequences elicit cancerous changes in cells in artificial media and in animals. In addition to containing such regulatory codes and tumor-promoting codes, DNA sequence and composition are often correlated with physical properties of the DNA such as the DNA melting temperature.

Fairly detailed comparisons between DNA sequences are useful and can be achieved by a variety of brute-force statistical computations, but sometimes at a cost of the loss of an intuitive feeling for the structures. Differences between sequences may obscure the similarities. Even determining whether a particular sequence is *random* is curiously difficult. The approaches described in this section provide a way for simply representing and comparing random and DNA sequences in such a way that several sequence features may be detected by the analyst's eye.

4.15.2 DNA Vectorgram

The "vectorgrams" sometimes look like the steps a drunkard would take wandering in an open field. They can also be used to search for patterns in the sequence of bases in DNA. The method involves the conversion of the DNA sequence to binary data and subsequent mapping of the data to a two-dimensional pattern on a cellular lattice. For the example presented in this section, triply bonded bases (GC) are differentiated from doubly bonded bases (AT) by assigning nucleotide input values as follows: G=1, C=1, A=0, T=0. As the sequence generated by this means are strings of 0's and 1's, the human observer may find difficulty in distinguishing between different sequences (Figure 4.17).

A technique which has proved useful in overcoming this drawback involves the transformation of the digit strings into characteristic two-dimensional patterns traced out on a unit cellular lattice. This approach was applied to the shift-registers of digital computers by D.H. Green (1968). The simple conversion pattern I use follows that of Green (Figure 4.18). Three digits at a time are inspected and assigned a direction of movement over a cellular lattice. "010" would indicate to move up and to the right. Therefore, each of the three digit combinations causes a vector to be drawn from a point on the lattice to one of the eight points immediately adjacent according to the coding system shown. This procedure is repeated using serial overlapping windows of length three, and therefore a pattern characteristic of the DNA sequence is drawn on the lattice.

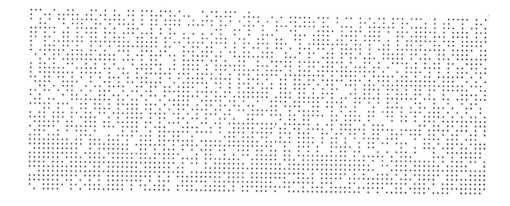

Figure 4.17. *Representation of DNA by dots.* G's and C's are mapped to dots in this representation of a 4000-base cancer gene. The human observer may have difficulty in distinguishing between different sequences using this representation. The DNA vectorgram makes this clear.

Using this approach, sequences with a predominance of repeating G's or C's, for example, will show a net movement along the right lower diagonal. In general, sequences with high G-C content will show a downward tendency. Using the transformation diagramed in Figure 4.18 – you can see that if for each combination of 3 bases found in the sequence, there exists at some other region another

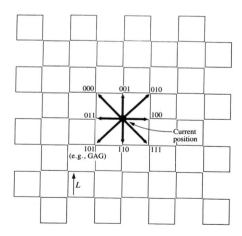

Figure 4.18. *DNA transformation.* The mapping of the digit strings into characteristic two-dimensional patterns traced out on a cellular lattice of cell length *L*. Each of the three digit combinations causes a vector to be drawn from a point on the lattice to one of the eight points immediately adjacent according to the coding system shown.

combination which is the logical inverse (e.g. G and A interchanged; 010 vs. 101), then the net movement will be zero. A repeating sequence such as ...GGGGAAGAATACGAGGGGAA... generates a trace that returns to its starting point.

Figure 4.19 shows a DNA vectorgram for a random input sequence. This is useful for comparison with the DNA sequence to follow which is visually far from random. The radius of the circle centered at the origin indicates how far the sequence is expected to travel by chance.

It was quite startling to see such a large difference in the vectorgram produced by a real DNA sequence as compared with the vectorgram in Figure 4.19. An example of the output of the graphics system for a large DNA sequence represented by the dots in Figure 4.17 is presented in Figure 4.20. The calculation was performed for a human bladder oncogene consisting of about 4000 bases (Reddy, 1983). The vectorgram, far from being random, travels a mostly downward course indicating strings containing a predominance of 1's (011,101,111). The most prominent feature on the map is the "kink" (global shift in direction) at about 1350, and interestingly this feature corresponds to a biologically important area of the DNA sequence. Magnifications of the fine structure of the vectorgram reveal additional interesting patterns (loops, hairpins, etc.). The authors's current work using 3-D lattices indicates the usefulness of intricate 3-D spatial patterns to represent genetic sequences and other kinds of data (Figure 4.21).

One can study a number of other cancer genes with this approach and examine the usefulness of the vectorgram in capturing patterns not easy to find using other traditional approaches. (See: Pick87a, *IBM J. of Res. and Dev.* for magnifications of the regions in bubbles in Figure 4.20. Also see: Pick89, *Speculations in Science and Tech.*)

4.16 Reading List for Chapter 4

Several excellent reference books describing prior work in the field of unusual graphic representations were listed in the beginning of this chapter. In addition, there is a growing literature on the Chernoff face representation. For some good references, see: Chernoff, H. (1973), Chernoff and Rizvi (1975), Flury and Riedwyl (1981), and Jacob et al. (1976).

For more information on the fractal characterization of natural objects, see Mandelbrot's work (Mandelbrot, 1983). For information on $1/f$ noise in music and speech, see the various papers by Voss (e.g., Clark and Voss (1975), Voss and Clarke (1978), and Voss (1979)). The bibliography at the end of this book has additional references.

```
ALGORITHM: Create a DNA Vectorgram

Variables:
 (x,y) - current position in lattice
  s    - step size for walk on lattice

select(argument);
 when('000') do; x=x-s;y=y+s; end;
 when('001') do; y=y+s; end;
 when('010') do; x=x+s;y=y+s; end;
 when('011') do; x=x-s; end;
 when('100') do; x=x+s; end;
 when('101') do; x=x-s;y=y-s; end;
 when('110') do; y=y-s; end;
 when('111') do; x=x+s;y=y-s; end;
end;/*select*/
call MovePen(x,y);
```

Pseudocode 4.4. *Create a DNA vectorgram.*

Cancer genes (oncogenes) continue to be of significant interest to molecular geneticists, and the reader should consult Bishop (1982) for an introductory description of these genes. For a more recent discussion of oncogenes, see Holden (1987). The sequence data for the oncogene graphics experiments in this book come from Reddy (1983). The search for patterns in DNA is also an active research area for molecular geneticists, and the reader should see Friedland and Kedes (1985), and Lewin (1986) for more information.

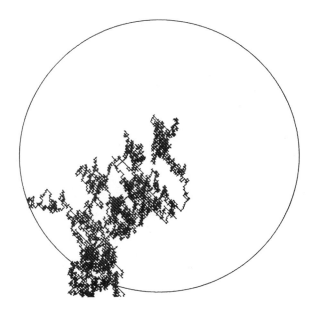

Figure 4.19. *Random nucleotide-base input sequence.* This is useful for visual comparison with the DNA sequence in Figure 4.20, which is far from random.

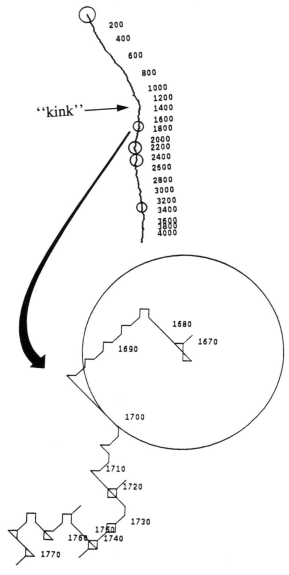

Figure 4.20. *Human bladder oncogene (cancer gene).* The vectorgram, computed from the same data as Figure 4.17, is far from random; it travels a mostly downward course indicating strings containing a predominance of 1's (011,101,111) (see top part of this figure). The most prominent feature on the map is the "kink" at about 1350, and interestingly this feature corresponds to a biologically important area of the DNA sequence. The uppermost circle is centered at the origin of the sequence and indicates how far the sequence is expected to travel if it were composed of a random sequence of bases. The four circles along the strand indicate coding regions, or "exons." The uppermost coding region, comprised of 109 bases, is magnified in the lower part of this figure to show various structural details.

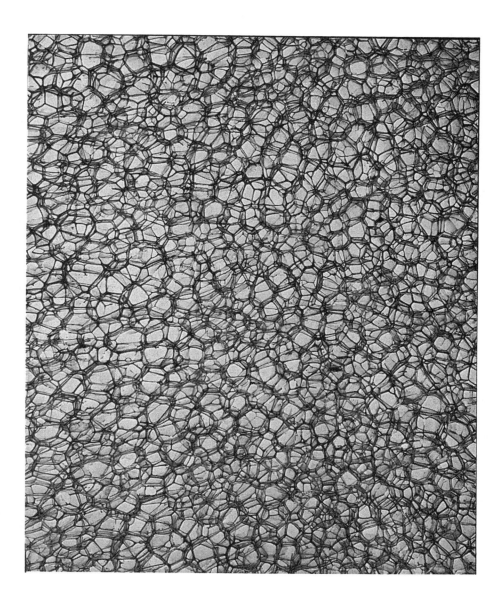

Figure 4.21. *Example of an irregular 3-D lattice.* Readers may wish to extend the DNA vectorgram concept in this chapter to patterns traced out on a more complicated, asymmetrical 3-D lattice, such as shown here.

Chapter 5

Image Processing of the Shroud of Turin

5.1 Image Processing

This chapter and Chapter 6 describe curious and artistic ways of representing images. The methods are reviewed because: 1) the techniques are useful in a variety of applications in Part III of this book, and 2) some of the techniques are easy to implement on a home computer (particularly the methods in Chapter 6).

This section introduces the reader to image processing, and as one interesting example, an application to the famous Shroud of Turin is shown. Picture processing, a subfield of computer graphics, has had a number of different goals, among them television bandwidth compression, image enhancement and restoration, and pictorial pattern recognition. In this section, several image processing techniques are used to render the Shroud of Turin for *artistic* purposes.

5.2 The Shroud

The Shroud of Turin is among the most famous, controversial, and enigmatic of all archeological artifacts. Currently residing in Turin, Italy, the Shroud is an ancient linen fabric clearly imprinted with the image of a bearded man who lies prone with his hands crossed before him. Various marks resembling wounds are visible on the body. Ever since its discovery in France in the mid-1350s, the Shroud has attracted wide-spread interest among scientists and laypeople. It appears that the Shroud contains the image of a crucified man, but it is not clear precisely how the image was formed. Interestingly, the image appears to be chemically stable (it cannot be dissolved by standard chemical agents). Some have believed the Shroud is the authentic 2000-year-old burial cloth used to wrap the body of Jesus Christ after crucifixion. Although the authenticity of the Shroud has been questioned in the past (Mueller, 1982), it is nevertheless an interesting subject for image processing. Recent radiocarbon experiments indicate that the Shroud was fabricated in the late Middle Ages, between A.D. 1260 and A.D. 1390 (Waldrop, 1988; Damon et al., 1989).

5.3 A Sampling of Results of Past Scientific Examination

Since 1978, various physical, chemical, and image processing tests have been applied to the Shroud in order to learn more about its origin (see references at the end of this book). Microscopic examination of the cloth has failed to find any sign of pigment, dye, ink, or powder. In addition, some of the microscopic pollen spores on the Shroud have been determined to come from plants grown only in Israel or Turkey. Photomicrographs indicate that the weave of the linen is a type common in the Middle East during the first century A.D. The image is essentially the discoloration of the very topmost fibers of the linen threads. The "bloodstains" have been subject to microspectrophotometry, and the results suggest that hemoglobin is a component of the color. Other tests suggest the presence of iron, a component of blood.

For additional material on scientific tests – including optical and UV reflectance, fluorescent spectroscopy, IR spectroscopy and thermography, X-radiography, X-ray fluorescence and chemical analysis – see Jumper (1982).

5.4 Past Image Processing Studies

Computer image processing studies (investigations involving mathematical operations on pictures) include the Jackson and Jumper investigation, which suggests that the brightness of the shroud image is mathematically related to the distance of the body from the cloth. They have since produced a 3-D reconstruction of the image. Lorre and Lynn have applied a computer technique of the kind that they used to study images transmitted from the surface of Mars by the Viking lander in 1976. They could find no "directionality" to the image – that is, the image had been applied to the surface of the cloth in a random and dimensionless fashion (e.g. no hand application of paint). In addition, a microdensitometer experiment, which measured the densities of the image on a photo, could detect no difference between the color of the Shroud image and the color of scorched linen – suggesting that the image could possibly be formed by heating the linen. Finally, a 1982 image processing study done by a group at the Jet Propulsion Laboratory involved filtering and color reconstruction of the image. Their color reconstruction experiment enhanced the actual color distribution in color photos of the Shroud and indicated distributions of chemical composition.

Figure 5.1. *Shroud of Turin.* The Shroud image prior to the pseudo-color modifications. A crease in the cloth is indicated by the arrow.

5.5 Present Study

We see contours when there is a contrast, or difference, in brightness or color between two areas. Contours are so dominant in our visual perception that when we draw an object, it is almost instinctive for us to begin by sketching its outlines. On the other hand, the Shroud image is a noisy image which lacks sharp boundaries between image and non-image areas, and therefore it is an interesting candidate for image processing techniques which reduce noise or enhance contours. Described in this section are techniques for making such contours more obvious. One goal of this section is to study the effect of novel non-monotonic gray-scale

Figure 5.2. *Jesus in art.* The image on the Shroud has many of the facial features of the standard bearded face of Jesus in art. This engraving by Albrecht Durer entitled "Man of Sorrows by the Column" was created in 1509 and displays Christ with the traditional long nose and hair, and full beard. The Shroud either reflects or has influenced the way most artists have portrayed Jesus for centuries.

mappings of the Shroud's original image in order to help make clear potentially interesting features of the image.

Figure 5.1 is an example of the Shroud image prior to the pseudo-color modifications. It is actually the negative of what appears on the Shroud and was produced by flipping the bits which make up the original digitized image (i.e., making dark areas light and light areas dark). Others have noted that the image in the negative appears to be a much clearer one than the original. This feature was first discovered in 1898 by Secondo Pia when the Shroud was first photo-

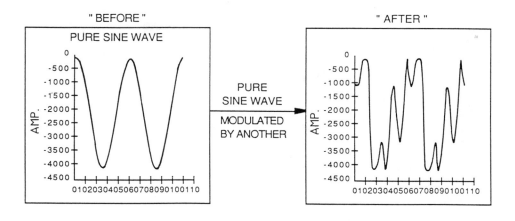

Figure 5.3. *FM modulation.* By modulating a sine wave by another with a different frequency a large variety of complex waveforms can be generated.

graphed. Pia accidentally noticed that the negative of his photograph revealed a positive image of the body which was far more lifelike than the original image.

Note that the image appears to have many of the facial features of the standard bearded face of Jesus in art (Figure 5.2), and this has been discussed by other authors (Stevenson and Habermas, 1982). The Shroud either reflects or has influenced the way most artists have portrayed Jesus for centuries.

5.6 Pseudo-Gray Transformation via Look-up Table (LUT)

In an attempt to enhance some of the contours of the image and to emphasize certain features in the presence of noise, the following protocol was followed. A monochrome photo was first digitized and represented in the computer by an array of 720 by 576 pixels. The digitized image was transformed via a look-up table (LUT) computed from a function of the form often found in frequency modulation synthesis applications (see Pickover and Evanglisti, 1987 *IBM Tech. Discl. Bull.* 29(9) 3761-3764):

$$f(\alpha, \rho, k) = \beta \sin[\alpha k + \sin(\rho k)] + \beta \qquad (5.1)$$

where $k \in [0°, 255°]$. $\beta = 125$ (for the purpose of scaling the sine wave close to the full range of gray levels where 0 is white and 255 is black). By modulating a sine wave (often called the "carrier") by another with a different frequency (controlled by ρ), a large variety of complex waveforms can be generated. Figure 5.3 is a picture of one sinewave modulated by another (where $\rho = 3\alpha$). Using this

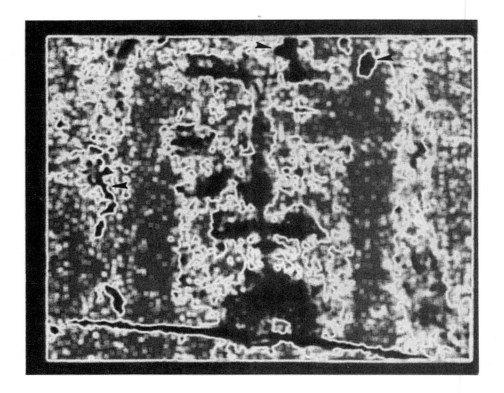

Figure 5.4. *Non-monotonic look-up table.* Image produced by a non-monotonic look-up table defined by $f(\alpha, \rho, x) = \beta \sin[\alpha x + \sin(\rho x)] + \beta$ where $\alpha = 1$ and $\rho = 1$. This figure visually brings out those parts of the face which touched the cloth or were in contact with it the longest. Note that certain well-defined closed regions ("bloodstains") on the forehead and hair at the side of the face are also made evident – and these are precisely where hemoglobin is said to have been found (see arrows).

technique, a graphically "rich" look-up table function can be produced with only a small number of input parameters. By exploring a variety of α and ρ certain features can be made to visually contrast well with others. In order to use $f(\alpha, \rho, x)$ to transform the Shroud, the value of each (x,y) element of the resultant picture is obtained by taking the k'th element in $f(k)$, where k is the value (intensity) of the element at (x,y) in the original image. This approach produces a continuous

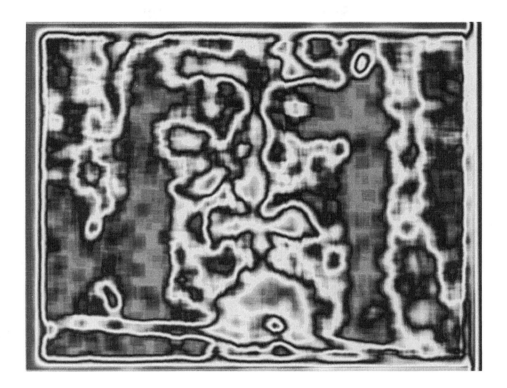

Figure 5.5. *Non-monotonic look-up table.* Image produced by a non-monotonic look-up table defined by $f(\alpha, \rho, x) = \beta \sin[\alpha x + \sin(\rho x)] + \beta$ where $\alpha = 3$ and $\rho = 3$. In addition, a strong local averaging is performed ($n = 23$). This figure appears to visually bring out the region where coins are suggested to have been placed over the eyes, a first-century Jewish custom.

gray scale change, but the fact that the LUT is non-monotonic can help to bring out certain low contrast features (Figure 5.4).

Next, *histogram equalization* is performed in order to visually emphasize various subtle features in the map (Pratt, 1978).[14] Histogram equalization takes a raster of intensities, plots the number of times each intensity occurs, and then

---

[14] This image processing technique is used to render various portraits of equations in Part III of this book

Figure 5.6. *Clipped sinusoid.* Image produced by using a clipped sinusoid ($\alpha = 2, \rho = 3$). Many figures produced by this approach have an artistic appeal reminiscent of the works of Picasso and other abstract painters.

creates a mapping from the original intensities to a new set so that each intensity level occurs with approximately equal frequency. In some of the figures, *local averaging* is performed. Finally the map is halftoned using *damped error diffusion* (Newman and Sproull (1979)). Halftoning is a method of presenting an image that has pixels of a great many different intensity-values on a display with only two levels (black and white). The basic idea is to use patterns of black and white to give the impression of intermediate intensities, and the approach relies on the spatial integration our eyes perform. Error diffusion compensates for some of the error in this process by distributing it to neighboring pixels. Other image processing techniques were tried, including high pass filtering of the image as well as

Laplacian operations; however, the protocol just described appears to give the best images in terms of distinctness of features.

In some of the figures, the sinusoid in Equation (5.1) is clipped in a particular manner so that the resultant picture is bi-level after the LUT transformation is performed:

$$f(\alpha, \rho, k) = 0 \text{ if } \mathbf{int} \; f(\alpha, \rho, k) \leq 125$$
$$f(\alpha, \rho, k) = 255 \text{ if } \mathbf{int} \; f(\alpha, \rho, k) > 125$$
$$\text{(5.2)}$$

where 0 represents white, and 255 represents black (Figure 5.6).

5.7 Processing via Pseudocolor LUT

A potentially powerful method of image processing is the use of pseudocolor for image display and enhancement. The motivation for using color is the eyes' better ability in seeing and interpreting color information compared with gray levels. (Gonzalez and Wintz, 1977). With pseudocolor, processing starts with a monochrome image. The objective is then to assign a color to each pixel based, for example, on intensity. For the Shroud, the most striking images are the ones created using a pseudo-color look-up table for mapping gray scale images to color. The look-up table was generated from three sine waves (one each for red, green, and blue) each with random phase (ϕ) and frequencies (α). For example,

$$f_{\text{red}} = \beta \sin(\alpha x + \phi) + \beta \tag{5.3}$$

where $\beta = 125$. Like the previous method, this protocol produces continuous color change, and the non-monotonic LUT is useful in revealing various low-contrast features. Local averaging is also performed for these pictures. Note that this approach produces well-saturated colors (i.e., pure colors not diluted with much white light). β allows the user to control the color changes in a picture; for example, reducing the β parameter gives a more correlated image with fewer color extremes and less rapid changes in color (see color pate at end of book).

For additional artistic renditions and for local averaging effects which fill in (smooth) the gaps in the face and cheeks, see Pickover, C. (1988c) Rendering of the Shroud of Turin using sinusoidal pseudocolor, *Computers and Graphics* (also see Color Plates).

5.8 Reading List for Chapter 5

Several good books on image processing and related computer graphics techniques are available, and these include: Gonzalez and Wintz (1977), Newman and Sproull (1979), Pratt (1978), and Foley and van Dam (1984).

Chapter 6

Physics: Charged Curves

"For those, like me, who are not mathematicians, the computer can be a powerful friend to the imagination. Like mathematics, it doesn't only stretch the imagination. It also disciplines and controls it. "

Richard Dawkins, *The Blind Watchmaker*

Part II: Representing Nature is concluded on a light touch − with easy-to-implement methods of representing voltage potentials on unusually-shaped discontinuous curves.

Today many important special functions of mathematical physics may be computed by recurrence formulas. The goal of this section is to give a flavor of the subject of recurrence relations and graphic representations. (See "Numerical Approximation Methods" on page 275 for more on recurrence relations.) The tools presented should be useful for home-computer *artists*, and they may also serve as a pedagogical device for *students* of physics. In this section computer graphics are applied in order to aid in the visualization of the solution of Laplace's equation by iteration. The solution of problems such as these by iterative methods occurs frequently in science and engineering.

A large variety of two-dimensional physical problems are governed by the *Laplacian Equation*

$$\nabla^2 u = \frac{\partial^2 u}{\partial x^2} + \frac{\partial^2 u}{\partial y^2} = 0 \tag{6.1}$$

Laplace's equation is useful in many fields, including electrostatics and thermodynamics. As an example of how the Laplacian equation can be solved by numerical methods, consider the problem of finding the voltage, at points of a square lattice of mesh size h, near a charged body. Happily for personal-computer users, there is a convenient way to solve Equation (6.1): one may simply average the lattice point values above, below, right, and left of a grid point. The voltage at grid i is given by:

$$u_i = (u_a + u_b + u_r + u_l)/4 \tag{6.2}$$

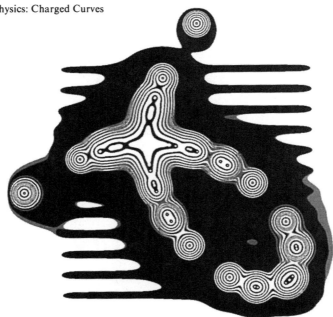

Figure 6.1. *Charged curve.* The solution to Laplace's equation for points on a curve known as the folium of Descartes. The contours were created using a look-up table based on a sinusoid as described in the text.

Equation (6.2) is derived from the mean value theorem (Salvadori and Baron, 1952; Cole, 1986); Starting with an initial value of u at the grid points, and averaging successively the voltage at four adjoining corners, iterated values for u_i are obtained in a very simple manner. A paper by R. Cole (1986) shows how a simple spreadsheet program on a microcomputer can be used to solve Laplace's equation for a small charged sphere.

In this section, a charged planar curve was placed on a grid and the voltage potentials solved for. In particular, a folium of Descartes was placed on a plane using

$$x^3 + y^3 = 3axy. \tag{6.3}$$

Points which satisfy this equation were set to 10 volts with each iteration of Equation (6.2). The four edges of the plate on which the folium was placed were grounded (forced to 0 volts with each iteration). This is schematically illustrated as:

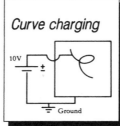

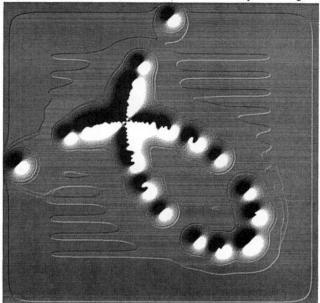

Figure 6.2. *Shaded surface.* Intermediate solution to Laplace's equation for a charged curve, shaded to emphasize regions of high voltage potential.

[To make the problem more graphically interesting, the initial folium was made discontinuous using a computer program and the following equation: if $abs((i - 50)^3 + (j - 50)^3 - 100(i - 50)(j - 50)) < \tau$ then $c(i,j) = 10$ (see Pseudocode 6.1). $c(i,j)$ is an array which holds the voltage values. For example, $\tau = 200$ creates a discontinuous curve where only about 30 charged points on the folium are used. Loop counters i and j go from 1 to 200.] To perform Equation (6.2) on a computer: $c(i,j) = c(i + h,j) + c(i - h,j) + c(i,j - h) + c(i,j + h)$, where $h = 1$. To speed convergence of the iteration process, it is important to start with good initial values. One way these have been obtained is by a *multigrid* approach which starts the program with a larger mesh size, h, and then decreases h gradually to 1 after a hundred iterations.

To display the resultant pictures, the grid was evaluated with several different look-up tables which map voltage to darkness (intensity) on the plot. For Figure 6.1 a square wave color look-up table was used (the table contains just two-states, black and white). This table can be produced from a sine wave. To use the table, the value of each (x,y) element of the final picture is obtained by taking the k-th element in the look-up table, where k is the voltage value of the element at (x,y) in the initial picture. This operation creates contour lines and helps to visually emphasize different regions of behavior of the function. Figure 6.2 uses shading techniques to produce a continuous gray scale image and to emphasize the high voltage regions. Figure 6.3 maps the value of u to height on a 3-D map and shows how convergence is gradually achieved using Equation (6.2)

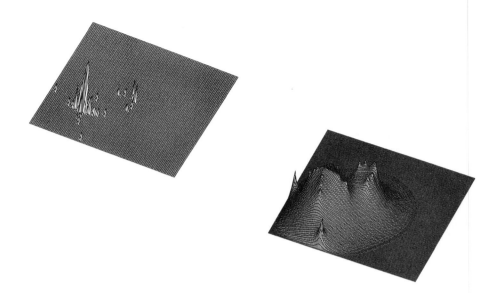

Figure 6.3. *Three-dimensional representations.* 3-D plots where height indicates the value of the voltage potential. Left: 3 iterations, far from convergence. Right: several 100 iterations.

The computer can plot the data as the calculation progresses. Seeing the solution graphically evolve in real time is quite fascinating and helps to visualize the convergence process, as the voltage potential spreads. Another advantage of these programs is that properties of the iterative approximations to Laplace's equations that might not be apparent from the mathematics stand out clearly when viewing the graphics. For example, if the boundary conditions are not fixed, the entire plane gradually becomes charged to 10 volts. Future experiments include: the use of different special plane curves, such as the Witch of Agnesi and the Tractrix (see *Glossary*), the use of different boundary conditions, and the use of curve-charging to smooth images and render scientific data. From an *artistic standpoint*, equations such as these provide a reservoir from which artists can draw. As can be seen, generation of interesting terrains can be accomplished using these methods. The recipes function as the artist's helper, quickly taking care of much of the repetitive and sometimes tedious detail.

6.1 Recipe for Accelerating the Iterative Process

In order to encourage reader involvement, pseudocode is given. Typical parameter constants are given within the code. The reader is urged to modify the equations to create a variety of voltage potential patterns. The purpose of "h" is to quickly spread the initial potential for faster convergence. Pseudocode 6.1 is an imple-

```
ALGORITHM: CALCULATION OF VOLTAGE POTENTIALS
Variables: c, ch = arrays holding the voltage values
k = iteration counter
h = step size
Typical Parameter Values:
iter=2000, res = 200, thresh = 200, volt=100

c,ch=0;                         /*   initialize arrays */
do k = 1 to iter;               /*    iteration loop   */
 if k = 1   then h = 50;        /* initial grid size   */
 if k = 200 then h = 10;
 if k = 300 then h = 5;
 if k = 400 then h = 1;
 do i = 2 to res-h by h;  /* loop in x direction */
  do j = 2 to res-h;      /* loop in y direction */
   if abs((i-50)**3+(j-50)**3-100*(i-50)*(j-50))  < thresh
   then c(i,j)= volt;
   ch(i,j) = c(i+h,j) + c(i-h,j) + c(i,j-h) + c(i,j+h);
  end; /* j */
 end; /* i */
 c=(ch)/4;                      /* average the values */
end; /* k */
```

Pseudocode 6.1. *Calculation of voltage potentials.*

mentation of the mean value theorem in Equation (6.2). A curve defined by Equation (6.3) is charged to 100 volts and the voltage potentials are solved for. (Pick88r, *Comput. Lang.*)

6.2 Reading List for Chapter 6

Much has been written on the use of Laplace's equation in a variety of fields. For example, two references are Cole (1986) (useful for beginners) and Salvadori and Baron (1952), which gives more detailed information.

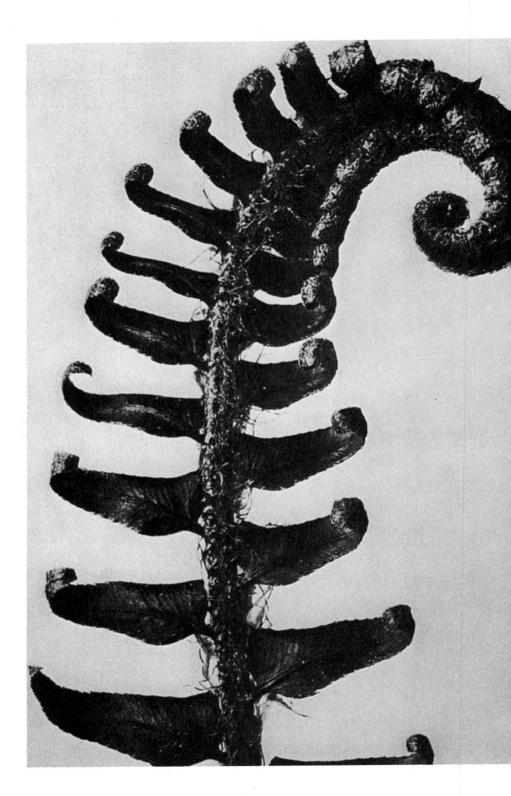

Chapter 7

Summary of Part II

Part II (Representing Nature) illustrates just a few of the many ways to cope with the vast quantities of data generated by modern instruments and computer techniques. Particular attention was given to identifying patterns and trends in various types of data. The displays were a mixture of old ideas used in new contexts and new ideas brought to bear on long-standing data analysis problems. Some of the displays described included: the DNA vectorgram, auto-correlation face, symmetrized dot-pattern, phase vectorgram, and random dot-display. Notice that the choice of data representation depends on the attributes of the phenomena under study, what the researcher is looking for, and the intended target audience (e.g. technical colleagues vs. children vs. general public). For a survey of the work described in this chapter and references to work in related fields, see Peterson's article in *Science News* (131: 392-394, 1987).

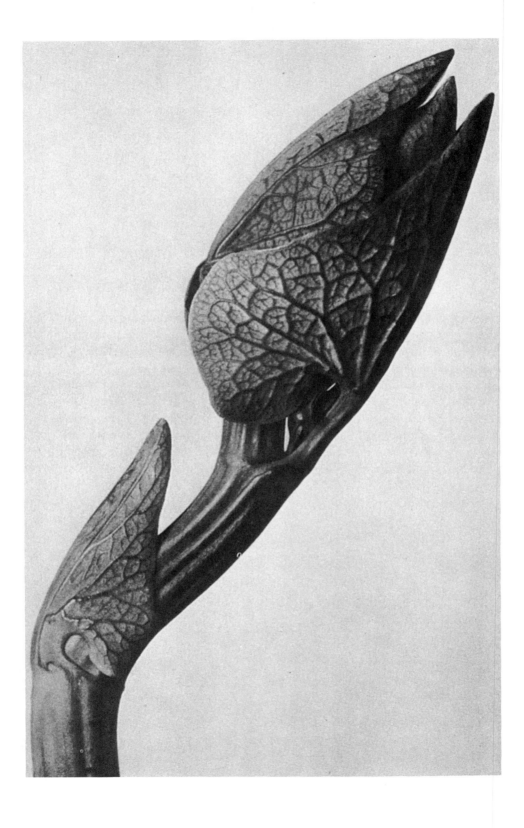

Part III

PATTERN, SYMMETRY, BEAUTY

"Some people can read a musical score and in their minds hear the music ... Others can see, in their mind's eye, great beauty and structure in certain mathematical functions ... Lesser folk, like me, need to hear music played and see numbers rendered to appreciate their structures."
Peter B. Schroeder, scientific consultant, 1986

As suggested in Chapter 2, in much of the work in this book, the line between art and science has become indistinct. Computer graphics makes this particularly apparent and adds a new element to the field of mathematics. The following chapters describe research in a "Mathematics and Beauty" series of publications (see bibliography for a listing). For references on work in this area (including fractals, chaos, and graceful geometric forms reminiscent of soap-film surfaces), see I. Peterson's article (*Science News*, Vol. 132, 1987, pgs. 184-186), Peterson's book *The Mathematical Tourist*, and this book's bibliography.

Traditionally when physicists or mathematicians saw complicated results, they often looked for complicated causes. In contrast, many of the shapes which follow describe the fantastically complicated behavior of the simplest of formulas. The results should be of interest to artists and non-mathematicians, and anyone with imagination and a little computer programming skill. Some readers may wonder why *scientists* and *mathematicians* use computer graphics to display mathematical results. Science writer James Gleick said it best in his 1987 book:

"Graphic images are the key. It's masochism for a mathematician to do without pictures... [Otherwise] how can they see the relationship between that motion and this. How can they develop intuition?"

The purpose of this part of the book is to illustrate simple graphics techniques for visualizing graphically interesting manifestations of chaotic, or irregular, behavior arising from simple formulas. Get set for the erratic side of nature and mathematics – the discontinuous monstrosities.

Chapter 8

Genesis Equations
(Or Biological Feedback Forms)

"There is no excellent beauty that hath not some strangeness in the proportion."

Francis Bacon

"Whatever can be done once can always be repeated," begins Louise B. Young in *The Mystery of Matter* when describing the shapes and structures of nature. From the branching of rivers and blood vessels, to the highly convoluted surface of brains and bark, the physical world contains intricate patterns formed from simple shapes through the repeated application of dynamic procedures (Figure 8.1). Questions about the fundamental rules underlying the variety of nature have led to the search to identify, measure, and define these patterns in precise scientific terms. Our seemingly chaotic world is actually highly structured. From an evolutionary standpoint, biological themes, structures, and "solutions" are repeated when possible, and inanimate forms such as mountains and snowflakes are constrained by physical laws to a finite class of patterns. The apparently intricate fabric of nature and the universe is produced from a limited variety of threads which are, in turn, organized into a multitude of combinations.

This section begins with a recently discovered class of beautiful and intricate geometric shapes produced by mathematical feedback. These kinds of shapes are called fractals and were first extensively characterized by B. Mandelbrot (Mandelbrot, 1983) and later by many others (see Reading List at the end of this Chapter). These techniques can be extended to the creation of biological shapes. (Pick87k, *Computer Graph. Forum;* Pick85g, *Computers and Graph.*)

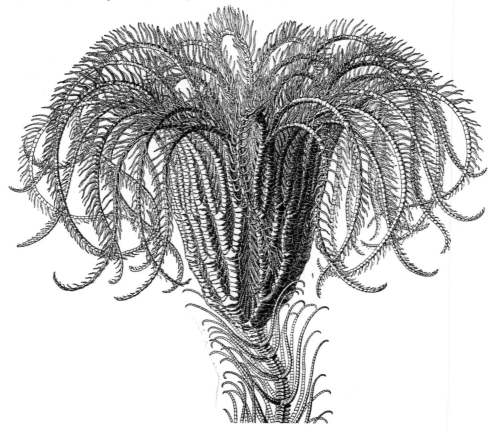

Figure 8.1. *Intricate biological shapes.* The physical world contains complicated patterns formed from simple shapes through the repeated application of dynamic procedures. Shown here is a sea-lilly.

8.1 Feedback

The earthworm burrowing through the soil encounters another earthworm and says "Oh, you're beautiful! Will you marry me?" and is answered: "Don't be silly! I'm your other end." Robert Heinlein

Feedback is a term we often hear today in a variety of settings; for example, amplifier feedback during rock concerts, biofeedback in medicine and psychology, and chemical feedback in the field of biochemistry. Generally, feedback means that a portion of the output of a system or machine returns to the input. In electronic amplifiers feedback can occur if the microphone is placed too close to the speaker. In the world of mathematics, feedback is often the result of an "iteration" or "recursion." By iteration, we mean the repetition of an operation or set of operations. In mathematics, composing a function with itself, such as in

Figure 8.2. *A Julia set.* The equation defining the set is $z = z^2 + \mu$, where μ is constant.

$f(f(x))$, can represent an iteration. The computational process of determining x_{i+1} given x_i is called an iteration. Take for example the simple act of squaring a number. Let's presume we have a magic box that squares whatever numbers are fed to it – if we put in 2, out comes 4. Now let's take the output, 4, and feed it to the input. Out comes 16. This self-squaring process is an example of mathematical feedback, and it may be simply described by the following equation: $z \rightarrow z^2$.

This particular squaring feedback seems rather uninteresting. The progress of the iteration is monotonic. Even if we add a constant (which can be designated by the Greek letter μ) to the squaring process, the numbers still follow a rather uninteresting and ever-increasing progression: $z \rightarrow z^2 + \mu$.

Gaston Julia (1893-1978) was one of the first mathematicians to notice that, under certain conditions, this feedback loop produces startling results. These results arise when "complex"[15] z values are used as input (complex numbers are of

---

[15] If real numbers are taken to represent points on a line, then complex numbers can represent points in a plane. Complex numbers are often represented by the symbols z or ζ.

Figure 8.3. *Shape produced by a mathematical feedback loop.* This figure was produced by the equation $z = z^2 + 0.5$ and is sometimes referred to as a filled "Julia set." Successive magnifications reveal the "self-similar" nature of the big black objects. This is a magnification of part of Figure 8.2.

the form $a + ib$ where $i = \sqrt{-1}$).[16] However, the striking beauty and complexity of "maps" representing such iterative Julia calculations have only recently been explored in detail, due in part to advances in computer graphics. B. Mandelbrot

---

[16] A note on complex numbers: If you were asked to find an x such that $x^2 + 1 = 0$ you would quickly realize that there was no real solution. This fact led early mathematicians to consider solutions involving the square root of negative numbers. Heron of Alexandria (c. A.D. 100) was probably the first individual who formally presented a square root of a negative number as a solution to a problem (for trivia aficionados, it was: $\sqrt{-63}$). These numbers were considered quite meaningless and hence the term "imaginary" was used. Today, imaginary numbers are indispensable to several branches of mathematics and physics. Carl Friedrich Gauss (1832) coined the word "complex" to describe numbers with a real and imaginary component.

Figure 8.4. *One of the author's first attempts at mathematical feedback.* The equation used was $z = z^z + \mu$.

has extended the theory and graphic presentation of iterated functions as a special class of the new geometry called "fractal" geometry. Fractals represent rough-edged objects or patterns that often appear self-similar; i.e., no matter what scale is used to view the pattern, the magnified portion of the fractal shape looks just like the original pattern (see "Fractal Characterization of Speech Waveform Graphs" on page 57 and also *The Beauty of Fractals*, Springer, 1986).

To familiarize yourself with the appearance of Julia set maps, see Figure 8.2. To create this figure, start with an array of complex values (z) and have the computer follow the outcome of the squaring process defined by $z \rightarrow z^2 + \mu$, where μ is constant. Once the initial points are selected, each iteration represents a step along a path that hops from one complex number z to the next. The collection of all such points along a path constitutes an orbit. The basic goal is to understand the ultimate fate of all orbits for a given system. For example, for certain initial z values, the z^2 equation produces larger and larger values; i.e., the function explodes or diverges. For other values, it does not explode (it is bounded). This behavior can be characterized by computer graphics. (See Mandelbrot's book

Figure 8.5. *Feedback plot.* The equation used was $z = z^5 + \mu$. Note that some of these plots are printed in reverse (black and white regions interchanged) for aesthetics.

(1983) for fascinating computer graphic representations of Julia sets. Also see Brooks and Matelski (1981) for some early graphic representations of Julia and Mandelbrot sets).

Some of the work in this book focuses on new equations which have particularly "beautiful" and complicated behavior and on slightly unusual ways of implementing, testing, and portraying their behavior. Insight into the complexity of nonlinear systems may be gained from experimentation on the computer by iterating functions:

$$z_n = f(z_{n-1}, \mu); \quad n = 1, 2, 3, \ldots \tag{8.1}$$

To reiterate, for certain values of z_0 the sequence z_n may diverge (grow increasingly large). For other values, the iteration converges to a small number, or hops between a set of several small numbers (this hopping behavior is called a "limit cycle"), or seems to display random behavior (known as "chaos"; see

Figure 8.6. *Feedback plot.* A typical biomorph is shown.

"Mathematical Chaos" on page 141). For monochrome graphic displays, regions which do not grow large are differentiated from regions in the z plane which explode upon iteration by black and white coloration. One way of implementing this on a computer is to take an initial z value, and perform the iteration in Equation (8.1) until the magnitude of z reaches a certain threshold value, τ. If after a large number of iterations, n, the magnitude of z is less than τ, place a black dot on the screen. For color figures, the number of iterations needed to reach the threshold is mapped to different colors to indicate the rate of explosion. Notice that an intricate structure evolves from a very simple equation! Also notice that the figure exhibits detail with repeated magnifications (Figure 8.3).

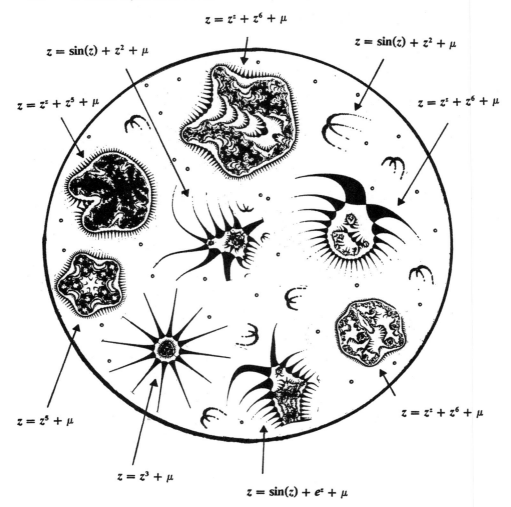

$$z = z^2 + z^6 + \mu$$

$$z = \sin(z) + z^2 + \mu$$

$$z = \sin(z) + z^2 + \mu$$

$$z = z^2 + z^5 + \mu$$

$$z = z^2 + z^6 + \mu$$

$$z = z^5 + \mu$$

$$z = z^2 + z^6 + \mu$$

$$z = z^3 + \mu$$

$$z = \sin(z) + e^z + \mu$$

Figure 8.7. *The Biomorph zoo.* Several examples are chosen to illustrate the diversity of biological forms which can result from the iteration of mathematical transformations. The forms were found in the abstract geometric space indicated by the equations. It should be stressed that their organic quality has not been arrived at through the use of random perturbations, explicit rules based on the laws of nature, or artistic intervention by hand. A joystick-driven cursor allows the researcher to search for and magnify particular pockets in a vast mathematical space which literally teems with these forms.

8.2 A Computer Program "Bug"

After a computer graphics program was written (with E. Khorasani) to explore these kinds of iterative methods, the resultant figures looked strangely different from those previously published. In fact it seemed impossible to duplicate prior

Figure 8.8. *A variety of simple, symmetrical natural forms (jellyfish).*

published graphics. One of the first attempts is shown in Figure 8.4. Notice the complicated network of triangular-shaped objects in the figure. We soon realized that a mistake in the computer program was responsible for producing these diverse forms, but by that time we were intellectually and aesthetically "hooked." Shapes produced by the bug were explored in more detail. Figure 8.5 and Figure 8.6 show examples of the visually striking class of displayable objects that can be produced. Basically, the bug involves a non-traditional divergence test. Points in the z plane are considered non-divergent (bounded) if either the real *or* imaginary component of z is small after n iterations. Normally, the magnitude of z is tested. The application of this weird "divergence" criterion gives rise to the triangular network of shapes seen in each of the figures. Without this specific test, most of the figure can disappear. What's nice about this approach is the amount of fine detail produced in the plot after only 10 iterations (making it easy for

```
ALGORITHM: Complex Iteration Map Generator

Note: Use ConvergenceTest b for Biomorph Creation
f is a polynomial with a transcendental component
such as z**z + z sup 5.
Variables: rz, iz = real, imaginary component of complex number
i = iteration counter
u, z = complex numbers

DO rrz = -4 to 4 by 0.08; /* real axis divided into 800 pixels */
  DO iiz = -4 to 4 by 0.08;/* imag axis divided into 800 pixels */
  z = cplx(rrz,iiz);            /* cplx returns a complex number*/
  InnerLoop: DO i = 1 to 30;    /* iteration loop              */
    z = f(z) + u;               /* main computation            */
    /* convert to real and imag component */
    rz = real(z); iz = imag(z);
    /* determine if magnitude is above threshold value of 100  */
    if sqrt(rz**2 + iz**2) > 100 then leave InnerLoop;
  END;                          /* InnerLoop                   */
  color = i;                    /* assign color index based on i*/
  /* Plot a colored point using either of two test options     */
  if ConvergenceTest = a then PrintDotAt(rrz,iiz,color);
  if ConvergenceTest = b then
  if abs(rz)<100 OR abs(iz)<100 then PrintDotAt(rrz,iiz,color);
  END;                          /* iz loop                     */
END;                            /* rz loop                     */
```

Pseudocode 8.1. *Complex iteration map generator.*

home-computer generation). For additional examples of these forms and a deeper explanation of the computer "bug," see *Computers and Graphics*.[17]

The next section describes an extension of similar equations that produce biological forms resembling primitive aquatic organisms.

8.3 Genesis Equations

"Life survives in the chaos of the cosmos by picking order out of the winds. Death is certain, but life becomes possible by following patterns that lead like paths of firmer ground through the swamps of time. Cycles of light and dark, of heat and cold, of magnetism, radioactivity, and gravity all provide vital guides – and life learns to respond to even their most subtle signs. The emergence of a fruitfly is tuned by a spark lasting one thousandth of a second. The breeding of a bristle worm is coordinated on the ocean floor by a glimmer of light reflected from the moon... Nothing happens in isolation. We breathe and bleed, we laugh and cry, we crash and die in time with cosmic cues."
                                                Lyall Watson, *Supernature*

---

[17] Pickover, C. and Khorasani, E. (1985) Computer graphics generated from algebraic transformations in the complex plane. *Computers and Graphics* 9: 147-151.

Figure 8.9. *An intricate abstract space.* This geometric space, defined by $z \rightarrow \sin(z) + z^2 + \mu$, is particularly rich in features. A magnification of the region denoted by a small box appears in Figure 8.10.

8.3.1 The Leeuwenhoek Program

The last section gave several example representations of feedback in simple systems. At some point, it seemed natural to extend these feedback equations to more complicated equations which contain polynomial and transcendental terms. In addition, features were added to the program to magnify any section of a picture by simply pointing with a joystick. The program was nicknamed the Leeuwenhoek Program after the inventor of the microscope and discoverer of microbes. When the program finally ran, it was quite startling to see complicated forms resembling invertebrate organisms. The next few hours were spent searching a variety of "spaces" defined by complex polynomials using the joystick controlled cursor. Examples of these forms are shown in this chapter.

Before turning our attention to these biological forms, let's first briefly explore a sampling of other work in the scientific literature where computer graphics has been used to create natural objects.

Figure 8.10. *What's inside the belly of the crab?* This is a magnification of Figure 8.9. The crab has organelles within organelles in an infinite hierarchy of decreasing sizes and infinitely increasing numbers. Probably by many criteria, a Biomorph is more complicated structurally than any real natural life form. The region in the box is magnified further in Figure 8.11.

8.3.2 Brief Sampling of Past Work in Natural Object Creation

Algorithms for natural object creation sometimes use random numbers to obtain irregularity and fuzziness. "Random fractals" have been used to generate mountains with startling realism (Mandelbrot, 1983). The peaks and valleys of these mountain ranges, as well as the texture of their slopes, are randomly determined. Other natural objects successfully generated by algorithms using random perturbations include wood grains and stone walls (Yessios, 1979). Researchers have also used rules based on the laws of nature, such as logarithmic spirals for sea shells (Kawaguchi, 1982), or tree branching patterns determined from the study of living specimens (Aono, 1984) (also see "Synthesizing Nature" on page 195). For research on the fractal characterization of the lung's bronchial tree and the fractal surfaces of protein molecules see West and Goldberger (1987), and Aqvist and Tapia (1987), respectively.

8.3.3 Biological Forms Generated from Mathematical Feedback Loops

The method for creating the biological forms in this section uses neither random perturbations nor natural laws, as employed by many algorithms in the literature for other natural forms. These biological morphologies are generated through the iteration of mathematical transformations. The term "Biomorph" encompasses

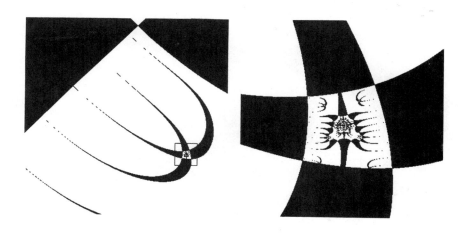

Figure 8.11. *A magnification of previous figure (left).* The figure on the right is a magnification of the region in the box at left.

organismic morphologies created by small changes to traditional Julia set calculations. In many of these creations, the mathematics has given rise to structures on the screen which resemble cilia (short hair-like features on the edges of a living cell), and various appendages (Figure 8.7).

The structures shown in Figure 8.7 have been chosen as examples of the variety of organic morphologies produced by this technique. While the resemblance of these "creatures" to their natural counterparts is only in spirit rather than detail, many resemble unicellular protozoa with their various organelles, or aquatic crustaceans and starfish (Figure 8.8). The bilaterally symmetric z^z shapes resemble ciliated larvae of several marine organisms. The 12-armed, radially symmetric structure (z^3) is similar to the Sarcodines, protozoa with thin, pointed pseudopods. Other Biomorphs contain features which resemble the crystalline projections of fossil adult echinoid (sea urchin) skeletons. Many of the Biomorphs have imperfect bilateral symmetry (if we were to draw a line down the middle of their long axis, both sides would be similar).

8.3.4 The Habitation of Abstract Geometric Space

In nature, organisms are constructed upon patterns of organization that have been tested and proved through immense periods of competition and differential survival. In the Biomorph Zoo, bio-forms are generated in certain pockets of

Figure 8.12. *Biomorph produced by recursion of* $z = z^z + z^5 + \mu$.

geometric space from mathematical feedback loops.[18] The Biomorph Zoo has a mysterious quality, partly due to the fact that in some sense the mathematical creatures *exist*. These objects inhabit the complex plane – though they resemble microscopic organisms that we could easily imagine flourishing in the ooze of a mist-covered swamp. Perhaps, as computer graphics expert Peter Sorenson says about certain fractal shapes, this familiarity results from the fact that these objects are shaped by laws that have molded the environment we live in. Their complexity, both in nature and the Biomorph Zoo, result from repeated application of simple dynamical rules.

8.3.5 Creation and Search in the Manifold Dimensions of Space

"The ascent of life is a hierarchy of organizations continually becoming more complex and more versatile. And so with the ascent of matter, from the single electron or proton to the numerous and enormously complicated colony of electrical particles which make up the bacterium – it too is a hierarchy of continually increasing complexity, or relationships, of organization."   George W. Gray, 1937

Like ancient ants trapped in amber, the Biomorphs remind us of the fossils of primitive life. If such complicated shapes can be found in the fabric of mathematical space formed from relatively simple equations, we might wonder if even "higher" life shapes could be found by searching spaces defined by more complicated equations. Perhaps more "advanced" forms could indeed be found in pockets of more complicated abstract geometric space, had we the computer time to carry out such a search. Whether they might resemble the structures of an insect or the gut of a rodent is not known.

The mathematics of iteration does have a more practical side, and fractal geometry, of which mathematical feedback is just one part, may help us gain an understanding of the complex shapes of nature. These shapes include mountains, clouds, and coastlines – in addition to the seemingly chaotic shapes of smoke, and the blossoms and eddies of water formed from a stream entering a stagnant pool. Apart from their curious properties, self-similar fractals have an immense attraction to physicists because of the role they play in understanding certain phase transitions and the interfaces of liquids of different densities (Robinson, 1985). In addition, work has been done in the characterization of speech waveforms using similar techniques (see Section "Fractal Characterization of Speech Waveform Graphs" on page 57). References for all of these applications are provided at the end of the book.

The Biomorph work demonstrates that a non-random algorithm can be used for the creation of diverse and complicated forms resembling invertebrate organisms. These shapes have both smooth and infinitely convoluted edges

---

[18] For more information, and color Biomorphs, see: Pickover, C. (1987) Biomorphs: computer displays of biological forms generated from mathematical feed back loops, *Computer Graphics Forum* 5(4): 313-316.

(Figure 8.10). They do not have the predictability of biological forms generated by rules based on explicit laws of nature. It will be possible for readers who have access to a home computer to generate their own Biomorphs (see Pseudocode 8.1). Also see "More Beauty from Complex Variables" on page 113 for easy-to-implement complex multiplication with programming languages with no complex data types. It is hoped that the techniques and system briefly described here will provide a useful tool for future exploration of this intricate space and will further graphic characterization of iterative transformations in general. The reader should consider that it might be possible to design a program to *automatically* search abstract geometric space for signs of structures resembling living forms, in the same spirit as scientists search for extraterrestrial life.

In the next chapter, more graphic forms are generated from the recursion of complex functions. See Color Plates for additional Biomorphs.

8.4 Reading List for Chapter 8

"It seems that nobody is indifferent to fractals. In fact, many view their first encounter with fractal geometry as a totally new experience from the viewpoints of aesthetics as well as science."

Benoit B. Mandelbrot, *The Beauty of Fractals*

The Julia set fractals in this chapter were generated using iterative methods which were first introduced by G. Julia and P. Fatou around 1918 (see Julia, (1918) and Fatou (1919)). However, this field remained somewhat dormant until B. Mandelbrot revealed the striking beauty and intricacy of these shapes in the complex plane (see Mandelbrot's 1983 book *The Fractal Geometry of Nature*).

In 1980, Benoit Mandelbrot described another self-similar fractal which consists of all values of μ that have connected Julia sets, and John Hubbard subsequently named this fractal the Mandelbrot set. The Mandelbrot set has emerged as one of the most scintillating stars in the universe of popular mathematics and computer art. The set also has an important connection with stability and chaos in dynamical systems. Mathematicians such as J. Hubbard, J. Milnor, and H.-O. Peitgen have explored this set's intricacies, developing and proving mathematical conjectures in the course of their computer-aided explorations (e.g. Hubbard (1986), Douady and Hubbard (1982)). Several beautiful computer graphics renditions of the Mandelbrot set were printed in *Scientific American* in August 1985.

There are many other references which may be mentioned. For example, Brooks and Matelski presented some early Julia and Mandelbrot set computer graphics in the Proceedings of the 1978 Stony Brook Conference (Brooks and Matelski, 1981). Crowe and colleagues have explored a set related to the Mandelbrot set called the *Mandelbar* set.[19] Robert Devaney of Boston University

---

[19] Crowe, W., Hasson, R., Rippon, P., Strain-Clark, P. (1989) On the structure of the Mandelbar set. *Nonlinearity* 2: 541-553. The term "bar" is used because the mathematical notation for the complex conjugate uses a bar. The Mandelbar set is derived from

has studied the dynamical behavior of Julia sets for certain trigonometric functions (Devaney, 1986). Since the time of Brooks and Matelski, many excellent papers and books on the subject have been published, and these are listed in the reference section of the present book. Some of these interesting books are singled out in the following list:

1. Peitgen, H., Richter, P. (1986) *The Beauty of Fractals*. Springer: Berlin.

2. Barnsley, M. (1988) *Fractals Everywhere*. Academic Press: New York.

3. Feder, J. (1988) *Fractals*. Plenum: New York.

4. Peitgen, H., Saupe, D. (editors) (1988) *The Science of Fractal Images*. Springer: Berlin.

---

the equation $z \to \bar{z}^2 + c$. Readers are urged to experiment with this fascinating set which is described in detail in this article.

Chapter 9

More Beauty from Complex Variables

"Mathematics is the only infinite human activity. It is conceivable that humanity could eventually learn everything in physics or biology. But humanity certainly won't ever be able to find out everything in mathematics, because the subject is infinite. Numbers themselves are infinite." Paul Erdös

This chapter presents additional complex-plane fractals. The reader should see "Reading List for Chapter 8" on page 109 for background references and some historical information. Like the forms in Chapter 8, the shapes in this section were generated using iterative graphics methods developed by Mandelbrot (1983) and later by Peitgen and Richter (1986). In addition to the z^2 sets, more complicated functions are used to generate the graphic forms.

9.1 Turbulent Complex Curls

From the tiny twisted DNA molecules in all living cells to the gargantuan curling arms of many galaxies, both mathematical and physical realms contain a startling repetition of spiral patterns (see "Synthesizing Nature" on page 195 for more information on spirals). In this section, spiral forms resulting from the iteration of complex equations are presented.

The figures for this section were generated using a constant μ, in the region of the μ plane indicated in Figure 9.1 (see previous chapter for background on complex iteration). In this figure, μ values selected outside the central body diverge upon iteration. Exploration on the computer indicates that the tiny region indicated by the arrow, in particular, gives rise to beautiful curling patterns. Since these μ are chosen *close* to the edge of the bounded region in Figure 9.1 they are delicately poised between connectedness and disconnectedness which helps to give the figures their intricate features. Because the μ values are on the *outside* of the bounded shape, repeated iteration yields structures with a dusty, evanescent quality – and in fact, structures such as these are known as "Fatou dusts." The

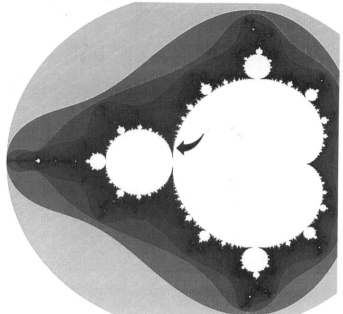

Figure 9.1. *Boundedness plot (Mandelbrot set) for the μ plane.* This set controls the Julia sets in the following plots. The boundaries for this figure are (−2.0, 0.5, −1.25, 1.25) (in the order of: real min, real max, imag min, imag max). All other maps in this section are generated using a constant μ in the black crevice indicated by the arrow. This tiny region gives rise to beautiful curling patterns when the various convergence (boundedness) tests in the pseudocode are used (see references by Peitgen and Richter, and Mandelbrot for additional background information). In this plot, the white areas correspond to non-exploding behavior.

further μ is from the bounding central shape in this figure, the thinner the dust of points.

Note that the triangular network of shapes in some of the figures is caused by the weird convergence test (see Pseudocode 9.2). The striped effect in some of the figures is produced by plotting points using an additional convergence test (plotting points only if the iteration counter, i, is even; see convergence test 3 in Pseudocode 9.2). Like a photographic negative, some of the figures are plotted in reverse; i.e., black is represented as white and vice versa. This not only provides visual variety but also allows certain mathematical structures to be more clearly visualized. All sets shown here have infinitely many buds and bays, and although the equations seem to display what might be called "bizarre" behavior, there nevertheless seems to be a limited repertory of recurrent patterns.

Recipes are included to encourage reader involvement. Typical parameter constants are given within the code. Readers are encouraged to modify the equations to create a variety of self-squared patterns of their own design. Keep in mind, however, that for each of these pictures, there are roughly 400 million

Figure 9.2. *Chaotic curl produced from convergence test 2* (See Pseudocode 9.2.)

z-squared operations (2000 by 2000 by 100 iterations). This can take several minutes of CPU time on an IBM mainframe computer. If the reader uses fewer iterations, it is quite easy to obtain a beautiful picture on a personal computer without waiting a long time. As we saw in the last chapter, convergence tests generally follow the value of z as a function is iterated. The position of z in the z-plane after n iterations determines whether a dot is printed on the graphics screen. Usually, if z grows very large the values produced by the equation are considered to have diverged, and no dot is printed. However, other tests are also given within the code. In addition, possible color parameters are given. If no color options are available, printing a black dot works almost as well. It is also possible to map the iteration number, i, to halftones; that is, the higher the value of i the darker or lighter the shades. For some of the halftoned images, a variety of image processing techniques have been used, including histogram equalization and damped error diffusion (see also "Synthesizing Nature" on page 195). A "back-lighting" effect was also used (see "Quaternion Images" on page 163).

Figure 9.3. *Chaotic curl produced from convergence test 3* (See Pseudocode 9.2.)

For readers without access to programming languages with complex data types, the squaring process can be easily implemented. [Consider the complex number Z with real and imaginary components R and B ($Z = R + Bi$), where R and B are real numbers. Let $I = Bi$. When z is squared, we get $(R + I)^2 \rightarrow R^2 + 2RI + I^2$. The final term turns out to be a real number, $-B^2$. This is because: $I^2 = B^2i^2$ and $i^2 = -1$. Collecting real and imaginary terms we get $R^2 - B^2$ for the real part and $2RB$ for the imaginary part. As a result, we can write a program even when complex data types are not supported (see Pseudocode 9.1).] (For more pictures, see Pick87e, *Computers and Graph.* For a simple introduction for beginners, and for some unusual plots, see Pick89, *Algorithm.*)

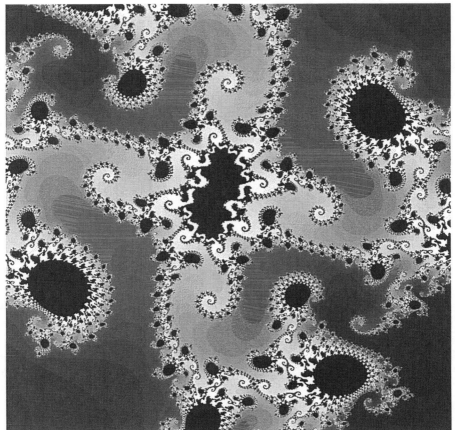

Figure 9.4. *Chaotic curl produced using halftones for gray levels.*

9.2 Transcendental Functions in the μ Plane

"Computer graphics methods have provided crucial assistance in many mathematics problems: new minimal surfaces have been found with the aid of computer graphics, and the visual displays of iterative maps make visible patterns that would never have been noticed by analytic means alone."

Lynn Steen, In "The science of pattern"

The stability plots for polynomials (last Chapter) and the usual quadratic equation naturally lead to curiosity about what similar sets are like for simple transcendental functions. Members of the family of transcendental functions include the exponential, sine, and cosine functions. See "Genesis Equations" on page 104 for an introduction to complex iteration.

In this section, computer graphics is used to explore the dynamical behavior of the iterates of the transcendental function $\cosh(z)$. Convergence maps of the μ plane reveal a visually striking and intricate class of displayable objects produced

```
ALGORITHM: Complex Squaring
INPUT: Two Real Numbers: the real (REAL) and imaginary (IMAG)
component of a complex number.
OUTPUT: The real and imaginary component after squaring, and the
magnitude squared.
REALTEMP = REAL * REAL - IMAG * IMAG
IMAG = REAL * IMAG * 2
REAL = REALTEMP
SIZE = REAL * REAL + IMAG * IMAG
```

Pseudocode 9.1. *Complex squaring.*

by recursion of the complex cosh. As a review, the study of the dynamics of complex analytic maps started in the early twentieth century and, since about 1980, there has been world-wide increasing interest in complex dynamical systems (for more information, see "Dynamical Systems" on page 249). The term "chaos" is often used to describe the complicated behavior of nonlinear systems, and complex maps are useful in describing certain aspects of dynamical systems exhibiting irregular ("chaotic") behavior. Algorithms for the generation of beautiful and complicated structures describing dynamic properties of complex recursion are currently being studied, and their popularity is evidenced by the proliferating number of articles in the scientific and popular literature (see "Mathematical Chaos" on page 141 for more on "chaos"). Recently, Devaney (1984) has provided an excellent mathematical description of the dynamics of $\exp(z)$ for Julia sets.

The goal of this section is to examine the dynamical behavior of a specific complex analytic map that is not rational, namely the hyperbolic cosine function mapping $z \rightarrow \cosh(z) + \mu$. Another goal is to demonstrate how research in iterated complex maps reveals an inexhaustible reservoir of magnificent shapes and images. The graphics experiments presented are good ways to show the complexity of the transition region between boundedness and divergence, and a variety of "views" are provided.

9.2.1 What is "cosh"?

The transcendental hyperbolic cosine is defined as:

$$f(z) = \cosh(z) = \frac{e^z + e^{-z}}{2} \tag{9.1}$$

In nature, this is the curve assumed by a heavy uniform flexible chain suspended from fixed points, or the cross-section of sails bellying in the wind. This shape, also known as a "catenary," is not a conic-section curve, although it is closely related to a parabola. If one were to cut a parabola out of wood and roll it along a straight line, the path traveled by its focus is a catenary.

```
ALGORITHM: Calculation of chaotic dusty curls

Variables: rz, iz = real, imaginary component of complex number
i = iteration counter
u, z = complex numbers
Note: Choose one of the three different tests for divergence.

u = -.74 + .11 i;                   /* typical u value
DO rrz = -1 to 1 by .001; /*real axis divided into 2000 pixels */
 DO iiz = -1 to 1 by .001;/*imag. axis divided into 2000 pixels*/
  z = cplx(rrz,iiz);                /* cplx returns a complex number*/
  InnerLoop: DO i = 1 to 100;      /* iteration loop            */
   z = z**2 + u;                    /* main computation          */
   rz = real(z); iz = imag(z);      /* get real and imag component */
   if sqrt(rz**2 + iz**2) > 2  then leave InnerLoop;
  END;                              /* InnerLoop                 */
  color = i;                        /* assign color index based on i*/
  if convergence_test = 1 then
     if rz**2 + iz**2 > 4 then  PRINTDOT(rrz,iiz,color);
  if convergence_test = 2 then
     if ((abs(rz)<2 ) & (abs(iz)<2)) then PRINTDOT(rrz,iiz,color);
  if convergence_test = 3 then
     if rz**2+iz**2>4 & mod(i,2) = 0 then PRINTDOT(rrz,iiz,color);
 END;                               /* iiz loop                  */
END;                                /* rrz loop                  */
```

Pseudocode 9.2. *Calculation of chaotic dusty curls.*

We wish to consider the *iteration* of cosh for *complex z* plus a *complex* constant, μ:

$$f(z): \ z \rightarrow \cosh(z) + \mu. \tag{9.2}$$

Insight into the complexity of this nonlinear system may be gained from experimentation on the computer. Here the goal is to describe the behavior of points under recursion of $f(z)$. For each selected initial point, μ, the function $f(z)$ is iterated

$$z_n = f(z_{n-1}, \mu); \quad n = 1, 2, 3 \ldots \tag{9.3}$$

where $z_0 = 0 + 0i$. For certain values of μ the sequence z_n may diverge (grow increasingly large), and for others the function does not diverge. Black regions in the figures represent those μ in the plane which do not explode upon iteration. In other words, μ belongs to the set we plot if and only if the point $z_0 = 0$ (called a "critical point") fails to diverge to infinity:

$$z_\infty \neq \infty \tag{9.4}$$

Traditionally, convergence (boundedness) is checked by testing whether z goes beyond a certain threshold, τ, after n iterations:

$$|z_n| < \tau \ \rightarrow \text{convergent} \tag{9.5}$$

where

Cosh (Z) vs. Z for Real Z

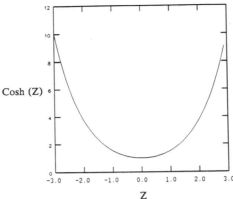

Figure 9.5. *Catenary*. cosh(z), for real z, is an even function with no period. For real *z*, the graph looks simple, somewhat like a parabola with minimum at $f(0) = 1$. In nature, this is the curve assumed by a heavy uniform flexible chain suspended from fixed points, or the cross-section of sails bellying in the wind. This shape is also known as a "catenary."

$$| z_n | = \sqrt{[\mathrm{Re}(z)]^2 + [\mathrm{Im}(z)]^2} \, . \tag{9.6}$$

However, sometimes other convergence tests are used, and these are outlined in the "Recipes" section.

9.2.2 Review of Some Definitions of Terms Used in This Chapter

Mappings from one space, of dimension greater than one, into a second space are often called *transformations*. A *linear transformation* is a transformation satisfying two conditions:

$$F(\vec{p} + \vec{q}) = F(\vec{p}) + F(\vec{q}) \tag{9.7}$$

$$F(r\vec{p}) = rF(\vec{p}) \tag{9.8}$$

The transformation ($z = \cosh(z) + \mu$) is therefore *nonlinear*. We often refer to $F(\vec{p})$ as the *image* of $\vec{p}$. And $\vec{p}$ is the *preimage* of $F(\vec{p})$. As suggested in the previous section, μ *maps* are plots of those μ (in closed black areas bounded by a fractal curve) such that iterates of $z_0 = 0$ under $z \rightarrow \cosh(z) + \mu$ fail to diverge to infinity. *Fractal curves* are curves which exhibit increasing detail ("bumpiness") with increasing magnification. With complex number fractals, "magnification" is accomplished by examining a smaller region of the complex plane.

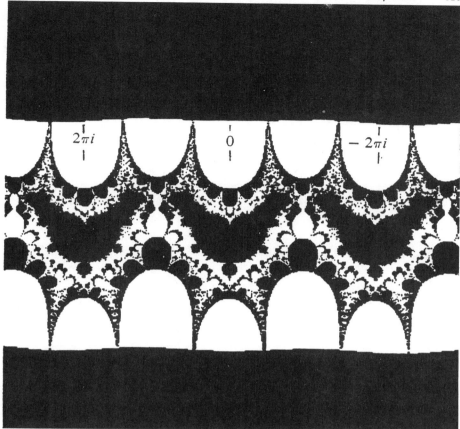

Figure 9.6. *Hyperbolic cosine.* μ plane map for $z \rightarrow \cosh(z) + \mu$ where z and μ are complex numbers. The real axis in all of the cosh complex-plane pictures is the vertical axis, and the imaginary axis is the horizontal axis. $\cosh(z)$ is periodic with imaginary period $2\pi i$. Only three (black) "continental molecules" are shown; however, they occur periodically out to $\pm\infty$ on the imaginary axis.

9.2.3 Graphics Gallery and Observations

Several observations can be made regarding the resulting graphics. Note that cosh (z) for real z is an even function (i.e., $\cosh(z) = \cosh(-z)$). Even though hyperbolic functions are not periodic (for real arguments), cosh (for complex arguments) is nevertheless periodic with an *imaginary* period of $2\pi i$. This periodicity is visually suggested by convergence maps (Figure 9.6). The dynamics of $\cosh(z)$ are quite complicated. Note that the shape of the main cosh body (called a "continental molecule" when the quadratic mapping is used) is reminiscent of the classic cardioid-shaped Mandelbrot set for z^2. There are however significant morphological differences which can be seen in the plots. The cosh set is about twice as large as the quadratic M-set, and there also seems to be a diversity of new shapes – especially near the two tail regions. Interestingly, a magnification of some of the tiny cosh dot-islands reveals a classic quadratic M-set. Upon closer magnification of the central body (Figure 9.7), one sees a highly convoluted surface and many tiny island-molecules which themselves contain a wealth of detail when magnified even higher (Figure 9.9 to Figure 9.14).

As with the quadratic M-set, μ values gleaned from transition regions in the cosh μ set give rise to visually striking Julia sets (examination of the z-plane with μ held constant (see "Genesis Equations" on page 104). Figure 9.15 gives an illustrative example for a real μ ($\mu = (-2.25,0)$). This curve is called the "San Marco" curve (Mandelbrot, 1983) for the quadratic case, where μ would equal (-0.75,0). The notable difference in the cosh case is the myriad tiny San Marco curves which surround the main body. Some of the tiny San Marco curves can be easily seen in the magnification (Figure 9.16). Many of the "dust specks" which surround the San Marco curve along its entire periphery are also miniature San Marco curves which are too small to be seen at these magnifications.

In order to facilitate comparison and characterization of complicated cosh dynamics, it is important to single out parameters which can be followed in a detailed and an objective fashion. Radius of gyration (R_g) measurements appear to be a sensitive way to characterize global structural changes and are a direct measure of the spatial extent of the iterate bodies (see Pseudocode 3.3 for information on R_g). Figure 9.17 shows plots of R_g vs. iteration number for both the quadratic and cosh case. Both plots indicate a large initial change in the size and shape of the structures at low iteration with eventual asymptotic behavior starting at about $n = 40$. Final R_g values ($n = 1000$) for the quadratic M-set and cosh set are 0.36 and 1.37, respectively. The center of gravity for both the M-set and cosh set is ($-0.14, 0$).

"A mathematician, like a painter or a poet, is a master of pattern," wrote English mathematician G.H. Hardy. Indeed, well after Hardy's death in 1947, computers with graphics have played a role in studying iterated sets and in helping mathematicians form the intuitions needed to prove new theorems about convergence of sequences of points in the complex plane. The process of iteration can be likened to pulling layers from a fruit whose center contains a hard kernel. The cosh set is such a "kernel" which remains after infinite recursion, and it has a boundary of extreme convolution and complexity. The cosh-explorer program and its joystick-driven cursor allow the researcher to search for and magnify pockets of abstract geometric space. The richness of resultant forms contrasts with the simplicity of the generating formula ($z \rightarrow \cosh(z) + \mu$).

In the present section, the periphery of the various shapes correspond to a magnificently complicated transition region which no one could fully have appreciated or suspected before the age of the computer. The term "transition region" denotes the fact that points inside the black boundaries have different fates upon iteration than those on the outside. Like classic fractal structures, some of the boundaries remind one of coastlines and, in fact, structural themes are repeated at different size-scales. See color plates for additional renditions of cosh. (For more color pictures, see Pick88e, *The Visual Computer*.)

Figure 9.7. *Magnification of previous map.* The μ values in the central closed black area (bounded by a fractal curve) are such that iterates of $z_0 = 0$ under $z \rightarrow \cosh(z) + \mu$ do not diverge to infinity. The main continental island is symmetric with respect to $\text{Im}(z) = 0$. This figure also includes the tail regions from two adjacent cosh bodies on the top and bottom edge of the map. Convergence test D was used (see "Recipes").

9.2.4 Recipes for Cosh Pictures

In order to aid the reader in reproducing the figures in this section, "recipes" are provided. For each picture there are roughly 6 million cosh operations (400 by 400 by 40 iterations). Some useful graphic techniques are also presented which help create visually and mathematically interesting pictures even on a monochrome display.

Square picture boundaries, B, will be given by four numbers: $B =$ (real minimum, real maximum, imaginary minimum, and imaginary maximum). The threshold, τ, above which z values are considered divergent, is about 50 for each picture. The number of iterations is given by n.

Boundedness tests (sometimes called convergence tests) generally examine the value of z as a function is iterated. Depending on where z lies in the complex

Figure 9.8. *Same as previous figure but using convergence test C.*

z-plane after n iterations, either no dot or a black dot is printed on the graphics screen. If z grows very large, the values are considered to have diverged, and no dot is printed. Otherwise the value is considered bounded, and a dot is printed.

9.2.4.1 Boundedness Test A

The "standard" test. Boundedness is detected by checking if the magnitude of z goes beyond a certain threshold, τ, after n iterations:

$$\sqrt{[\text{Re}(z_n)]^2 + [\text{Im}(z_n)]^2} < \tau \;\; \rightarrow \;\; |z_n| < \tau \;\; \rightarrow \text{bounded.} \qquad (9.9)$$

9.2.4.2 Boundedness Test B

Often to speed assessment of boundedness, with little or no change to the resultant map, the following test is checked which avoids the square and root in Test A. $\wedge$ symbolizes a logical "AND."

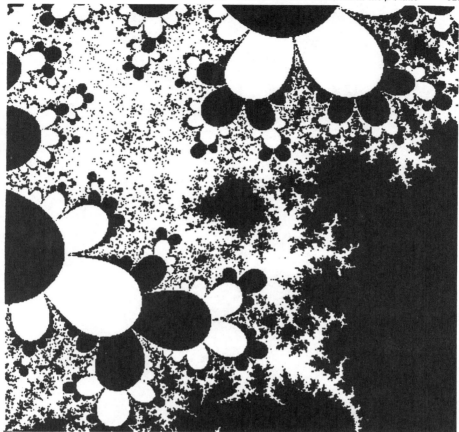

Figure 9.9. *A view of the cosh boundary in a piece of the tail section.* Notice the deformed replica of the quadratic M-set and the detailed periphery of the main cosh continent.

$$\text{abs}[\text{Re}(z_n)] < \tau \ \wedge \ \text{abs}[\text{Im}(z_n)] \ < \ \tau \ \ \rightarrow \text{bounded} \qquad (9.10)$$

9.2.4.3 Boundedness Test C

Boundedness tests may be used which reveal preimage corridors of the real and imaginary axis in graphically interesting ways. Instead of using a circular aperture, as in Test A, a cross-shaped aperture of width τ is used. This boundedness test, and several graphic examples, are presented in detail in Pickover (1987) (see also previous sections). From a purely artistic standpoint, this test is useful since visually intricate shapes are produced even at low iteration with little computation. [However, from a scientific view, the preimages may guide experimenters in locating visually and mathematically interesting regions of a set, can call attention to periodicities which may exist, and can give an idea of what low iteration values may yield. (The solid black or white preimage features do not cover the tight approximation set ($n = \infty$) but surround it and sometimes "point" to impor-

A

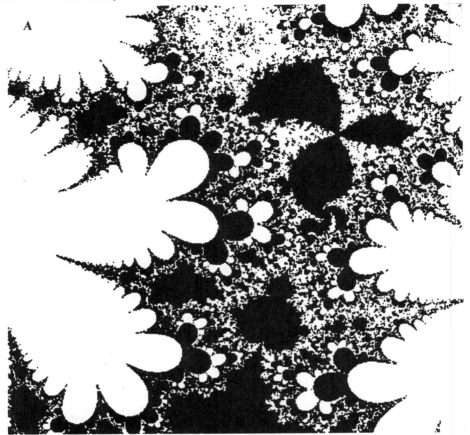

Figure 9.10. *Spears and propellers.* A quadratic M-set is nestled between a spear of the continental cosh and a propeller-shaped island.

tant regions which are revealed upon higher magnification).] ∨ symbolizes a logical "OR."

$$\text{abs}[\text{Re}(z_n)] < \tau \; \lor \; \text{abs}[\text{Im}(z_n)] < \tau \quad \rightarrow \text{bounded} \tag{9.11}$$

9.2.4.4 Boundedness Test D

This boundedness test, which has many of the graphical and mathematical features of Test C, has been used for many of the figures in this section. Basically it gives an idea of what lower iteration numbers (n) yield, while at the same time displaying the "tight approximation." Pictures computed with a lower iteration count are generally less detailed, and the main non-divergent structures are larger. The iteration loop in Equation (9.3) is performed, and if z grows too large (as tested by 1 and 2 below, in sequence) the loop is left:

B

Figure 9.11. *Magnification of region in previous figure.* The area magnified is between the tip of the M-set and the propeller-like structure. The island, a deformed replica of the quadratic M-set, is connected to other structures by superstable strings which remain upon even higher iteration.

1.   If abs[Re(z_n)] $\vee$ abs [Im(z_n)] are greater than threshold, τ, then leave the z iteration loop.

2.   If

$$\sqrt{[\mathrm{Re}(z_n)]^2 + [\mathrm{Im}(z_n)]^2} > \tau, \tag{9.12}$$

then leave the iteration loop.

3.   The loop counter, i, at the point the loop is left ($i < n$) is checked, and black and white regions are alternated depending on the current value of i. For example, if $i = 3$, there is a "pen-down." $i = 4$ causes "pen-up." $i = 5$ causes "pen-down," and so on. In some of these applications, only about 6 "layers" are used, and $i = n$ (the "tight approximation") always causes a pen-down. Step 1 (above) is used only for computational speed and for preventing numerical overflows that might be caused by squaring in Step 2.

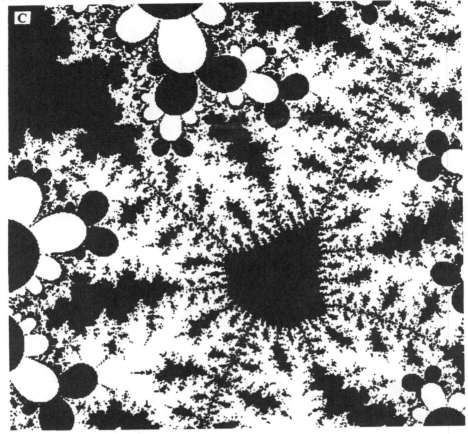

Figure 9.12. *Magnification of deformed M-set in previous figure.*

9.2.5 Maps

Unless stated otherwise, the picture resolution is 400 x 400 grid units. For Figure 9.6, the window coordinates, B, (described in "Recipes") are ($-10, 10, -10, 10$), and the maximum number of iterations, N, is 40. Boundedness Test D is used. For Figure 9.7, $B = (-4, 4, -4, 4)$, $n = 40$, and boundedness Test D is used. For Figure 9.9, $B = (0.411, 1.099, -1.75, -1.058)$, $n = 35$, and boundedness Test D is used. For Figure 9.10, $B = (1.0126, 1.916, 1.447, 2.353)$, $n = 40$, and boundedness Test D is used. For Figure 9.11, $B = (1.369, 1.424, 0.744, 1.799)$, $n = 30$, and boundedness Test D is used. For Figure 9.12, $B = (1.369, 1.387, 1.778, 1.796)$, n=40, and boundedness Test D is used. For Figure 9.13, $B = (0.377, 1.981, 2.491, 4.095)$, $n = 60$, and boundedness Test B is used. The resolution is 500 x 500. For Figure 9.14, $B = (0.350, 0.508, 0.974, 1.132)$, $n = 40$, and boundedness Test C is used. For Figure 9.15, a z-plane map, $B = (-2.8, 2.8, -2.8, 2.8)$, $n = 40$, and boundedness Test D is

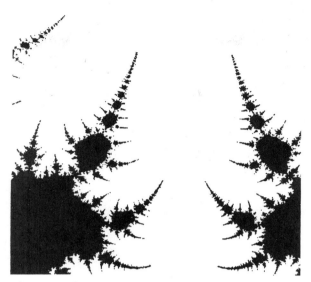

Figure 9.13. *Are adjacent cosh continents connected?* Here a high-resolution magnification of the region between two continental bodies is presented. From this picture, it appears that there are no connecting strings, but mathematical research is needed to properly answer this question.

used. For Figure 9.16, a z-plane map, $B = (0.876, 1.785, 1.592, 2.501)$, $n = 35$, and boundendess Test D is used.

9.3   How to Design Textures Using Recursive Composite Functions

"One sign of an interesting program is that you cannot readily predict its output."
   Brian Hayes, "On the bathtub algorithm for dot-matrix holograms" (1986)

In this section, the concept of "controlled accident" in computer art is explored. Only relatively recently has the break between artistic and scientific pursuits become so apparent. Whereas earlier thinkers such as Leonardo da Vinci pursued science and art in the light of guiding principles such as harmony and proportion, today some hold the view that the scientific way of life stifles the artistic spirit. Nevertheless, the computer is, in fact, a machine capable of creating images of captivating beauty and power. The current section illustrates several artistic textural effects discovered in the course of studying certain iterated equations. In somewhat the same spirit of the paintings of Jackson Pollack and Louis Daguerre, and the music of John Cage, these figures represent "controlled accidents." "Controlled accident" has found its place in many areas of the modern arts (O'Brien, 1968).

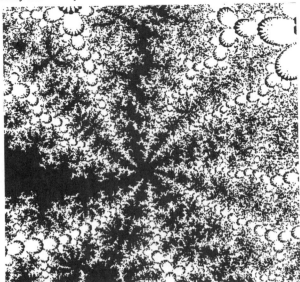

Figure 9.14. *A detail offshore from the cosh continental island.*

9.3.1 Secrets and Tricks

We wish to consider the recursion of

$$f(z): z \rightarrow \lambda \left[(\lambda z - \lambda/z) - \frac{1}{(\lambda z - \lambda/z)^2} \right] \qquad (9.13)$$

The notion of using mathematical feedback loops on real or complex numbers to produce artistic results is not new – as evidenced by the growing number of papers in the scientific and popular literature (see previous sections). The secret or "trick" often is to find just the right equations to produce interesting behavior. For example, Figure 9.18 was created using a fairly simple-looking equation $z = \lambda z - \lambda/z^2$. λ is held constant while z is iterated. λ is then changed and the equation iterated again. Here, the black regions represents those λ regions which do not explode upon repeated application of the equation. While the figure is certainly appealing aesthetically, compare this with the remaining figures created using Equation (9.13) (see also Color Plates). Equation (9.13) produces figures with a beautiful frothy look and with extremely intricate textures. For the Color Plates, the different colors indicate different rates of divergence. Figure 9.22 is a Julia set (a map of the z plane for a particular constant value of λ).

One question comes immediately to mind: how do we arrive at such an intricate equation easily? The trick here is to use composite functions when programming a computer. Let f be a function which maps set X into set Y, that is, $y = f(x)$, and let g be a function which maps set Y into set Z, that is, $z = g(y)$. The composition of a function g with function f is a composite function denoted by $g \circ f$ which maps set X into set Z. [For each element $x \in X$ there corresponds

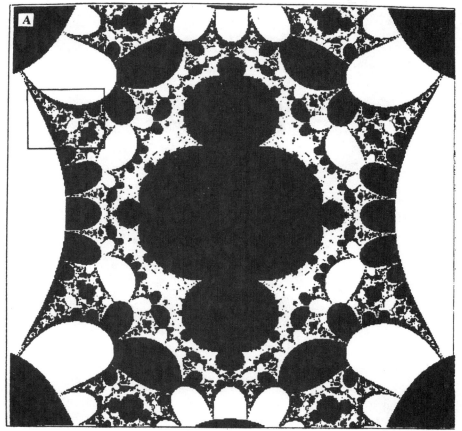

Figure 9.15. *San Marco wonderland.* An illustrative Julia set (z-plane picture with μ held constant) for $\mu = (-2.25,0)$. This curve is called the "San Marco" curve for the quadratic case. The San Marco curve is the lobed black shape in the middle of the figure. Notice the myriad tiny San Marco curves which surround the main body.

an element $z \in Z$ through the intermediary element $y \in Y$.] For example, take two simple functions: $z \to \lambda z - \lambda z^{-1}$ and $z \to \lambda z - \lambda z^{-2}$. Their composite is Equation (9.13). For the rest of this section, a composite function of this type is denoted as C_o. In a computer program, the composite is implemented merely by having one equation follow the other. The reader is encouraged to try some equations, either found in the literature or found by the user's personal experimentation, and to form C_o of two or three functions, and compute the resulting textures.

For more mathematical interest, let me note that it is possible to determine the collective behavior of starting points in the various non-exploding regions simply by selecting a point in the region and following its fate. The different visually-distinct black regions generally contain collections of points that all have the same behavior. Figure 9.23 is a sketch which shows the period of the limit cycles for certain indicated regions in Figure 9.19 (see also "Feedback" on

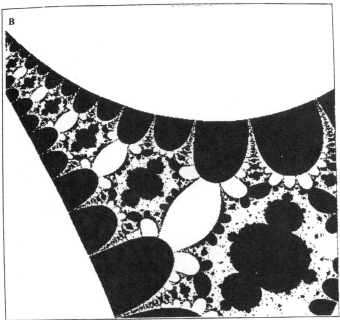

Figure 9.16. *A magnification of the cosh San Marco curve.* (See box in Figure 9.15.) The reader is urged to explore this "tube" by magnifying its different sections.

page 96). The λ maps for Equation (9.13) start with an initial value $z_0 = 0.5$ and they subsequently reveal a visually striking and intricate class of patterns indicative of behavior ranging from stable points, to a bifurcating hierarchy of stable cycles, to apparently random fluctuations.

9.3.2 Chaos and Pattern

The total absence of structure, such as in the visual noise produced by a TV set turned to an unused channel, is not very appealing from an artistic standpoint. Similarly, the vertical-bar test pattern on the TV set is also aesthetically uninteresting. In fact, the precise balance of randomness and order in a picture can often control the degree to which the human eye considers the pattern "beautiful." The computer is a tool which allows us to explore and produce art by playing with this mix of chaos and order. This is done by 1) altering the equations, 2) altering the various parameters, or 3) by focussing on regions of the complex plane which have a interesting mix of textures. Most often one can explore by first quickly producing low-resolution maps and then zooming into regions and using a finer sampling of the plane.

In this section, texturing by complex mappings is an effective method of simulating modern-art surface detail. It took Jackson Pollock to recognize the visual appeal of the dropping of paint – and to declare that dribbled paint could be

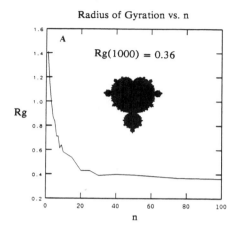

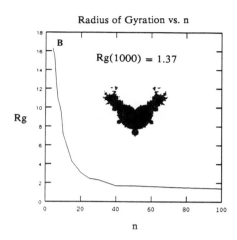

Figure 9.17. *Radius of gyration measurements as a function of iteration, n.* The radius of gyration gives an idea of the spatial extent of an object. The cosh set (b) and quadratic M-set (a) are compared.

appropriate subject matter for art. Likewise, controlled accident in computer graphics is emerging as an important art form. Past work by others in natural object creation by computer includes wood grains and stone walls (Yessios, 1979). Commercial techniques for producing textures without the aid of a computer are numerous. For example, manufacturers of paper products traditionally create "marble-paper" by dripping oil paint into a large vat of water (see "Synthesizing Ornamental Textures" on page 227). Other methods of realistic texture generation involve mapping of scanned images onto the surface of an object; the technique is simple and versatile but can sometimes lead to distortions.

9.3.3 Where Do We Go From Here?

"In my experience in architectural design, use of the 'thumbnail' sketch, done with a crayon really too large for the job, introduced frequent 'accidentals', which I believe were communications from the subconscious."

Geddes H. Jackson, *Science News*

By using composite maps, and by varying parameters such as the picture boundaries, thresholds (τ), z_0, or λ, the mathematician/artist can display results in a compelling fashion dictated as much by a sense of aesthetics as the needs of logic. From a purely artistic standpoint, some of the figures in this section are reminis-

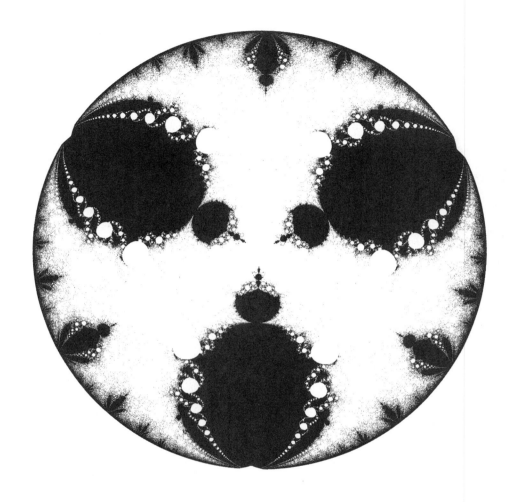

Figure 9.18. λ *map for the simple non-composite equation in the text.*

cent of the crawls and dribbles of paint on an "incompatible surface," or the foaming of liquids (Figure 9.24). This resemblance is due to the mixture of stochasticity and periodicity produced by the algorithm, and the reader should explore the various parameters to achieve artistic control and a variety of visual effects.

Figure 9.19. λC_o *map.* (This is computed for Equation (9.13).) The λ values in the closed large circle $|\lambda| < 1$ are such that the iterates of z_0 fail to converge to infinity.

9.3.4 Recipe

To compute the pictures in this section, Equation (9.13) was iterated 80 times for Figure 9.19, and 30 times for the other figures. After each iteration, the magnitude of z is computed and compared to a threshold value. This is shown in Pseudocode 9.3. This pseudocode loop is repeated for each pixel in the complex plane. RZ is the real part of z, and IZ is the imaginary part of z. For the pictures in this section, cutoff = 4, $z_0 = 0.5$, and $f \circ g$ is a composite function. If the loop is left before completion ($n \neq 80$), then no dot is plotted (the values have exploded). n can also be mapped to different colors, or it can be mapped to grey levels if halftone techniques such as dithering or error diffusion are available (see "Image Processing of the Shroud of Turin" on page 73). (Pick89, *Leonardo*.)

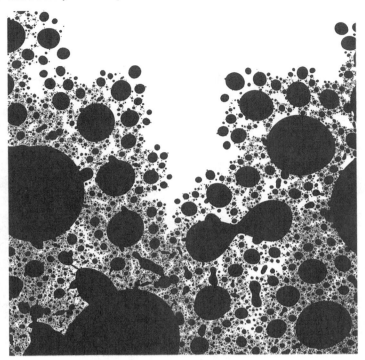

Figure 9.20. *A magnification of the previous figure.* The region magnified is $-0.1577 < \mathrm{Re}\,\lambda < 0.1902$, $-0.551 < \mathrm{Im}\,\lambda < -0.2078$.

9.3.5 Networks, Repeller-Towers

"Mathematical Chaos" on page 141 contains additional material dealing with complex numbers, including the propagation of complex numbers through networks of interconnections and also "towers" made from processes of complex variable arithmetic.

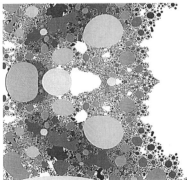

Figure 9.21. *A magnification of previous figure.* The region magnified is $0.115 < \mathrm{Re}\,\lambda < 0.239$, $-0.283 < \mathrm{Im}\,\lambda < -0.159$.

Figure 9.22. *Julia set for* λ = (0,0.2). (This set uses Equation (9.13).) Outside the boundary of the set are z-points that converge to infinity. The picture boundaries are $-2 < \text{Re } \lambda < 2, -2 < \text{Im } \lambda < 2$.

9.4   Reading List for Chapter 9

The reader should see "Reading List for Chapter 8" on page 110 for background references and some historical information.

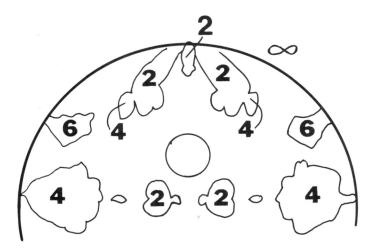

Figure 9.23. *Period of limit cycles for indicated regions.* In the open disc $|\lambda| > 1$ the iteration of Equation (9.13) converges to infinity. For reference, see Figure 9.19.

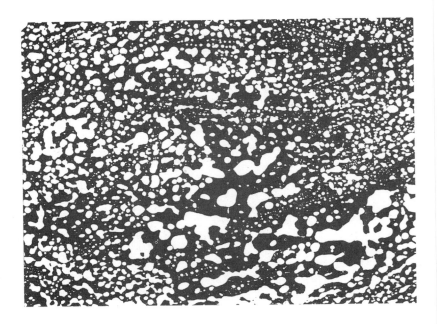

Figure 9.24. *Paint upon plastic.* The plastic "rejects" the paint, which forms small, irregular puddles (From O'Brien (1968) Dover: New York).

Algorithm: Create Composite-Equation Textures

Note: RZ is the real part of z, and IZ is the imaginary part of z. For the pictures in this section, cutoff = 4, z0=0.5, and f(g) is a composite function.

```
z = z0;
LOOP: DO N = 1 to 80
 z= f(z, lambda) ; z = g(z, lambda)
 IF (SQRT( RZ**2 + IZ**2 ) > CUTOFF) THEN LEAVE LOOP;
END;
color = N;
PlotDot(color,rz,iz);
```

Pseudocode 9.3. *How to create composite equation textures (main computation).*

Chapter 10

Mathematical Chaos

"If we wish to make a new world we have the material ready. The first one, too, was made out of chaos."
Robert Quillen

"Chaos and chance are words to describe phenomena of which we are ignorant."
Sven G. Carlson

10.1 What is Chaos?

The term "chaos" was mentioned in the last two chapters without providing much background. As review, chaos theory today usually involves the study of a range of phenomena exhibiting a sensitive dependence on initial conditions. This means that if you very slightly change a parameter in an equation or system, very different behavior can result. From chaotic toys with randomly blinking lights to wisps and eddies of cigarette smoke, chaotic behavior is generally irregular and disorderly; other examples include weather patterns, some neurological and cardiac activity, the stock market, and certain electrical networks of computers (Fisher, 1986). Although chaos often seems totally "random" and unpredictable, it actually obeys strict mathematical rules that derive from equations that can be formulated and studied. One of the principal research tools for the study of chaos is the computer with graphics. Today, there are several scientific fields devoted to the study of how complicated behavior can arise in systems from simple rules and how minute changes in the input of a nonlinear system can lead to large differences in the output; such fields include chaos and cellular automata theory (see "Tesselation Automata Derived from a Single Defect" on page 295).

Many chaotic systems that people investigate are expensive to set up and rather complicated to study. Of course, there is special interest in systems from which researchers can easily collect experimental data. In the next few sections, the reader will see more examples of the irregular side of nature and mathematics.

Figure 10.1. *Chaos.* To ancient man, Chaos represented the unknown, the spirit world – menacing, nightmarish visions that reflected man's fear of the irrational and the need to give shape and form to his apprehensions. Displayed here is a fantastic creature from *Les Animaux*, drawn by J. Grandville (1803-1847).

10.2 Pattern Formation and Chaos in Networks

"In a world as crazy as this one, it ought to be easy to find something that happens solely by chance. It isn't."
Kevin McKeen, in "The Orderly Pursuit of Pure Disorder"

The purpose of this section is to stimulate the reader's imagination in formulating new equations which generate beautiful graphical behavior. The network diagrams described in the following paragraphs are convenient ways for readers to build and represent feedback pathways which are more complicated than the simple $z = z^2 + \mu$ formula discussed in previous chapters. The reader should consult the reading list at the end of Chapter 5 for historical and other backround information to this class of iterative shapes. The pictures which can result from this approach should be of interest to computer artists. The term *network* signifies a structure specifying the interconnections of basic computations such as addition or multiplication.

The aesthetic and functional appreciation of complicated patterns involving the interconnection of rings, knots, and lines dates back to early civilizations. These forms appear in sculptures, mosques, floor and ceiling tilings, rugs, braided

Figure 10.2. *"Creating chaos from order using simple rules"*. (Cartoon ©1988 by Jacques Boivin).

coiffures and formal gardens. Only within the last century, however, did topologists begin the first systematic study and cataloging of such interconnections, or "networks." In fields such as chemistry and genetics (Wasserman and Cozzarelli (1986)) these classifications have flourished; however, as of yet, there has been little description of the rich fractal patterns produced by complicated networks as a result of the propagation of signals through them. In this section, computer graphics is used to represent the chaotic behavior of networks in response to the propagation of complex input.

Past studies have looked at "mathematical feedback" (the output of an equation returning to the input) in an attempt to quantify the characteristics of chaotic dynamical systems in general (see last two chapters). As we said, the most famous example is "self-squared" complex feedback in the new field of fractal geometry. Dewdney (1985) summarizes this work in his article in *Scientific American* on the behavior of Mandelbrot's function $z = z^2 + \mu$ for complex values of z and the constant μ. However, past work has usually involved only the simplest of topologies – for example, the iteration of one function with only one feedback path. However, the feedback topology need not be so simple, and the behavior of one-step transformations naturally leads to curiosity about the patterns generated by more complicated networks.

What happens when a complex signal is propagated through a network with feedback or feedforward paths? For what input values do the values on points of the network remain stable and for what inputs do the network values "explode"? One goal of the current section is to answer questions such as these by graphically

Figure 10.3. *2-D stability plot for propeller skeleton.* (The network and skeleton are shown in section 10.2.2.2.) Wiggly lines in the network diagrams for this and following figures refer to the process of squaring. White represents stable regions. Magnifications of certain areas are presented in following figures. The number of iterations is 30.

examining the dynamical behavior of networks involving several steps, feedback paths, and intermediate nodes. The stability of the network's behavior can be plotted in response to a range of complex input values as the network is iterated (i.e., as signals are stepped synchronously through the net).

10.2.1 Networks

Network connectivity representations help generate and define algorithms available for artistic pattern-generation. Symbolic representations provide a "language" to systematize and classify the interconnections of pathways and feedback loops – the flows of which are in general nonlinear and difficult to conceptualize.

Figure 10.4. *Magnification of central white stable region in previous figure.* The very tip of the "bud" pointed to by the arrow is magnified in the following figure. Notice the infinitely many bays and buds that surround the central white convergent region.

10.2.2 Drawing the Network

A function of one variable, $b = f(a)$, where the function is, for example, the process of squaring, can be written as a simple assignment as one would write in a computer program:

$$b = a^2 \tag{10.1}$$

The network for this process can be drawn as:

where solid lines represent variables and wiggly lines indicate a transformation (much of this nomenclature is adapted from Sinanoglu's papers (1975, 1981) for representations of chemical networks). ρ is defined as the number of transforma-

Figure 10.5. *Magnification of a small projection (arrow) in previous figure.*

tions (in this case 1); the network therefore has ρ wiggly lines. σ is the number of variables (in this case 2).

One aspect of a network involves how line blocks (the smooth lines in the diagrams that represent the variables) are interconnected by ρ wiggly lines which represent the operations performed on the variables. These topological features of a network can be shown by drawing a more condensed picture: the skeleton (S) of a network (N). To form the skeleton, simply convert each line block in N to a "dot point" and each wiggly line to a solid line. In other words, in skeletons, the nodes represent variables, and the lines (or arcs) represent operations. The network above gets compressed to the skeleton below:

A function of more than one variable, $c = f(a,b)$, such as in:

$$c = (a + b)^2 \tag{10.2}$$

has a network:

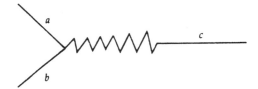

Figure 10.6. *Magnification of small organismic shape.* (Original tiny shape is seen in Figure 10.3.) Notice that inside the "belly" of the shape are infinitely many deformed replicas of the parent shape.

and skeleton:

Note that variables a and b become one node in the skeleton since they are connected and on the same side of the wiggly line and "=" sign. Also, the "plus" operation is used only as an example, and, in general, any operation involving variables a and b could be used for the above example. Several quite different networks may lead to the same skeleton; this can make apparent their inherent similarity in regard to feedback aspects and connectivity which may be obscured in the intricate-looking networks (see following examples).

10.2.2.1 Feedback

Feedback, as in a=f(a), is exemplified by the following transformation:

$$a = a^2 \tag{10.3}$$

This equation has the following network and skeleton:

Note the ring or "loop" in the skeleton of feedback networks. The classic Mandelbrot and Julia set generating equations then, which are often written in terms of the complex variable z and complex constant μ,

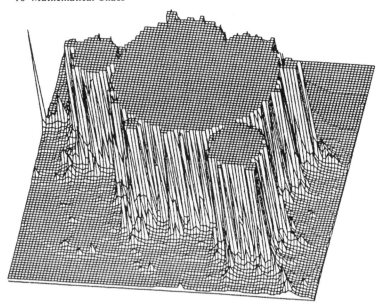

Figure 10.7. *3-D convergence plot.* This is for roughly the same region as depicted in Figure 10.3. 3-D maps provide an alternative way to look at the stability plots as a function of iteration. Although the lower resolution of these plots obscures the infinitely convoluted peripheries seen in the 2-D maps, the effects of iteration are sometimes conceptually clearer. The vertical axis is the number of iterations, and the horizontal plane is the complex plane.

$$z = z^2 + \mu \tag{10.4}$$

can be drawn as

where "i" denotes the set of complex plane variables which are used as *input*, and "o" is the *output* variable which is tested for convergence and divergence. For example, in the M-set, the equation is iterated and the value of z is tested in response to all values of complex μ. In the J-set, z itself is tested in response to scanning of the z-plane.

10.2.2.2 Propeller in Skeleton

The network and skeleton for

$$b = a^2 \; ; \; b = (a + b)^2 \; ; \; c = (b + d)^2 \tag{10.5}$$

Figure 10.8. *2-D stability plot for the network and skeleton shown.* The number of iterations is 30.

is drawn as: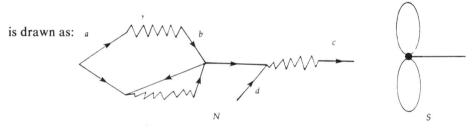

Again, the "recipe" for creating skeletons from networks is to shrink all smooth lines in N to 0 length (bringing the variables together) and changing the wiggly operation lines in N to smooth lines in S. As in electrical diagrams, directionality is missing, although it need not be (as indicated).

10.2.3 Some Examples

The propagation of complex input through the example networks which contain feedback (shown as rings in the skeletons) such as those described above, leads to chaotic (nonlinear and irregular) behavior. For certain initial input values, the signal at a particular test node explodes. Here the goal was to describe the behavior of points under recursion of the network. A few simple examples are provided. Wiggly lines refer to the process of squaring.

The author's 1988 paper in the *Communications of the ACM* goes into more detail, covering such topics as: multistep "laminar" and turbulent networks, linear chains, trees, stars, roses and non-planar networks. The figures in this section show graphics for a few simple representative example networks.

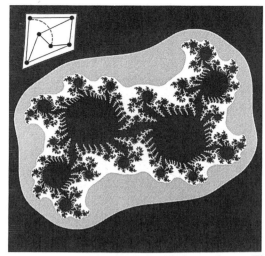

Figure 10.9. *2-D stability plot for the non-planar skeleton shown.* The number of iterations is 25.

10.2.4 Summary

This section described an approach to fractal structure generation. Networks were easily specified which lead to intricate fractal behavior. The introduction of the network flow representations may in the future be a useful way to systematize the search for visually and mathematically interesting patterns. Though the networks seem to display what might be called "bizarre" behavior, there nevertheless seems to be a limited repertory of recurrent patterns. Experimentation with more networks is needed to generalize this observation.

10.2.5 Recipes for Generating Networks

Computer graphics "artists" are sometimes interested in the rapid automatic generation of symmetrical and/or visually pleasing networks which in turn lead to patterns of extreme aesthetic appeal. Two simple programs are provided.

10.2.6 Automatic Computer Generation of Networks

Symmetrical Networks - Upon viewing some of the more intricate symmetrical networks and skeletons, many colleagues have inquired about the computer-controlled generation of large symmetrical topologies for testing. In this way, a large number of interconnections might be generated with few controlling parameters, and the effect of symmetry group classification on the artistic and mathematical properties of the stability plots can be assessed. The easy-to-implement skeleton generator (in Pseudocode 10.1) can be used to produce visually intricate

Figure 10.10. *Example output of the symmetric network-generator pseudocode.*

stability plots. Figure 10.10 shows some examples of networks generated with this approach.

Random Networks - Random networks are easy to generate automatically. Pseudocode 10.2 demonstrates one way of forming the networks. The program begins by randomly positioning the network nodes, and then each node sends out probes within a specified search radius to make contact with neighbor nodes. If the search radius is very large, the interconnections will be totally random. If the search radius is moderate, nodes will tend to be linked to nearby nodes. The program has various controls and accepts as input the following parameters: the number of nodes, search radius, and number of connections for each node. The connectivity is then calculated based on the number of cells and number of connections. Figure 10.11 is an example diagram produced by this approach which can be used as a network or skeleton. (For further information: Pick88g, *Commun. ACM.*)

10.3 Graphics, Bifurcation, Order and Chaos

This section outlines graphic representations with both exquisitely fine structure superimposed by structures which are indistinguishable from noise. As background, meteorologist E.N. Lorenz and many researchers after him have studied the behavior of simple equations which produce "deterministic chaos" (i.e. disorderly behavior produced by a simple rule). One of the early examples was:

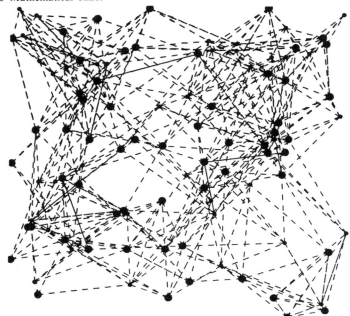

Figure 10.11. *Example output of the random network-generator pseudocode.*

$$X_{t+1} = \lambda X_t (1 - X_t) \tag{10.6}$$

(Lorenz believed that the unpredictability of the weather should be compatible with simple deterministic equations – see Glossary for the Lorenz equations.) This is a nonlinear rule that maps a point X_t to a new point X_{t+1} and can be thought of as a discrete-time dynamical system, such as is produced whenever a system of differential equations is simulated on a digital computer. For any given parameter λ and initial conditions X_0, a sequence of numbers $\{X_1, X_2, \ldots X_N\}$ is generated. A "bifurcation diagram" of an equation indicates the position of points in this sequence (discussed below). For certain intervals of λ, X_N converges to specific values known as predictable "attractors." *Predictable attractors* correspond to the behavior to which a system settles or is "attracted" (for example, a point or a looping closed cycle; see "A Note on Rendering 3-D Strange Attractors" on page 160 for further definitions of attractors and limit cycles). For other values of λ, X_N does not converge and takes on apparently random behavior. A *chaotic attractor* is represented by an unpredictable trajectory where a minute difference in starting positions of two initially adjacent points leads to totally uncorrelated positions later in time or in the mathematical iteration.

[This section focuses on a little-studied equation and includes pseudocode to encourage reader involvement. It should be stressed that graphic studies of the branching behavior of these diagrams ("period doubling," demonstrated below) and chaotic behavior have a more practical side. Despite the figures' complexity, they possess universal features shared by entire classes of nonlinear processes. For example, similar behavior is exhibited in a range of real physical systems

```
ALGORITHM: Symmetric Network Generator
```
```
INPUT: (Angle, length, repeat) arrays, and overall repetition.
For example, angle could be an array of the 3 numbers: 30, 45, 60.
Length could be an array of 3 numbers: 10, 5, 10.
Repeat could be an array of 3 numbers: 4, 5, 6.
OUTPUT: Interconnections of the vertices of the network.
```
```
theta=0; l=0;
do i = 1 to irep; /*irep is overall repetition            */
  do j = 1 to num  /*num = number of (angle, length, repeat) sets*/
    do k = 1 to repeat(j);
    l=l+1;                        /* l is number of vertices in network */
    theta=theta+angle(i); if theta >= 360 then theta=theta-360;
    x = length(j)*sin(theta)+ x; y=length(j)*cos(theta)+y;
    x_coord(l)=x; y_coord(l)=y;
    end;
  end;
end;
```

Pseudocode 10.1. *Symmetric network generator.*

including: biological populations and a large variety of noisy mechanical, electrical and chemical oscillators (Levi, 1981).]

The "one-dimensional map" that this section concentrates on was first presented briefly by R. May (1976) as a mathematical curiosity in his paper on complicated dynamics; however, May used little graphics. Here the goal is to graphically explore the dynamical behavior of:

$$X_{t+1} = \frac{\lambda X_t}{[1 + X_t]^\beta} \tag{10.7}$$

where β is a constant.

[In a useful computer tool, several variables may be entered at the terminal keyboard; these include the picture boundaries, the number of iterations (N), β values, picture resolution (λ step-size), and X_0. Any coordinate values of interest on the bifurcation diagram may be queried and printed simply by pointing on the screen with the joystick-driven cursor. This is useful for estimating such parameters as λ_c (defined below). The resolution ("res") for the maps ranges between 400 and 600 points (in other words the λ range is divided into 400 to 600 increments). The number of iterations ranges between 300 and 400, giving 240,000 dots for the most dense picture.]

The bifurcation diagram of Equation (10.7) indicates the position of points in the attracting set (X_t) on the x-axis and the bifurcation parameter λ on the y-axis. Figure 10.12 was made by fixing the parameter λ and then iterating. λ is changed and the equation is iterated again. In nearly all previous studies, dots are only plotted when transients have disappeared (i.e., t is large), so that X is near its attractor. In this section all X_t are plotted in order to show the trajectories of low iterations as well. Indeed these transients provide visually and mathematically interesting features, show how convergence is gradually achieved, and emphasize

```
ALGORITHM - Random Network Generator
INPUT: Number of nodes, number of transformations for each node,
search radius
OUTPUT: Interconnections of the vertices of the network.
/* Generate num vertices at positions x,y */
do i = 1 to num;
 call rand; x(i) = rand*100+1;   /*rand generates random num*/
 call rand; y(i) = rand*100+1;
end;
/* calculate connectivity matrix, c */
do i = 1 to num;
 kk=0;
 jloop:do j = 1 to num;
  if abs(x(j)-x(i))<=irad & abs(y(i)-y(j))<=irad &
  x(i)¬=x(j) & y(i)¬=y(j) then do; /*irad is search radius*/
  kk=kk+1; neighbor(kk)=j;
 end; /*then do*/
end;/*jloop*/
/*numcon is number of connections for each node*/
do k = 1 to numcon;
 call rand; pickn=rand*k+1;
 c(i,neighbor(pickn)) = c(i,neighbor(pickn))+1;
 MoveTo(x(i),y(i)); /*draw network*/
 PenTo(x(neighbor(pickn)),y(neighbor(pickn)));
 end;
end; /* do i = 1 to num*/
```

Pseudocode 10.2. *Random network generator.*

the fractal (self-similar) structure of these maps. The graphics system has color capability; when low iteration trajectories are plotted in red, and high iteration trajectories ($t > 10$) plotted in blue, the resultant plots are particularly illuminating in that the eye can more easily differentiate the structures of low iteration from those of high iteration. If a range of colors are available, the iteration number, t, may index into gradually changing values of a color table to provide additional insight.

The judicious choice of λ *resolution* and maximum iteration number, N, is important so that structures of interest can be revealed on the map. If these parameters are too low, important features will not show up, and if these parameters are set too high, sometimes significant features can be obscured (e.g. low iteration features and other trends – particularly in the region where attractive behavior is superimposed on chaotic behavior). An interactive system allows the user to choose parameters best suited for visual demonstrations of features of interest.

A bifurcation diagram for Equation (10.7) is shown in Figure 10.12. $\beta = 5$ is used because this produces a range of dynamic behavior (orderly and chaotic). For $\lambda < 13$ there is a unique attracting fixed point (i.e., the stem at the bottom right). Above $\lambda \sim 13$ the solution bifurcates into a period-two limit cycle (P2); in other words two convergent points are found. These two branches are marked by arrows. Following upward across the diagram, the period-doubling cascading

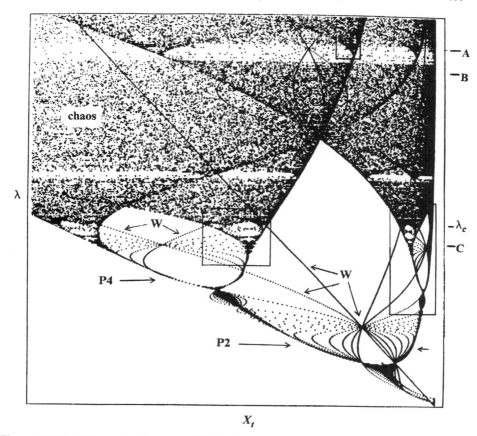

Figure 10.12. *Bifurcation diagram.* (This is for Equation (10.7).) The picture boundaries are: $(0 < \lambda < 125, \ -0.1 < X_t < 5.0)$. $\beta = 5$, $N = 300$, and res = 400. For values of $\lambda > 59$, chaotic solutions are intricately interspersed with limit cycles. Some of the webbing (W) produced by low iteration trajectories is marked. Boxes denote regions magnified in: Pickover, C. (1987) Graphics, bifurcation, order and chaos, *Computer Graphics Forum*, 6: 26-33.

eventually accumulates as the period goes to infinity at $\lambda_c \sim 59$. For values of $\lambda > 59$ chaotic solutions are intricately interspersed with limit cycles. Like classic fractal structures, the maps for these transformations are "self-similar." If we look at any one of the bifurcation branches we notice that the same shape is found at another place in another size (Figure 10.13).

Figure 10.14 has a change in the β parameter to $\beta = 3$. Note the vast difference in the behavior of this function compared to the behavior shown in Figure 10.12. Even though the λ axis is 10 times as long in this figure, no chaos has evolved. In this plot two bifurcations can be seen. Figure 10.15 shows a magnification of a region delimited by the box in Figure 10.14. As the iteration number, t, increases, the low iteration webbing converges to an attractor. If the

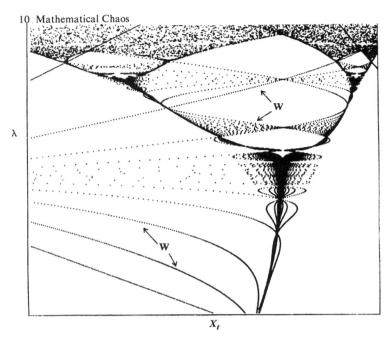

λ

X_t

Figure 10.13. *A magnification.* The area delimited by the box in Figure 10.12 is magnified. Like classic fractal structures the maps for these transformations are "self-similar" (see "Genesis Equations" on page 104, "More Beauty from Complex Variables" on page 113, and "Fractal Characterization of Speech Waveform Graphs" on page 57). If we look at any one of the bifurcation branches we notice that the same shape is found at another place in another size. Some of the webbing (W) produced by low iteration trajectories is marked. For this figure, the picture boundaries are: $(43 < \lambda < 61, 2.0 < X_t < 2.9)$. $\beta = 5$, $N = 400$, and res = 600.

lower iterations were peeled away like layers of an onion, the map would look like a thin "Y."

While the bifurcation diagrams in this section for Equation (10.7) have many similarities to previous diagrams for Equation (10.6) (see for example Campbell (1985)) there are both qualitative and quantitative differences. For example, the plots here appear much less symmetrical about a line drawn perpendicular to the X_t axis, and $\lambda_c \sim 59$ instead of $\lambda_c \sim 3.6$. Interestingly, Equation (10.7) has been used to fit a considerable amount of data on insect populations (Hassell (1974)). In contrast to previous systems where mathematical and aesthetic beauty relies on the use of imaginary numbers, these calculations use real numbers – facilitating their study with programming languages having no complex data types on small personal computers.

The richness of resultant forms contrasts with the simplicity of the generating formula. Apart from their curious mathematical properties and artistic appeal, bifurcation maps with chaotic dynamics and fractal characteristics are interesting because of the role they play in understanding heart failure, meteorology, economics, population biology, neural networks, arrays of parallel processors, noisy

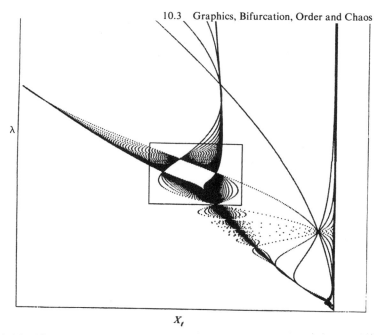

λ

X_t

Figure 10.14. *Change in β parameter to β = 3.* Note the vast difference in the behavior of this function compared to the behavior shown in Figure 10.12. Even though the λ axis is 10 times as long in this figure, no chaos has evolved. Much of the figure is composed of webbing produced by low iteration trajectories. In this plot two bifurcations can be seen. The picture boundaries are: $(0 < λ < 1000, \ -10 < X_t < 100)$. $β = 3$, $N = 300$, and res = 400.

Josephson junctions, and leukemia. As May (1976) points out, the fact that simple, deterministic equations (such as those presented here) can possess trajectories which look like random noise has disturbing practical implications. For example, apparently erratic fluctuations in an animal population may simply derive from a rigidly deterministic population growth relationship.

It is hoped that the systems described here will provide a useful tool and stimulate future studies in the graphic characterization of the morphologically rich structures produced by the iteration of simple one-dimensional transforms. As David Ruelle, chaos specialist, has stressed: "There is a whole world of forms still to be explored and harmonies to be discovered" (Fisher (1985)).

10.3.1 Recipe for Bifurcation Plot Generation

Pseudocode 10.3 gives a recipe for producing the plots in this section. Suggested is a color assignment based on the number of iterations needed to produce a particular point on the plot. If color options are not available, line 5 may be omitted. See Color Plates for color rendition. (Pick87f, *Computer Graphics Forum*.)

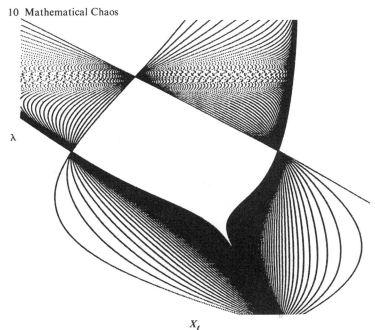

λ

X_t

Figure 10.15. *A magnification.* The region is delimited by a box in Figure 10.14. As the iteration number, t, increases, the low iteration webbing converges to an attractor. If the lower iterations were peeled away like layers of an onion, the map would look like a thin "Y." The graphical method is illustrating the transient approach of an orbit onto its attractor. For this figure, the picture boundaries are: $(319 < \lambda < 500,\ 29 < X_t < 59)$. $\beta = 3$, $N = 400$, and res = 600.

10.4 Image Processing Techniques and Deterministic Chaos

This section is a light introduction to contemporary computer graphic tools which can improve the perception and understanding of complicated processes. The same types of pseudo-gray and pseudo-color mappings in "Image Processing of the Shroud of Turin" on page 73 can also be used in mathematics, in particular in the area of bifurcation map representation. This is an example of lateral thinking mentioned in Chapter 1. In the last section, a judicious choice of λ resolution and maximum iteration number (N) was important to reveal structures of interest on the map. If these parameters were too low, important features did not show up, and if these parameters were set too high, sometimes significant features were obscured. In contrast, the image processing techniques below overcome some of these difficulties.

The region of (λ, x) space is subdivided into 1600 by 1600 pixels, and the histogram (P) of the equation's trajectory wandering through a pixel is represented by simply summing the number of times an orbit intersects a pixel:

$$P_{\lambda, x} = \sum_{i=1}^{\nu} n \tag{10.8}$$

```
ALGORITHM : Bifurcation Plot Generator
INPUT: Min and Max picture boundaries, beta, resolution,
iteration, X0
Typical Parameter Values: min=0, max=125, N=300, res=400,
beta=5, X0=0.9
OUTPUT: Bifurcation-Plot ( Lambda vs. X(time) )
1 do lambda = min to max by (max-min)/res; (* Scan lambda *)
2   x=x0;                          (* Set initial point, X0 *)
3   do i = 1 to N;                 (* Iteration loop        *)
4     x = lambda*x*(1+x)**(-beta); (* Generating equation     *)
5     SetColor(i)                  (* Set color based on iteration *)
6     PlotDot(lambda,x);           (* Plot dot at point (lambda,x) *)
7   end;                           (* End Iteration loop      *)
8 end;                             (* End lambda loop         *)
```

Pseudocode 10.3. *Bifurcation Plot Generator.*

where ν is the number of intersections (for the applications here, we set $n = 1$ so that the above equation simply gives ν). $P_{\lambda, x}$ is eventually mapped to intensity on a bi-level graph using the following protocol. First, all values of P above 255 are mapped to zero to help reveal structures in the most intense regions of the map which would normally be saturated:

$$P_{\lambda, x} = 0 \quad if \quad P_{\lambda, x} > 255 \tag{10.9}$$

These values can be mapped to gray levels using histogram equalization and damped error diffusion as mentioned in "Image Processing of the Shroud of Turin" on page 73.

Figure 10.16 is a bifurcation diagram for Equation (10.7) for $\beta = 5$. For $\lambda < 13$ there is a unique attracting fixed point (i.e., the stem; large arrow at the bottom left). This is an example of an orbit that behaves relatively tamely. This is stable behavior: all sufficiently nearby initial choices of X_0 lead to the same fate for the orbit. Above $\lambda \sim 13$ the solution bifurcates into a period-two limit cycle (next arrow in figure). The rightmost arrow indicates a period-four cycle. Figure 10.17 represents Equation (10.7) in an (x, β) plot; in other words, λ is held constant while β is scanned along the horizontal axis. This plot clearly demonstrates that for increasing values of β the system becomes chaotic.

Finally, a concrete example suggests that maps such as these have practical implications. The discrete phase-locked loop (DPLL), shown in Figure 10.18, is a simple circuit which nevertheless has complicated dynamics. With this circuit, the internal voltage controlled oscillator (VCO) becomes synchronized with the incoming waveform. The VCO's frequency Ω is dependent upon the voltage across the capacitor, C. At instants of time, α, $(\alpha = \omega t/(2\pi))$ the switch closes, and the successive instants of closing satisfy the following recurrence relation, T,

$$\alpha = \alpha + \left[\frac{b}{1 + \lambda \sin(2\pi\alpha)} \right], \quad where \quad \alpha_{n+1} = T(\alpha_n) \tag{10.10}$$

Figure 10.16. *Halftone bifurcation diagram* (for Equation (10.7)). The x-axis represents increasing values of λ, and the y-axis represents X_t. The picture boundaries are: ($0 < \lambda < 125$, $-0.1 < X_t < 5.0$). $\beta = 5$, and $N = 300$.

where λ is the input voltage, and $b = \omega/\Omega$. For a derivation of this formula, and more details of this circuit, see Kudrewicz, et al. (1986). The x-axis in Figure 10.19 is voltage (λ) and the y-axis is the switching rate, α. As can be seen in Figure 10.19, for smaller voltages the rate of switching is fairly constant but at larger λ the behavior becomes chaotic. See Color Plates for an additional rendition. (Pick88o, *The Visual Computer*.)

10.5 A Note on Rendering 3-D Strange Attractors

The purpose of this section is to illustrate a very simple graphics technique whereby chaotic attractors can be clearly visualized. Here, we'll be interested in systems that almost repeat themselves but never quite succeed. As mentioned in the last section, *predictable attractors* represent the behavior to which a system

Figure 10.17. (X, β) *plot.* λ is held constant while β is scanned along the horizontal axis.

settles down or is "attracted" (for example, a point or a looping closed cycle). An example of a *fixed point attractor* is a mass at the end of a spring, with friction. It eventually arrives at an equilibrium point and stops moving. A *limit cycle* can be exemplified by a metronome. The metronome will tick-tock back and forth – its motion always periodic and regular. A *"strange attractor"* has an irregular unpredictable behavior. Its behavior can still be graphed, but the graph is much more complicated. With "tame" attractors, initially close points stay together as they approach the attractor. With strange attractors, initially adjacent points eventually follow widely divergent trajectories. Like leaves in a turbulent stream, it is impossible to predict where the leaves will end up given their initial positions.

The figure in this section is created by a trajectory governed by three simple functions of x, y and z which are particularly useful in demonstrating chaos (see Pseudocode 10.4). An initial point (0,0,0) is selected and the equations are iterated 5 million times. Figure 10.20 is an x-y projection of the resultant points' trajectory. The darkness of a region of the graph relates to how many times a trajectory crosses a particular pixel in the display. Unfortunately, simply plotting the result leads to a graph dominated by certain high intensity regions, with almost no other features visible. Of course, a logarithmic scaling helps to show the low intensity values, but does not exhibit them in as vivid a manner as in the method described below.

The following example protocol describes one useful way of displaying the curve. The display region is subdivided into 1600 by 1600 pixels, and the histogram (P) of the equation's trajectory wandering through a pixel is represented by simply summing the number of times an orbit intersects a pixel:

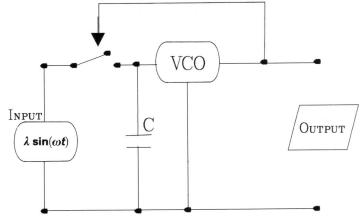

Figure 10.18. *Model of a discrete phase-locked loop.* See Kudrewicz et al. (1986) for more on this circuit.

$$P_{x,y} = \nu \qquad\qquad (10.11)$$

where ν is the number of intersections. As demonstrated earlier, occasionally it is useful to map all values above a threshold intensity to zero to help reveal structures in the most intense regions of the map which would normally be saturated:

$$P_{x,y} = 0 \quad if \;\; P_{x,y} > \tau \qquad\qquad (10.12)$$

where τ is some threshold value. $P_{x,y}$ is mapped to intensity on a bi-level graph using the following protocol. As in other sections of this book, histogram equalization and damped error diffusion is performed in order to visually bring out various subtle features in the map.

10.5.1 Recipe

If image processing techniques are not available, the reader can compute a simpler map by decreasing the number of iterations and simply plotting dots at the positions in the "p" array where $p(x,y) > 0$. Note that if the dynamical system producing this plot led to totally random output, then the plot would be a diffuse random scattering of points in 3-space. If the system were absolutely periodic (like a sine wave), then the figure would consist of a thin curve in 3-space. This curve is delicately poised somewhere between the two extremes and has a potential infinity of values. Although $(x,y,z) = (0,0,0)$ was used as a starting point, the starting point makes little difference; this indicates that the resulting figures are attractors for the dynamics. As long as you're somewhere near the

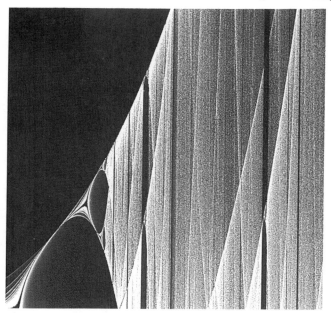

Figure 10.19. *Chaotic behavior in the discrete phase-locked loop.* As the voltage increases (horizontal axis) bifurcation and chaos arise.

attractor, the next few points will quickly converge to the attractor.[19] (Pick88j, *Computers and Graphics.*)

10.6 Quaternion Images

In this section, image processing of the beautiful and intricate structures resulting from the iteration of quaternion equations is examined. Quaternions are an extension of the complex plane and were discovered in 1843 by William Hamilton while attempting to define three-dimensional multiplications (reprinted in Hamilton, 1969). Quaternions have since been used to describe the dynamics of motion in 3-space. The Space Shuttle's flight software uses quaternions in its computations for guidance, navigation, and flight control for reasons of compactness, speed, and avoidance of singularities.

Quaternion representations are so complicated that it is useful to develop methodologies to aid in their display. Such methods reveal an exotic visual universe of forms.

---

[19] Note that some scientists look for strange attractors wherever nature is irregular. Some argue that the earth's weather might lie on a strange attractor. Even though it may never be possible to precisely predict phenomena like the weather or the stock market, one might foresee the global patterns of their behavior – the "order within the chaos."

Figure 10.20. *3-D chaotic attractor rendered using the techniques described.*

10.6.1 Quaternion Julia Sets

Alan Norton is the pioneer in three-dimensional representations of quaternion iteration, and he has displayed the surface texture of 3-D "slices" of 4-D quaternions (Norton (1982)). In contrast to the 3-D images which give important global information on quaternion structures (but at a cost of losing some of the fine structure), in this section image processing techniques are presented for the rendering of 2-D slices of these four-dimensional objects.

Quaternions define a four-dimensional space which contains the complex plane. Quaternions can be represented in four dimensions by

$$Q = a_0 + a_1 i + a_2 j + a_3 k \tag{10.13}$$

where i, j and k are (like the imaginary number i) unit vectors in three orthogonal directions, and they are perpendicular to the real axis.

```
ALGORITHM 3-D Strange Attractor Generator

TYPICAL PARAMETER VALUES:
xxmin=-2; xxmax=2, yymin=-2, yymax=2   (* picture boundaries  *)
pres  = 1600                           (* picture resolution   *)
iter1 = 1000; iter2 = 5000;
(* iter1*iter2 = total number of iterations *)
METHOD: A 5-parameter Dynamical System
OUTPUT: Pixel array containing the output picture intensities.
NOTES:  Try experimenting with different values of e which
can control the degree of randomness of the system.

xinc=pres/(xxmax-xxmin);         (* controls x-pixel position *)
yinc=pres/(yymax-yymin);         (* controls y-pixel position *)
a=2.24;b=.43;c=-.65;d=-2.43;e=1; (* control parameters        *)
p(*,*)=0;                        (* initialize p array        *)
x,y,z=0;                         (* starting point            *)
do j = 1 to iter1;
 do i = 1 to iter2;
  xx = sin(a*y)  -z*cos(b*x);
  yy = z*sin(c*x)-cos(d*y);
  zz = e*sin(x);
  x = xx; y=yy; z=zz;
  if xx<xxmax & xx>xxmin & yy < yymax & yy > yymin then do;
   xxx= (xx-xxmin)*xinc;         (* scale to range (0, pres) *)
   yyy= (yy-yymin)*yinc;         (* scale to range (0, pres) *)
   p(xxx,yyy) = p(xxx,yyy) + 1;
  end; /* then do */
 end;        (* i          *)
end;         (* j          *)
(*P now contains the intensities for each pixel in the picture*)
```

Pseudocode 10.4. *3-D strange attractor generator.*

To add or multiply two quaternions, we treat them as polynomials in i, j and k, but use the following rules to deal with products:

$$i^2 = j^2 = k^2 = -1 \qquad (10.14)$$
$$ij = -ji = k \quad jk = -kj = i \quad ki = -ik = j \qquad (10.15)$$

In order to produce the patterns in this section, "mathematical feedback loops" were used (similar in spirit to those of Julia set theory; see "Genesis Equations" on page 104). Here one simply iterates $F(Q,q)$

$$F(Q,q): \quad Q \rightarrow Q^2 + q \qquad (10.16)$$

where Q is a four-dimensional quaternion, and q is a quaternion constant. The computer algorithm for squaring a quaternion involves keeping track of the four components in Equation (10.13) and is given in Pseudocode 10.5.

In the present section several image processing techniques are used to render the complicated quaternion Julia sets in order to make their features obvious to the human analyst. This approach uses shades of gray to indicate the rate of explosion of the function. As is standard with Julia sets, "divergence" is checked by testing whether Q goes beyond a certain threshold, τ, after many iterations. For these figures, the function is iterated 100 times and the iteration count, n, is

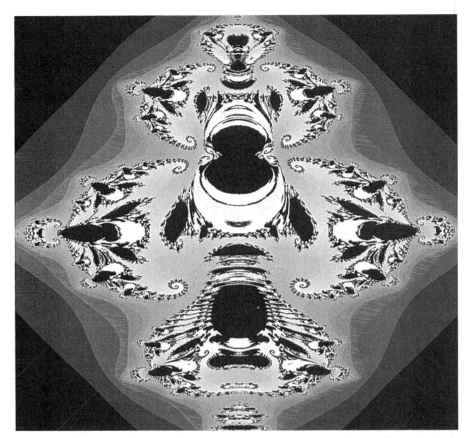

Figure 10.21. *A 2-D slice of a four-dimensional quaternion Julia set.* Note the "back-lighting" halo effect around the black bodies. This technique is described in the text.

stored when $|Q| \sim \tau$. The *logarithm* of the iteration counter, n, is then mapped to intensity in the picture. Without the log, higher iteration values can dominate too strongly (the picture will not clearly show shades of gray associated with low iterations). Next, $\log(n)$ is scaled to the range (0,255) where 255 is black and 0 is white. The maximum number of iterations (255) is changed to a value of 1; this abrupt change has the effect of giving a halo around the central convergent body *(as if the body were back-lighted)*. Without this, the graphically interesting structures are often obscured by the adjacent dark gray levels. Histogram equalization and error diffusion are then performed (see "Image Processing of the Shroud of Turin" on page 73).

Figure 10.21 represents a 2-D slice of a four-dimensional Quaternion Julia set. The slice is in the (a_0, a_2) plane at level $(a_1, a_3) = (0.05, 0.05)$. The constant $q = (-0.745, 0.113, 0.01, 0.01)$ and $\tau = 2$. The initial value of Q is $(a_0, a_2, 0.05, 0.05)$, where a_0 and a_2 correspond to the pixel position in a figure. All figure boundaries are within -2 and 2; i.e., $(-2 < a_0 < 2, -2 < a_2 < 2)$. The

Figure 10.22. *A magnification of the top portion.* (See Figure 10.21.)

selection of τ is not critical as long as it is large enough to differentiate bounded and unbounded behavior of the iterates of Q. A good rule of thumb is that $\tau > 1/2 + 1/2 (\sqrt{1 + 4|q|}\,)$ (see Mandelbrot, 1983). Note that the figures often display a slight asymmetry. Traditional complex Julia sets contain a mirror or inversion symmetry. The Quaternion Julia set slices do not necessarily have such symmetries. The figures show the beginning of symmetry break down as the observation plane (a_1, a_3) leaves the origin. For the slices in this book, as a_1, a_3, μ_1 or μ_2 increases, asymmetry increases. The quaternion constant q was chosen because exploration on the computer indicates that this value gives rise to beautiful curling self-similar patterns. Because the q value is close to and on the *outside* of the quaternion Mandelbrot set, repeated iteration yields structures with a dusty, evanescent quality. The other figures show magnifications of portions of Figure 10.21. See Color Plate for an additional rendition. (Pick88n, *Image and Vision Comp.*)

Figure 10.23. *A magnification of a right portion.* (See Figure 10.21.)

10.7 A Note on Rendering Chaotic Repeller Distance-Towers

This section illustrates another simple graphics technique for visualizing a large class of graphically interesting manifestations of chaotic behavior arising from complex analytic dynamics. When in color, the results sometimes resemble flames and are quite beautiful.

To compute a gallery of artistic forms (see Color Plates), two simple formulas were used. The color plates are maps created by computing Julia sets (also known as Julia repellers) for $f(\zeta)$: $\zeta \rightarrow \cosh(\zeta) + \mu$ and stacking them vertically for continuously changing real values of μ (stacking them like a tower of pancakes). ζ is a complex variable. Simple techniques for computing Julia repeller curves are discussed in Peitgen and Richter (1986) and Mandelbrot (1983). As is well-known, the edges of such curves have a complicated self-similar structure. For certain values of μ the curve is closed and for others the curve degenerates and no longer has a nicely defined inside and outside. Once this edge is computed, the reader can then compute a distance parameter as a function of real coordinates in the complex plane, $\delta(\zeta,)$. $\delta(\zeta,)$ is the distance from a line outside the repeller set (and parallel to the real axis of the complex plane) to the closest point on the edge of

Figure 10.24. *A magnification of one of the spirals.* (See Figure 10.21).

the repeller with the same ζ_r. This δ is then mapped to color giving a visual idea of the parameter dependance of the Julia edge. Various different color assignments for the δ values reveal complicated boundaries which provide a reservoir of magnificent shapes (see color figures). Some figures use a monotonic, gradual,

```
ALGORITHM - Compute quaternion, main computation
```
```
Variables:
a0,a1,a2,a3,rmu are the real, i, j, and k coefficients
Notes:
This is an 'inner loop' used in the same spirit as in traditional
Julia set computations. No complex numbers are required for the
computation. Hold three of the coefficients constant and examine
the plane determined by the remaining two. This code runs in a
manner similar to the other complex number routines in this book.
rmu is a quaternion constant.
```
```
DO i = 1 to NumberOfIterations
  savea0 =      a0*a0 - a1*a1 - a2*a2 - a3*a3 + rmu0;
  savea1 =      a0*a1 + a1*a0 + a2*a3 - a3*a2 + rmu1;
  savea2 =      a0*a2 - a1*a3 + a2*a0 + a3*a1 + rmu2;
  savea3 =      a0*a3 + a1*a2 - a2*a1 + a3*a0 + rmu3;
  a0=savea0;a1=savea1;a2=savea2;a3=savea3;
  if (a1**2+a2**2+a3**2+a0**2) > CutoffSquared then leave loop;
end; /*i*/
PlotDot(Color(i));
```

Pseudocode 10.5. *Compute quaternion, main computation.*

rainbow color table to map δ to color. This permits the human analyst to clearly visualize the continuously varying distances. Other figures use color tables which are non-monotonic and periodic (e.g. alternating light and dark colors) to emphasize contours in the image. Note that a good way to display these images on a black and white device is simply to alternate even and odd pixel-intensities with black and white colors.

The final picture's axes are μ (vertical) vs. the real ζ axis (horizontal). A "repeller distance-tower," or δ -tower, for another equation $f(\zeta)$: $\zeta \rightarrow \zeta^2 + \mu$ is also provided. The bottom of both the cosh and ζ^2 δ -towers corresponds to smaller values of $|\mu|$, where the Julia repeller is "fat." As $Re(\mu)$ is varied up along the δ tower the set becomes thinner and rougher, the various protuberances finally evaporating (Figure 10.25).

One note on the computation: to reduce the CPU time for $\zeta \rightarrow \cosh \zeta + \mu$ (at a resolution of 1024 x 1024 pixels), an inverse iteration method was used for approximating the boundary of the Julia repeller. See Peitgen and Richter (1986) for a detailed discussion of the method. For cosh , this approach involves iterating $\zeta = \zeta - \mu$ followed by $\zeta = \log(\zeta \pm \sqrt{(\zeta^2 - 1)}\,)$ and choosing a branch ($\pm$) of the square root at random. To verify that this approach gives a fair approximation to the δ tower, for comparison parts of the tower were also computed using other methods and essentially the same graphic results were obtained. See Color Plates for an example of repeller distance-towers. (For additional color renditions, see Pick88h, *Computers in Physics.*)

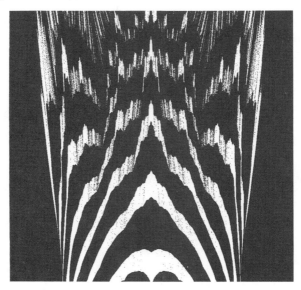

Figure 10.25. *Repeller distance-tower.* This tower is computed for $\zeta \rightarrow \cosh(\zeta) + \mu$. μ values continuously vary from top to bottom ($-3 < \mu < -2.25$). The horizontal axis is $-2.8 < Re(\zeta) < 2.8$. δ is mapped to the striping pattern using a sinusoidal look-up table. Various thin ridges are seen which vary continuously with μ.

10.8   Reading List for Chapter 10

The computer graphics experiments in this chapter were inspired by a number of researchers' work over the past few decades. For example, chaos in real physical systems was clearly demonstrated in 1963 by MIT scientist E.N. Lorenz. This atmospheric scientist proposed a simple model for convection in the atmosphere which displayed unpredictable behavior, and the reader should see his landmark paper for details (Lorenz, 1963). Hofstadter (1986) gives a detailed and quite readable description of various problems in nonlinear iteration, bifurcation maps, and strange attractors. He also mentions some of the scientists and mathematicians who have studied, discovered, and popularized many of the important features inherent in phenomena exhibiting bifurcating behavior. (These scientists include: S. Ulam, J. Eckmann, J. Myrberg, P. Stein, P. Collet, H. Koch, M. Stein., M. Feigenbaum, R. May, and D. Ruelle, just to name a few.) The discovery of the recursive regularity of bifurcation maps, first made by Feigenbaum using a little calculator, was one of the major recent advances in the chaos field (Feigenbaum, 1979).

Readers may also be interested in a recent lively (1989) article by M. Hirsch entitled "Chaos, Rigor, and Hype" which appeared in the *Mathematical Intelligencer*. Hirsh notes that many important chaotic systems were first identified and explored not by computer simulation but by mathematical proof, and he cites the work of Poincare, Birkhoff, Levinson, Smale, Anosov, Kolmogorov, Arnold, and Moser as examples. Readers interested in both the history and mathematics of chaos should consult the many papers and books in the Reference section. Some personal favorites on the subject are:

1. Gleick, J. (1987) *Chaos: Making a New Science*. Viking: New York.

2. Moon, F. (1987) *Chaotic Vibrations*. John Wiley and Sons, New York. (Moon gives many practical examples of chaos in real physical systems.)

3. Shaw, A. (1984) *The Dripping Faucet as a Model Chaotic System*. Aerial Press: California.

"Reading List for Chapter 14" on page 266 contains additional historical and bibliographical background material on the field of chaotic dynamics.

Chapter 11

Number Theory

"The trouble with integers is that we have examined only the small ones. Maybe all the exciting stuff happens at really big numbers, ones we can't get our hands on or even begin to think about in any very definite way. So maybe all the action is really inaccessible and we're just fiddling around. Our brains have evolved to get us out of the rain, find where the berries are, and keep us from getting killed. Our brains did not evolve to help us grasp really large numbers or to look at things in a hundred thousand dimensions."

Ronald Graham, mathematician

11.1 Introduction

"The primary source of all mathematics are the integers."

Herman Minkowski

"Mathematics, rightly viewed, possess not only truth, but supreme beauty — a beauty cold and austere, like that of sculpture."

Bertrand Russell, *Mysticism and Logic, 1918*

This chapter outlines some artistic and easy-to-implement ways of representing patterns in number theory. Number theory – the study of properties of integers – is an ancient discipline. Much mysticism accompanied early treatises; for example, Pythagoreans based all events in the universe on whole numbers (Spencer, 1982). Only a few hundred years ago courses in numerology[20] were required by all college students, and even today such numbers as 13, 7, and 666 conjure up emotional reactions in many people. Today integer arithmetic is important in a wide spectrum of human activities. It has repeatedly played a crucial role in the evolution of the natural sciences (for a description of the use of

---

[20] Numerology is the study of mystical and religious properties of numbers.

number theory in communications, computer science, cryptography, physics, biology and art, see Schroeder (1984)).

11.2 Exotic Symmetries from Large Pascal's Triangles

One of the most famous integer patterns in the history of mathematics is Pascal's triangle (PT).[21] The first 7 rows of Pascal's triangle can be represented as:

```
1                                           1
1 1                                      1    1
1 2 1                                 1    2    1
1 3 3 1          or                1    3    3    1
1 4 6 4 1                        1    4    6    4    1
1 5 10 10 5 1                 1    5   10   10    5    1
1 6 15 20 15 6 1          1    6   15   20   15    6    1
```

Each number in the triangle is the sum of the two above it. The role that Pascal's triangle plays in probability theory, in the expansion of binomials of the form $(X + Y)^N$, and in various number theory applications has been discussed extensively by Martin Gardner (Gardner, 1977).

Mathematician Donald Knuth once indicated that there are so many relations in Pascal's triangle that when someone finds a new identity, there aren't many people who get excited about it anymore, except the discoverer. Nonetheless, several novel approaches have revealed patterns in the triangle. These include: geometric patterns in the diagonals, the existence of perfect square patterns with various hexagonal properties, and an extension of the triangle and its patterns to negative integers (see bibliography).

Researchers have noted that the Pascal sequence contains within it a variety of patterns, some very obvious, others extremely subtle and hard to recognize. Computer graphics is a good method by which patterns in Pascal's triangle can be made obvious. Unfortunately, computer graphics has been little exploited in past Pascal triangle work. In other areas of number theory, graphics has been useful in revealing patterns in prime numbers (Stein et al., 1964) and in $3n+1$ ("Collatz") numbers (see next section). In this section, computer graphics is used to reveal patterns in Pascal's triangle. For some related work, see Holter (1986).

11.2.1 Computation

The figures represent Pascal's triangle computed with modular arithmetic. For example, Figure 11.3 is Pascal's triangle, mod 2 ; i.e., points are plotted for all even numbers occurring in the triangle. This can be accomplished in many programming languages by the conditional "If mod(i,2) = 0 Then PlotDot," where i

---

[21] Blaise Pascal was the first to write a treatise about this progression in 1653 – although the pattern had been known by Omar Khayyam as far back as 1100 A.D.

Figure 11.1. *Pascal's triangle, mod 2.* The arrows indicate a size change in the internal triangles every k^m *rows* ($m = 0,1,2,3 \ldots \infty$) where k is the mod index (in this figure, $k = 2$). This size change relation holds for all PT's mod p where p is a prime number. The arrows shown indicate 2^3, 2^4, 2^5, 2^6 and 2^7.

is the number in Pascal's triangle. Patterns computed in this way reveal many surprises, some of which are discussed later.

There are many different ways to compute the triangle: trigonometric methods, combinatorial methods, or the binomial theorem method (Spencer, 1982). Presented here are two methods which the reader should be able to implement in most programming languages. Method 1 is an easy way of constructing the triangle using the REXX programming language (IBM Manual, 1984). REXX was used primarily because of its exact arithmetic with arbitrarily large integers, allowing the user to compute the triangle to any depth (the programming language LISP also has this feature). Indeed, as Figure 11.2 shows, the integers become extremely large very rapidly.

The values in Pascal's triangles grow so fast (Figure 11.2) that it would be possible to only compute a few score rows before exceeding the precision of variables in most programming languages. In Method 1 (Pseudocode 11.1), 100-digit

```
ALGORITHM - Compute Pascal's Triangle Mod 2   (Method 1)
─────────────────────────────────────────────────────────
Variables: c has the value of the Pascal triangle for a given
           row, n, and column, r.
Notes: This pseudocode is written in the REXX programming
language. However, this method works well even in
BASIC if the triangle is not very large.
─────────────────────────────────────────────────────────
numeric digits (100)   /* set the precision of variables    */
do n = 0 to 200        /* n = number of rows                */
  string = ' '         /* initialize output row             */
  do r = 0 to n        /* r = number of columns             */
    c=1                /* initialize entry in triangle      */
    do x= n to n-r+1 by -1/*generate all the entries in a row*/
    c=c*x/(n-x+1)
    end
    /* check remainder after division by 2 */
    /* write a dot if c is an even number  */
    if c // 2 = 0 then string = string || '*'
    else string = string || ' '
  end /*r*/
  /* Write the line of the triangle                 */
  EXECIO 1 DISKW 'PASCAL DECK A 0 F 255 (STRING' STRING
end  /*n*/
```

Pseudocode 11.1. *Compute Pascal's triangle mod 2 (Method 1).*

precision was used. Nevertheless, the code is so simple to implement that the reader is encouraged to use whatever language is available, such as BASIC, since low-order Pascal's triangles also yield fascinating shapes. (For a similar program in BASIC, see Spencer, 1982). Color capability further enhances the graphics presentation and allows the human analyst to detect important features in the data. For example, points mod 2 and mod 3 can be displayed in different colors in the same triangle.

Method 2 (Pseudocode 11.2) for computing Pascal's triangle does not allow the user to compute actual values for entries in the triangle but rather computes the triangle using modular arithmetic. Methods 1 and 2 can both be used to plot the figures in this section; however, using Method 2, super-large integers are not generated, and Method 2 is faster. The figures display the triangle for a variety of modularities.

Pascal portraits contain a beauty and complexity which corresponds to behavior which mathematicians may not have been able to fully appreciate before the age of computer graphics. As in other sections in this book, this complexity makes it difficult to objectively characterize structures such as these, and therefore it is useful to develop graphics systems which allow the maps to be followed in a quantitative and qualitative way.

1
255
32385
2731135
172061505
8637487551
359895314625
12801990477375
396861704798625
10891649009473375
267934565633045025
5967633507281457375
121341881314722966625
2268159781498283145375
3920676193732746 5798625
6299219751263946 17164575
9448829626895919257468625
13283942828400 7335443235375
17564324406440 96990860556625
21909183601718472991260627375
25852836650027798 1296875403025
28930555298840631240 36462843375
30771590636039580501115104788625
31172959209553140246781 8235467375
30133860569234702238555 76276184625
27843687165972864868425524791945935
24630954031437534306684 1180851829425
20890698048885908726780 23348706256975
170109969826642399632353329823 22378225
1331550453470614645398076064 47833788175
100310134161452969953321730 1907014537585
728057425365384459338625461 0615428095375
509640197755769121537037822 74307996667625
344393224544050042735634649 914263128996375
224868517202291498492090859649 9012195211625
1419884065763040604764345142 3608048432621975

Figure 11.2. *Beginning entries in row 255 of Pascal's triangle.* For convenience, the numbers are printed vertically down the page.

11.2.2 Nomenclature

Before considering the figures, it is useful to provide additional background to traditional Pascal's triangle nomenclature. Each entry in the triangular array consisting of n rows and r columns can be denoted by the symbol:

$$\binom{n}{r} \tag{11.1}$$

For example,

$$\binom{3}{2} = 3 \tag{11.2}$$

```
Algorithm: Compute Pascal's Triangle using Modular Arithmetic
Variables: c has the modular value of the Pascal triangle for a
given row, n, and column, r.
p(*)=0;c(*)=0;                    /* initialize c and p arrays   */
do n = 1 to 255;                 /* 255 rows                    */
  do r = 2 to n;                 /* generate the entries in a row*/
    c(r)=mod(p(r)+p(r-1),imod);/*imod=modulus index chosen   */
    if c(r)= 0 then PLOTDOT(n,r);  /*place at position (n,r)*/
  end;
  p(*)=c(*);                     /* update p array for next row */
end;
```

Pseudocode 11.2. *Compute Pascal's triangle using modular arithmetic (Method 2).*

(the second element of the third row). These patterns can be defined algebraically when $n \geq 0$ and $0 \leq r \leq n$ that is:

$$\binom{n}{r} = \frac{n!}{r!(n-r)!} \tag{11.3}$$

Other authors have extended the triangle to negative values of n (Bidwell, 1973).

In this section, high-resolution graphs are constructed by drawing a dot at positions:

$$\binom{n}{r} = \frac{n!}{r!(n-r)!} \quad when \ \binom{n}{r} = 0 \ \text{mod} \ k \tag{11.4}$$

for ($0 < n < 255$), where k is the modulo index. "Anti-triangles" are computed by plotting the inverse of the triangle defined in Equation (11.4), i.e. by plotting points when

$$P(n,r) \neq 0 \ \text{mod} \ k \tag{11.5}$$

(These look like a photographic negative.) Values of k for the figures range from 2 to 666.

11.2.3 Gaskets

The resulting shapes are of interest mathematically, and they reveal a visually striking and intricate class of patterns which make up a family of regular, fractal networks (see also "Tesselation Automata Derived from a Single Defect" on page 295, "Genesis Equations" on page 104, and "Fractal Characterization of Speech Waveform Graphs" on page 57). Often the fractals of most interest are ones that are self-similar; for example, if we look at any one of the triangular motifs within Pascal's triangle we notice that the same pattern is found at another place in another size. The two-dimensional networks revealed in the figures in this section are known as Sierpiński gaskets (Mandelbrot, 1983) which share impor-

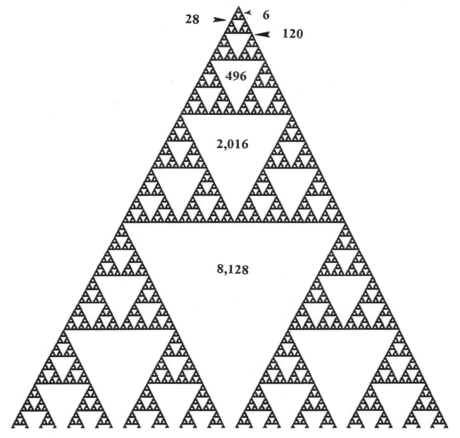

Figure 11.3. *Pascal's triangle, mod 2, anti version.* This results from a logical "not" operation on Figure 11.1. The numbers on the figure indicate the number of dots which make up each triangle in the central stack. All perfect numbers appear in this central pattern (see text).

tant geometrical features with percolation problems (Gordon et al., 1986) and cellular automata. The Sierpiński gasket consists of triangles nested in one another "like Chinese boxes or Russian dolls" (Kadanoff, 1986).

11.2.4 Size Changes of Internal Triangles

By studying the figures in this section, several interesting observations can be made. Starting with Figure 11.1 (mod index, $k = 2$), we observe that internal triangles undergo a size change (starting at the top triangle with one dot) every 2^m rows where m is an integer. Note in Figure 11.4 ($k = 3$) a size change occurring at 3^m rows. The relationship for Figure 11.6 is not as simple: a size change occurs not at 4^m but at 2^m. In fact, for non-prime k, size changes occur at one of the prime factors raised to a power. Also, once a size change occurs for non-prime

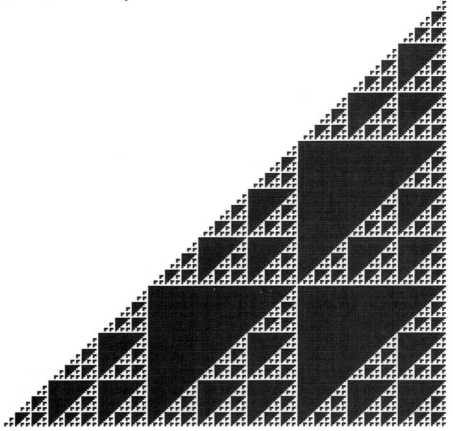

Figure 11.4. *Pascal's triangle, mod 3, right-triangle plot.* This and following figures are plotted so that the 1's which make up the first entry in each row fall beneath one another. Note the size change in internal triangles every 3^m rows ($m = 0,1,2,3 \ldots \infty$).

PT's, smaller triangles still remain intricately interspersed with the new larger breeds.

In general, the Pascal's triangles with the simplest symmetries and patterns are of the form

$$\binom{n}{r} = 0, \bmod p, \tag{11.6}$$

where p is a prime number. Starting from the top of these p-Pascal's triangles, notice that the internal triangular motif undergoes its first size change after $p - 1$ triangles (or p triangles in the anti version). Check this for yourself by observing other triangles.

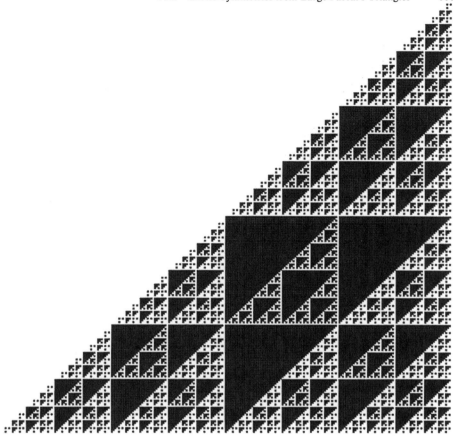

Figure 11.5. *Pascal's triangle, mod 4.*

11.2.5 Symmetries

The figures indicate self-similarity of the gaskets for several orders of dilational invariance, and they possess what is known as nonstandard scaling symmetry, also called dilation symmetry, i.e. invariance under changes of size scale (for a classification of the various forms of self-similarity symmetries, see "Fractal Characterization of Speech Waveform Graphs" on page 57). As alluded to in various sections of this book, Mandelbrot (1983) established geometric scale invariance as a general property of nature. Dilation symmetry is sometimes expressed by the formula $(\vec{r} \rightarrow a\vec{r})$. Thus an expanded piece of Pascal's Sierpiński gasket can be moved in such away as to make it coincide with the entire gasket, and this operation can be performed in an infinite number of ways. Other more trivial symmetries in the figures include the bilateral symmetry of all equilateral PT's, the various rotation axes, and other mirror planes.

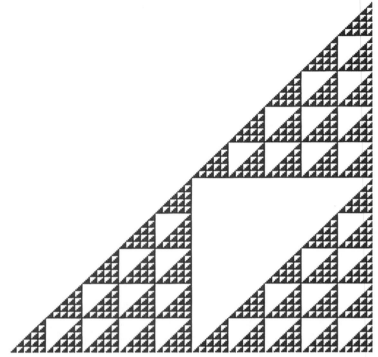

Figure 11.6. *Pascal's triangle, mod 5, anti version.*

Another observation is that, in general, the higher the modulus index, k, the more intricate and harder-to-define are the symmetries. Figure 11.8 shows Pascal's triangle for a large k ($k = 666$).

By visually familiarizing oneself with the basic internal motifs for various modulus indices, it is possible at a glance to determine the prime factors of k for many Pascal's triangles. For example, in Figure 11.7 one can see a "2-motif" (triangle surrounded by 3 dots), and a "3-motif" (3 triangles touching at their vertices). On a similar line of thought, it is possible to construct higher-k PT's from several lower-k PT's. As just one example, let P_{12} be the PT for $k = 12$. Let $\neg P_{12}$ be the corresponding "anti" triangle (black dots interchanged with white dots). We can then perform logical operations on PT's for $k = 4$ and $k = 3$ (note: 4 and 3 are factors of 12), obtaining:

$$\neg P_4 \vee \neg P_3 = \neg P_{12} \tag{11.7}$$

where $\vee$ is a logical "or." Equivalently, $P_4 \wedge P_3 = \neg P_{12}$. The reader is encouraged to explore this by constructing pictures of $\neg P_4$ and $\neg P_3$ and holding the pictures, one behind the other, up to a light and observing the resultant portrait. This is a simple way for performing a logical "or," and it reveals $\neg P_{12}$! This approach only works if the two generating PT's do not have factors in common. For example, $\neg P_{12} \neq P_6 \wedge P_2$ since 6 has as one of its factors, 2.

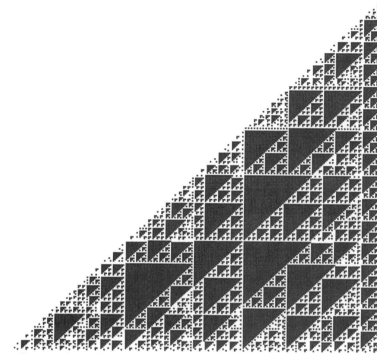

Figure 11.7. *Pascal's triangle, mod 6.*

11.2.6 Plotting a Complete PT

How far (to how many rows, n) should the PT be computed to yield a useful, "complete," and aesthetically pleasing pattern? By observing the figures, one finds that

$$n_{\text{max}} = k^m \tag{11.8}$$

(where k is the modularity index and m an integer power) provides an artistically and mathematically useful stopping point since the internal triangular network terminates on the tips of internal triangles rather than being cut off somewhere in between. If this is not possible, due to size, resolution and computation limitations, then any prime factor raised to a power provides a useful stopping point.

11.2.7 Perfect Numbers

Finally, an additional interesting observation by Martin Gardner (1977) is made obvious in Figure 11.3. If one were to count the number of dots in the central triangles starting from the top, one would find that each is made up entirely of an even number of dots. At the top is 6, then 28, 120, 496 ... dots. 6, 28, and 496 are perfect numbers because each is the sum of all its divisors excluding itself

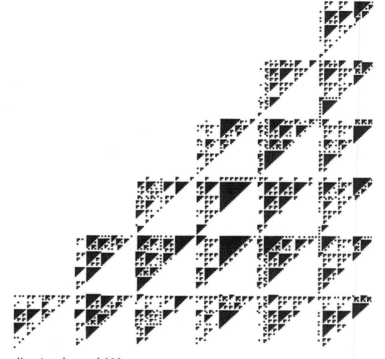

Figure 11.8. *Pascal's triangle, mod 666 .*

(6=1+2+3). The formula for the number of dots in the nth central triangle, moving along the central axis, is

$$2^{n-1}(2^n -1) \tag{11.9}$$

Because every even perfect number is of the form $2^{n-1}(2^n -1)$, where $(2^n - 1)$ is prime, all even perfect numbers appear in the central stacked triangular pattern in Figure 11.3. Other patterns and curious relations can be found in these figures, and these are left for the reader's discovery. The "endpiece" of this chapter contains a triangle mod 100.

11.2.8 Practical Importance

Dilation symmetry has been discovered and applied in different kinds of phenomena in condensed matter physics, diffusion, polymer growth and percolation clusters. One example given by Kadanoff is petroleum-bearing rock layers. These typically contain fluid-filled pores of many sizes, which, as Kadanoff points out, might be effectively understood as Sierpiński gaskets (Kadanoff (1986)).

These figures may have a practical importance in that they can provide models for materials scientists to produce new structures with novel properties.

For example, Gordon et al. (1986) have created wire gaskets on the micron size scale almost identical to the mod 2 structure in Figure 11.3. The area of their smallest triangle was $1.38 \pm 0.01 \ \mu m^2$, and they have investigated many unusual properties of their superconducting Sierpiński gasket network in a magnetic field. In addition, because of modular PTs' dilation symmetry, statistical-mechanical and transport problems are exactly solvable on these fractals – making them attractive candidates as model systems.

11.2.9 Future Work

Provocative avenues for future graphics include the plotting of figures for: Pascal's pyramid (a 3-D extension presented by Liu Zhiquing of the Peoples Republic of China (1985)), negative Pascal's triangle (presented by James Bidwell of Central Michigan University (1973)), hexagonal clusters (presented by Zalman Usinskin of the University of Chicago (1973)), and complex number Pascal's triangles. Lastly, interactive programs which allow the user to view Pascal's pyramids from within, like a worm tunneling through Swiss cheese, will provide an amusing, artistically interesting, and possibly mathematically useful exploration tool. One can only speculate that Blaise Pascal would have been intrigued by the beauty and complexity of the infinite spaces represented by these graphs. As Pascal once said, *"When I consider ... the small part of space which I can touch or see engulfed by the infinite immensity of spaces that I know not and that know me not, I am frightened and astonished...."* (Pick90, *Leonardo.*)

11.3 Patterns in Hailstone (3n+1) Numbers

"The external world exists; the structure of the world is ordered; we know little about the nature of the order, nothing at all about why it should exist."
Martin Gardner, 1985, paraphrasing Bertrand Russell

A particularly famous problem in number theory, the hailstone problem (Hayes (1984)),[23] has fascinated mathematicians for several decades (Legarias (1985), Wagon (1985), Garner (1981), Crandall (1978)). It has been studied primarily because it is so simple to state yet apparently intractably hard to solve. The hailstone algorithm is defined by the function $h:N \rightarrow N$ on the set of positive integers:

$$h(n) = \begin{cases} n/2 & \text{if } n \text{ even,} \\ 3n + 1 & \text{if } n \text{ odd} \end{cases} \qquad (11.10)$$

---

[23] This problem is also known as the $3n+1$ problem, the Collatz algorithm, and the Syracuse problem.

where n is any initial positive integer. Let $h^k(n)$ be the kth iterate of $h(n)$. A sequence of hailstone numbers is generated in a mathematical feedback loop where

$$h^k(n) = h(h^{k-1}(n)) \quad \text{for } k \in N \tag{11.11}$$

and can be represented as

$$H(n) = \left\{ h^k(n) \right\} \quad k = 1,2,3, \ldots \tag{11.12}$$

For example, the hailstone sequence for 3 is: $H(3) = \{3, 10, 5, 16, 8, 4, 2, 1, 4, \ldots \}$.

Like hailstones falling from the sky through storm clouds, this sequence drifts down and up, sometimes in seemingly haphazard patterns (Figure 11.9 and Figure 11.10). Also like hailstones, hailstone numbers always seem eventually to fall back down to the ground (the integer "1"). In fact, it is conjectured that *every* hailstone sequence ends in the cycle 4,2,1,4,... This hailstone conjecture has been numerically checked for a large range of n, and the current record has been set by N. Yoneda who has checked all integers less than $2^{40} \sim 1.2 \times 10^{12}$ (see Legarias (1985)).[24] A variety of cash awards have been offered for a solution to the hailstone problem.

A number of researchers have noted that the hailstone sequence gives rise to a mixture of regularity and disorder: it is definitely not random, but the pattern resists interpretation. This problem in number theory can be placed in a much larger context of chaos theory which involves the study of a range of mathematical and physical phenomena exhibiting a sensitive and often irregular dependence on initial conditions (see "Mathematical Chaos" on page 141). Computer graphics is a good method by which patterns in this hailstone sequence can be made more obvious to the mathematician. Unfortunately, computer graphics has been little exploited in $3n+1$ work .

The figures represent plots of $H(n)$ *vs.* n where $H(n)$ is the trajectory of hailstone numbers for a range of starting positive integers n.

Figure 11.9 is a plot of $H(n)$ *vs.* k for $n = 54$, in other words, a hailstone sequence for just one starting value, 54. Its path length (before settling back down to 1) is 112 and the maximum value reached is 9,232. Figure 11.10 is the same plot with an initial $n = 649$. Its path length is 144 and also has a maximum value of 9,232. Note that in both these plots that there is a seemingly chaotic trajectory and that both trajectories eventually settle back down to 1.

---

[24] High-speed computers have allowed investigators to check the validity of many mathematical conjectures, and various mathematical evidence now goes into unimaginably large numbers. However, numerical evidence should be viewed with caution and is sometimes inadequate. For example, consider the fact that $\int_2^x 1/\ln t \, dt - \pi(x)$ is positive for all $x \le 10^{12}$ and probably far beyond ($\pi(x)$ is the number of prime numbers less than or equal to x) (Wagon, 1985)). This massive amount of evidence previously led researchers astray; however, it is now known that a sign change does occur, but all that is currently known is that the first sign change occurs below 1.65×10^{1165}.

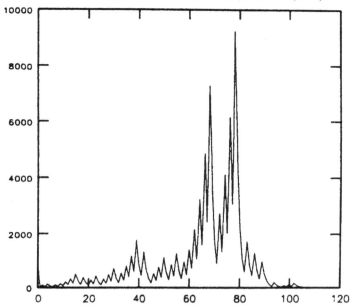

Figure 11.9. *H(n) vs. k for n = 54.* This is a hailstone sequence for just one starting value, 54.

Figure 11.11 is an *H(n) vs. n* plot for a range of starting positive integers ($1 < n < 1000$). The y-axis is cut off at $H(n) = 1000$. Figure 11.12 is the same plot with a cutoff of $H(n) = 10,000$. Figure 11.13 is an *H(n) vs. n* plot for ($1 < n < 10,000$), and the y-axis cutoff is $H(n) = 10,000$. Notice that all these plots reveal a pattern of diagonal lines of varying density which pass through the origin, a pattern of horizontal lines (visually reminiscent of preferred energy state diagrams in quantum mechanics) and a diffuse "background" of chaotically positioned dots. In Figure 11.12 and Figure 11.13 the "preferred" states (horizontal lines) are particularly obvious.

An interpretation of the existence of the horizontal lines is immediate: they represent certain values which are much commoner than others and far too common to be explained by any statistical process. Other mathematicians have noted preferred states in the hailstone numbers (Hayes, 1984), and an outstanding example is state 9,232. Of the first 1,000 integers more than 350 have their maximum at 9,232.

The existence of the pronounced diagonal lines is probably indicative of "likely" transformations which the 3n + 1 sequence naturally gives rise to. For the hailstones, we are often multiplying by 3 and then dividing by 2. Therefore, the linear transformation $y = (3/2)x$ is quite common (we can eliminate the + 1 in n+1 for large x). In order to test this hypothesis, lines of the form:

$$y = \frac{3^n}{2^m} x \tag{11.13}$$

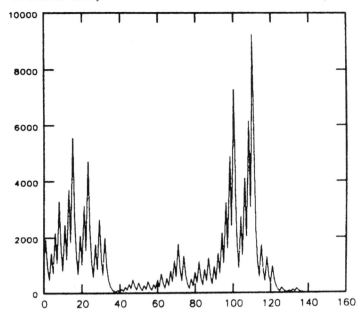

Figure 11.10. *H(n) vs. k for n = 649.* This is a hailstone sequence for just one starting value, 649. Note in this figure and the previous that there is a seemingly chaotic trajectory and that both trajectories eventually settle back down to 1.

were plotted for $(0 < n < 5,\ 0 < m < 5)$ (Figure 11.14). Several of the lines which correspond to densely populated transforms in Figure 11.11 are indicated on the plot. Figure 11.14 accounts for many but not all of the diagonal lines seen in Figure 11.11. In fact, higher order lines $(0 < n < 10,\ 0 < m < 10)$ are needed to account for all the diagonal patterns seen in Figure 11.11. Note that in Figure 11.11 the diagonal lines are of varying density – dark lines indicate more probable transforms. Figure 11.14 demonstrates that all of the darker lines are accounted for by low order transforms (multiplication by 3/2 and 1/2 are among the most probable). The various probabilities of multiplication are discussed in (Hayes, 1984; Legarias, 1985).

Watching the figures evolve dynamically upon the screen helps to give an appreciation of the complicated behavior of $3n+1$ numbers. The $H(n)$ maps clearly display preferred states, but exactly why these states and clusters of states exist is unclear. Every possible integer state and trajectory length (path before returning to 1) can be produced – but again some numbers appear more often than others. As Paul Erdös commented on the complexity of $3n+1$ numbers, *"Mathematics is not yet ready for such problems."* (Pick89, *J. Recr. Math.*)

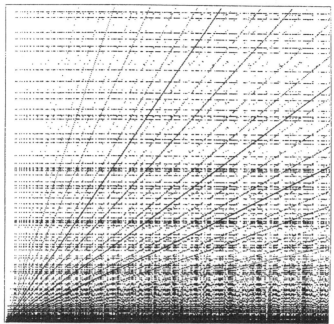

Figure 11.11. *H(n) vs. n.* This is a plot for a range of starting positive integers (1 < *n* < 1000). The y-axis is cut off at *H(n)* = 1000. This plot reveals a pattern of lines of varying density and a diffuse "background" of chaotically positioned dots.

11.4 Is There a Double Smoothly Undulating Integer?

This is perhaps the only topic in this book without accompanying graphics. The topic is included because, like the hailstone number problem, this unsolved problem is also simple to state and challenging for computer programmers to investigate. The reader can imagine that there may also be interesting graphic patterns produced by undulating regions in the decimal representations described below.

The term "smoothly undulating integer" was used by C. Trigg in a paper on palindromic octagonal numbers, where he defines an integer as smoothly undulating if two digits oscillate, for example 79797979. The term "smooth" differentiates this kind of number from an undulating integer where the alternating digits are consistently greater or less than the digits adjacent to them, for example 4253612 (Trigg, 1982).

Let us define a *double* smoothly undulating integer as an integer that undulates in both its decimal and binary representation. For example, 1010 is an undulating binary number. For this section, we exclude the trivial case of double digit decimal numbers which might ordinarily fall into the category of smoothly undulating. Therefore, a number such as 21 (10101) is not included.

In this section, the reader is invited to ponder the question: Does there exist a double smoothly undulating integer? I have searched for such an integer for all

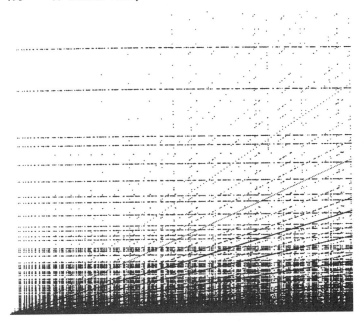

Figure 11.12. *Same as previous figure with a cutoff of H(n) = 10,000.*

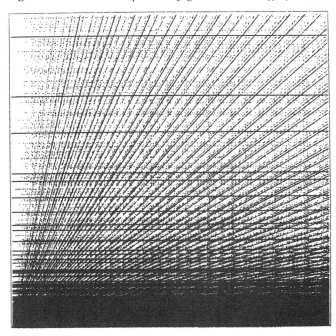

Figure 11.13. *H(n) vs. n plot.* (1 < n < 10,000). The y-axis cutoff is H(n) = 10,000.

```
Algorithm: Generate 500 hailstone numbers
n=starting_number;
do i = 1 to 500;
  if mod(n,2)=0 then n=n/2; else n=3*n+1;
Print(n);
end;
```

Pseudocode 11.3. *How to generate 500 hailstone numbers.*

decimal integers n ($1 \leq n \leq 10^{100}$) and have found no such integer, and it is conjectured that no such number exists. Of course, numerical evidence such as this provides no real answer to the question, and it would be interesting to prove the conjecture that there is no double smoothly undulating integer, or to find such a number. It is also interesting to speculate whether there is anything special about the arrangement of digits within a decimal number corresponding to a binary undulating number. Casual inspection suggests that the arrangement is random.

As a final observation, note that if an n-digit decimal number is selected at random, the chance that it will be smoothly undulating is $81/9x10^{n-1}$ which is approximately equal to $1/10^n$ for large n. This means that if the decimal equivalent of a smoothly undulating binary integer could be considered as a random arrangement of digits, the probability of it being smoothly undulating becomes exceedingly small. Note also the interesting fact that there is a constant number, 81, of possible undulating integers for any given n-digit decimal number. This speeds the search for double smoothly undulating integers using a computer.

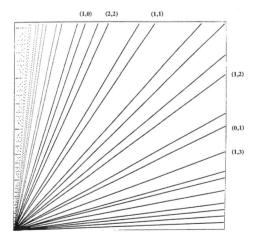

Figure 11.14. *Diagonal lines produced by a linear relationship.* The relationship is described by $y = (3^n/2^m)x$ for ($0 < n < 5$, $0 < m < 5$). Numbers in parentheses represent certain (n,m) values.

You may wish to use computer graphics to find patterns in the undulation of even/odd numbers in the decimal equivalents. (Pick90, *J. Recr. Math.*)

11.5 Reading List for Chapter 11

Various papers on the fractal properties of Pascal's triangle (mod 2) have been published by Lakhtakia (see References). Mandelbrot on page 329 of his book discusses the relationship between Pascal's triangle and the Sierpiński gasket (Mandelbrot, 1983).

The Reference section of this book lists many general references to the field of number theory. Two personal favorites are:

1. Spencer, D. (1982) *Computers in Number Theory*. Computer Science Press: Maryland. (An easy-to-read book with computational recipes.)
2. Schröder, M. (1984) *Number Theory in Science and Communication*. Springer: New York (This book is recommended highly. An interesting book, by a fascinating author).

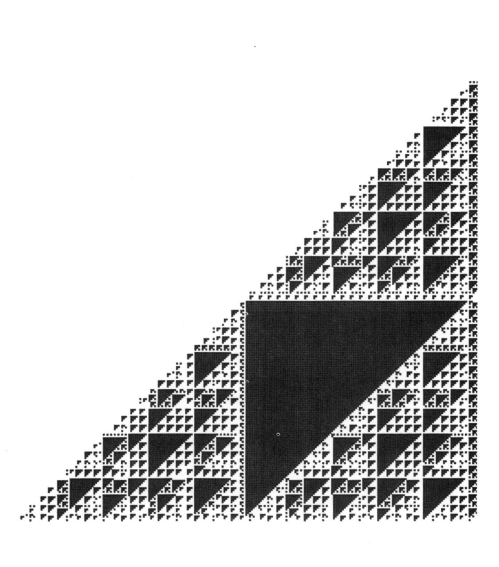

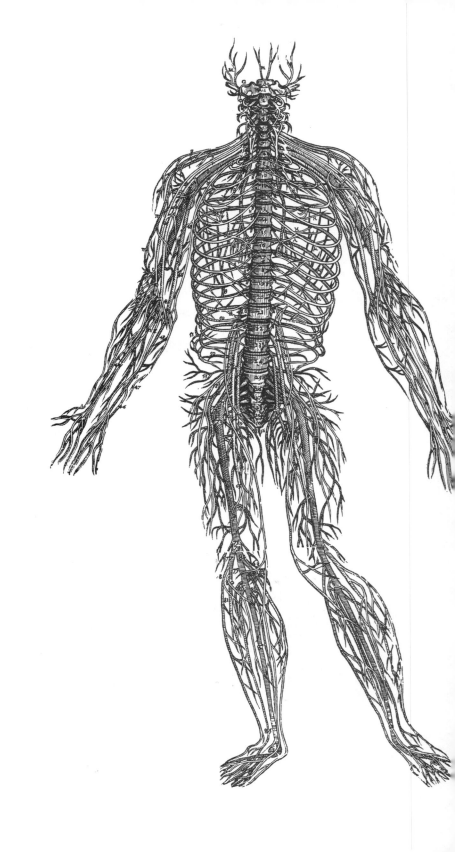

Chapter 12

Synthesizing Nature

"Nature's great book is written in mathematical symbols."　　　　Galileo

"Perhaps an angel of the Lord surveyed an endless sea of chaos, then troubled it gently with his finger. In this tiny and temporary swirl of equations, our cosmos took shape."　　　　Martin Gardner

Nature is a kaleidoscope of shapes. As we saw in "Genesis Equations" on page 104, mathematical formulas can sometimes be used to simulate natural forms. This chapter focuses on the simulation of botanical shapes and also provides a sampling of spirals in nature, science, and art. The last section describes some simple terrain generation techniques. (Pick88k, *Leonardo*; Pick87j, *Computer Graph. World*.)

12.1 Wild Monopodial Tendril Plant Growth

The idea that nature and mathematics are inextricably linked is not new – and neither is the application of that idea in computer graphics. The Fibonacci sequences, as well as a number of published papers, address the generation of mathematically derived morphological models for plants (Jena, 1984). These and other successes provide continuing incentive for more research on the mathematical basis of plant structure. This section emphasizes the role of recursive algorithms in generating plantlike forms and shows the reader how to create such shapes using a computer.

Computer graphics, in general, provides a way to represent biological objects (for an excellent book on techniques for simulating nature, see Rivlin (1986)). Researchers have explored the use of rules based on the laws of nature, such as logarithmic spirals for sea shells (Kawaguchi, 1982) or tree branching patterns determined from the study of living specimens (Aono, 1984). Other papers describe the generation of plant leaf vein patterns (Kolata, 1987) and woodgrains (Yessios, 1979). Bloomenthal (1985) describes methods for simulating tree bark,

Figure 12.1. *Immature stalk rises from the mud after only about 10 iterations.* Various buds can be seen from which lateral branches will grow in a direction different from the main stalk. Striations and rings, reminiscent of growth marks on corals or plants, are also evident. With each iteration another growth ring forms. The arrows indicate the direction of future growth at selected points, and the size of the arrow is roughly proportional to the rate of growth at the indicated node. Note that growth is more extensive toward the outer edge of the main stalk.

leaves, and limbs. Many of these algorithms involve the use of random numbers to obtain irregularity and fuzziness. In this section, algorithms (using neither random perturbations nor natural laws) are used for the creation of complicated forms resembling "monopodial" tendril plant growth and branching patterns.

From a morphological standpoint, there are only two basic categories of plant branching patterns: dichotomous branching patterns and monopodial branching patterns (Aono, 1984) (see next section for some pictures of natural plants). With the monopodial branching simulated here, a branch divides in two at the growth point, and one follows the direction of the main axis while the other goes in a different direction to form a lateral branch. Dichotomous branching is discussed in "How to Design with Directed Random Walks" on page 202.

Figure 12.2. *After 25 iterations monopodial branching has taken place.* While the resemblance of these tendril plants, or corals, to their natural counterparts is only in spirit rather than details, many have the appearance of the Pteropsida (ferns) and related plants which are most successful in moist environments.

12.1.1 Spirals in Nature

Spirals in nature are ubiquitous and have a range of botanical and zoological manifestations (Dixon (1983)). Spirals are evident in the arrangement of seeds of many plants (sunflower and daisy), and the scales of a pinecone. Other clear examples of spirals in plants (also known as green spirals) occur in the purple cornflower (Braun, 1986), pineapples, cacti, and the arrangement of buds in a pussywillow stem. It appears that some general regulatory agent is at work producing common spiral forms in plants as disparate as sunflowers and pines, and biological experimentation is underway in search of the source of these patterns. Dixon gives several equations for computing these spirals based on the logarithmic and Fibonacci spirals.

Figure 12.3. *After 55 iterations, the structure has a very filamentous appearance.* The figure is plotted in reverse video.

12.1.2 Graphics Gallery of Plant Forms

In order to produce the patterns in this section, it is possible to use "mathematical feedback loops" similar in spirit to those of Julia set theory (see "Genesis Equations" on page 104), with interesting equations and/or with novel convergence tests. Here equation networks are used instead of a single equation (as discussed in "Pattern Formation and Chaos in Networks" on page 142). The figures in the section illustrate the diversity of forms produced by the technique described by Pseudocode 12.1. The particular equations given produce biological structures, and small changes to parameters, such as μ, allow the user to produce fine distinctions in the overall morphology.

Figure 12.4. *Super ramification.* After 200 iterations the spiral structure has become so ramified that the structure has lost some of its biological appearance.

12.1.3 Natural Growth

The patterns and forms of organisms are their most immediate and obvious properties. One of the basic problems raised by the descriptive study of biological form is to understand how these structures are generated. Self-similar spirals with spiral ramification are in the branching patterns of even the most primitive plants. It it has been suggested that the relationship between phylotaxis and simple mathematical relations points to some deep mechanism of morphogenic control.

The mathematical concept of similarity holds one of the keys to understanding the processes of growth in the natural world. As a member of a species grows to maturity it generally transforms in such a way that its parts maintain approximately the same proportion with respect to each other (Kappraff, 1986), and this is probably a reason why nature is often constrained to exhibit self-similar spiral growth. The figures in this section show different magnifications of a complex space defined by the network of equations outlined in the "Recipe" section. With increasing iteration of the network of equations, monopodial

Figure 12.5. *A far-away view of a wild plant jungle for high iterations.* This figure, along with Figure 12.6, has lost some its biological appearance, although the fine feathery material attached to the various strands reminds observers of some organic matrix. The lower central spiral tendril is the same structure shown in the previous figures.

branching takes place – branching characteristic of most higher plants. In fact, if the structures here are plotted for increasing iterations (10-200 iterations), and the successive frames viewed in animated sequence, the result would reveal the gradual formations of buds and growth of lateral branches. This complicated budding pattern is most plant-like over a definite range of iterations – too high an iteration and the plant becomes too filamentous, too low and there are no branches. Magnification is also an important parameter. For example, with too small a magnification of the complex plane less plant-like structures are seen – although the patterns are often quite beautiful. For this reason, an interactive research station allows for the generation of these functions using a variety of input data scaling and windowing parameters. Other equations also yield plant-like forms, and as an example, Figure 12.7 shows a tendril computed from $z = e^{(i \times \theta)} z (1 - z)$, where θ is a constant.

Figure 12.6. *A further-away view revealing the various neighbor tendrils.*

Interestingly, the bark-like pattern on the trunk of the "plants" in the figures is caused by the weird convergence test used. In addition, as with certain aspects of true plant morphologies, these math-plants are inherently regular and deterministic throughout their "life cycle." As with the Biomorphs, these forms have a mysterious quality, partly due to the fact that in some sense the mathematical creatures exist. These objects inhabit the complex plane – though they resemble forms we could easily imagine in some primeval forest.

While the resemblance of these tendril plants to their natural counterparts is *only in spirit* rather than in details, many have the appearance of the Pteropsida (ferns) and related plants which are most successful in moist environments. Coral growths also come to mind when viewing the pictures. Some of the methods explored in "Pattern Formation and Chaos in Networks" on page 142 illustrate the ideas discussed here. An example of a network is given in the following section. Of course, the specific network of equations demonstrated in this section can only be used to represent a small subset of the large variety of natural plant forms.

Figure 12.7. *Coral-like forms.* These forms were produced from iteration of $z = e^{(i \times \theta)} z (1 - z)$, where θ is a constant.

12.1.4 Recipe for Picture Computation

Typical parameter constants are given within the Pseudocode 12.1. The reader is encouraged to modify the equations to create a variety of self-similar growth patterns. Possible color parameters are also given. If no color options are available, the program prints black dots on a white background, which works well. (Pick87j, *Computer Graphics World.*)

12.2 How to Design with Directed Random Walks

> *"Mathematicians are inexorably drawn to nature, not just describing what is to be found there, but in creating echoes of natural laws. "*   Roger Lewin

> *"Evolution is chaos with feedback."*   Joseph Ford, physicist

"How to Design Textures Using Recursive Composite Functions" on page 129 mentions that "controlled accident" has found its place in many areas of the

```
Algorithm:   Calculation of spiral plant forms

Variables: rz, iz = real, imaginary component of complex number
i = iteration counter
u, z = complex numbers
Notes: This approach iterates the network of 9 equations below.
Some of the equations are not necessary when in this order, but
are left in the code since the reader may wish to shuffle the
order of equations and view the results.

u = .35 + .35 i;
DO rrz = -2 to 2 by .005;  /* real axis       */
 DO iiz = -2 to 2 by .005; /* imaginary axis */
  a,b,c,d,e,f,g=0;
  z = cplx(rrz,iiz);          /* cplx returns a complex number  */
  InnerLoop: DO i = 1 to 30;/* iteration loop                 */
   a=z;                       /* main computation in next 2 lines*/
   b=a**2+u; e=a**2+u; c=e**2+u; b=c**2+u; f=c**2+u; d=f**2+u;
   d=b**2+u; e=d**2+u; a=f**2+u;
   z=a;
   /* convert to real and imag component*/
   rz = real(z); iz = imag(z);
   if sqrt(rz**2 + iz**2) > 10 then leave InnerLoop;
  END;                        /* InnerLoop                       */
  color = i;                  /* assign color index based on i   */
  if abs(rz) < 10 OR abs(iz) < 10 then PrintDot(rrz,iiz,color);
 END;                         /* iz loop                         */
END;                          /* rz loop                         */
```

Pseudocode 12.1. *Calculation of spiral plant forms.*

modern arts (O'Brien, 1968). For example, Dadaist and Surrealist painters such as Miro, Masson, and Arp capitalized on the elements of chance, and the works they created provide challenges for the mind as well as the eye. Perhaps the greatest artist, Mother Nature, also exhibits intricacy and beauty in partially-ordered structures, and examples include clouds, oceans, blood vessels, cracked mud, minerals, and trees. The current section illustrates several "accidental" artistic and botanical effects discovered in the course of studying certain geometrical aspects of random walks. Similar botanical designs can be created by the reader with the barest and simplest of algorithms. Other sophisticated approaches to botanical structure generation exist, for example, beautiful "particle systems" consisting of trajectories of particles influenced by the pull of gravity (Reeves, 1985). See also (Viennot et al., 1989; Prusinkiewicz et al., 1988).

12.2.1 Directed Random Walk

In the classical one-dimensional random walk in physics, transition probabilities p and q are defined as the probability that a particle will go from point k to $k + 1$ or $k - 1$ respectively. Here, we consider a special kind of random walk with transition probabilities that depend on the direction of motion. For a detailed mathematical treatise on this kind of random walk, see (Cohen, 1964). In particular, a particle changes direction or does not change direction with probabilities α and β respectively ($\alpha + \beta = 1$) dependent upon the previous direction it was travelling. If the

Figure 12.8. *Monopodial branching in the Kentucky coffee tree.* With monopodial branching a branch divides in two at the growth point, and one follows the direction of the main axis while the other goes in a different direction to form a lateral branch.

particle does change direction we then say that it is *reflected*, and if it does not we say it is *transmitted*.

12.2.2 The Algorithm

Random walks can be used, with transition probabilities that depend on direction of motion in polar space (r, θ), to create a variety of botanical forms. A particle advances in radius from a central point by a constant positive amount, with the angle θ changing in a controlled random way:

1. Choose a constant probability, α, the probability that the particle will be reflected.

2. If the previous θ change was in a negative direction, then a threshold τ is set to α, otherwise the threshold is set to β (of course the first step has no previous history and is chosen randomly as outlined in Pseudocode 12.2).

Figure 12.9. *Polychotomous branching in a dandelion gone to seed.* With dichotomous (or polychotomous) branching, a "branch" divides into two (or many) directions, and each branch goes in a different direction from the original.

3.   A random number generator on $(0,1)$ is used. If the result is greater than the threshold, then *direc* $= 1$, otherwise *direc* $= -1$ (direc keeps track of the direction for the next iteration). The random number generator is called again and the result, R, multiplied by *direc*. The particle moves by an amount (r, θ) where $\theta = R \times direc$.

Steps 2 and 3 are repeated N times, where N controls the overall length of the walk. Using this method, a particle can have a tendency to continue in the same direction as the previous step (e.g. $\alpha = 0.1$) or be continually reflected in direction (e.g. $\alpha = 0.9$). $\alpha = 0.5$ *would be a true random walk.* Other parameters which control this process are: the number of tendrils emanating from a starting point (to create a bundle of tendrils), and a scale factor controlling the size of the (r, θ) steps.

Smaller size bundles of tendrils are then placed randomly at some of the tips of the mother tendrils. This produces "self-similarity" in the design: we see in the same object similar structural themes which are repeated at different size scales. Many of the figures here contain three or four size scales. This placement also produces polychotomous branching. With dichotomous (or polychotomous)

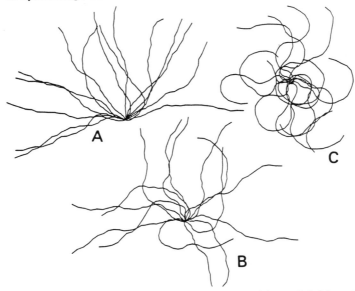

Figure 12.10. *Growth bundles.* (a) $\alpha = 0.9$, (b)$\alpha = 0.5$, (c) $\alpha = 0.1$. Note that in (a) the particle is continually reflected because of the high value of α. This tends to give rise to long, straight structures. On the other hand, curvy tendrils are created when there is a high probability of transmission, as seen in (c). Fig. (b) is a true random walk.

branching, a branch divides into two (or many) directions, and each branch goes in a different direction from the original (see Figure 12.8 and Figure 12.9). Pure polychotomous branching is rare in higher plants although it is often seen in lower forms such as algae and marine plants.

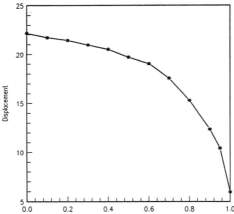

Figure 12.11. *Length vs. transmissivity.* Average tendril length (displacement of a tendril tip from its starting point) as a function of the transmissivity. As β increases, particles tend to have shorter net displacements from the origin due to their curvy shapes (see previous figure). The following two figures were produced using different values for the parameters described in the text.

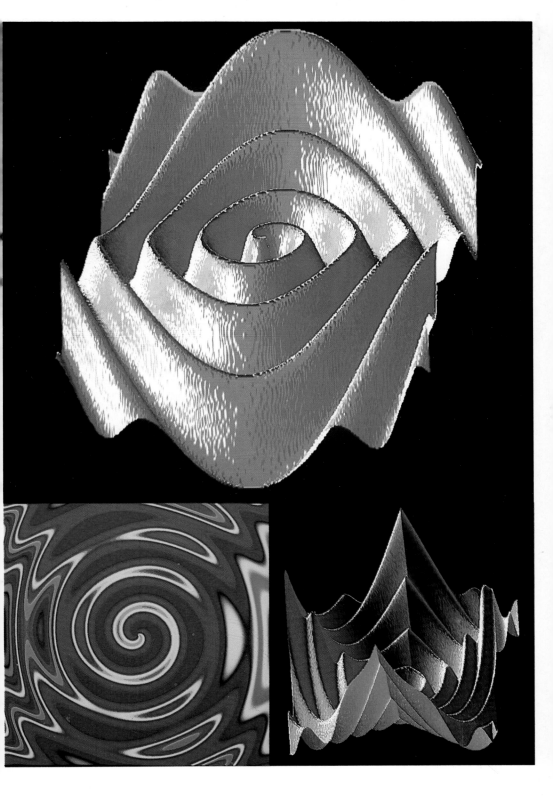

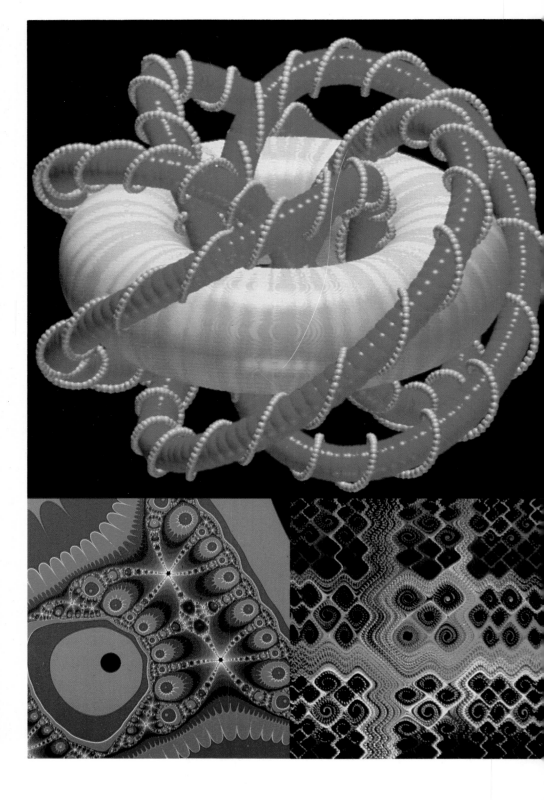

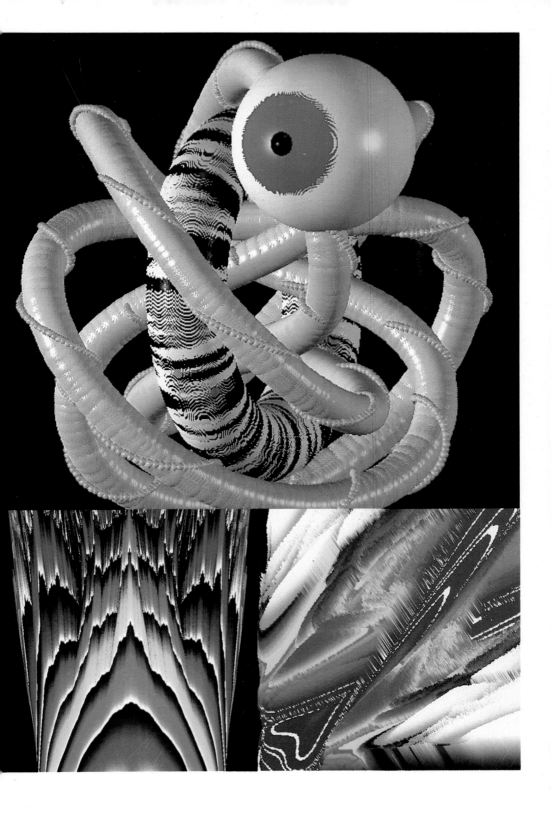

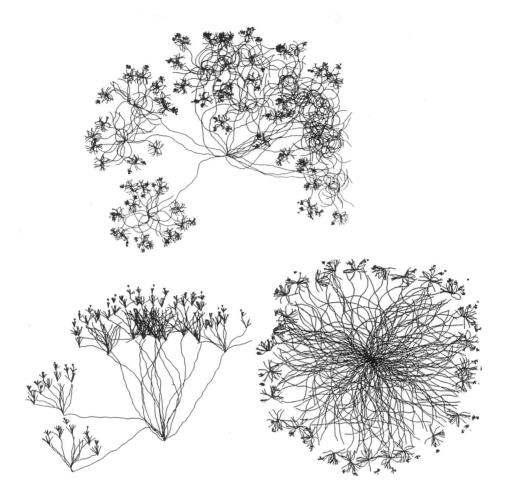

Figure 12.12. *Sample botanical forms produced by transition probabilities.*

Figure 12.10 indicates the effect of α on some simple bundles. Figure 12.11 is a plot of average tendril length (displacement of a tendril tip from its starting point) as a function of the transmissivity. It can be shown that the standard deviation of displacements generally increases as a function of β. The remaining figures illustrate the diversity of polychotomous forms which can be produced using the random walk technique described.

```
Algorithm: Calculation of plant forms

METHOD: Random walk with transition probabilities that depend
on the direction of motion.
INPUT: BranchNum - number of fibers in the bundle   (20)
DelTheta   - scale factor for theta              (0.5)
Delr       - scale factor for r                  (0.05)
Alpha      - probability of transmission         (0.1)
N          - number of steps                     (35)
x0, y0     - initial position
```
```
do j = 1 to branchnum;
  x=x0; y=y0; r = 0;                             (* initialize *)
  theta=0;
  do i = 1 to N;                                 (* number of steps *)
   if i = 1 then do;                             (* first time      *)
    Random(result);           (* create random num. between (0-1) *)
    if result > .5 then direc=1; else direc=-1;
    Random(result); result=result*direc;
    theta=theta+(result*deltheta);
    r=r+delr;
    x=r*cos(theta)+x; y=r*sin(theta)+y;  (* convert from polar *)
    MoveTo(x,y);
    last_direc=direc;
   end;
   else do;
    (*- determine threshold - *)
    if last_direc=-1 then thresh=alpha; else thresh = 1-alpha;
    Random(result);
    if result > thresh then direc=1; else direc=-1;
    Random(result); result=result*direc;
    theta=theta+(result*deltheta);
    r=r+delr; x=r*cos(theta)+x;  y=r*sin(theta)+y;
    DrawTo(x,y);
   end;
   last_direc=direc;
  end; /*i loop */
end;   /*j loop */
```

Pseudocode 12.2. *Calculation of plant forms based on random walk.*

12.2.3 Recipe for Transition Probability Plants

Pseudocode 12.2 gives typical parameter constants for the figures in this section. The program produces one bundle of tendrils, and the number of tendrils is controlled by the variable "branchnum." Variable N controls the number of steps taken in the directed random walk. Together with the step size for theta and r in polar space ("DelTheta" and "Delr"), N controls the length of each tendril. The reader is encouraged to experiment by moving "theta=0" outside the first loop. In this way the initial orientations are less constrained and correlated. (Pick89, *Comput. Lang.*)

12.3 A Sampling of Spirals in Science, Nature, and Art

"If the cosmos were suddenly frozen, and all movement ceased, a survey of its structure would not reveal a random distribution of parts. Simple geometrical patterns, for example, would be found in profusion – from the spirals of galaxies to the hexagonal shapes of snow crystals. Set the clockwork going, and its parts move rhythmically to laws that often can be expressed by equations of surprising simplicity. And there is no logical or a priori reason why these things should be so."

Martin Gardner, "Order and Surprise," 1985

We have seen spirals in a number of settings in previous chapters. This section emphasizes the important and conspicuous role that spirals play in nature, civilization, and art. The term "spiral" is used generically to describe any geometrical smooth curve that winds about a central point or axis while also receding from it. When you think of examples of spirals, both the mundane and the exotic easily come to mind, for example: the gentle curl of a fern tendril, the shape of an octopus's retracted arm, the death-form assumed by a centipede, the spiral intestine of a giraffe, the shape of a butterfly's tongue, the spiral cross-section of a scroll, the shape of the Yellow Brick Road in Munchkinland in the film classic *The Wizard of Oz*, and even the characters of several written languages (Figure 12.13).

This section is divided into four parts, which deal with: traditional mathematical spirals, spirals in nature, spirals made by humans, and "strange spirals." Here the term "strange spiral" denotes entities that have many of the visual properties one normally associates with spirals as defined above, yet also have other interesting features such as being infinitely convoluted, being infinitely discontinuous or simply having several novel geometric and visual properties, such as those described later in the text.

12.3.1 Traditional Mathematical Spirals (Clothoid, Littus, et al.)

Generally, plane curve spirals are of the form

$$r = f(\theta) \tag{12.1}$$

in polar coordinates (where f is monotonic), and they possess a simple beauty which humans have copied in their arts and tools, and nature has used in the creation of many structures of life. All the mathematical forms presented in this section were first discovered in the seventeenth and eighteenth centuries, except for the simplest form, the *Archimedes spiral*, which was first discussed by Archimedes in 225 B.C. The *Archimedes spiral* is expressed by the equation

$$r = a\theta \tag{12.2}$$

The most commonly observed spirals are of the Archimedian type: tightly wound springs, edges of rolled-up rugs and sheets of paper, and decorative spirals on

Figure 12.13. *Simple spiral forms.* Written languages often contain several spiral forms. From top to bottom of the figure: (a) Thai printing (Haas, 1956). (b) This ornate design represents the word for spiral in Farsi (pronounced "mar-peach," which literally means "snake curl"). (c) Sample of Tamil script (from southern India), which is famous for its spiral forms. (d) Spiral representations ("spirons") of sub-atomic particles. Very small particles, such as electrons, have been postulated to be composed of these spiral structures (Boivin, 1978). (e) Sample "doodle" taken from a page of a phone book. (f) Repeated attempts of a three-year-old boy to draw a spiral.

jewelry. Practical uses of the Archimedes spiral include the transformation of rotary to linear motion in sewing machines (Gardner, 1969).

The *logarithmic spiral* (also known as the *equiangular spiral* or *Bernoulli spiral*) can be expressed as

$$r = ke^{a\theta} \tag{12.3}$$

This spiral was first discussed by Descartes in 1638. The angle between the straight line, $\theta =$ constant, and the tangent to the curve is constant. Examples of the logarithmic spiral found in nature are mentioned in "Spirals in Nature" on

Figure 12.14. *Examples of spirals in nature.* Several shells of various ammonites (extinct shellfish) are shown.

page 213. Other more exotic spirals include the *hyperbolic spiral* (or *reciprocal spiral*), which is of the form

$$r = \left(\frac{a}{\theta} \right) \tag{12.4}$$

A *littus* has the form

$$r^2\theta = a \tag{12.5}$$

A *Cornu spiral* (or *clothoid* or *Euler's spiral*) has a parametric representation:

$$x = a\sqrt{\pi} \int_0^t \cos\left(\frac{\pi t^2}{2} \right) dt \tag{12.6}$$

$$y = a\sqrt{\pi} \int_0^t \sin\left(\frac{\pi t^2}{2} \right) dt \tag{12.7}$$

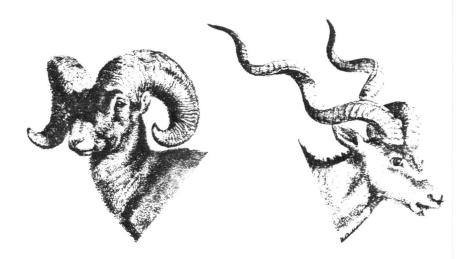

Figure 12.15. *Spiral horns on a bighorn sheep and African kudu antelope.*

This curve was discovered by Euler in 1744, and M.A. Cornu later used this curve in the representation of optical diffraction.

Some of these families of spiral curves can perhaps be more simply defined by

$$r^m = a^m \theta \tag{12.8}$$

which includes the Archimedes spiral ($m = 1$), Fermat's spiral ($m = 2$) (first discussed by Fermat in 1636), the hyperbolic spiral ($m = -1$) (first discussed by Pierre Varignon in 1704), and the littus ($m = -2$) (originated by Cotes in 1722).

The *involute of a circle* with parametric equations

$$x = a(\cos \phi + \phi \sin \phi) \tag{12.9}$$
$$y = a(\sin \phi - \phi \cos \phi) \tag{12.10}$$

was first taken into account by Huygens when he was formulating his ideas for clocks without pendulums, which might be of service on seagoing vessels. This is the curve described by the endpoint of a string as it unwinds from a circle of radius a while held taut. The curves traced by all points along the plank of a seesaw or the path of a goat tied to a cylindrical post as it winds tightly around it are both involutes of a circle.

Finally, the *cochleoid* (or snail form) is given by

$$r = a \left(\frac{\sin \theta}{\theta} \right) \tag{12.11}$$

Figure 12.16. *Artists' spirals.* Ornamental alphabets often contain spirals such as seen here in several letters from graphic designer Carol Grafton.

Apart from their mathematical differences, and also the varied natural forms these spirals help to describe, many of these spirals are quite different *visually*. For example, perhaps the most exotic-looking of the group is *Euler's spiral*, which consists of two spirals connected together, giving it the appearance of a mustache with two curled ends. The only other spiral of the group with more than one center is the *Cochleoid* which contains two directly adjacent spirals. *Fermat's spiral* is the only member that consists of two concentric lines, and it resembles the paths of two tracks of a stereo record groove. Finally, the *littus* is the only spiral of the group with a long, almost linear section; it looks like a fern tendril with a very long stem.

12.3.1.1 Spirals in Nature

Spirals in nature are ubiquitous and have a range of botanical and zoological manifestations. Probably the most common examples are the logarithmic spirals of Nautilus shells and other sea shells (Figure 12.14), the horns of a variety of mammals including the African kudu antelope (Figure 12.15), the arrangement of seeds of many plants (sunflower and daisy), and the scales of a pinecone (see previous section for spirals in plants). Other algorithms for recreating shells, horns, tusks and claws are described by Kawaguchi (1982). Body parts with spiral structures include the spiralling fibers at the apex of the heart.

Martin Gardner has noted that *Eperia*, a common variety of spider, spins a web in which a strand coils around the center in a logarithmic spiral. Aquatic life often manifest spiral bodies or appendages. The branchial filaments of *spirographics* (tube-worms) play spirally in the water, and when stimulated they jerk spontaneously back into a tube along a screw-like form. The tube-worms' gill filaments form a perfect spiral (Schwenk, 1976). In the intestine of *Protopterus* and other lung-fishes there exists a spiral fold. On a smaller scale, many unicellular animals have incorporated spiral shapes; for example, the infusoria are creatures with spherical form and have screw-like spiralling motions for

Figure 12.17. *Spirals in art.* Spirals often appear in artists' drawings of the creatures of mythology, legend or religion (Huber, 1981). Clockwise from top left: (a) Maori drawing of spiral facial tattoos, New Zealand, 19th C. (b) Gargoyle from the Milan Cathedral. (c) Spiral nose on a cittern by Girolamo de Virdis, 1574. (d) German helmet with spiral horns, 1511-14. (e) Lion with spiral Dragon's tail and tongue, from a Victorian border design. (f) Water dragon, from a print. (g) This "voice amplifier" appears in "Gabinetto Armonico," first printed in 1716, by Jesuit Filippo Bonanni. Bonanni wrote on art and folk instruments of all levels of European society, and here it is suggested that a large spiral tube would considerably magnify the sound of the voice.

locomotion. On even smaller scales, spirals also abound: for example, the α helix, the supercoiled α helix, the helical packing of subunits in viruses and in DNA, and the coiling of DNA strands in a nucleosome (Vaneschtein, 1986). (Technically the helix is not a spiral, but we include it here because it is closely related to

Figure 12.18. *Spirals made with straight lines.* Top: Random segment spirals. These figures were created by connecting pairs of points with straight lines. The eye perceives spiral patterns by observing the correlated pairs. Bottom: Trigonometric "bushy" spirals. Here, an infinite variety of spiral-like patterns were created by the author using a complicated hierarchy of trigonometric functions.

the spiral.) Still smaller yet, sub-atomic particles, such as electrons, have been represented by spiral structures called "spirons" (Boivin, 1978) (Figure 12.13).

Other examples in nature include the patterns on *Spiriferida* (certain fossilized shells), *spiral cleavage* (a pattern characterized by formation of an embriological cell mass showing spiral symmetry), the *spiral valve* (a spiral fold of mucous membrane in the small intestine of sharks which increases the area for absorption), fingerprint whorls, and the axoneme (bundle of fibers in a flagellum) (Doczi, 1986).

Examples of natural non-living spiral motifs are galactic formations and the vortices of water and air waves. These vortices include vertical spiralling columns of air which carry gliding birds to great heights and the whirling path of air in organ pipes.

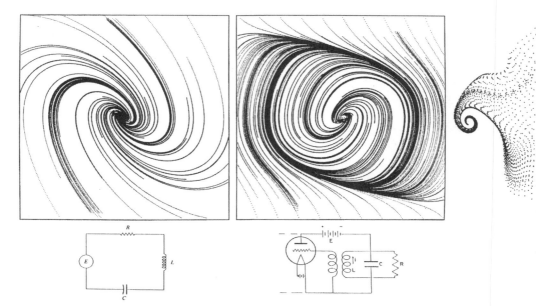

Figure 12.19. *Dynamical systems involving real numbers.* These figures were created by plotting trajectories through time. Left to right: (a) Phase portrait of an RLC circuit. (b) Phase portrait of an oscillator. (c) Phase portrait of coupled differential equations (see Appendix).

12.3.2 Spirals Made by Humans

In modern technological society, spiral devices play an invaluable role. Examples include the spiral bevel gear (a gear with oblique teeth), spiral chutes for conveying material, the spiral cutterhead (a rotary digging device), spiral mold cooling (to cool an injection mold by passing liquid through a spiral cavity), and the spiral staircase. Other spiral devices include a variety of gauges, heat exchangers, thermometers, pipes, distillation equipment, and intrauterine devices for birth control. The spiral spring (an Archimedian spiral) is particularly interesting in its unique ability to respond to both torsional and translational force. In musical instruments, spirals also abound. Examples include the posthorn and many modern brass instruments. Children's toys often are comprised of spirals (e.g. the Slinky and Chinese yo-yos), and spiral forms also are used in vending machine dispensers, record grooves, ornamental alphabets (Figure 12.16), written languages (Figure 12.13), and the curse-word symbols that cartoonists use. Extremely intricate spirals can be made chemically by coating a glass sheet with carbon black and various liquids (Zvilna, 1986).

Doodles – those designs we make by idle, unconscious scribbling when our thoughts are occupied elsewhere – often contain a remarkable number of spiral forms (Figure 12.13). Just what this unconscious tendency to draw spirals tells us about the unconscious human mind and its inner images is not clear, but from ancient times the spiral has been used in art and dance to induce a state of ecstasy (Samuels, 1982). The actual mental and physical ability permitting humans to draw spirals probably begins around age 3. Figure 12.13 shows several attempts of a three-year-old boy to draw a spiral. Today, psychologists have used the spiral for deepening relaxation and bringing about a "deeper level of mind" (Samuels, 1982).

Ancient examples of spirals include prehistoric spiral mazes, Stone Age animal ornaments, terracotta pot spiral designs from the 6th century B.C. (Rozsa, 1986), decorations from ancient Altaic works (middle of the first millennium B.C.) (Mamedov, 1986), engravings on threshold stones of initiation chambers in the Bronze Age in Ireland, Tibetan Tanka art work, and scrollworks for Irish manuscripts (Makovicky, 1986). Spirals also often appear in artists' drawings of the creatures of mythology, legend, or religion (Figure 12.17). A beautiful example of an 18th century engraving depicting a spiral musical instrument is also shown in Figure 12.17. This "voice amplifier" appeared in Jesuit Filippo Bonanni's book "Gabinetto Armonico." Spirals also are found in modern surrealist art (for famous examples, see the works of Joan Miro, Matta, and Alfred Jarry (Rubin, 1975)).

12.3.3 Strange Spirals

As mentioned in the Introduction, "strange spiral" is a term coined to denote entities that have many of the visual properties one normally associates with spirals as defined above, yet have other novel features such as being infinitely convoluted, being infinitely discontinuous, or simply having more complicated generating formulas (see below).

12.3.4 Galaxies

The logarithmic spiral's most impressive appearance is in the arms of many galaxies. Although it is clear that the overall mass distribution and motions of the components of a galaxy are determine by gravity, it not clear what is responsible for the striking spiral morphology of galaxies (Schulman and Seiden, 1986). Spiral arms extend over 20,000 parsecs (1 pc = 3.26 light years), and the traditional view is that it is necessary to have a long-range interaction like gravity to create such long-range order. In spiral galaxies, the spiral arms are sites of active star formation.

Spiral galactic shapes are relatively easy to program on the computer, as they consist of dots forming a double logarithmic spiral. One arm is 180° out of phase with the other. To obtain a picture of a galactic distribution of dots, simply plot dots at (r, θ) according to:

$$r_1 = e^{[\theta \tan \phi]}$$

(12.12)

```
Algorithm: How to produce a galaxy

Notes: The program produces a double logarithmic spiral.
The purpose of the random number generator is to add
jitter to the distribution of stars.
Variables: in = curvature of galactic arm (try in=2)
maxit = maximum iteration number
scale = radial multiplicative scale factor
cut = radial cutoff
f = final scale factor

loop1:Do i = 0 to maxit;
 theta=float(i)/50;
 r=scale*exp(theta*tan(in));
 if r > cut then leave loop1;
 x=r*cos(theta)+50;  y= r*sin(theta)+50;
 call rand(randx);  (* return a random number between 0 - 1 *)
 call rand(randy);  (* return a random number between 0 - 1 *)
 PlotDotAt(x+f*randx,y+f*randy);
end;
loop2:Do i = 0 to maxit;      (* Create second arm of galaxy *)
 theta=float(i)/50;
 theta2=(float(i)/50)-3.14;
 r=scale*exp(theta2*tan(in));
 if r > cut then leave loop2;
 x=r*cos(theta)+50;  y= r*sin(theta)+50;
 call rand(randx);  (* return a random number between 0 - 1 *)
 call rand(randy);  (* return a random number between 0 - 1 *)
 PlotDotAt(x+f*randx,y+f*randy);
end;
```

Pseudocode 12.3. *How to produce a spiral galaxy.*

$$r_2 = e^{[(\pi+\theta)\tan\phi]} \tag{12.13}$$

where r_1 and r_2 correspond to the two intertwined spiral arms. The curvature of the arms is controlled by ϕ which should be about 0.2 radians for realistic results. In addition, $0 < \theta < 1000$ radians. For greater realism, a small amount of random jitter may be added to the final points.

12.3.5 Seashells

The seashell on the cover of the book was based upon the logarithmic spiral,

$$r = ke^{a\theta}; \quad (x, y) = f(r, \theta) \tag{12.14}$$

```
Algorithm: How to produce a bushy spiral
Variables: (l,d,g,k,u1,u2,w1,w2); Try: (10,10,10,10,3,3,3,3)
Notes: This basic algorithm follows that of Jacobson (1982).
The main difference is the use of random numbers (see text).
pi = 1.5707;  (* a constant = pi/2 *)
s = atand(w1,w2);   (* arctangent, input is in degrees *)
t = 360*(w1*sind(S)+w2*cosd(s));
call uwindo(-t,t,-t,t);   (* scale window size *)
do b = 0 to 360 by d;
 do a = 0 to 360 by g;
  z = k*pi*(u1*sind(l*a)+u2*cosd(l*a));
  r = b*(w1*sind(z)+w2*cosd(z));  (* d means degrees *)
  call rand(randx); call rand(randy);  (* random numbers *)
  x = r*cosd(a)+randx*0.1*r;     y = r*sind(a)+randy*0.1*r;
  if a > 0 then LineTo(x,y); else call MoveTo(x,y);
 end;
end;
```

Pseudocode 12.4. *How to produce a bushy spiral.*

where the θ range is $-12\pi < \theta < 6\pi$.[24] Some past work has presented 2-D graphics of spirals (e.g. Kawaguchi, 1982); however, here some of the shapes have a (helical) axis, z, around which the shell grows. Two z functions were used, $z = \alpha\theta$ where $(\alpha > 1)$, or $z = \beta r$ where $(\beta \sim -2)$ (the latter creates more realistic seashells). In all cases the radius of the "tube", R, which makes up the shell is a function of r, i.e., $R = r/\gamma$, where γ is a constant in the range $(0.01 < \gamma < 3)$. The shells were rendered on a graphics supercomputer with sophisticated lighting and shading facilities. (Pick89, *IEEE Computer Graphics and Appl.*)

12.3.6 Fuzzy Spirals

If a pattern of random dots is superimposed on itself and rotated by a small angle, concentric circles are perceived about the point of rotation (see "Another Dot-Display Used in Molecular Biophysics" on page 45). Figure 12.18 shows "fuzzy" spirals created by a procedure related to random-dot spirals. To reproduce these figures, first plot about 5000 randomly positioned dots. Then rotate these same 5000 dots by 2° to 30° and expand slightly. Connect the dots to their respective original dots. Your eye perceives spiral patterns by observing the correlated pairs. By varying the angle and specific type of random numbers used, you can generate a variety of visually exciting patterns. For some of the figures, Gaussian white noise is used. This can be generated by:

$$Noise = \left(\frac{1}{n}\right) \sum_{i=1}^{n} \delta_i \tag{12.15}$$

---

[24] Perhaps not intuitively obvious is the fact that negative angles are essential in producing the most interesting and realistic seashell shapes. Readers can check this for themselves.

where δ_i is a random number in $(0,1)$ and n is about 6.

12.3.7 Spiral-Like Forms from Differential Equations

12.3.7.1 RLC Circuit

The differential equation

$$L\ddot{x} + R\dot{x} + \left(\frac{1}{C}\right) x = 0 \tag{12.16}$$

governs the behavior of a simple RLC electric circuit, where x represents the charge on the capacitor, and $\dot{x}$ represents the current in the loop. R is the resistance, L the inductance, and C the capacitance. The equivalent first order system is:

$$\dot{x} = y \tag{12.17}$$

$$\dot{y} = -\left(\frac{1}{LC}\right) x - \left(\frac{R}{L}\right) y \tag{12.18}$$

This can easily be implemented on a computer:

$$x_t = x_{t-1} + \lambda y_{t-1} \tag{12.19}$$

$$y_t = y_{t-1} + \lambda\left[\left(\frac{-1}{LC}\right) x_{t-1} - \left(\frac{R}{L}\right) y_{t-1}\right] \tag{12.20}$$

where $\lambda > 0$ is a constant known as the *step size* of the numerical solution. Here, λ is kept small ($\lambda \sim 0.1$) $-3 < x < 3$ and $-3 < y < 3$ and R, L and C can be set to 1.0. Figure 12.19 reveals that all initial points (x,y) have spiral trajectories that converge at the fixed point in the center of the figure. Watching this shape dynamically unfold on the cathode ray tube (CRT) is especially useful for revealing the damped response of the RLC circuit (see Glossary for *damp*).

12.3.7.2 Self-sustained Oscillations

In this class of problems, we have a nonlinear vibration where the damping is also nonlinear. One of the best known cases encountered in practice is that of the triode vacuum tube. An electrical circuit containing such a tube (Stoker, 1953) is shown in Figure 12.19 with its accompanying phase "portrait."

Figure 12.19 was generated from the differential equation governing the current in an oscillator:

$$CL\ddot{X} + F(\dot{x}) + x = 0 \tag{12.21}$$

The function $F(\dot{x})$ is a nonlinear function (caused by the nonlinear relation between current and voltage in the tube). The function used here was suggested by Stoker (1953):

$$F(\dot{x}) = \varepsilon \left[-\dot{x} + \left(\frac{1}{3} \right) \dot{x}^3 \right] \tag{12.22}$$

This system was implemented on a computer by deriving the following coupled discretization using the forward Euler approximation (Finney and Ostberg, 1976):

$$x_t = x_{t-1} + \lambda y_{t-1} \tag{12.23}$$

$$y_t = y_{t-1} + \lambda \left[x_{t-1} - R \left(-y_{t-1} + \left(\frac{y_{t-1}^3}{3} \right) \right) \right] \tag{12.24}$$

where $\lambda > 0$. λ is kept small ($\lambda \sim 0.05$). L and C have been set to 1.0. Also: $-3 < x < 3$, $-3 < y < 3$, and $\varepsilon = 1.0$.

From a mathematical standpoint, the graph in Figure 12.19 is fascinating. If one watches as it evolves on the graphics screen, one can see that all initial points (x,y) contained within the bounding ovoid shape (known as an attractor) spiral outward to the attractor surface, while all points outside the attractor spiral inward toward it. Once a point in the path meets the attractor, it circulates along the attractor forever. As λ is increased, more stochastic behavior is observed. The reader is encouraged to experiment with this parameter and to observe the results.

As the reader may imagine, an infinite variety of spiral patterns can be computed from differential equations (see "Dynamical Systems" on page 249). In addition, the iteration of complex functions also produces a number of spiral forms (see "More Beauty from Complex Variables" on page 113). For more specific information on how to create figures such as these, see "More Beauty from Complex Variables" on page 113.)

12.3.8 Trigonometric Iteration (Bushy Spirals)

An infinite variety of spiral-like patterns can be created using a complicated hierarchy of trigonometric functions (Pseudocode 12.4). The user enters a series of eight parameters l, d, g, k, u_1, u_2, w_1, w_2. In order to produce the "bushy" designs in Figure 12.18, first parameters s and t are computed for the pictures:

$$s = \tan^{-1} \left[\frac{w_1}{w_2} \right] \tag{12.25}$$

$$t = 360[w_1 \sin(s) + w_2 \cos(s)] \tag{12.26}$$

t is a parameter which controls the window of the graphics screen – the lower left hand corner is set to $(-t, -t)$, and the upper right hand corner is set to (t,t). The following sets of equations are then iterated for $0 < b_i < 360$ and $0 < a_j < 360$. The step size for the i loop is d, and the step size for the j loop is g. Nested inside these two loops are the following equations:

Figure 12.20. *Iteration of a complex function.*

$$z = k\pi\,[u_1\,\sin(l\,a_j) + u_2\,\cos(l\,a_j)] \tag{12.27}$$

$$r = b_i\,[w_1\,\sin(z) + w_2\,\cos(z)] \tag{12.28}$$

$$x = r\,\cos(a_j) + \beta_1 \tag{12.29}$$

$$y = r\,\sin(a_j) + \beta_2 \tag{12.30}$$

where

$$\beta = 0.1r\gamma, \tag{12.31}$$

and γ is a random number on $(0,1)$. The bushy spirals in Figure 12.18 results from plotting (x,y) coordinates. The eight parameter values are all set to values near 3 for Figure 12.18. This system of equations follows that of (Jacobson, 1982), the significant difference being the β parameter which gives the resulting patterns a much more "natural" look. The spiral nature of these patterns is clearer when the viewer watches the figures plotted dynamically on the screen.

12.3.9 Concluding Remarks on Spirals

The forms described by geometry and mathematics are not just abstract ideas. As far as the physical universe is concerned, spiral shapes are one of nature's most fundamental forms. As science writer Kathleen Stein (Omni Magazine) once pointed out, spirals appear early in the chain of animal evolution: cilia, worms' gills, fly larvae, and some shark egg capsules have them. The cochlea in the ear of every mammal is screw-shaped, and so are many corals. Like the forms in other chapters of this book, some of the spiral shapes in this section are magnificently complicated structures which few could have appreciated fully or even suspected before the age of the computer. Again, the richness of resultant forms often contrasts with the simplicity of the generating formulas.

Precisely *why* the spiral is ubiquitous in nature and in civilization is a profound question. Whether one is considering the movement of stars, the development of an embryo, the motion of a pencil on a page, or many of the phenomena that make up the fabric of our universe, it is clear that symmetry operations are often nature's guiding hand. Spiral patterns often occur spontaneously in matter that is organized through symmetry transformations: change of size (growth) and rotation. Form follows function, and the spiral form can allow for the compaction of a relatively long length. Long-yet-compact tubes are useful in spiral molds, brass instruments, mollusks, and cochleas for obvious reasons including physical strength and increased surface area. For some phenomena, such as in doodles, written languages, and spiral galaxies, the precise "reason" for spiral forms is less clear.

The mathematical concept of similarity holds one of the keys to understanding the processes of growth in the natural world. As a member of a species grows to maturity it generally transforms in such a way that its parts maintain approximately the same proportion with respect to each other (Kappraff, 1986), and this is probably a reason why nature is often constrained to exhibit self-similar spiral growth. Through time, *humans have imitated the spiral motifs around them in their art forms and sciences*, and occasionally they invent new spirals not known to have specific counterparts in the natural world. It is probable that catalogues of "traditional" and "nontraditional" spiral formulas will help scientists better understand the fundamental rules underlying the apparent spiral repetition of nature, since they can generate, define and predict these patterns in precise scientific terms. (Pick88k, *Leonardo*.)

12.4 A Vacation on Mars

It is indeed fascinating that complicated and artistic mountainscapes can be fully computed and rendered in under 2 minutes using a Stellar GS1000, a member of the new class of graphics supercomputers which have become readily available in 1989. This new breed of computer can typically plot more than 50,000 shaded triangular facets in a second. (For a review of such kinds of computers, see Anderson, 1988.) The color plates show an imaginary planet which, like Mars, is scarred and rust colored. The figure was fully computed and rendered in under 2 minutes. This speed may make such hardware and software systems of interest to both artists and computer graphics scientists.

Various methods have been used in the past to generate terrain, and many of these methods have used Brownian (or Brownian-like) noise functions (described later) to create an irregular surface. To generate the noisy surfaces, the methods sometimes involve the addition of randomly placed and randomly oriented faults in a plane, or the use of fast Fourier transform filtering, or the displacement of points on a grid (for a review see (Voss, 1988)). The originator of fractal landscapes in computer graphics is IBM Fellow B. Mandelbrot. The reader is directed to *The Fractal Geometry of Nature* for details of this work in "Brownian and fractional Brownian surfaces", and for more information on fractals. Voss (1985, 1988) used fractal concepts to create very convincing representations of nature. See Musgrave (1989) for interesting recent work and for a directed reading list on this topic.

The method used for the pictures in this book involves the use of circular disks with equal radii which are randomly moved on a plane in order to approximate a Brownian surface. I've not seen this precise method in the published literature, but considering the simplicity of the approach, I expect others have used the same techniques. Although this approach sacrifices both the mathematical purity and graphic detail of traditional fractals, the process is conceptually simple and easy to implement – and attractive pictures result.

The foreground terrain shown in the Color Plates was generated using a Brownian distribution of filled circles. To produce this distribution, have your computer take a circular disk of height 1 unit and randomly walk the disk over a plane. Have the moving circle leave behind an irregular trail of circles. After the walk continues for a long time, a bumpy pile of disks finally result. The mountains were generated by viewing (with the aid of a graphics supercomputer) the "bumpy pile" from an angle specified by the user. Red lights were used to illuminate the terrain. For this scene, approximately 35,000 circular disks were used. The size of the plane is 512 by 512 units. Of course, most readers will not have access to a graphics supercomputer, but even if sophisticated graphics computers are unavailable, the resulting Brownian intensity profiles look quite marvelous if the pile height is represented as color in a 2-D representation.

Informally speaking, the landscapes are fractals – rough-edged objects which continue to exhibit structural details upon increasing magnification. Note that since a constant radius of 25 was used for the circle size, these landscapes will not show detail at small size scales. However, the simple numerical methods used here are not intended to create realistic models of earthly terrain which have been rendered so skillfully in the past (Mandelbrot, 1983), but rather provide a rapid means for generating artistically interesting panoramas. The rising planet effect was achieved by randomly positioning circular disks on a plane to form an irregular pile. As with the random-walk methods for the mountains, sum the accumulated intensities of the circles, but instead of viewing the profile from the side, view it from above. The height of the pile at any given point on the plane can be color coded to produce an artistically interesting pattern. This pattern is then projected onto the surface of a sphere.

12.5 Reading List for Chapter 12

Aside from the various papers and books in the Reference section at the back of this book, the reader may find the following books of particular interest:

1.   Rivlin, R. (1986) *The Algorithmic Image.* Microsoft Press, WA.
2.   Thompson, D. (1961) *On Growth and Form.* Cambridge: England.

Rivlin's book indicates recent advances in the computer synthesis of natural forms, while Thompson's older book discusses various mathematical properties of biological structures (such as cell aggregates, horns, teeth, and tusks).

Chapter 13

Synthesizing Ornamental Textures

"Mathematics is order and beauty at its purest, order that transcends the physical world."
Paul Hoffman, 1987, "The Man Who Loves Only Numbers"

"The job of the artist is always to deepen the mystery. "　　Francis Bacon

The line between science and art is a fuzzy one; the two are fraternal philosophies formalized by ancient Greeks like Eratosthenes and Aristophanes. Computer graphics helps reunite these philosophies by providing scientific ways to represent natural and artistic objects. In this section, real numbers are used to generate a surprising variety of beautiful and unpredictable textures and ornaments on small computers. See also related material in the Chapters on "Synthesizing Nature" on page 195 and "Numerical Approximation Methods" on page 275.

13.1 Self-decorating Eggs

"I look at mathematics pretty globally. It represents the ultimate structure and order. And I associate doing mathematics with control."　　Paul Erdös

High on a green hilltop in Vegreville, Canada, stands a huge model of a Ukranian Easter egg. The surface of the egg-monument is covered by what appears to be symmetrical designs of colored tiles, and the reflection of the gargantuan egg in the nearby lake enhances the monument's beauty. It is clear that many of the ornaments of modern man and his ancient cultures consist of symmetrical and repeating designs. Consider the beautiful Moorish, Persian, and other motifs in tiled floors and cloths shown in Figure 13.1 and Figure 13.2.

Figure 13.1. *Pattern of a woven carpet depicted in a miniature painting (Bagdad, 1396).*

Today, we continue to be fascinated with symmetry and repetition in design. As modern examples, there are the isometric designs of John Locke and the geometrical ornaments of Russian artist Chernikow (where simple forms create complex interweavings), and a variety of popular art deco designs:

Figure 13.3 shows a modern symmetrical design by artist William Rowe. Even nature often expresses itself in terms of repeating symmetries – and the cross section of plants, phase transitions, standing waves on metal plates, muscle striations, snow crystals, and dendritic ice are just a few examples (Figure 13.4 and Figure 13.5) (see also Chapter on "Synthesizing Nature" on page 195).

How can the beauty of the symmetrical ornaments and designs of various cultures be simulated with the aid of a computer? One way is by the use of mathematical equations. Indeed, structures produced by the equations in this section include shapes of great intricacy. The egg shapes generated for this section have

Figure 13.2. *Japanese "Diaper ornaments".* Diaper Ornaments contain features occurring at regular intervals, enclosed or connected by geometrical or flowing lines.

been called *"chaos-eggs"* by some observers because of their intricate designs and hard-to-predict behavior (see "Summary of Egg Tiling Patterns" on page 232). The graphics experiments presented, with the variety of accompanying parameters, demonstrate the complexity of such behavior.

13.1.1 The Algorithm

To compute the tiling patterns, first z is calculated:

$$z_{xy} = \alpha(\sin x + \sin y) \tag{13.1}$$

where α is a constant, and where

$$x = \beta_1 + (\gamma i), \quad i = 0, 1, 2, 3 \ldots R \tag{13.2}$$
$$y = \beta_2 + (\gamma j), \quad j = 0, 1, 2, 3 \ldots R. \tag{13.3}$$

Therefore, $\{\beta_1 \leq x \leq \beta_1 + (\gamma R)\}$ and $\{\beta_2 \leq y \leq \beta_2 + (\gamma R)\}$. β controls the phase of the two sine waves, while γ controls the frequency. This surface function (Figure 13.6), even for different phases and frequencies, is rather dull and uninteresting. The excitement comes by implementing the following few steps.

The resulting z value (Equation (13.1)) is truncated (made an integer) and divided by another integer, m. If the remainder is zero, a dot is plotted on the graphics screen at point (x, y). In other words,

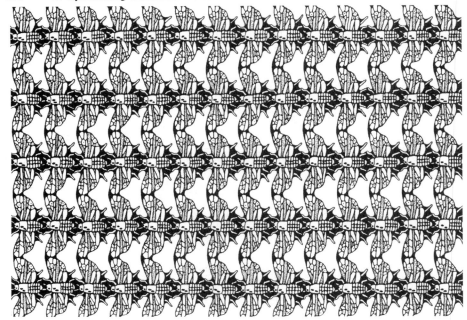

Figure 13.3. *Modern symmetrical design.*

$$\psi_{xy} = trunc(z_{xy}) \tag{13.4}$$

A dot is plotted if and only if

$$\psi_{xy} \bmod m = 0 \tag{13.5}$$

This approach was described previously in relation to exotic tiling patterns.[25] In the present section, a second transformation is sometimes applied to map this pattern to a sphere or ellipsoid (algorithms for spherical and other coordinate systems are not discussed here since they can be found in many computer graphics and mathematics texts (see references).

13.1.2 Graphics Gallery

The figures are the resulting maps for a variety of values for α, β, γ, and m. When mapped to ellipsoidal surfaces, some of the figures remind observers of Russian Easter eggs and Christmas ornaments, in addition to various weavings, rugs, and mosaic tile patterns. Aside from the fact that the maps are complex and aesthetically pleasing, several mathematical observations can be made. For one,

---

[25] Pickover, C. (1987) Blooming Integers: An elegantly simple algorithm generates complex patterns (Mathematics and Beauty III) *Computer Graphics World* (March), 10(3): 54-57.

Figure 13.4. *Snow crystals.*

the α multiplier can be considered as an entropy factor. As α increases, the disorder (entropy) of the map increases until it looks almost random to the eye. For low values of α the pattern becomes perfectly ordered – somewhat crystalline in appearance. This phenomenon can be simply understood, in part, by noting that for smaller alpha the range of values for resultant ψ is smaller, and therefore the pattern is obviously more repetitive, simple, and ordered. Figure 13.7 contains patterns for several values of α suggesting this entropic effect.

Another simple observation is that as the modulus factor, m, increases, the *density* of the system decreases. This too can be simply understood since there are fewer numbers in Equation (13.1) on page 229 evenly divisible by 10 (for example) than there are by 3. Figure 13.8 and Figure 13.9 contain patterns for several values of m which suggest this density effect, and Figure 13.10 shows the density fluctuation for a typical system as a function of m. The existence of the periodic lines seen for many modularities is due to the periodic occurrences of $\sin(x) + \sin(y) = 0$, since $0 \bmod(m) = 0$ for all m. In fact, experiments with large m ($m > 1000$) reveal plots whose only features are the honeycomb of straight lines.

When the dot-size for a tile portrait is decreased, a visually interesting half-toning is accomplished (Figure 13.11).

Note that although the figures in this section were computed for $z_{xy} = \alpha(\sin x + \sin y)$ other trigonometric equations yield visually rich patterns. For example, Figure 13.12 was computed for $z_{xy} = \alpha(\sin x + \cosh y)$. The striped pattern is due to an artifact of computation: $\cosh(z)$ grows very large very quickly, and when z becomes too large, significant digits are lost and the behavior

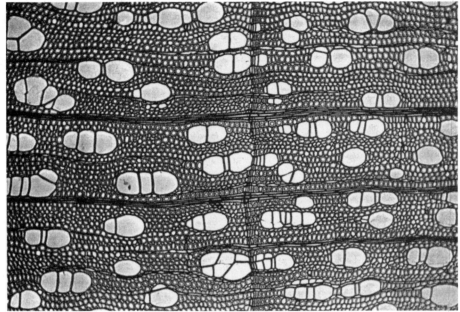

Figure 13.5. *Cross section of sweet (black) birch wood (x 80).*

of the mod function becomes erratic. Nonetheless, observers of this pattern have found it artistically interesting.

The additional figures show tiling patterns for a range of input parameters for $z_{xy} = \alpha(\sin x + \sin y)$. Typical input parameter values for α, β, γ, and m are given in the pseudocode.

13.1.3 Summary of Egg Tiling Patterns

"No two are alike!" the saying goes, when describing the intricate patterns found in snowflakes. Likewise, the few illustrations of the chaos-eggs here are a small set of the remarkable panoply of designs made possible by the algorithm. By "turning a dial" which controls m or α (or the other parameters described in the pseudocode), an infinite variety of attractive designs is generated with relative computational simplicity For this reason, the chaos-eggs may be of interest to designers of museum exhibits and other educational displays for both children and adults.

In this section patterns reminiscent of the ornaments of a variety of cultures (ornaments with a repeating motif in at least two nonparallel directions) are generated. These patterns are derived from the equation $z_{xy} = \alpha(\sin x + \sin y)$, and their behavior includes a network of periodic lines and patterns, and visually-random fluctuations. The computer-based system (outlined in Pseudocode 13.1) is special in that its primary focus is on the fast characterization of simple tiling generators, using an interactive graphics system with a variety of controlling

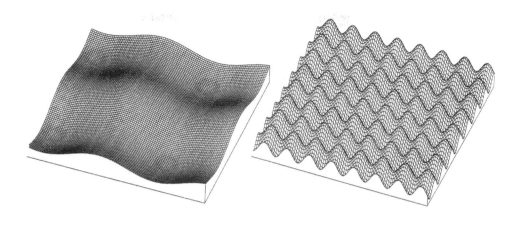

Figure 13.6. *The function $z_{xy} = \alpha(\sin x + \sin y)$ for two different frequencies (see text).*

parameters. In contrast to previous systems where mathematical and aesthetic beauty relies on the use of imaginary numbers, these calculations use real numbers – facilitating their study with programming languages having no complex data types and on personal computers.

The idea of investigating the ornaments and decorations of various cultures by consideration of their symmetry groups appears to have originated long ago. From a purely artistic standpoint, some of the figures in this section are reminiscent of Persian carpet designs, ceramic tile mosaics, Peruvian striped fabrics, brick patterns from certain Mosques, and the symmetry in Moorish ornamental patterns. This resemblance is due to the mixture of stochasiticity and periodicity produced by the algorithm, and it is suggested that the reader manipulate the various parameters to achieve artistic control of the visual effect most desired.

Since the original research in this section was done, an excellent article on a similar technique by Brian Hayes in *Computer Language* came to my attention (Hayes, 1986). B. Hayes introduces the use of the truncation approach as applied to the parabolic equation $z = x^2 + y^2$. His patterns look different from the figures in the present section, and the reader is encouraged to compare the figures in this section with the beautiful figures in the Hayes article.

(Pick87h, *Comput. Lang.*; Pickover, 1987g, *Comput. Graph. World.*)

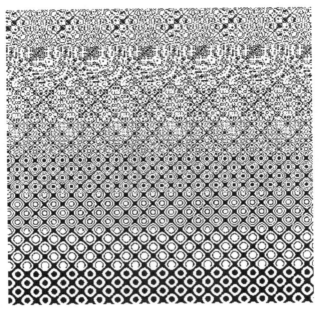

Figure 13.7. *Effect of entropic factor* α. As α decreases down the page, the disorder of the ψ map (Equation (13.5)) decreases until the pattern becomes perfectly ordered and is somewhat crystalline in appearance. This figure was computed with $m = 3$, and $(2 < \alpha < 50)$.

13.2 Self-Decorating Surfaces (Beauty from Noise)

Over the years, people in various professions have shown remarkable ingenuity in developing ways to create patterns that resemble natural and artistic textures. Commercial techniques for producing textures without the aid of a computer are numerous. For example, manufacturers of paper products traditionally create "marble paper" by dripping oil paint into a large vat of water. The craftsperson swirls or blows on the surface, and when the appearance is judged "interesting" the paper is carefully placed on the liquid's surface to transfer the pattern. Another example of a labor-intensive texture process – still in use today – is in the area of commercial cake decoration. One major company applies icing to the cake by machine, and a human is instructed to drag three spoons on top of the icing, each spoon oscillating at a different frequency, so that the cakes have a different appearance and look homemade. Other methods of realistic texture generation involve mapping of scanned images onto the surface of an object; the technique is simple and versatile but can sometimes lead to distortions. In this section, a computer algorithm for parameterized control of intricate texture generation is discussed, and it allows a large variety of textures to be produced with relative computational ease.

Recent work in computer texturing includes research on methods to texture complex surfaces (Peachy, 1985), and to simulate surfaces such as marble, rip-

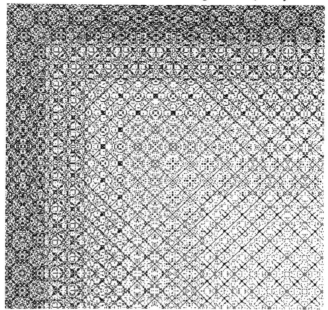

Figure 13.8. *Density as a function of m, rectangular plot.* As the mod factor, *m*, increases, the density of the system decreases (see text for explanation). *m* = 2 at the upper left corner, and *m* increases as the plot proceeds in both the *x* and *y* directions.

pling water, and fire (Perlin, 1985). In this section, in order to give both home-computer users and commercial artists the greatest chance of creating and comparing textures of their own design, an algorithm is outlined which creates interesting and detailed surface textures *from the barest and simplest of algorithms*. In fact, to compute the textures here, all one really needs is to have access to a random number generator and a simple averaging computer subroutine.

13.2.1 Recipe

The algorithm is as follows. First, create an array of random numbers ranging from 0 to 255, where 0 indicates white in the final picture and 255 indicates black. Intermediate values represent gray levels. To create the figures in this section, a local averaging of this noise is performed. This function produces an image in which each pixel represents the average of the neighborhood about the corresponding point in the original image:

$$I_{x,y} = \left(\frac{1}{(2n + 1)^2} \right) \sum_{i=x-n}^{i=x+n} \sum_{j=y-n}^{j=y+n} I_{i,j} \tag{13.6}$$

n defines the size of the neighborhood. Larger values for *n* force more correlations in the noise. $I(x,y)$ is an image and refers to a 2-dimensional light intensity function where *x* and *y* denote spatial coordinates, and the value of *I* at any point

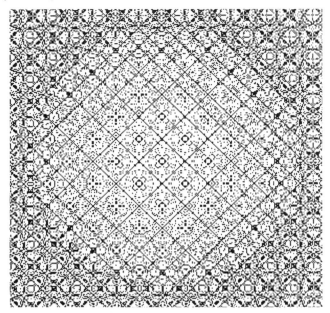

Figure 13.9. *Density as a function of m, radial plot.* This abstract design was created by having *m* increase as the distance of the pattern from the center of the rectangle grows smaller.

(*x*,*y*) is proportional to the brightness or gray level of the image at that point. This procedure acts as a low pass filter, and I call this image a *noise-gram*. In an attempt to enhance some of the contours of the image and to bring out certain features the following protocol was followed. First, the noise-gram was transformed via a look-up table (LUT) computed from a sinusoidal function of the form

$$f(l) = 255 \times |\sin(g \times l)| \tag{13.7}$$

where $l \in [0°, 255°]$. Using this technique, a graphically continuous look-up table function can be produced with only a small number of input parameters. By exploring a variety of frequencies (*g*) for the sine wave, certain trends in the noise-gram can be visually emphasized. In order to use $f(l)$ to transform the noise-gram, the value of each (*x*,*y*) element of the resultant picture is obtained by taking the *l*-th element in $f(l)$, where *l* is the value (intensity) of the element at (*x*,*y*) in the original image. This approach produces a continuous gray scale change. Subsequent to using the look-up table transformation, histogram equalization and damped error diffusion are performed in order to achieve a contrast in the texture's features.

The figures in this section are the resulting maps for a variety of values for *g* and for different local averages, controlled by *n*. Some of the figures remind observers of various weavings and rugs in addition to marble or organic patterns such as tree cross-sections. From a purely artistic standpoint, some of the figures

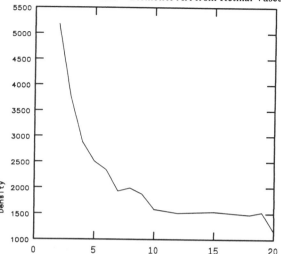

Figure 13.10. *Density fluctuation for a typical system as a function of m.*

in this section are reminiscent of Peruvian and other fabrics (Makovicky, 1986; Grunbaum, 1986), marble textures, and wood grains.

In this section, we see that the computer is a tool which allows us to explore and produce art by controlling this mix of chaos and order. Texturing is an effective method of simulating surface detail at relatively low cost. Maps are derived from simple image processing techniques: 1) local averaging of a noisy distribution to force visual correlations, followed by 2) a sinusoidal look-up table to produce a gray-scale image. It should be noted that techniques such as these have a practical role. They allow us to see correlations and contour levels in a noisy grey-scale picture, and similar techniques have been used to enhance features in the "Shroud of Turin" image (see "Image Processing of the Shroud of Turin" on page 73). Interestingly, some of the figures in this section have been created starting from "real" data: namely a very noisy distribution of both metal atoms within a polymer, and chemical bases within a DNA sequence. Aside from the plots' beauty, they can give researchers an indication of metal density and DNA base content by observation of the contours. (Pick88l, *Computer Graphics World*)

13.3 Biometric Art from Retinal Vascular Patterns

"Biometric art" is a term coined by the author to denote computer art which is derived from measurements of unique characteristics associated with a living organism. Biometric input devices are commercially available and can quantify the shape of one's hand, the lines of the palm, the fingerprints, the voice, the forces generated when signing a name, etc. For example, parameters derived from the blood vessel patterns in a retinal eye-scan can be converted to computer art. The vascular parameters used involved angular measurements of the major blood vessels with the optic nerve as the origin. These parameters were then used for

Figure 13.11. *Halftoning effect created by decreasing the dot size.*

coefficients of equations in complex polynomial iterations or dynamical systems. The resulting patterns are startlingly attractive. Although the system used took some time to produce a picture, one may imagine future systems with special-purpose hardware that allow a user to gaze into a retinal scanner, wait a few seconds, and see a beautiful pattern produced by the user's unique vascular pattern. Figure 13.24 displays simple biometric art produced by a variation of the equations in "Trigonometric Iteration (Bushy Spirals)" on page 221. The system of equations follows that of Jacobson (1982). Note that the symmetrized dot patterns produced from cardiac sounds ("Medicine: Cardiology and SDPs" on page 41) are another form of biometric art.

13.4 Reading List for Chapter 13

Although some readers might have thought that a computer art book written in 1969 would be of little use today, J. Reichardt's book *Cybernetic Serendipity: The Computer and the Arts* contains a very stimulating collection of papers on the alliance of art and technology. This book is still of considerable interest and highly recommended. For more recent works, see the list of books and papers under "Ornaments, Artistic Textures, Symmetry" in the Reference section of this book. Readers should also examine the various SIGGRAPH Conference Proceedings published by The Association for Computing Machinery, 11 West 42nd Street, New York, New York 10036.

Figure 13.12. *Tiling pattern produced by* $z_{xy} = \alpha(\sin x + \cosh y)$ *(see text for explanation).*

Figure 13.13. *Self-decorating egg 1.*

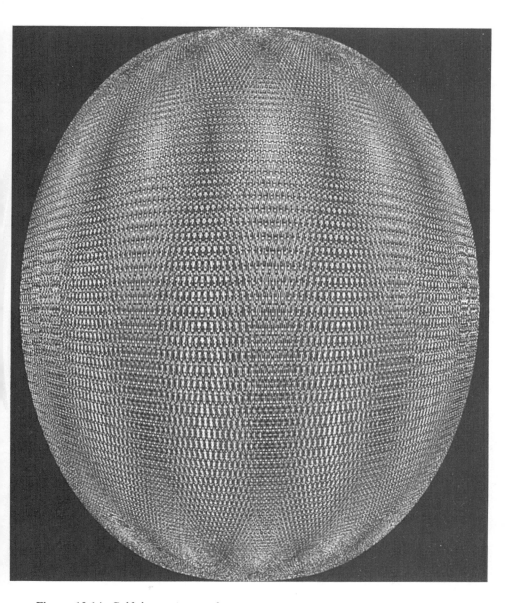

Figure 13.14. *Self-decorating egg 2.*

Figure 13.15. *Self-decorating egg 3.*

```
ALGORITHM Egg Tile Generator

INPUT: Res, Beta1, Beta2, Gamma, Alpha, Modf
TYPICAL INPUT PARAMETER VALUES:
 Beta1=-11, Beta2=-12, Gamma=60,  Alpha=10,  Res=500, Modf=3
 Beta1=-16, Beta2=-21, Gamma=87,  Alpha= 4,  Res=500, Modf=2
 Beta1=-11, Beta2=-12, Gamma=200, Alpha= 4,  Res=500, Modf=3
OUTPUT:  Tile patterns composed of dots at positions (i,j).
These designs can subsequently be mapped to ellipsoids to
produce Russian Easter egg ornaments.

do i = 1 to res;                   (* loop in x direction       *)
  do j = 1 to res;                 (* loop in y direction       *)
    x = Beta1 + (Gamma*i);         (* compute x                 *)
    y = Beta2 + (Gamma*j);         (* compute y                 *)
    z = Alpha*(sin (x) + sin (y)); (* compute z                 *)
    c = trunc (z);                 (* convert z to an integer   *)
    if mod(c,modf) = 0          (* if c evenly divisible by modf *)
       then PlotDot(i,j);       (* plot a point at position (i,j)*)
  end;                             (* End j loop                *)
end;                               (* End i loop                *)
```

Pseudocode 13.1. *Egg Tile Generator.*

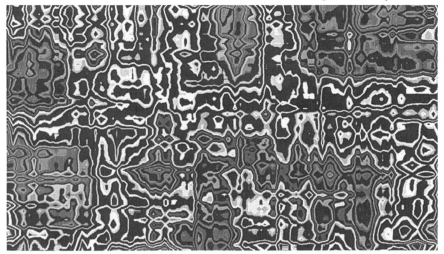

Figure 13.16. *Noise surface.* Surface produced by local averaging of noise followed by use of a sinusoidal look-up table, histogram equalization, and error diffusion.

Figure 13.17. *Same as previous figure except with lower frequency sine wave.*

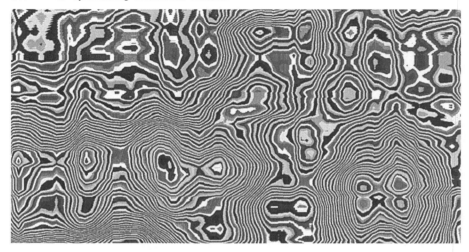

Figure 13.18. *Metal atoms.* Surface produced by a different starting "noise-gram" (in this case, a noisy distribution of metal atoms within a polymer).

Figure 13.19. *Clipped sinusoid.* Same as previous figure except a clipped sinusoid is used, as described in the text.

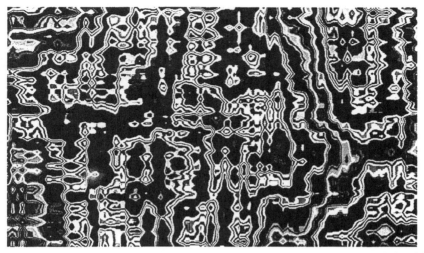

Figure 13.20. *DNA.* Another textured surface. The noise-gram generator for this was a noisy distribution of bases in a DNA sequence.

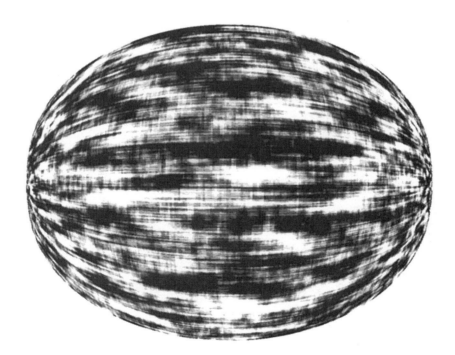

Figure 13.21. *Watermelon-like surface.* This figure is produced by superimposing two identical noise-grams, each with a different local average factor, *n*. The result is then mapped to an ellipsoid's surface.

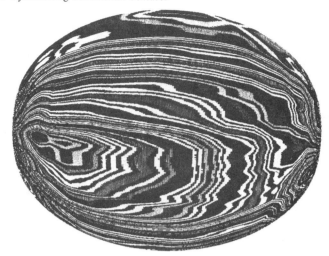

Figure 13.22. *Modern art surface 1 generated from the protocol described in the text.*

Figure 13.23. *Modern art surface 2 generated from the protocol described in the text.*

Figure 13.24. *Biometric art from the author's eyes.* Shown here are artistic patterns derived from parameters characterizing blood vessel patterns in the author's right and left eyes.

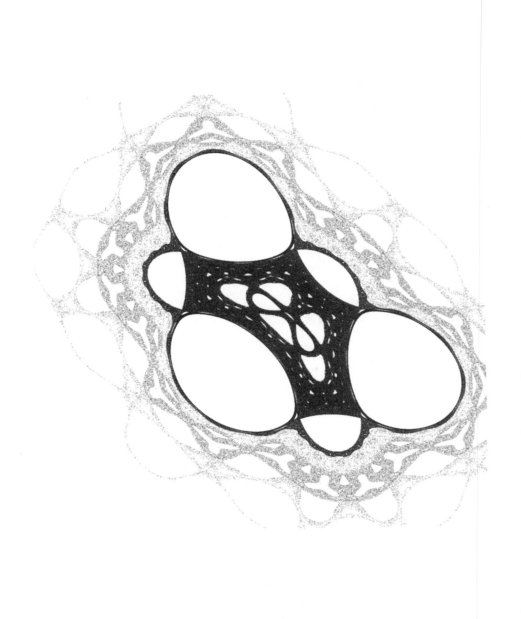

Chapter 14

Dynamical Systems

"It's like asking why Beethoven's Ninth Symphony is beautiful. If you don't see why, someone can't tell you. I know numbers are beautiful. If they aren't beautiful, nothing is."
Paul Erdös

"That mathematics could be a jewel may come as a surprise to those of us who struggled with multiplication tables as kids and now need help completing W-4 forms."
Paul Hoffman (1987) In "The Man Who Loves Only Numbers"

Another deep reservoir for striking images is the *dynamical system.* Dynamical systems are models containing the rules describing the way some quantity undergoes a change through time. For example, the motion of planets about the sun can be modelled as a dynamical system in which the planets move according to Newton's laws. Generally, the pictures presented in this section track the behavior of mathematical expressions called *differential equations.* Think of a differential equation as a machine that takes in values for all the variables and then generates the new values at some later time. Just as one can track the path of a jet by the smoke path it leaves behind, computer graphics provides a way to follow paths of particles whose motion is determined by simple differential equations. The practical side of dynamical systems is that they can sometimes be used to describe the behavior of real-world things such as planetary motion, fluid flow, the diffusion of drugs, the behavior of inter-industry relationships, and the vibration of airplane wings.

"Dynamics" and "chaos theory" are fields which are now emerging somewhere between mathematics and physics (see "Mathematical Chaos" on page 141). The early days of modern dynamics span half a century, starting with French mathematician Poincare and Russian mathematician Lyapunov in the early 1900's. After undergoing a relatively quiet period, the study of dynamics was revived between 1961 and 1971, partly as a result of the increasing use of computer graphics strategies of doing mathematics. (Pick87i, *Computers and Graph.*; Pick89, *Visual Computer.*)

"A Non-Linear Dynamical System"

Figure 14.1. *"A nonlinear dynamical system".* (Cartoon © 1988 by Jacques Boivin).

14.1 Time-discrete Phase Planes Associated with a Cyclic System

"If math is about structures that are part of the real world, it is not surprising it is a powerful tool, not surprising that what we find as beautiful are those things that match the real world. Our minds have evolved to find this pleasing."   David Gross

In this section, time-discrete phase planes associated with the cyclic systems are studied:

$$\begin{cases} \dot{x}(t) = -f(y(t)) \\ \dot{y}(t) = f(x(t)) \end{cases} \tag{14.1}$$

The dot above the x and y indicates a derivative with respect to time. In *phase space* each dimension can represent one of the variables in the differential equation. In the pictures in this section, the trajectories of variables (x,y) are plotted to reveal complicated motions. This system of differential equations was studied in Nussbaum and Peitgen's paper (1984) where the authors restricted their f to functions which have two positive zeros. The present section extends the range of functions to include more general nonlinearities, i.e. oscillating functions with more than two positive zeros. Here, these functions are generally of the form often found in frequency modulation synthesis applications:

$$f(x) = \sin[x + \sin(\rho x)] \tag{14.2}$$

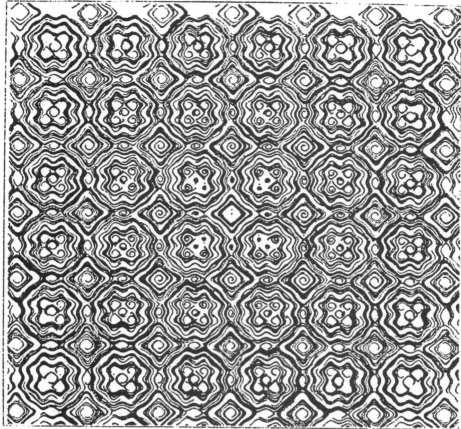

Figure 14.2. *Portrait of a time-discrete dynamical system T(f,h).* The phase plane diagram of Equation (14.3) indicates the trajectories of points through time. For this portrait, $f(x) = \sin[x + \sin(3x)]$. This plane tesselation is reminiscent of some of the work of artist M.C. Escher.

By modulating a sine wave (often called the "carrier") by another with a different frequency (controlled by ρ), a large variety of complex waveforms can be generated (for graphs, see "Pseudo-Gray Transformation via Look-up Table (LUT)" on page 76). Using this technique, a graphically "rich" function can be produced with only a small number of input parameters.

The discretization of Equation (14.1) for implementation on a computer takes the following simple form (known as the forward Euler approximation (Finney and Ostberg, 1976)):

$$\begin{cases} x_{t+1} - x_t = -hf(y_t) \\ y_{t+1} - y_t = hf(x_t) \end{cases} \tag{14.3}$$

where $h > 0$ is a constant known as the *step size* of the numerical solution. In this section, h is kept small ($h \sim 0.1$). Other methods yielding greater accuracy can

Figure 14.3. *A magnification.* (The magnification is of the repeating motif in Figure 14.2.) Notice the remarkable detail resolved by magnifying this segment.

also be used with essentially the same approach, but with increases in technical (and computer programming) complexity (Nussbaum and Peitgen, 1984).

Finally, it should be stressed that graphic studies of the phase plane behavior may have a more practical side. Despite the phase portraits' complexity, they possess universal features shared by entire classes of nonlinear processes. For example, a range of real physical systems can be described by similar systems of differential equations (Campbell et al., 1985).

Studied in this section is the phase portrait for the time-discrete dynamical system $T(f,h)$ given in Equation (14.3). As mentioned before, in this section the phase plane diagram of Equation (14.3) indicates the trajectories of points in the x-y plane. The equations are iterated with initial values given by the starting-point position on the plane. For example, Figure 14.2 was made by fixing the parameter (x_0, y_0) and then iterating. (x_0, y_0) is changed and the equations are iterated again. (x_t, y_t) are plotted in order to show their trajectories through time. Indeed, these trajectories provide visually and mathematically interesting features

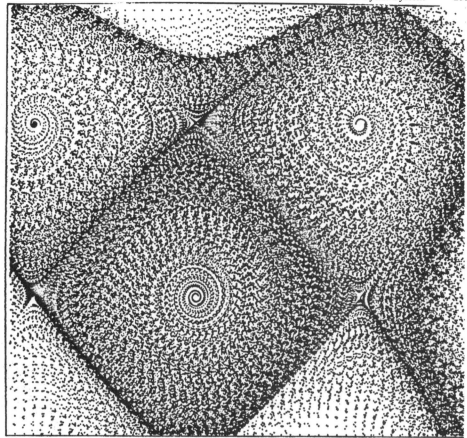

Figure 14.4.   *A further magnification.* (Spiral patterns in the upper right corner of Figure 14.3 are magnified.)

and can show how convergence is gradually achieved. The graphics system has color capability; when low iteration trajectories are plotted in red and high iteration trajectories ($t > 10$) plotted in blue, the resultant plots are particularly illuminating in that the eye can more easily differentiate the structures of low iteration from those of high iteration. If a range of colors is available, the iteration number may index into gradually changing values of a color table to provide additional insight.

The judicious choice of resolution and maximum iteration number, N, is important so that structures of interest can be revealed on the map. If these parameters are too low, important features will not show up, and if these parameters are set too high, sometimes significant features can be obscured. An interactive computer system allows the user to choose parameters best suited for visual demonstrations of features of interest.

Figure 14.2 is an (x,y) diagram for Equation (14.3) where $f(x) = \sin[x + \sin(3x)]$. The picture boundaries are ($-20 < x_t < 20$, $-20 < y_t < 20$), and $h = 0.1$. The number of iterations, N, is 50, and the resolution ("res") is 50

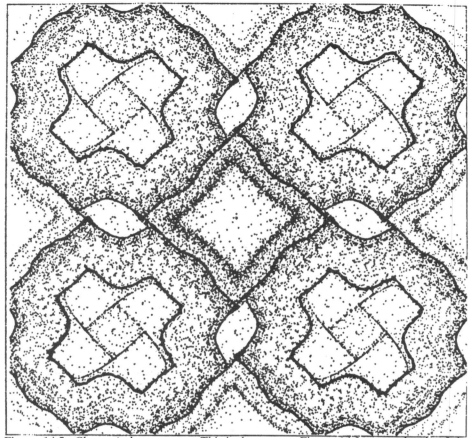

Figure 14.5. *Change in h parameter.* This is the same as Figure 14.3 except that $h = 0.4$ instead of $h = 0.1$.

(which means the range (20,20) is divided into 50 intervals). This plane tesselation is reminiscent of some of the work of artist M.C. Escher (Lockwood, 1978) which contains interesting symmetries. Figure 14.3 is a magnification of the repeating motif in Figure 14.2. Notice the remarkable detail resolved by magnifying this segment. The picture boundaries are ($-6 < x_t < 6$, $-6 < y_t < 6$), and $h = 0.1$, $N = 50$, *res* = 50. Figure 14.4 is a magnification of the right-hand corner of Figure 14.3 showing spiral patterns. Figure 14.5 is the same as Figure 14.3 except that $h = 0.4$. Note that some of the main symmetries remain, but there is also stochastic behavior in some regions. The dark lines represent several trajectories superimposed ("attractive" behavior). Figure 14.6 is the same as Figure 14.3 except that $f(x) = \sin[x^2 + \sin(3x)]$. For Figure 14.7, the following equations were used:

Figure 14.6. $f(x) = \sin[x^2 + \sin(3x)]$. This is the same as Figure 14.3 with a different equation.

$$
f(x) = \left[\begin{array}{l} \sin(x), \quad -\pi < x \le \pi \\ \sin(x^2 + \sin(3x)), \quad (-2\pi < x < -\pi) \cup (\pi < x < 2\pi) \\ \sin(x + \sin^2(3x)), \quad |x| \ge 2\pi \end{array}\right. \qquad (14.4)
$$

The symbol $\cup$ stands for union. The picture boundaries are ($-8 < x_t < 8$, $-8 < y_t < 8$), and $h = 0.1$, $N = 50$, $res = 50$. Figure 14.8 is the same as Figure 14.7 except that the boundaries for computation are ($-8 < x_t < 8$, $-8 < y_t < -2$). By computing the picture for a limited region of phase space, it becomes possible to observe the evolution of individual features of interest. Figure 14.9 is a magnification of the bump containing a spiral in the lower right of Figure 14.7. Figure 14.10 is the same as Figure 14.9 except that $h = 0.01$. Figure 14.11 is computed for the function $f(x) = \sin[x + \tan(3x)]$. The picture boundaries are ($-6 < x_t < 6$, $-6 < y_t < 6$), and $h = 0.05$, $N = 50$, $res = 50$. Figure 14.12 is a magnification of a group of 9 tendrils in Figure 14.11. Figure 14.13 is computed for the function $f(x) = \sin[x^6 + \sin^4(3x)]$ with the

Figure 14.7. *Phase plane portrait.* (This is computed from (Equation (14.4).)

same picture parameters as Figure 14.11. Note apparently random regions surrounding regular canal-like structures. Figure 14.14 is computed for the function

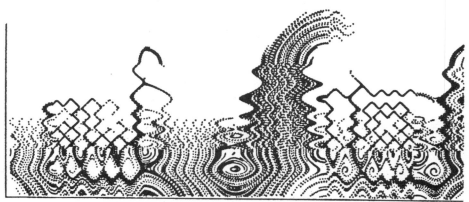

Figure 14.8. *Boundary restriction.* This is the same as Figure 14.7 but the boundaries
for computation are restricted in one direction. By computing the picture for a limited
region of phase space, it becomes possible to observe the temporal evolution of individual
features of interest.

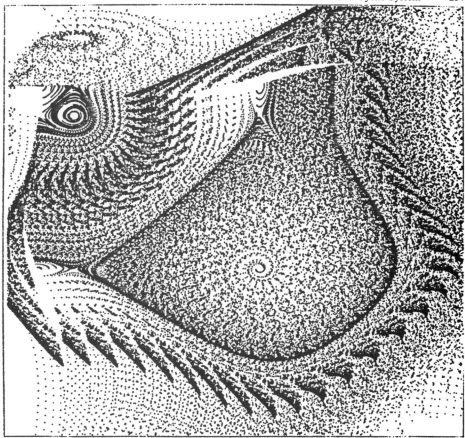

Figure 14.9. *A magnification.* This is a magnification of the bump containing a spiral in the lower right of Figure 14.7.

$f(x) = \sin[x + \sin(x) \sin(3x)]$ with the same picture parameters as Figure 14.11, except that $h = 0.6$. Figure 14.15 is a magnification of the region delimited by the box in Figure 14.14.

Using modulated sine functions for f, a graphically "rich" function (and resultant map) can be produced with only a small number of input parameters. The possible dynamics of solutions, even for very simple-looking fs, are very complicated. Some of the forms generated by the time-discrete systems are reminiscent of the plane tesselations of various artists or woven artistic textiles containing somewhat lesser symmetry (Nimann et al., 1978). In painting and sculpture, perfect symmetry is more often avoided than pursued, being generally replaced by a sense of "balance" rather than highly repetitive motifs. However, some modern artists, notably M.C. Escher and M. Vasarely, have used various degrees of plane and point symmetry. Whether or not the algorithm here evolves into a practical tool for synthesizing decorative patterns is a matter for further study. For the present, we can appreciate the elegance of a strikingly simple formula that generates highly complex, rich patterns.

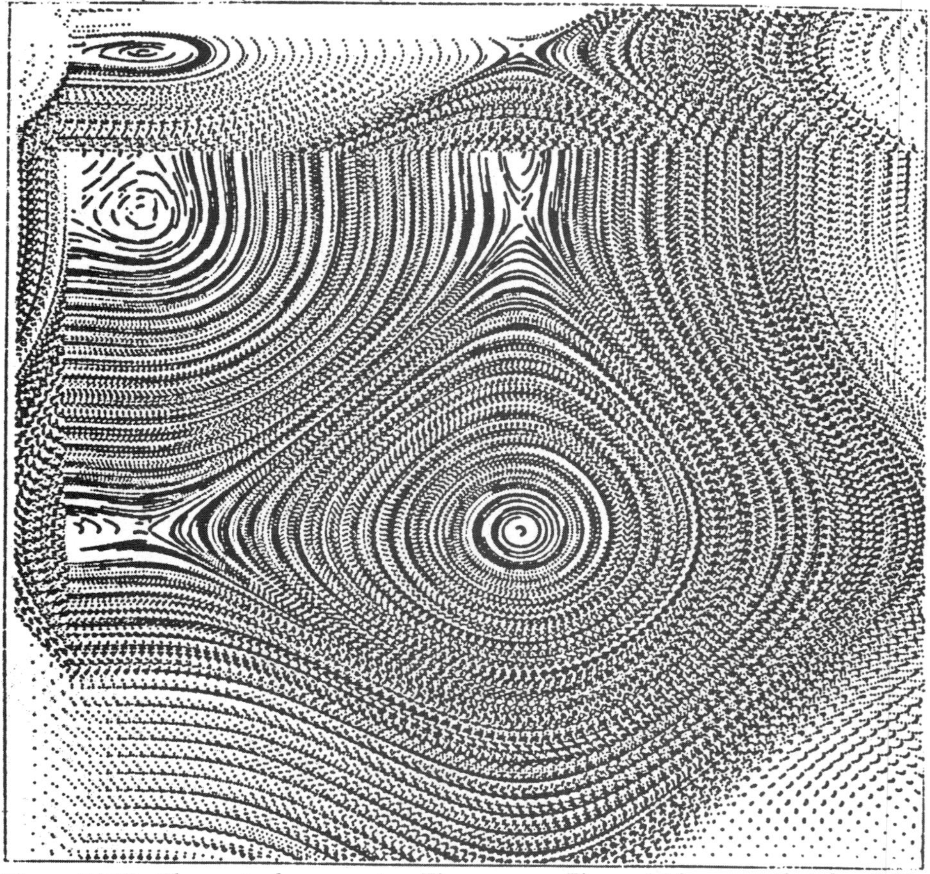

Figure 14.10. *Change in h parameter.* The same as Figure 14.9 except that $h = 0.01$ instead of $h = 0.1$.

14.1.1 Recipe

To produce these figures, an initial point in the x-y plane is selected and the four lines in Pseudocode 14.1 are repeated, giving rise to the trajectories through time. Think of the initial point as a leaf in a stream. Steps 2 and 3 describe the motion in the stream. See color plates for additional renditions.

14.2 Cycles and Centers in Time-Discrete Dynamical Systems

There has been considerable success in the literature of the last five years in understanding the dynamics of one-dimensional mappings (see "Graphics, Bifurcation, Order and Chaos" on page 151), and very simple discrete dynamical systems can exhibit extremely complicated behavior. This naturally leads to curiosity about two-dimensional systems (such as in this section and the previous)

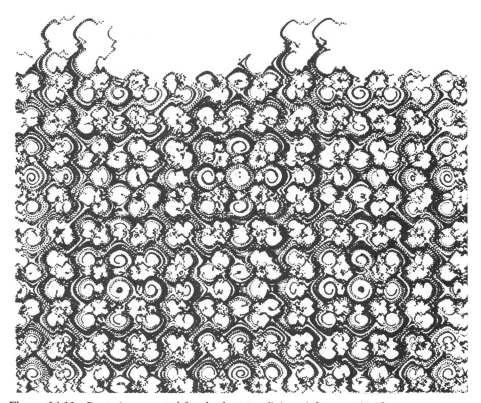

Figure 14.11. *Portrait computed for the function f(x) = sin[x + tan(3x)].*

which show both orderly and chaotic behavior. Like the last section, this section describes some aspects of the dynamically rich behavior of time-discrete phase planes associated with the cyclic systems. However, the approach now is different in that: the discretization is modified (see following), only a small number of initial points is used (5-15 points), and h, the step size, is chosen so that the picture is delicately poised between order and chaos. This entire approach facilitates the demonstration of cyclical and chaotic behavior.

The discretization of Equation (14.1) for implementation on a computer can take another simple form (known as an implicit Euler approximation)

$$\begin{cases} x_{t+1} - x_t = -hf(y_t + hf(x_t)) \\ y_{t+1} - y_t = hf(x_t) \end{cases} \tag{14.5}$$

where $h > 0$ is a constant known as the *step size* of the numerical solution. In this section, h ranges between 0.2 and 0.4. See Nussbaum and Peitgen (1984) for a motivation of the particular discretization given in Equation (14.5). The resolution ("res") for the maps is about 10 points per axis (i.e., the x_0 and y_0 axes are

Figure 14.12. *A magnification.* (Magnified is a group of 9 tendrils in Figure 14.11).

each divided into 10 increments). The number of iterations for each point is approximately 2500. Color capability further enhances this system's usefulness and allows the human analyst to detect important features in the data. Trajectories are color coded by initial point thereby allowing the user to identify periodic patterns which a specific point gives rise to, even when such patterns are separated by considerable distance in x-y space.

14.2.1 A Review of Some Definitions of Terms

In order to aid the reader, some of the technical terms used in this section are briefly reviewed. For a more detailed description, see Abraham and Shaw (1985). A *fixed point* is a point which is invariant under the mapping (i.e., $x_t = x_{t+1}$). An *invariant curve* is a generalization of a fixed point and is also invariant under the map or flow.

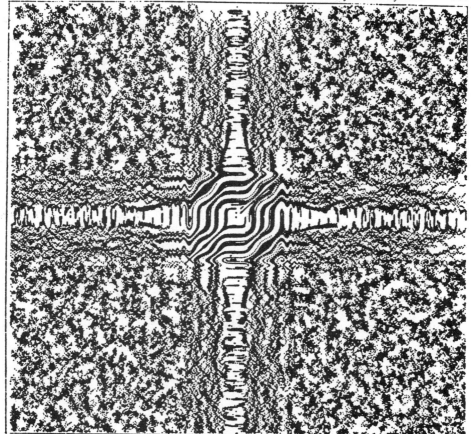

Figure 14.13. *Portrait computed for the function* $f(x) = \sin[x^6 + \sin^4(3x)]$. Note the apparently random regions surrounding more regular canal-like structures.

A particular kind of fixed point is a *center*, or limit, which can be illustrated as:

The concentric smooth lines surrounding the center in this illustration are known as *cycles* which have predictable periodic motions, like circular orbits. *Hyperbolic points* have nearby flows in and out as follows:

The smooth horizontal line is known as a *stable manifold* or *attractor*. The vertical line is an *unstable manifold*. Center points are non-hyperbolic. A *strange attractor* is an unpredictable trajectory where a minute difference in starting positions of two initially adjacent points leads to chaos.

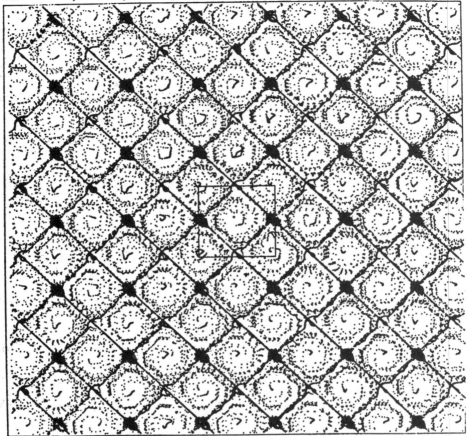

Figure 14.14. *Repeating beehive-like pattern.* This was computed from the function $f(x) = \sin[x + \sin(x)\sin(3x)]$.

As in the last section, the phase plane diagram of Equation (14.5) indicates the trajectories of points in the x-y plane. The equations are iterated with initial values defined by the user. For example, Figure 14.16 was made by fixing the parameter (x_0, y_0) and then iterating. (x_0, y_0) is changed and the equations are iterated again. As Figure 14.16 indicates, a variety of limit points and cycles may be distributed through the state space. In this and the following paragraph some of these structures are cataloged simply to give the reader a flavor of the terminology in the field; however, the goal of this section is to demonstrate the role of mathematics in producing *artistic* designs. For a review of the mathematical terms, see Abraham and Shaw (1983). Figure 14.16 is an (x,y) diagram for Equation (14.5) where $f(x) = \sin[x + \sin(3x)]$. The picture boundaries are $(1.6 < x_t < 4.7, 1.6 < y_t < 4.7)$, and $h = 0.4$. The number of iterations, N, is 2000, and the resolution is 10. On the plot are five prominent center fixed points (cfp), two of which are labelled. Smooth concentric cycles appear around these cfp's, and some cycles are denoted by "c." In the top left and bottom right

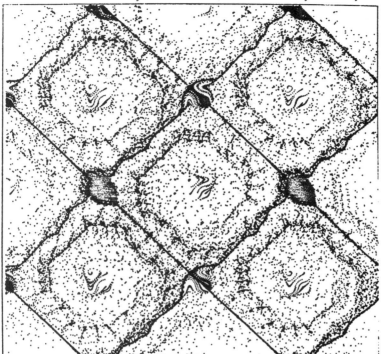

Figure 14.15. *A magnification.* (Magnified region is delimited by the box in Figure 14.14).

ellipsoid are periodic center points (pcp) (of period 7). There are four major hyperbolic fixed points, the top one denoted by "hfp." The thick dark regions can be thought of as "strange attractors" (sa). Surrounding the prominent large cycle (which itself surrounds the 5 cfp's) are periodic center points (pcp) of period 24.

```
ALGORITHM: Dynamical Orbits

Note: first choose an (xx,yy) coordinate. Then repeat the
following four lines to plot the trajectory. f is a
frequency modulation function as described in the text.

1. xold=xx; yold=yy;
2. xx = xold-h*f(yold);
3. yy = yold+h*f(xold);
4. PlotDotAt(xx,yy);
```

Pseudocode 14.1. *How to produce orbits of dynamical systems.*

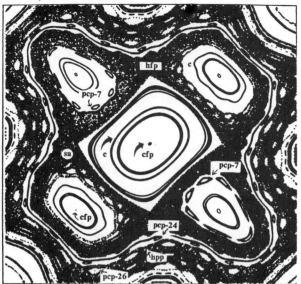

Figure 14.16. *Portrait of the time-discrete dynamical system, $T(f_p, \alpha)$.* This phase plane diagram is computed for Equation (14.5). For this portrait, $f(x) = \sin[x + \sin(3x)]$. Limit points and cycles are distributed through the state space. Abbreviations: cfp (center fixed points), pcp (periodic center points), sa (strange attractor), hpp (hyperbolic periodic points), c (cycle).

Going outward, we encounter a twisted structure consisting of hyperbolic periodic points (hpp) and periodic center points (pcp) (of period 26):

Figure 14.17 is a magnification of the left two lobes separated by a hyperbolic fixed point (hpf) in Figure 14.16. Notice the remarkable detail resolved by magnifying this section. Surrounding the center fixed point (cfp) in the bottom lobe are periodic center points (pcp) and hyperbolic periodic points (hpp) of period 7. Surrounding the center fixed point of the top lobe are periodic fixed points of period 6. Figure 14.18 is a magnification of the lower lobe in Figure 14.17. Additional microstructure is revealed. Going radially outward from the center fixed point (cfp), one encounters: cycles, periodic fixed points (period 6), periodic fixed points (period 8), and so on. Squeezed between are additional periodic fixed and hyperbolic points. The graphics system allows the user to note the direction of the vector fields by watching the diagram dynamically unfold on the screen. For example, one cycle's direction of flow is indicated by a little arrow. Figure 14.19 is a magnification of the box in Figure 14.18. Three primary center fixed points and their accompanying cycles can be seen. Figure 14.20 is a magnification of

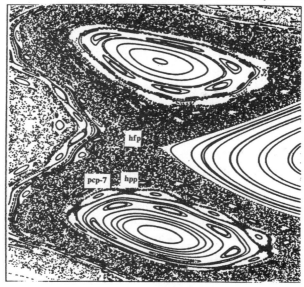

Figure 14.17. *Magnification.* (Magnified are the left two lobes separated by a hyperbolic fixed point (hpf) in Figure 14.16). Surrounding the center fixed point in the bottom lobe are periodic center points (pcp) and hyperbolic periodic points (hpp) of period 7. Surrounding the center fixed point of the top lobe are periodic fixed points of period 6.

the box in Figure 14.19 which focuses on the upper most center point. Concentric cycles surround this fixed point, and three periodic points of a period-4 grouping surround the cycles.

[Figure 14.21 is derived from $f(x) = \sin[x + \sin(10x)]$. The picture boundaries are $(2.2 < x_t < 4.1, \ 2.2 < y_t < 4.1)$, and $h = 0.2$. The number of iterations, N, is 2000, and the resolution ("res") is 10 (which means the range (2.2, 4.1) is divided into 10 intervals). Note that some of the main symmetries in Figure 14.16 remain, such as the central fixed point surrounded by four additional fixed points, but there are also considerable morphological differences. Proceeding outward from the central fixed point, we encounter a gray region, a large cycle, periodic fixed points (of period 28), and another gray region. The large cycle separates these gray regions, which are the stable and unstable manifolds generated by different sets of hyperbolic fixed points. Additional periodic fixed points are scattered throughout the figure. Figure 14.22 is a magnification of the region delimited by the box in Figure 14.21. A system of periodic fixed points (of period 4) can be seen surrounded by a dark region. The large cycle in Figure 14.21 is actually composed of infinitely many "thin" cycles revealed in this magnification. Figure 14.23 is a magnification of the region delimited by the box in Figure 14.22. A periodic center point (pcp) of period 2 is labelled. Its mate is to the lower right. An additional set of periodic points (period 5) is labelled. In Figure 14.24 a sequence of period-4 center points surrounds a central fixed point. Figure 14.25 is a magnification of the upper left lobe in Figure 14.21. Several periodic fixed points can be seen in the dark region (periods 4 and 5 are most prominent). Figure 14.26 is a magnification of one of the period-5 periodic fixed points delimited by the box in Figure 14.25

Figure 14.27 is derived from $f(x) = \sin[x + \sin(3x + \sin(2x))]$. All parameters are the same as for Figure 14.21. Again the basic symmetry of the map is preserved. Six periodic center points (pcp) surround the central fixed point. A number of other periodic fixed points can also be seen in this map. Figure 14.28 is a magnification of the region surrounding a hyperbolic fixed point delimited by the box in Figure 14.27. Figure 14.29 is a magnification of the region surrounding a central fixed point delimited by the box in Figure 14.28. Periodic fixed points (of period 4) surround the main center.]

In this section, we have seen yet another example of graphically rich maps produced with only a small number of input parameters. Increasing magnifications reveal a never-ending collection of limit points and cycles which are distributed through the state space. See color plates for additional renditions.

14.3 Reading List for Chapter 14

The geometry of chaotic dynamical systems was firmly established by French mathematician Jules Henri Poincare in his research in celestial mechanics (1892). G. Birkhoff's 1932 paper on remarkable curves was one of the first papers in the mathematical literature to discuss chaotic attractors. Much later, digital simulations of the properties of periodic motions in nonlinear oscillations have become increasingly important, especially since the experimental discovery of chaotic attractors in 1962 by Lorenz. There has been considerable research by a number of scientists in dynamical systems and chaotic dynamics. Some pioneers in this field include: Duffing, Van der Pol, Levinson, Cartwright and Littlewood, Lorenz, Stein, Ulam, Smale, Rössler, Ueda, Shaw, Farmer, and Feigenbaum – just to name a few. (See Abraham and Shaw (1985) for additional historical information.) "Reading List for Chapter 10" on page 171 gives a useful reading list and some historical background for many of the topics in this chapter. The reader may wish to consult the following interesting introductions to the subject:

1. Stewart, I. (1987) The nature of stability. *Speculations in Science and Tech.* 10(4): 310-324.

2. "Symmetries and Asymmetries" (1985) *Mosaic* Volume 16, Number 1, January/February. (An entire issue on the subject of fractals, symmetry and chaos. *Mosaic* is published six times a year as a source of information for scientific and educational communities served by the National Science Foundation, Washington DC 20550).

3. Abraham, R., Shaw, C. (1985) *Dynamics – The Geometry of Behavior, Part 3: Global Behavior.* Aerial Press: California. (Actually, the entire book collection of Aerial Press, including the Visual Math Series, is an educational wonderland).

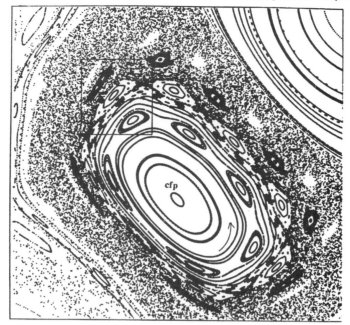

Figure 14.18. *Magnification.* (Magnified is the lower lobe in Figure 14.17.) One cycle's direction of flow is indicated by an arrow.

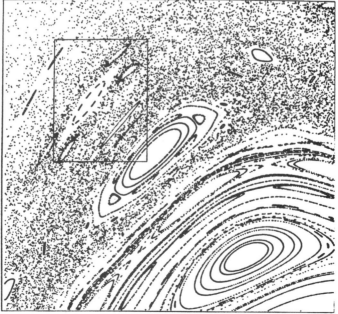

Figure 14.19. *Magnification.* (Magnified is the box in Figure 14.18.) Three primary center fixed points and their accompanying cycles can clearly be seen.

Figure 14.20. *Magnification.* (Magnified is the box in Figure 14.19.) This focuses on the uppermost center point. Concentric cycles surround this fixed point, and three periodic points of a period-4 grouping surround the cycles.

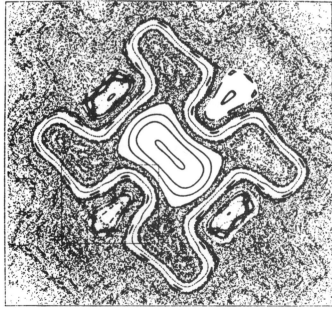

Figure 14.21. *Portrait derived from* $f(x) = \sin[x + \sin(10x)]$. Some of the main symmetries seen in Figure 14.16 remain. Proceeding outward from the central fixed point, we encounter a gray region, a large cycle, periodic fixed points (of period 28), and another gray region. The large cycle separates these gray regions, which are the stable and unstable manifolds generated by different sets of hyperbolic fixed points. Additional periodic fixed points are scattered throughout the figure.

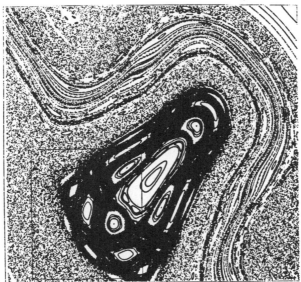

Figure 14.22. *Magnification.* (Magnification of the region delimited by the box in Figure 14.21). A system of periodic fixed points (of period 4) is surrounded by a dark region. The large cycle in Figure 14.21 is actually composed of infinitely many "thin" cycles, revealed in this magnification.

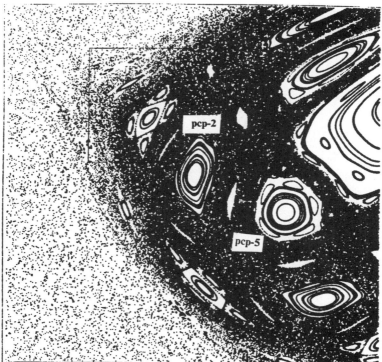

Figure 14.23. *A periodic center point (pcp) of period 2 (labelled).* Its mate is to the lower right. An additional set of periodic points (period 5) is labelled.

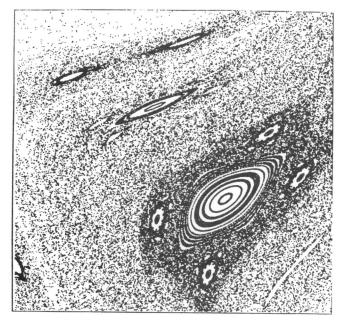

Figure 14.24. *A sequence of period-4 center points surrounds a central fixed point.*

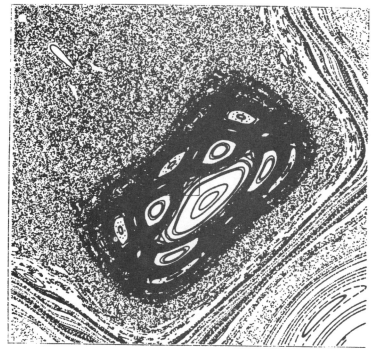

Figure 14.25. *Magnification of the upper left lobe.* (Magnified is Figure 14.21.) Several periodic fixed points can be seen in the dark region (periods 4 and 5 are most prominent).

Figure 14.26. *Magnification.* (Magnification of one of the period-5 periodic fixed points delimited by the box in Figure 14.25).

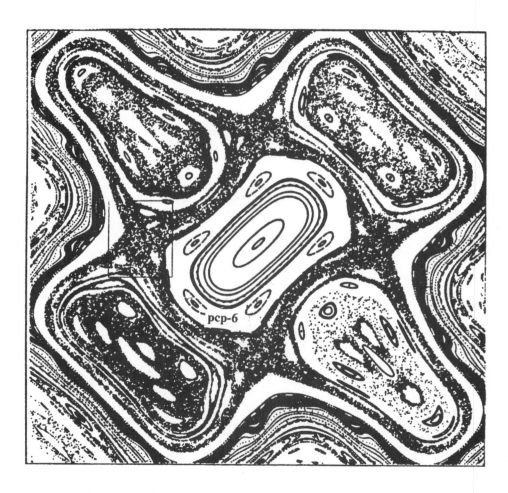

Figure 14.27. *Portrait derived from* $f(x) = \sin[x + \sin(3x + \sin(2x))]$. All parameters are the same as for Figure 14.21. The basic symmetry of the map is preserved. Six periodic center points (pcp) surround the central fixed point. Other periodic fixed points are in this map.

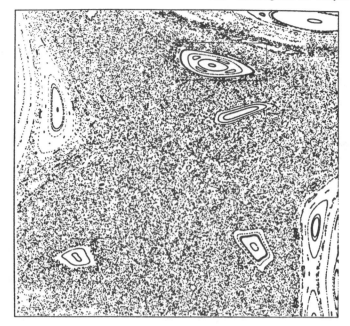

Figure 14.28. *Magnification.* (Magnified region surrounds a hyperbolic fixed point delimited by the box in Figure 14.27.)

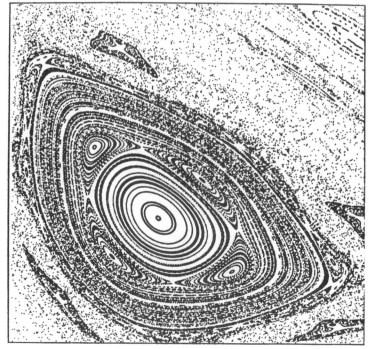

Figure 14.29. *Magnification.* (Magnified is the region surrounding a central fixed point delimited by the box Figure 14.28.) Periodic fixed points (of period 4) surround the main center.

Chapter 15

Numerical Approximation Methods

"Erdös has made me and other mathematicians recognize the importance of what we do. Mathematics is there. It's beautiful. It's the jewel we uncover."

Joel Spencer, mathematician

The use of computational techniques based on recurrence relationships can be traced back to the dawn of mathematics. The Babylonians used such techniques to compute the square root of a positive number, and the Greeks to approximate π (Wimp, 1984). Today many important special function of mathematical physics may be computed by recurrence formulas. "Numerical methods" use numbers to simulate mathematical processes, which in turn usually simulate real-world situations (Hamming, 1973). The choice of a particular algorithm influences not only the process of computing but also how we are to understand the results when they are obtained. An interesting numerical technique (for the purpose of graphical characterization) is *Halley's method*. (Pick88p, *The Visual Computer*; Pick88q, *Commun. ACM*; Pick88s, *Phys. Lett. A*; Pick89, *Comput. and Math. with Appl.*; Pick89, *Physica Scripta*, and the book *Symmetry 2*.)

15.1 Halley Maps for a Trigonometric and Rational Function

The goal of this section is to give a flavor of the subject of recurrence relations and chaos, and the computer graphics reveals the beauty that can be found in such relationships. This section addresses the process of solving equations of the form $f(x) = 0$. The problem of finding the zeros of a continuous function by iterative methods occurs frequently in science and engineering (Peterson, 1987; Grove, 1966). These approximation techniques start with a guess and successively improve upon it with a repetition of similar steps. The graphs in this section give an indication of how well one of these iterative methods, Halley's method, works, and it shows where Halley's method can be relied upon and where it behaves strangely. Halley's method is of interest theoretically because it converges rapidly relative to many other methods. Interesting recent work includes a study of the iterates of a related method, Newton's method (Benziger, 1987; Peitgen and Richter, 1986), for cubic polynomials. This section focuses on: 1) high-resolution graphics characterizing chaotic aspects of the behavior of Halley's method applied to functions with a root at the origin, 2) unusual convergence tests, and 3) the application of image processing techniques and other graphical methods in order to reveal the subtle structures of the maps. Each magnification of the behavior brings new surprises.

As suggested in the previous paragraph, Halley's method is in a class of algorithms that begins with a guess. The iteration is supposed to lead to a better guess, and the process is repeated. Halley's method behaves like a comet torn between conflicting tugs of two nearby planets. In some cases it might be difficult to determine which of the two nearby planets a comet will collide with even though we know the gravity equations. Of course, if we knew *exactly* how the comet is moving at any give time, then we could predict its future exactly. But we never do know anything exactly....

Let $F(\zeta)$ be a complex-valued function of the complex variable ζ. The *Halley map* is the function

$$H(\zeta): \zeta_{n+1} = \zeta_n - \left[\frac{F(\zeta_n)}{F'(\zeta_n) - \left(\dfrac{F''(\zeta_n)\, F(\zeta_n)}{2F'(\zeta_n)} \right)} \right] \tag{15.1}$$

This iteration is used to find the zeros of F and is derived in Grove (1966).

[In brief, we may develop the Halley method by truncating the Taylor series expansion of $F(\zeta)$ about a point ζ_n after the second derivative:

$$F(\zeta) = F(\zeta_n) + F'(\zeta_n)\, (\zeta - \zeta_n) + \left(\frac{F''(\zeta_n)\, (\zeta - \zeta_n)^2}{2} \right) \tag{15.2}$$

If we substitute $\zeta = \zeta_{n+1}$ and assume ζ_{n+1} is a good approximation to the root so that $F(\zeta_{n+1}) = 0$ we get

$$0 = F(\zeta_n) + F'(\zeta_n)\, (\zeta_{n+1} - \zeta_n) + \left(\frac{F''(\zeta_n)\, (\zeta_{n+1} - \zeta_n)^2}{2} \right) \tag{15.3}$$

To finish the derivation of Equation (15.1), solve for ζ_{n+1}.

$$(\zeta_{n+1} - \zeta_n)\left[F'(\zeta_n) + \frac{F''(\zeta_n)(\zeta_{n+1} - \zeta_n)}{2} \right] = -F(\zeta_n) \tag{15.4}$$

Figure 15.1. *Halley map portrayed for* $\zeta(\zeta^\alpha - 1) = 0$ $(\alpha = 6)$. The basins of attraction for the roots of the equation are displayed graphically for various initial values of ζ_0 in the complex plane. Light regions correspond to starting points where convergence is rapidly achieved (see text). Note: figures in this chapter appeared in a paper by the author in Hargittai, I., ed. (1989) *Symmetry 2, Unifying Human Understanding.* Pergamon Press: Oxford.

$$\zeta_{n+1} - \zeta_n = -\frac{F(\zeta_n)}{F'(\zeta) + \dfrac{F''(\zeta_n)(\zeta_{n+1} - \zeta_n)}{2}} \tag{15.5}$$

or

$$\zeta_{n+1} = \zeta_n - \frac{F(\zeta_n)}{F'(\zeta) + \dfrac{F''(\zeta_n)(\zeta_{n+1} - \zeta_n)}{2}} \tag{15.6}$$

At this point we recall the Newton-Raphson formulation

Figure 15.2. *Contour plot.* (This is for the same region of the complex plane as in Figure 15.1.) Note the complicated behavior along the boundary regions between roots and the various "nodules" along these high-iteration radial branches.

$$\zeta_{n+1} = \zeta_n - \frac{F(\zeta_n)}{F'(\zeta_n)} \tag{15.7}$$

or

$$\zeta_{n+1} - \zeta_n = -\frac{F(\zeta_n)}{F'(\zeta_n)} \tag{15.8}$$

In Equation (15.6) we replace $\zeta_{n+1} - \zeta_n$ from Equation (15.8) to get Halley's formula (Grove, 1966).]

Considered here are functions, F, that are analytic in the complex plane C. ζ_z is a zero of F and a fixed point of H: $H(\zeta_z) = \zeta_z$. The *basin of attraction* of ζ_z is the set of all points whose forward orbits by H converge to a ζ_z.

Figure 15.3. *Magnification.* (Magnified is one of the nodules near the origin in Figure 15.2.) Successive close-ups reveal self-similarity in the pictures: the pattern of nodules seems to repeat on all size scales. This is a characteristic property of "Julia sets" (see "Genesis Equations" on page 104).

To simplify the discussion, we can first consider, as an example, the one-parameter polynomial

$$\zeta(\zeta^6 - 1) = 0 \tag{15.9}$$

Polynomial problems occur frequently in practice, and polynomials are useful for theoretical study since a polynomial of degree M has exactly M zeros, and we therefore know when we have found all the zeros. This polynomial has seven roots; one is at the origin, and the others are at $\zeta = e^{2\pi i m/6}$. Also studied in this section is the simple trigonometric function $\sin(\zeta) = 0$ which has periodic roots on the real axis. In this section, the graphical behavior of Halley's method results from forward iteration. An initial point on the complex plane is selected and iterated N times. Traditionally a point is considered to have converged if

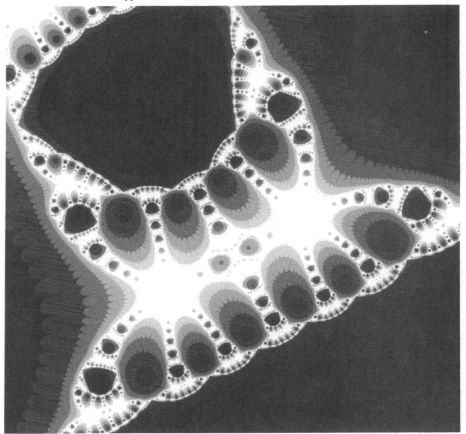

Figure 15.4. *Halley map.* (This is computed for the same complex plane region as in Figure 15.3.) Here, white areas indicate slow convergence.

$$|\zeta_{n+1} - \zeta_n|^2 < \varepsilon \tag{15.10}$$

where ε is a small value. To verify that this criterion for ending the iteration has actually allowed the system to converge to a root, $|F(\zeta)| < \varepsilon$ was used in conjunction with Equation (15.11) — producing visually identical plots. In this section, the following weird test was also sometimes used (discussed later):

$$||(\zeta_{n+1})|^2 - |\zeta_n|^2| < \varepsilon \tag{15.11}$$

The value of ε was 0.0001 and $N \sim 50$. The iteration for Equation (15.1) was performed on 4 million initial parameter values in a 2000-by-2000-point square grid. Note that the values being graphed are *not* the values of the function H. They are values of n for which ζ_n satisfies Equation (15.11). Also $H(\zeta)$ arises from setting $\zeta = \zeta_{n=0}$ and then using the recurrence relation in Equation (15.1) to get ζ_n.

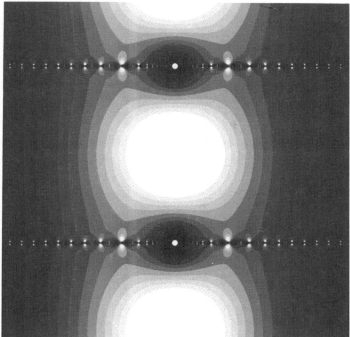

Figure 15.5. *Relaxed Halley map portrayed for* $\sin(\zeta) = 0$. The periodic roots are contained by the large white regions along the real axis. The two small white dots on the real axis are repulsive fixed points.

Three types of plots are presented. One is a bi-level plot, created by plotting a black dot if $n = 0 \bmod 2$. This operation creates contour lines and helps to visually emphasize different regions of behavior of the function. The second type of graph maps the value of n to darkness on the graph, thereby showing relative rates of convergence within each basin of attraction.

Figure 15.1 shows a graph of Halley's Map for $\zeta(\zeta^6 - 1) = 0$. The basins of attraction for the roots of the equation are displayed for various initial values of ζ_0 in the complex plane (between -2.5 and 2.5 in the real and imaginary directions). The six central white regions, and the region at the origin, contain the roots and correspond to starting points where convergence is achieved rapidly (within 3 iterations). Initial guesses in the tearshaped basins fanning out from the roots are safe; that is, any starting points selected from these regions come close to a root within a small number of iterations. Black regions converge much more slowly (about 50 iterations), and behavior on the black radial boundary region is considerably more complicated. These borders consist of elaborate swirls that can pull the calculations of Halley's method into any one of the seven roots. In this vicinity, a tiny shift in starting point can lead to widely divergent results.

Figure 15.2 is a contour plot of the same region of the complex plane as in Figure 15.1. Note the complicated behavior along the boundary regions and the various "nodules" along the high-iteration radial branches. The use of Equation (15.11) produces the whisker-like projections around each contour, and these

Figure 15.6. *Contour plot for* $\sin(\zeta) = 0$. Fixed points are at the center of the concentric rings.

whiskers generally point to the root (or to regions of fast convergence). Therefore, directionality now can easily be understood by observing the contour plots. Some contours do not contain whiskers, and these are regions which converge to the root at the origin. Figure 15.3 is a magnification of one of the nodules near the origin in Figure 15.2 and gives a high-resolution visual indication of the complexity of the behavior of Halley's map when applied to a simple function. The several large "bull's-eye" regions converge rapidly to a solution, and by testing the value of ζ_n after N iterations, one can determine to which root these areas converge. Using interactive computer graphics routines, one can simply point at the picture and extract the root. The results indicate that nearby points have different fates upon iteration. For example, Figure 15.10 indicates the final fates for points in the bull's-eye regions. The roots are: $R_0 = (0, 0\,i)$, $R_1 = (1/2 + i\sqrt{3}/2)$, $R_2 = (1 + 0\,i)$, $R_3 = (1/2 - i\sqrt{3}/2)$, $R_4 = (-1/2 - i\sqrt{3}/2)$, $R_5 = (-1 + 0\,i)$, $R_6 = (-1/2 + i\sqrt{3}/2)$.

Figure 15.7. *Close-up contour plot.* (The magnified area is near the thin chaotic boundary regions of Figure 15.6.)

Figure 15.3 also reveals miniature copies of the nodules and copies of the pattern in Figure 15.2. We have found that this self-similarity on all scales is characteristic of Halley's plot for polynomial equations. Figure 15.4 computed for the same region as Figure 15.3 and, like Figure 15.1, indicates the behavior of the function in gradations of intensity which make visually obvious the relative speed of convergence of different starting points. Here dark regions indicate areas of rapid convergence. The complexity and richness of resultant forms contrasts with the simplicity of the formula being solved.

Figure 15.5 through Figure 15.9 are plots for $\sin(\zeta) = 0$. To solve for the roots of this function, one can use

$$H(\zeta): \zeta_{n+1} = \zeta_n - \lambda \left[\frac{F(\zeta_n)}{F'(\zeta_n) - \left(\dfrac{F''(\zeta_n)\, F(\zeta_n)}{2F'(\zeta_n)} \right)} \right] \tag{15.12}$$

The coefficient λ in the modified Halley's method is known as a *relaxation coefficient* and is used to control stability of convergence where the method may be susceptible to overshoot. $\lambda = 0.1$ was used. Decreasing λ from 1 damps the Halley step and enlarges the domain of monotonic convergence (also tending to reduce the size of the area where self-similar chaotic fragmentation occurs between roots). The convergence test in Equation (15.10) was used for these figures. Roots are encompassed by the broad white regions and are separated by periodic thin chaotic regions. The 3-D plots show the attractive fixed points for the roots as holes in a surface since these represent low iteration points. In addition to attractive fixed points at the roots, the Halley map has repulsive fixed points where

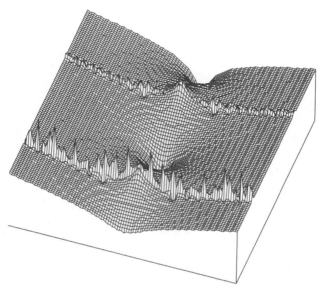

Figure 15.8. *3-D plot.* (This is computed for Figure 15.5.) Height indicates iteration (areas of slow convergence). Both attractive and repulsive fixed points are indicated by the wells and broad peaks, respectively. The two thin ridges are in the region of chaotic fragmentation between the roots.

$F'(\zeta) = 0$. For $\sin(\zeta)$ we can see these repulsive fixed points most clearly in the 3-D plots (as broad peaks) and in the half-tone plot as dark regions surrounding a small white fixed point.

15.1.1 Overrelaxation and Chaos

[The relaxation coefficient λ in the modified Halley's method can be greater than 1 in the *overrelaxed* case in order to speed the rate of convergence in some problems. Increasing λ above 1 increases the Halley step and decreases the domain of monotonic convergence (also tending to enlarge the size of the area where self-similar chaotic fragmentation takes place). As λ increases one observes that the Julia sets (see Glossary) become more complex. Note that $H'(\zeta)$ at a simple zero is $H'(\zeta) = 1 - \lambda$. Therefore, for $|1 - \lambda| < 1$, $H'(\zeta)$ is a contraction. As $1 - \lambda$ approaches 1, all zeros of $f(z)$ become less and less stable, and their immediate basins of attraction collapse to points. This explains the increasingly wild and chaotic behavior as λ increases: there are no more stable solutions to $H(\zeta) = \zeta$ when $|1 - \lambda| > 1$. Since there are likely to be no stable attractors for $|1 - \lambda| > 1$, the Julia set's Hausdorff dimension for such λ is 2.] (Quite startling pictures can be produced with overrelaxation, and examples can be found in Pick88s, "Overrelaxation and Chaos," *Phys. Lett. A*).

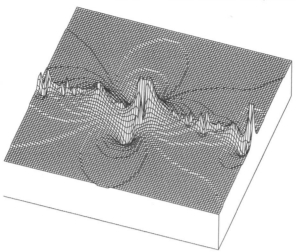

Figure 15.9. *3-D close-up of a piece of a chaotic boundary ridge for* sin(ζ) = 0. Wells indicate rapid convergence.

15.1.2 Buridan's Ass

As David Tritton has pointed out (Tritton, 1986), chaotic systems are a little like the legendary Buridan's ass. Buridan's ass died of starvation because it was exactly midway between a bunch of hay and an equally attractive pail of water. If the ass did in fact decide to eat or drink, who can say which it would have done first? Likewise, the pictures indicate that prediction is difficult when in the chaotic fragmentation between attractive roots in Halley's method. Provocative avenues of future research include extension to nonpolynomial equations and to related root-finding numerical methods such as Muller's method, Aitken's method, and the secant method. Hopefully the described techniques will stimulate future studies in the characterization of complicated behavior of numerical methods – methods which are being used in many branches of modern science with increasing frequency.

15.2 Beauty, Symmetry and Chaos in Chebyshev's Paradise

> *"We live in a non-linear world; how dull it would otherwise be! ... The Reagan-Gorbachov system has to be non-linear!"*   David Tritton, physicist

It's interesting to extend the Halley method to additional functions. The title of this section contains the name of the Russian mathematician Pafrutii L. Chebyshev (1821-1894) since all forms in this section are based on the "Chebyshev polynomials." Chebyshev polynomials of degree n are usually denoted by $T_n(x)$ (the notation comes from the French spelling, Tchebychef). $T_n(x)$ are given by the formula

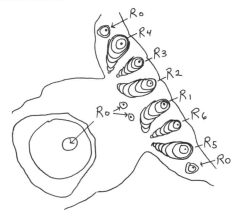

Figure 15.10. *Final fates for points in bull's-eye regions.*

$$T_n(x) = \cos(n \cos^{-1} x) \tag{15.13}$$

In practical applications, $T_n(x)$ are used for representing other functions in the form of a rapidly converging expansion (Hamming, 1973). Chebyshev polynomials are useful for demonstrating chaos and pattern formation since they have a non-constant period of oscillation (see Figure 15.11). In addition, it is very easy to compute Chebyshev polynomials, as explained in the Recipe section.

First consider, as an example, the Chebyshev polynomial, $T_7(x)$. We know that the zeros of $T_n(x)$ in the interval (-1,1) are located at

$$x = \cos\left[\frac{\pi(k - 1/2)}{n}\right]; \quad k = 1, 2, \ldots, n \tag{15.14}$$

As in the last section, the graphical behavior of Halley's method results from forward iteration. An initial point on the complex plane is selected and iterated 50 times. The convergence test in Equation (15.11) was used. The value of ε was 0.0001. The iteration in Equation (15.1) was performed on 4 million initial parameter values in a 2000-by-2000-point square grid. A bi-level plot is created by plotting a black dot if m is even the first time the convergence test is satisfied (m is the iteration number). This operation creates contour lines and helps to visually emphasize different regions of behavior of the function.

Figure 15.12 shows a contour plot of Halley's Map for $T_7(x)$. [The "basins of attraction" contain points which gradually "fall" into a fixed point, and the basins for the roots of the equation are displayed for various initial values of (ζ_0) in the complex plane (between -1 and 1 in the real and imaginary directions). The large central "bull's-eye" region represents those points which converge to (0,0). Other smaller bull's-eye regions along the real axis contain the other six roots and correspond to starting points where convergence is achieved rapidly. Initial guesses in the basins fanning out from the roots are "safe"; that is, any

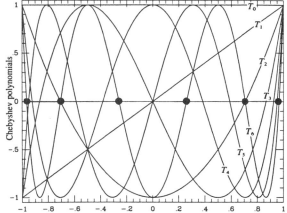

Figure 15.11. *Chebyshev polynomials.* $T_0(x)$ through $T_6(x)$ are shown for real values of x (figure adapted from Press et al., 1986). Note, in general, the non-constant period of oscillation, as indicated by the roots (dots) for $T_6(x)$.

starting points selected from these regions come close to a root within a small number of iterations.]

Figure 15.13 is a magnification of an intricate region of the complex plane shown in Figure 15.12. Figure 15.14 is a magnification of one of the small "nodules" in the chaotic region between roots. This magnification reveals miniature copies of the nodule in different sizes and at different locations.

15.2.1 Chebyshev Rings

To compute the ring patterns, a real number z is first calculated for a range of (x,y) pairs:

$$z_{xy} = \alpha \left(T_n x + T_n y \right) \tag{15.15}$$

where α is a constant. To create contour lines, the resulting z value is truncated (made an integer) and divided by another integer, m. If the remainder is zero, a dot is plotted on the graphics screen at point (x, y) (see Pseudocode 13.1). This approach was introduced in "Synthesizing Ornamental Textures" on page 227 where patterns reminiscent of the ornaments of a variety of cultures (ornaments with a repeating motif in at least two nonparallel directions) are generated.

15.3 Recipe for Chebyshev's Paradise

> *"A man must have chaos within him to be able to give birth to a dancing star."*
>   Friedrich Nietzsche

The following hints may help the reader to produce the plots in this section. Though the expression for $T_n(x)$ in Equation (15.13) may look trigonometric at

Figure 15.12. *Chebyshev-Halley map.* (This is computed for $T_7(x)$ for complex values of x.) Note the chaotic behavior along the boundary regions between roots (the roots are seen as bull's eyes on the vertical axis). The shapes in this chaotic fragmentation region between roots vary because the shape of the Chebyshev polynomial differs from period to adjacent period.

first glance, it actually can be combined with trigonometric identities to yield explicit expressions for $T_n(x)$ which facilitate their computation on personal computers:

$$T_0(x) = 1 \qquad\qquad (15.16)$$

$$T_1(x) = x \qquad\qquad (15.17)$$

$$T_2(x) = 2x^2 - 1 \qquad\qquad (15.18)$$

$$T_3(x) = 4x^3 - 3x \qquad\qquad (15.19)$$

$$T_{n+1}(x) = 2\,xT_n(x) - T_{n-1}(x) \qquad n \geq 1 \qquad\qquad (15.20)$$

Figure 15.13. *Magnification.* (Figure 15.12 is magnified.)

Chebyshev polynomials are also useful for generating intricate-looking dynamical systems (as in "Dynamical Systems" on page 249). To produce "Cheby-orbits" an initial point in the x-y plane is selected and four simple program lines are repeated, giving rise to the trajectories through time (see Pseudocode 15.1).

15.4 Reading List for Chapter 15

The Reference section of this book lists many papers and books on the subject of numerical methods. Two personal favorites are:

1. Grove, W. (1966) *Brief Numerical Methods.* Prentice-Hall: New Jersey (This has an excellent section on root-finding methods).

2. Press, W. Flannery, B. Teukolsky, S., Vetterling, W. (1986) *Numerical Recipes.* Cambridge University Press: New York.
   Several papers have been written on graphical representations of the behavior of Newton's method (this root-finding method uses the first derivative, while Halley's method also requires the second derivative). Peterson (1987) overviews some of this work in an excellent introductory article in *Science News.* See also Peitgen and Richter (1986), and Benzinger et al. (1987). It is interesting to note that British mathematician Arthur Caley in 1879 studied similar problems for cubic polynomials, but he found considerable difficulty in describing the chaotic

behavior – perhaps because computer graphics tools were not available to illustrate the complicated structures!

Figure 15.14. *Magnification.* (One of the small "nodules" (bubble-like structures) in Figure 15.12 is magnified.) Successive close-ups reveal self-similarity in the pictures: the pattern of nodules seems to repeat on all size scales.

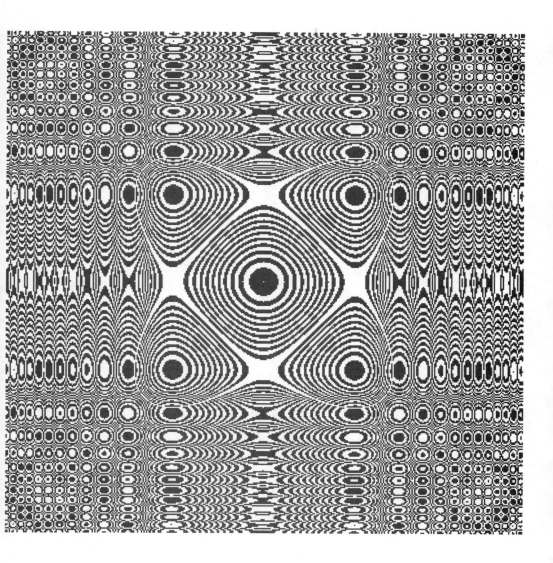

Figure 15.15. *Cheby-rings.* These were produced by $z_{xy} = \alpha(T_n x + T_n y)$. The picture boundaries are (-2,2) in the x-y direction. Only the rings in the central bull's eye are real contour lines; the rest are beautiful artifacts of the sampling process (known as "aliasing"); these artifacts dominate outside the central region on (-1,1).

Figure 15.16. *Cheby-rings.* (A region of Figure 15.15 is magnified.)

```
ALGORITHM: Cheby-Orbits

First, choose an (xx,yy) coordinate. Then repeat the
following 4 lines. The reader should
first experiment with cheb = T3(x) and follow the orbits
produced.

1. xold=xx; yold=yy;
2. xx = xold-h*sin(cheb(yold));
3. yy = yold+h*sin(cheb(xold));
4. PlotDotAt(xx,yy);
```

Pseudocode 15.1. *How to produce Cheby-orbits.*

Figure 15.17. *Cheby-orbits.*

Chapter 16

Tesselation Automata
Derived from a Single Defect

"The generation of random numbers is too important to be left to chance."
Robert Coveyou, mathematician, Oak Ridge National Laboratory

Tesselation automata (TA) are a class of simple mathematical systems which are becoming important as models for a variety of physical processes. They can exhibit random-looking behavior sometimes and highly ordered behavior at others – depending on the rules of the game. Interesting previous applications include the modeling of the spread of plant species, the propagation of animals such as barnacles, and the spread of forest fires. Referred to variously as "cellular automata," "homogenous structures," "cellular structures," and "iterative arrays," they have been applied to, and reintroduced for, a wide variety of purposes (Wolfram, 1983; Poundstone, 1985; Levy, 1985; Schrandt and Ulam, 1970). The term "tesselation" is used in this section for the following reason: When a floor is covered with tiles, a symmetrical and repetitive pattern is often formed – straight edges being more common then curved ones. Such a division of a plane into polygons, regular or irregular, is called a "tesselation" – and the term "tesselation" is chosen here to emphasize these geometric aspects often found in the figures in this section.

Usually tesselation automata consist of a grid of cells which can exist in two states, occupied or unoccupied. The occupancy of one cell is determined from a simple mathematical analysis of the occupancy of neighbor cells. Mathematicians define the rules, set up the game board, and let the game play itself out. One popular set of rules is set forth in what has become known as the game of "LIFE" (Poundstone, 1985). Though the rules governing the creation of tesselation automata are simple, the patterns they produce are very complicated and sometimes seem almost random, like a turbulent fluid flow or the output of a cryptographic system. In this chapter, the focus is on TA derived from a single defect using symmetrical rules. (Pick89, *Computers and Math. with Appls.*, and the book *Symmetry 2.*)

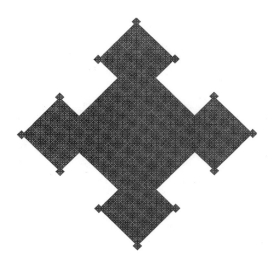

Figure 16.1. *TA Type 1 after "growing" for 200 generations.* This pattern starts with a single seed in the center of this figure. Note: figures in this chapter appeared in a paper by the author in Hargittai, I., ed. (1989) *Symmetry 2, Unifying Human Understanding.* Pergamon Press: Oxford.

16.1 Method and Observations

Tesselation automata (TA) are mathematical idealizations of physical systems in which space and time are discrete (Wolfram, 1983). Presented here are patterns exhibited by figures "growing" according to certain recursive rules. The growth occurs in a plane subdivided into regular square tiles. Note that with the rules of growth in this section, the designs will continue increasing in size indefinitely as time progresses. In each of the cases, the starting configuration is only one occupied cell, which can be thought of as a single defect (or perturbation) in a lattice of all 0's, represented by:

$$\begin{bmatrix} 0\,0\,0\,0\,0 \\ 0\,0\,0\,0\,0 \\ 0\,0\,1\,0\,0 \\ 0\,0\,0\,0\,0 \\ 0\,0\,0\,0\,0 \end{bmatrix} \tag{16.1}$$

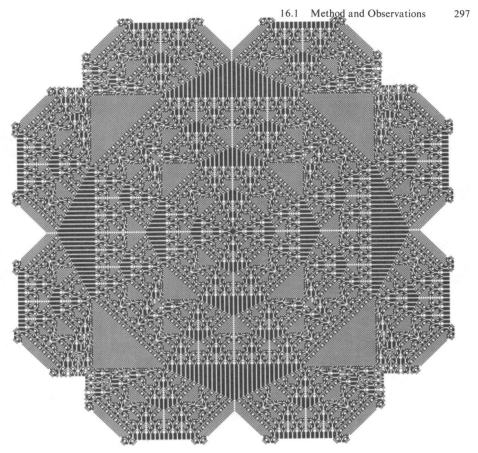

Figure 16.2. *TA Type 2A.* The TA presented here has a time dependency in its rules of growth.

16.1.1 TA Type 1

This is the simplest system to set up, yet the behavior is still interesting. Given the *n*-th generation, we can define the *(n+1)*th generation as follows: A cell of the next generation is born if it is orthogonally contiguous to one and only one square of the current generation. Starting with the pattern in Equation (16.1) for $n = 1$, the pattern for $n = 2$ would be:

$$\begin{bmatrix} 0\,0\,0\,0\,0 \\ 0\,0\,1\,0\,0 \\ 0\,1\,1\,1\,0 \\ 0\,0\,1\,0\,0 \\ 0\,0\,0\,0\,0 \end{bmatrix} \qquad (16.2)$$

Figure 16.1 indicates the result at $n = 200$. This TA is similar to the one described in Poundstone (1985) and Levy (1985). Note that no "deaths" of

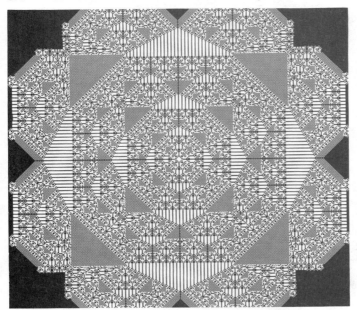

Figure 16.3. *Same as previous figure, but plotted as its negative.*

squares occur (i.e., no 1 → 0 transitions can occur; deaths are employed in many TA experiments). Note also that on the two perpendicular axes (which go through (0,0)), all the squares will be present. These are the stems from which branching occurs.

16.1.2 TA Type 2. Time Dependence of Rules

16.1.2.1 "Mod 2" TA

Given the *n*th generation, we can define the *(n+1)* th as follows. A cell of the next generation is occupied if:

1. It is orthogonally contiguous to one and only one square of the current generation for even *n* (i.e., *n* mod 2 = 0).

2. It is contiguous to one and only one square of the current generation, where the local neighborhood is both orthogonal and diagonal, for odd *n* (*n* mod 2 = 1).

In other words, for (*n* mod 2 = 0),

$$\text{if } \sum C_{\text{orth}} = 1 \text{ then } C_{ij} = 1 \tag{16.3}$$

where

$$C_{\text{orth}} = [C_{i,j+1}, C_{i,j-1}, C_{i+1,j}, C_{i-1,j}] \tag{16.4}$$

Figure 16.4. *TA Type 2B, with time dependent growth.*

For (n mod $2 = 1$)

$$\sum C_{\text{orth-diag}} = 1 \;\;\rightarrow\; C_{ij} = 1 \tag{16.5}$$

where

$$C_{\text{orth-diag}} = [C_{i,j+1},\, C_{i,j-1},\, C_{i+1,j},\, C_{i-1,j},\, C_{I+1,j+1},\, C_{i-1,j-1},\, C_{i-1,j+1},\, C_{i+1,j-1}]$$

Notice the discrete symmetrical planes running through these TA. For example, these planes in Figure 16.2 and Figure 16.3 look like:

We can use this observation to get a visual idea of resultant patterns, for large n, in a multi-defect system (see TA Type 3).

16.1.2.2 "Mod 6" TA

Given the nth generation, we can define the $(n+1)$th in the same manner as for Type 2A, except that n mod $6 = 0$ vs. n mod $6 \neq 0$ determines the temporal evolution of the pattern (Figure 16.4).

Figure 16.5. *Multi-defect system.* This is composed of three initial seeds of TA Type 2 (figure is magnified relative to Figure 16.6).

16.1.3 TA Type 3. Contests Between Defects

More than one initial defect can be placed on a large infinite lattice. We can let them each grow and finally merge (and compete) according to a set of rules. Figure 16.5 is a TA of Type 2A, and it shows three defects after just a few generations (this figure is magnified relative to others). Figure 16.6 shows the growth for large *n*.

To help see the numerous symmetry planes and to get an idea about the shape of the figure as it evolves, the reader can draw the primary radiating symmetrical discrete planes (see Type 2A); for example, for Figure 16.6:

For a recent fascinating article on competition of TA *rules*, see Brown (1987) which models biological phenomena of competition and selection by TA "subrule competition."

Figure 16.6. *Same as previous figure, except computed for longer time.*

16.1.4 TA Type 4. Defects in a Centered Rectangular Lattice

In this type of TA, a single defect is placed in a lattice of the form:

$$\begin{bmatrix} 0 & 1 & 0 & 1 & 0 \\ 1 & 0 & 1 & 0 & 1 \\ 0 & 1 & 0 & 1 & 0 \\ 1 & 0 & 1 & 0 & 1 \\ 0 & 1 & 0 & 1 & 0 \end{bmatrix} \tag{16.6}$$

This is known as a "centered rectangular lattice" (Lockwood, 1978). In some experiments, two different background lattices with adjacent boundaries are used, and the defect propagates from its beginning point in the centered rectangular lattice through the interface into the second lattice defined by:

$$\begin{bmatrix} 0 & 1 & 0 & 1 & 0 \\ 0 & 1 & 0 & 1 & 0 \\ 0 & 1 & 0 & 1 & 0 \\ 0 & 1 & 0 & 1 & 0 \\ 0 & 1 & 0 & 1 & 0 \end{bmatrix} \tag{16.7}$$

This is known simply as a "rectangular lattice." Adding a defect to these two-phase systems bears some similarity to seeding supersaturated solutions and watching the crystallization process grow and "hit" the boundary of a solution with a different composition. In the examples in this section, the two phases are also reminiscent of metal-metal interfaces – such as Silicon 100 (centered rectan-

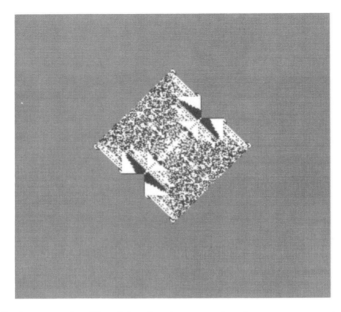

Figure 16.7. *TA Type 4A.* The defect has been growing from a center position in a centered rectangular lattice (which is seen as a diffuse gray background since the dot size is extremely small). Without the presence of the defect, the rules have no effect on the lattice.

gular) and Chromium (rectangular). Note that with no defect present, the rules described have no effect on either lattice! Only when the defect is placed in the lattice does any growth occur. The rules for growth of the defects are as follows (note that deaths of cells can occur in these systems).

16.1.4.1 TA Type 4A

$$\text{if } \sum C = 3 \ \wedge \ \text{if } C_{i,j} = 0 \quad \rightarrow C_{i,j} = 1 \tag{16.8}$$

$$\text{if } \sum C = 3 \ \wedge \ \text{if } C_{i,j} = 1 \quad \rightarrow C_{i,j} = 0 \tag{16.9}$$

where

$$C = [C_{i,j+1}, C_{i,j-1}, C_{i+1,j}, C_{i-1,j}, C_{i+1,j+1}, C_{i-1,j-1}] \tag{16.10}$$

The symbol $\wedge$ denotes a logical "and." Figure 16.7 shows a defect which has been growing from a central position in a centered rectangular lattice (which is seen as a diffuse gray background at this resolution). Figure 16.8 shows the propagation of the defect through a two-phase boundary. Note that the propagation behavior is visually different when in the second layer. For example, notice that the growth in the bottom layer appears to be constrained to planes 0 and 60 degrees with respect to the lattice.

Figure 16.8. *Magnification.* Magnified picture of the beginning of propagation of a Type 4A defect through a two-phase system. The top phase is a centered rectangular lattice, while the bottom phase is a rectangular lattice.

The introduction of "germ" cells appears to be useful in simulating real nucleation processes. An interesting paper in the literature describes solid-solid phase transformations of shape memory alloys, such as Cu-Zn-Al, using a 1-D cellular automata approach (Maeder, 1987). In this investigation, each cell represents several hundred atoms.

The search for multiphase systems, such as the ones in this section, which are unaffected by a rule system *until* a defect is added, remains a provocative avenue of future research.

16.1.4.2 TA Type 4B

This case (see Figure 16.12) is the same as for Subset 4A, except that

$$\text{if } \sum C = 3 \ \wedge \ C_{i,j} = 1 \quad \rightarrow \ C_{i,j} = 0 \tag{16.11}$$

$$\text{if } \sum C = 3 \ \wedge \ C_{i,j} = 0 \quad \rightarrow \ C_{i,j} = 1 \tag{16.12}$$

$$\text{if } \sum C \neq 3 \ \wedge \ C_{i,j} = 1 \quad \rightarrow \ C_{i,j} = 1 \tag{16.13}$$

$$\text{if } \sum C \neq 3 \ \wedge \ C_{i,j} = 0 \quad \rightarrow \ C_{i,j} = 0 \tag{16.14}$$

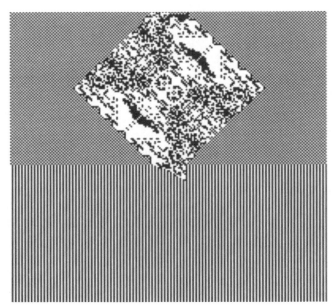

Figure 16.9. *Evolution of previous figure.* The figure is less magnified and computed for 20 generations. The defect has just "broken through" the boundary.

16.1.5 TA Type 5. Larger Local Neighborhood

In TA Types 1-4, the neighborhood was defined as being within one cell of the center cell under consideration. In this system, the local neighborhood is larger. The rule is as follows:

$$\text{if } \sum C \text{ mod } 2 = 0 \;\; \rightarrow \; C_{i,j} = 0. \tag{16.15}$$

$$\text{if } \sum C \text{ mod } 2 \neq 0 \;\; \rightarrow \; C_{i,j} = 1. \tag{16.16}$$

where
$$C = [C_{i-2,j+2}, \; C_{i+2,j+2}, \; C_{i,j+1}, \; C_{i-1,j}, \; C_{i+1,j}, \; C_{i,j-1}, \; C_{i-2,j-2}, \; C_{i+2,j-2}]$$

Figure 16.14 shows the evolution of a 2-state background defined by the lattices in Equation (16.6) and Equation (16.7) for several different snapshots in time. Unlike Type 4, the background without a defect is disturbed by this rule set. Notice the visually unusual behavior of this system with both symmetry and stochasticity present. Also note the interesting growth of the two defects which have been placed next to each other in the top layer.

As we have seen as a theme throughout this book, the forms in this section contain both symmetry and stochasticity, and the richness of resultant forms contrasts with the simplicity of the generating formula. Running TA at high speeds on a computer lets observers actually see the process of growth.

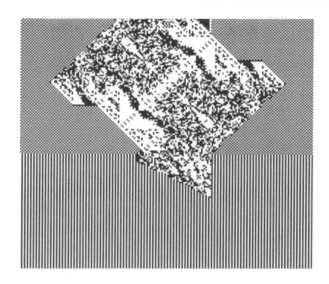

Figure 16.10. *Same as previous figure, for 80 generations.*

Also from a purely artistic standpoint, some of the figures in this section are reminiscent of Persian carpet designs, ceramic tile mosaics, Peruvian striped fabrics, brick patterns from certain Mosques, and the symmetry in Moorish ornamental patterns (Rozsa, 1986 (see also references in "Synthesizing Ornamental Textures" on page 227)):

The idea of investigating the ornaments and decorations of various cultures by consideration of their symmetry groups appears to have originated with Polya (Polya, 1924). This artistic resemblance is due to the complicated symmetries produced by the algorithm.

In natural phenomena, there are examples of complicated and ordered structures arising spontaneously from "disordered" states, and examples include: snowflakes, patterns of flow in turbulent fluids, and biological systems. As Wolfram points out, TA are sufficiently simple to allow detailed mathematical analysis, yet sufficiently complex to exhibit a wide variety of complicated phenomena, and they can perhaps serve as models for some real processes in nature.

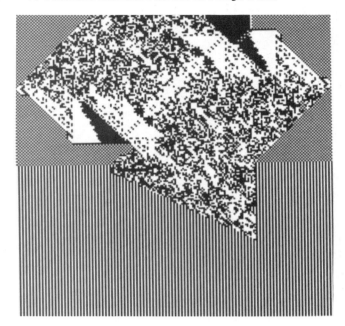

Figure 16.11. *Same as previous figure, for 100 generations.*

Figure 16.12. *Propagation for TA Type 4B in a two-phase system (n=120).*

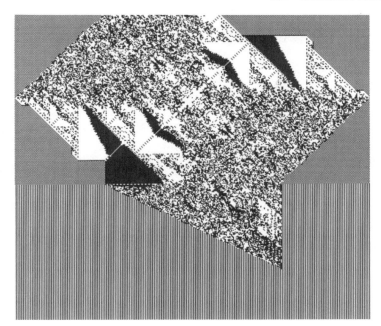

Figure 16.13. *Propagation for TA Type 4B in a two-phase system (n=200).*

Figure 16.14. *Evolution of a two-state background.* The background is defined by the lattices of Equation (16.6) and Equation (16.7) Two adjacent defects have been placed in the top layer, and the result for 2 generations (n=2) is shown.

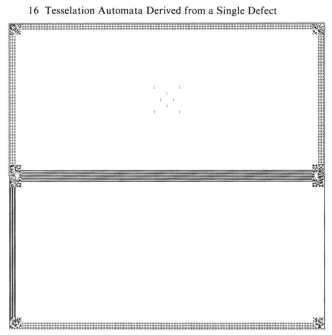

Figure 16.15. *Figure after 8 generations (n=8).*

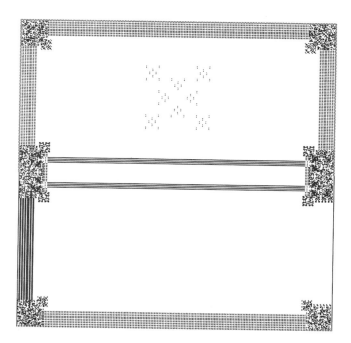

Figure 16.16. *n = 20.*

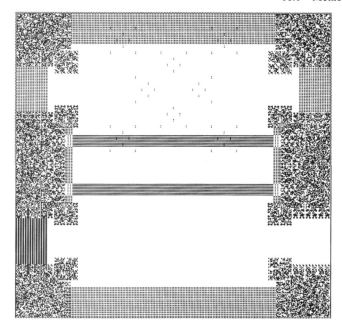

Figure 16.17. *n = 40.*

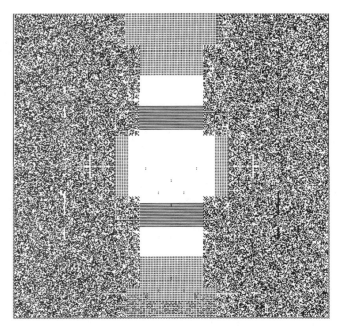

Figure 16.18. *n = 80.* Note that the pattern, previously well-ordered, appears to be on the route to "chaos."

16.2 Recipe for Tesselation Automata

Readers are encouraged to modify the equations to create a variety of patterns of their own design. In Pseudocode 16.1, the C array is initially 0 for all its elements, except for a value of 1 placed in its center. In the program, a temporary array, Ctemp, is used to save the new results of each generation. The routine would be called n=200 times in a typical simulation.

16.3 Reading List for Chapter 16

The cellular automata concept was introduced in the 1950s by John von Newumann and Stanislaw Ulam (they succeeded in proving that an abstract pattern could create a copy of itself by following a set of fixed rules). The cellular automata game called *Life* was invented in 1970 by British mathematician John Conway and popularized by Martin Gardner in the October 1970 issue of *Scientific American.*

The Reference section of this book lists many papers and books on the subject of cellular automata. Three personal favorites are:

1. Conway, J., Berlekamp, E., Guy, R. (1982) *Winning Ways for Your Mathematical Plays.* Academic Press: New York.

2. Gardner, M. (1983) *Wheels, Life, and Other Mathematical Amusements.* Freeman: New York.

3. Poundstone, W. (1985) The Recursive Universe. William Morrow and Company: New York.

Note that S. Wolfram has done extensive work in this field of cellular automata, and he has developed a scheme for using cellular automata in place of computer approximations of differential equations. Ivars Peterson described various aspects of Wolfram's work in: Peterson, I. (1988) *The Mathematical Tourist* Freeman: New York. Also see Wolfram (1983).

```
ALGORITHM:   TA GENERATION (TYPE 2A )

INPUT:       1 DEFECT, Centered in the C array
OUTPUT:      TA PATTERN
TYPICAL PARAMETER VALUES:
             Size = 400
             n is the generation counter - goes from 1 to 200

do i = 2 to size-1;                   (* X - direction          *)
   do j = 2 to size-1;                (* Y - direction          *)
    if C(i,j) = 0 then do;            (* Test for vacancy        *)
      if mod(n,2) = 0 then do;        (* Test for even number  *)
        sum = C(i,j+1)+C(i,j-1)+C(i+1,j)+C(i-1,j);
      else do
        sum = C(i,j+1)+C(i,j-1)+C(i+1,j)+C(i-1,j)
        C(I+1,j+1) + C(i-1,j-1)+ C(I-1,j+1)+C(i+1,j-1);
      end;
      if sum = 1 then Ctemp(i,j) = 1;
    end;                              (* test for vacancy       *)
   end;                               (* End j loop             *)
end;                                  (* End i loop             *)
C=Ctemp;
```

Pseudocode 16.1. *TA generation (Type 2A).*

Chapter 17

Summary of Part III
and Conclusion of Book

"Blindness to the aesthetic element in mathematics is widespread and can account for a feeling that mathematics is dry as dust, as exciting as a telephone book .... On the contrary, appreciation of this element makes the subject live in a wonderful manner and burn as no other creation of the human mind seems to do."　　　　　　　　　　　*P. J. Davis and R. Hersch*

In Part III we've seen that both richly organized and chaotic patterns can come from simple formulas. Note also that there is sometimes no faster way of finding out how a chaotic system will evolve than to watch its evolution. As other researchers have pointed out, the system itself is its own fastest computer.

The computer graphics experiments in Part III demonstrate an incompleteness in a traditional view that complicated results come from complicated causes. Throughout Part III the reader has been presented with simple techniques for visualizing graphically interesting manifestations of this kind of behavior. Many of the graphics function like a wood-stain helping to reveal the subtle textures and grains in an attractive manner. Hopefully, this part of the book will make a wider audience aware of the role of aesthetics in mathematics.

Let's sum up *Computers, Pattern, Chaos, and Beauty* by noting that a recent National Science Foundation study found that the sciences were in urgent need of government support for graphic tools to view the millions of bytes of data that computers are heaping upon researchers (Wolff, 1988). Today, visualization is being pursued in various university supercomputer centers and government labs. The commercial world is beginning to recognize the visualization needs of the scientific community and respond to them. Some specialized high-performance graphics computers are now available, for example from Pixar, Stellar, Silicon Graphics, and Ardent, but these have a heavy price tag.

Whether advertising a commercial product, visualizing complicated data, or creating art just for fun, computer graphics allows human creativity and imagination to soar in ways never before possible. Beyond the realm of art and games, computer graphics has exciting new practical applications ranging from flight simulators to image processing of pictures from outer space.

I conclude by adding my voice to the chorus of others which are suggesting there is only a fine line between science and art. Sven G. Carlson in his letter to *Science News* says it well:

> *"Art and science will eventually be seen to be as closely connected as arms to the body. Both are vital elements of order and its discovery. The word 'art' derives from the Indo-European base 'ar', meaning to join or fit together. In this sense, science, in the attempt to learn how and why things fit, becomes art. And when art is seen as the ability to do, make, apply or portray in a way that withstands the test of time, its connection with science becomes more clear."*

*"The chamois making a gigantic leap from rock to rock
and alighting, with its full weight, on hooves supported by an ankle
two centimeters in diameter: that is challenge and that is mathematics.
The mathematical phenomenon always develops out of simple arithmetic,
so useful in everyday life, out of numbers, those weapons of the gods:
the gods are there, behind the wall, at play with numbers."*

Le Corbusier, *The Modulor* (London: Faber, 1954), p. 220
Quoted by Ellis in *Number Power in Nature, Art, and Everyday Life*
(New York, St. Martin's Press, 1978).

Appendix A

Color Plates

Most of the color plates were produced on an IBM 5080 graphics display at a resolution of 1024 × 1024 pixels. The programming language was usually PL/I, and an IBM 3090 mainframe computer was often used to compute the images. For some of the 3-D images, a Stellar GS 1000 computer was used, and the programming language was C. Note that many of the color plates can be rapidly created using personal computers if a lower resolution picture is computed. The following lists Color Plate numbers and accompanying descriptions.

1. Computer rendition of a polyhedral model. In the past, complicated polyhedra were often hand-built and photographed in order to allow students and mathematicians to appreciate the complicated symmetries. Today, powerful graphics computers can render symmetrical models in seconds (Pick89, *Symmetry*).

2. Pseudocolor rendering of the Shroud of Turin. This figure visually enhances regions which touched the cloth or were in contact with it the longest, as well as "bloodstains" in the forehead and hair. For information on how to create this image, see "Image Processing of the Shroud of Turin" on page 73.

3. Soap bubbles in the moonlight. For more information on how to create this image, see "Circles Which Kiss: A Note on Osculatory Packing" on page 332.

4. Stability plot for $z \rightarrow \cosh(z) + \mu$. "Water colors" (blue, cyan, green) represent points which grow large with few iterations. Black regions do not explode. For more information on how to create this image, see "More Beauty from Complex Variables" on page 113.

5. Another stability plot for $z \rightarrow \cosh(z) + \mu$. $\mu = (-2.25, 0)$. Red areas represent non-exploding points. For more information on how to create this image, see "More Beauty from Complex Variables" on page 113.

6. Dynamical system. For more information on how to create this image, see "Dynamical Systems" on page 249.

7. Stability plot for a composite equation. For more information on how to create this image, see "How to Design Textures Using Recursive Composite Functions" on page 129.

8. Cross-section of a quaternion. For more information on how to create this image, see "Quaternion Images" on page 163.

9. 3-D spherical Lissajous curve generated from $x = r\sin(\theta t)\cos(\phi t)$, $z = r\cos(\theta t)$, $y = r\sin(\theta t)\sin(\phi t)$. Readers can try ratios of θ/ϕ such as $1/2$ or $1/3$.

10. Seashell produced using a logarithmic spiral, with large vertical displacement. For more information on how to create this image, see "Seashells" on page 218.

11. 3-D spherical Lissajous curve generated from $x = r\sin(\theta t)\cos(\phi t)$, $z = r\cos(\theta t)$, $y = r\sin(\theta t)\sin(\phi t)$.

12. Spiral *Ricard* surface produced by $z = \alpha + \cos(6\pi \sqrt{(x^2 + y^2)} + arctan(y/x))$ where $\alpha = 3y(3x^2 - y^2)/4$.

13. Spiral surface viewed in 2-D with color indicating height.

14. Spiral surface produced by $\alpha = 5\sqrt{|x| - |y|} + 2|xy|/(\sqrt{(x^2 + y^2)})$

15. A vacation on Mars. For more information on how to create this image, see "A Vacation on Mars" on page 223.

16. Sunset on Mars. For more information on how to create this image, see "A Vacation on Mars" on page 223.

17. Noise-sphere. By mapping the results of a random number generator to the position of points in a spherical coordinate system, certain bad random number generators are quickly found by visual inspection. This plate represents the output of a bad BASIC random number generator showing correlations (tendrils) which are not present in good (uniform) generators. Noise-spheres are quite easy to compute. This method is not discussed further in the book; however, more information is available from the author.

18. 3-D spherical Lissajous curve generated from $x = r\sin(\theta t)\cos(\phi t)$, $z = r\cos(\theta t)$, $y = r\sin(\theta t)\sin(\phi t)$.

19. Stalks within the Mandelbrot set. (Also see the frontpiece for Chapter 6).

20. Bifurcation plot. For more information on how to create this image, see "Image Processing Techniques and Deterministic Chaos" on page 158.

21. "Annelida" (From a collection of the author's mathematically derived sculptures entitled *I Have Dreams at Night*.)

22. Halley Map. For more information on how to create this image, see "Numerical Approximation Methods" on page 275.

23. Dynamical system. For more information on how to create this image, see "Dynamical Systems" on page 249.

24. "Night Vision" (From a collection of the author's mathematically derived sculptures entitled *I Have Dreams at Night*.)

25. Chaotic repeller distance-tower. For more information on how to create this image, see "A Note on Rendering Chaotic Repeller Distance-Towers" on page 168.

26. Lyapunov exponent, rivers and "snow-capped" mountains. The Lyapunov exponent (see Glossary) can reveal the enormously complicated behavior of certain simple formulas in an aesthetic and useful fashion. Here, high elevation (white) mountains represent chaotic regions, and blue water colors represent regions of stability.

27. Julia set for composite equation. For more information on how to create this image, see "How to Design Textures Using Recursive Composite Functions" on page 129.

28. Halley map for a seventh order Chebyshev polynomial. For more information on how to create this image, see "Numerical Approximation Methods" on page 275.

29. Biomorph produced from $z \rightarrow z^5 + \mu$. For more information on how to create this image, see "Genesis Equations" on page 104.

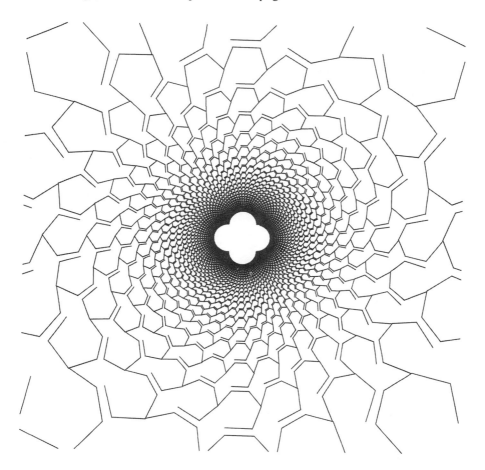

Appendix B

Additional Recipes

Included in this Appendix are a few additional computer graphics experiments and curiosities which are easy to implement. Some of the systems are illustrative of complicated behavior in simple systems.

B.1 Chaos from bits

The simple routine in Pseudocode B.1 produces complicated behavior as a result of examining a bit within an integer represented in its binary form. The integer is a function of $i^2 \times j$ where i and j are loop counters. Some similar work has been done by Neil J. Rubenking (Contributing Editor, *PC Magazine*) who has written to me about interesting patterns from other bit-checking routines. (For analysis: Pick89 and Lakh, *J. Recr. Math.*)

B.2 Dynamical Systems

The set of equations in Pseudocode B.2 produces visually interesting orbits from 2-D dynamical systems. An initial point in the *x-y* plane is selected and the four lines in the pseudocode are repeated – giving rise to the trajectories through time. Figure B.2 and Figure B.3 are portraits for different values of lambda.

B.3 Cartoon Faces for Multidimensional Data Portrayal

Pseudocode B.3 can be used to create the cartoon faces discussed in "Autocorrelation Cartoon-Faces for Speech" on page 47. The input arguments are 10 facial parameters (p1,p2,...,p10), whose values range from 0 to 10. All 5's generally produce a middle-setting face. The only drawing routines the reader must provide are MoveTo, LineTo, and Circle whose functions are to move to a

```
ALGORITHM: Chaos from Bits
─────────────────────────────────────────────────────────────
Variables: n = the position in the bit string
 The variable test is a bit.  Test2 is an 8-bit variable.
 Iprod is an integer.
Output : dots plotted according to the nth bit in the bit string
Notes: Try n=5.
─────────────────────────────────────────────────────────────
do fi = 1 to 200;
 do fj = 1 to 200;
  iprod=fi**2*fj;          (* compute an integer            *)
  test2=convert(iprod);    (* convert the integer to bits   *)
  test= substr(test2,n,1); (* take the nth bit in bit string *)
  if test then PrintDotAt (fi,fj);(* if the bit is 1, print *)
 End;
End;
```

Pseudocode B.1. *Chaos from bits.*

point, draw a line, and draw a circle, respectively. The graphics screen is assumed to range from 0 to 100 in the x and y directions. The face is centered at (50,50).

B.4 Symmetrized Random-Dot Patterns

The use of symmetry operations on dot patterns was discussed in several sections of Part II in this book. Presented here are symmetrized *random dot-patterns.* Since the patterns are so easy to compute, and so beautiful to look at, we spend a little space describing their generation.

B.4.1 Recipe

What happens if randomly positioned dots on a plane are subject to symmetry operations such as rotation and reflection? Will the resulting pictures also appear random, or will the eye find interesting structures? A number of visual demonstrations can be created by performing symmetry operations on a distribution of random dots. If a pattern of random dots is superimposed on itself and rotated by an angle several times, a variety of intricate global structures is easily perceived in the resultant pattern. Aesthetic figures can be produced with mirror planes at multiples of 60 degrees. To start, a random (r, θ) value is chosen. When a randomly positioned parent dot is selected by computer, it is subsequently reflected about the six mirror planes. This process is repeated n times. The symmetry creates organized patterns from randomness.

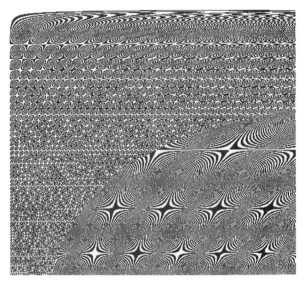

Figure B.1. *Chaos from Bits.* (See Pseudocode B.1).

B.4.2 Sqrt(r) Dot-Patterns

Since the selection of a random *r* and random *θ* for each initial dot naturally creates higher dot densities at lower *r* in polar space, an attempt can be made to suppress this feature. Instead of computing *r* directly from *δ* (*δ* is a random number from 0 to 1), *r* is computed from $\sqrt{\delta}$. For all such figures, it appears that global correlations are more easily perceived the further away one views the figure, and features not seen at all from close inspection may become apparent (test this for yourself).

```
ALGORITHM: Another dynamical system.

Suggested Parameters:
aa= 0.9;bb= 0.8;cc= 0.7;dd= 0.6
Note:  Choose an initial (xx,yy) coordinate, and loop through
these equations about 30 times. Then choose another coordinate...
By gradually changing lambda from 0.1 to 0.8 and assembling
a series of pictures, one can watch the evolution of a variety
of behaviors (fixed points, bifurcations, limit cycles...)
(see Figure B.2 and Figure B.3).

1. xold=xx; yold=yy;
2. xx =    ee*(i)+ (aa*xold-lambda*g(cc*yold));
3. yy =    ee*(i)+ (bb*yold+lambda*g(dd*xold));
4. PlotDot(xx,yy);
```

Pseudocode B.2. *Another dynamical system.*

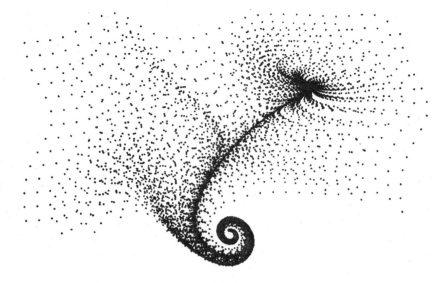

Figure B.2. *Dynamical system* See Pseudocode B.2.

B.4.3 Random Walk Dot-Patterns

An attempt to induce further order from the chaotically positioned dots is seen in Figure B.4. In these cases, a higher correlation between the *initially* selected random dots is achieved as described in the following equations:

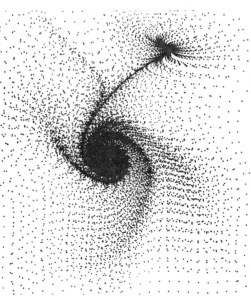

Figure B.3. *Dynamical system* See Pseudocode B.2.

```
ALGORITHM: Draw Chernoff-like faces

Notes: The computer generated faces in various sections of this
book were generated using the following subroutines.
Ten integer input parameters p(1)...p(10) control the facial
coordinates.

FACES:
(* 10 input parameters *)
PROCEDURE (p1,p2,p3,p4,p5,p6,p7,p8,p9,p10);
p(1)=p1; p(2) = p2; p(3) = p3; p(4) = p4;
p(5) = p5; p(6)=p6; p(7) = p7; p(8) = p8;
p(9) = p9; p(10) = p10;
    call head;
call eye;
call pupil;
call eyebrow;
call nose;
call mouth;
(* ----- Head Shape ----------*)
(* range 0-10.   5 is circle *)
head: proc;
eccenx=0;ecceny=0; radius = 30;
if p(1) > 5 then do;
  eccenx = (p(1)-5)*2;
end;
if p(1) < 5 then do;
  ecceny = abs((p(1)-5))*2;
end;
do theta = 1 to 360;
  x = (radius + eccenx)*cosd(theta) + 50;
  y = (radius + ecceny)*sind(theta) + 50;
if theta = 1 then call MoveTo(x,y);
else call LineTo(x,y);
end;
end head;
```

Pseudocode B.3 (Part 1 of 3). *How to draw Chernoff-like faces.*

$$r_{i+1} = r_i + \alpha\sqrt{\delta_{i+1}} \, ; \quad \theta_{i+1} = \theta_i + \beta\delta_{i+1}$$

where δ is a random number, and α and β are scale factors. Each new parent dot's position is related to the subsequent dot's position by a random walk process, and snowflake-like patterns are created. By varying α and β, a variety of distinct structural classes can be produced. In Figure B.4 the increment in r's walk is somewhat more restricted than the θ increment (i.e., $\alpha < \beta$). As might be expected, the higher the symmetry, the easier it is for most people to classify such patterns as organized, that is, non-random (Figure B.5). As the placement of dots on a vector-graphics display progresses during the course of creating the figure, a variety of geometrical forms evolve. After some time, original structures can no longer be perceived, as totally new forms take their place. An amusing avenue of future work would be to use dot distributions with different "second-order" characteristics. That is, each dot is disallowed from falling within a specified distance of another. (Pick89, *Recr. Educat. Comp. Newsletter.*)

```
(* ---- Eye Shape ------------*)
(* range 1-10.   5 is circle *)
eye: proc;
eccenx=0;ecceny=0; radius=5;
if p(2) > 5 then do;
 eccenx = (p(2)-5)*2;
end;
if p(2) < 5 then do;
 ecceny = abs((p(2)-5))*2;
end;
p(7) = p(7) - 5;      /* eye spacing */
p(8) = (p(8) - 5)/2; /* eye size    */
do theta = 1 to 360 ;
 x = (radius+p(8)+eccenx)*cosd(theta)+40-p(7);
 y = (radius+p(8) + ecceny)*sind(theta) + 60;
 if theta = 1 then call MoveTo(x,y);
 else call LineTo(x,y);
end;
do theta = 1 to 360;
 x = (radius+p(8)+eccenx)*cosd(theta)+60+p(7);
 y = (radius+p(8) + ecceny)*sind(theta)+60;
 if theta = 1 then call MoveTo(x,y);
 else call LineTo(x,y);
end;
end eye;
(*-------Pupil Size---------*)
pupil: proc;
dcl (k,pupilsize) float;
select(p(3));
when(0) do; pupilsize = .1;end;
when(1) do; pupilsize = .2; end;
when(2) do; pupilsize = .4; end;
when(3) do; pupilsize = .6; end;
when(4) do; pupilsize = .8; end;
when(5) do; pupilsize = 1; end;
when(6) do; pupilsize = 1.2; end;
when(7) do; pupilsize = 1.4; end;
when(8) do; pupilsize = 1.6; end;
when(9) do; pupilsize = 1.8; end;
when(10) do; pupilsize = 2.0; end;
when(11) do; pupilsize = 2.2; end;
end;
do k = pupilsize to 0 by - .2;
 (* draw circle centered at x,y with radius k *)
 call Circle (40-p(7),60,k);  (* pupil *)
 call Circle (60+p(7),60,k);  (* pupil *)
end;
end pupil;
```

Pseudocode B.3 (Part 2 of 3). *How to draw Chernoff-like faces.*

B.5 Burnt Paper

"Burnt paper" can be simulated by superimposing randomly positioned, randomly sized circles. The resulting summed intensity values are mapped to gray levels (see Figure B.6). Similar techniques have been used to simulate clouds (Ogden,

```
(*----------Eyebrow Slope-------------*)
eyebrow: proc;
y1 = 70;
y2 = 70;
y1 = (p(4)-5) + y1;
y2 = y2 - (p(4)-5) ;
call MoveTo(35,y1); call LineTo(45,y2);
call MoveTo(55,y2); call LineTo(65,y1);
end eyebrow;
(*---------Nose Size-----------------*)
nose: proc;
p(5) = (p(5)-5)*.5;
call MoveTo(50,55);    /* nose*/
call LineTo(46,45+p(5));
call LineTo(54,45+p(5));
call LineTo(50,55);
end nose;
(*-----------Mouth--------------------*)
mouth: proc;
p(9) = p(9) -5;   /* mouth size */
x1 = 40-p(9);y1=35;
x2 = 60+p(9); y2 = 35;
x3 = (x2-x1)/2 + x1;
y3 = (p(6) -5) +35;
(* construct mouth with parabolic interpolation *)
do k = 1 to 2;
  if k = 2 then y3 = y3 + p(10)/2;
  call MoveTo(x1,y1);
  denom=x1**2*(x2-x3)+x1*(x3**2-x2**2)+x2**2*x3-x3**2*x2;
  a=(y1*(x2-x3)+x1*(y3-y2)+y2*x3-y3*x2)/denom;
  bb=(x1**2*(y2-y3)+y1*(x3**2-x2**2)+x2**2*y3-x3**2*y2)/denom;
  c=(x1**2*(x2*y3-x3*y2)+x1*(x3**2*y2-x2**2*y3)
  +y1*(x2**2*x3-x3**2*x2))/denom;
  do i = x1 to x2;
    call LineTo (i,a*i**2+bb*i+c);
  end;
end; /* end k loop */
end mouth;
END FACES;
```

Pseudocode B.3 (Part 3 of 3). *How to draw Chernoff-like faces.*

1985). To achieve the ragged paper edge, confine the selection of circle center positions to a square boundary within the larger picture boundary.

B.6 Picturing Randomness with Truchet Tiles

This appendix section provides a light introduction to a simple graphics technique which uses tiles to visualize random data. In particular, Truchet-like tiles are used for representing graphically interesting manifestations of chaotic behavior. Interesting tiling patterns can be created using an orientable square tile with curved lines that join to produce continuous closures regardless of how the tiles are oriented.

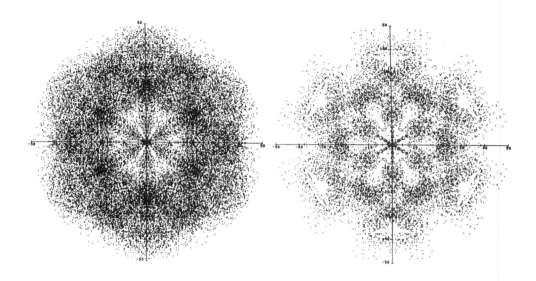

Figure B.4. *Random walk dot-displays.* r and θ are determined in a random walk manner (see text).

A generating tile can be represented as:

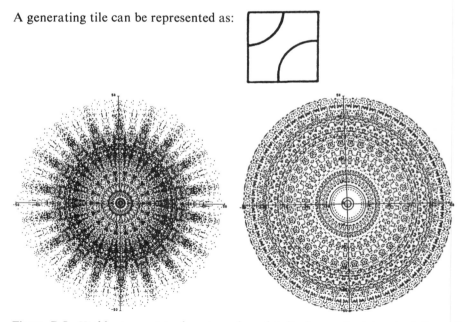

Figure B.5. *Highly symmetrized sqrt random dot-displays.* r is determined from the square root of a random number. The mirror planes occur more frequently than in the previous figure.

Figure B.6. *Burnt paper.*

To produce Figure B.7 simply orient the generating square randomly and place it within the corner of a large square lattice. Add successive adjacent tiles to the lattice for a particular row until it is filled, and start a new row. Continue this process until the lattice is filled. This is easily achieved with a computer program using binary values $\{B_i, \; i = 1,2,3, \ldots, N\}$, with random values of 0 and 1 for B_i. Simply map B_i to two different orientations of the tiles. For random orientations, the *circle fraction* is approximately 0.054 (number of closed circles in the pattern divided by the number of tiles). The *dumbbell fraction* is approximately 0.0125 (number of closed bilobed shapes divided by the number of tiles). Note that the eye perceives no particular trends in the design. This kind of pattern is reminiscent of the tiles of Sebastien Truchet (Smith, 1987). Truchet's paper, written in 1704, shows that numerous patterns can be generated by the assembly of single half-colored tiles in various orientations.

The tiles in Figure B.7 can be used to represent different kinds of noise distributions or experimental data. In particular, by using this approach, subtle differences in the noise distributions become visually apparent. For example, consider binary data $\{B_i, \; i = 1,2,3, \ldots, N\}$ where the 0/1 sequence is not "completely random" but can be described as a stationary Markov process with the transition matrix P:

$$P = \begin{bmatrix} P_0 & 1 - P_0 \\ 1 - P_1 & P_1 \end{bmatrix} \qquad (B.1)$$

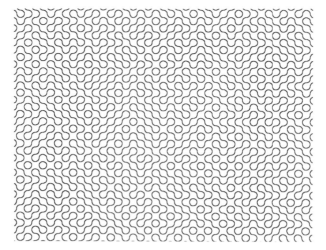

Figure B.7. *Truchet tile characterization of noise.*

P_0 and P_1 are the probabilities that B_i is equal to zero or one, respectively, if B_{i-1} is equal to zero. P_1 and $1 - P_1$ are the probabilities that B_i is equal to one or zero, respectively, if B_{i-1} is equal to one. Since the values of B_i depend on the values at B_{i-1}, even small deviations from randomness (P_0, $P_1 \neq 0.5$) are visually manifested in patterns in the tiles. The reader is encouraged to experiment with different probabilities and view the tiles. The resulting patterns for the Markov process are left as a puzzle and surprise to the reader. Enjoy! For maze aficionados, the random and Markov approach both provide a mechanism for generating an infinite variety of hard-to-solve mazes.

Note that the graphical detection and characterization of subtle patterns within random data is an area of active interest (Voelcker, 1988). Since the Truchet approach is so sensitive to certain deviations from randomness, it may have value in helping researchers find patterns in complicated data. (Pick89, *J. Recr. Math.*) For the relationship of similar kinds of tilings to fractals, see Roux et al., 1988. For historical background on similar tilings, see Smith, 1987.

B.7 Circles Which Kiss: A Note on Osculatory Packing

This appendix section provides several simple recipes for graphically interesting structures based on the osculatory packing of finite areas using circles and spheres. The problem of covering a finite area with a given set of circles has received frequent attention (Klausch-Becken et al., 1970). As background, the densest packing of non-overlapping uniform circles is the hexagonal lattice packing where the ratio of covered area to the total area (*packing fraction*) is $\phi = \pi/\sqrt{12} = 0.9069$. The limiting packing fraction for nested hexagonal packing of circles, with k *different* circle sizes is

```
ALGORITHM: Truchet tile generation.

Note: A method for generating a Markov process is included
(see text).  If p0 and p1 are 0.5, then simple random numbers are
generated and mapped to the tile orientations.

  xoff = 2.5; yoff=2.5;     /* parameters for tile placement     */
  dx,dy = 2.5;  r=dx/2;     /* a screen size of 100x100 is assumed */
  jump = 105/dx;  olddata = 0;

  get list(p1,p0);          /* enter the probability factors     */
  do j = 1 to N;            /* generate N tiles                  */
    Random(result);        /* return a random number on (0,1)   */
    if olddata=0 then if result < p0 then data = 0; else data=1;
    if olddata=1 then if result < p1 then data = 1; else data=0;
    if data = 1 then call up;   /* an orientation of the tile    */
    if data = 0 then call down; /* opposite orientation of tile  */
    /* ----- fill lattice in x and y directions --------------   */
    xoff = xoff+dx;             /* change x position of tile      */
    if mod(j,jump)=0 then do;yoff=yoff+dy; xoff=0; end;
    if yoff > 100 then stop; olddata=data;
  end;
  /* ------------ Draw "Up" Orientation of Tile -----------------*/
  up: proc;
    if olddata = 0 then xoff=xoff+dx;
    do i = 90 to 180 by 10;          /* units in degrees         */
      x = r*cosd(i)+xoff;  y = r*sind(i)+yoff;
      if i = 90 then Move(x,y); else Pen(x,y); /* draw the curve */
    end;
    xc=xoff-dx;yc=yoff+dy;
    do i = 270 to 360 by 10;   /* generate the other curved line */
      x = r*cosd(i)+xc; y = r*sind(i)+yc;
      if i = 270 then Move(x,y);  else Pen(x,y);
    end;
  end up;
  /* --------- Draw "Down" Orientation of Tile -----------------*/
  down: proc;
    if olddata = 1 then xoff=xoff-dx;
    do i = 0 to 90 by 10;
      x = r*cosd(i)+xoff;       y = r*sind(i)+yoff;
      if i = 0 then Move(x,y);   else     Pen(x,y);
    end;
    xc=xoff+dx;yc=yoff+dy;
    do i = 180 to 270 by 10;
      x = r*cosd(i)+xc;          y = r*sind(i)+yc;
      if i = 180  then Move(x,y); else Pen(x,y);
    end;
  end down;
```

Pseudocode B.4. *Truchet tile generation.*

$$\phi_k = 1 - (1 - 0.9069)^k \qquad\qquad (B.2)$$

This applies to cases where each of the uncovered areas, or *interstices*, is also hexagonally packed by smaller circles. For larger values of k, ϕ_k approaches unity (Kausch-Blecken et al., 1970).

Past work has usually defined a distribution of circles as *osculatory* if any available area is always covered by the largest possible circle (Kausch-Blecken et

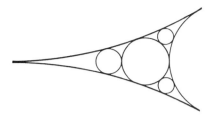

Figure B.8. *Tricuspid interstices in standard osculatory packing.*

al., 1970). If the original area to be covered is a tricuspid area (Figure B.8), then
the first circle to be placed must be tangent to the three original larger circles.
This kind of packing is also often referred to as *Apollonian packing* (Boyd, 1973;
Mandelbrot, 1983). In contrast to past work, the criterion for osculatory packing
is relaxed here: each successively placed circle on the plane need only be tangent
to at least *one* previous circle (*tangent-1 packing*). To generate the artistic figures
in this section, a circle center is randomly placed within the available interstice.
The circle then grows until it becomes tangent to its closest neighbor. The process
is repeated several thousand times. One easy way to simulate this on a computer
is to determine the distances d_i from the newly selected circle center to all other
circles i on the plane. Let

$$\delta_i = d_i - r_i \qquad (B.3)$$

where r_i is the radius of circle i. $\min\{\delta_i\}$ is then the radius of the new circle. Note
that if there exists a negative δ_i then the selected center is within a circle on the
plane. In this case the circle center is discarded, and a new attempt to place a
circle is made.

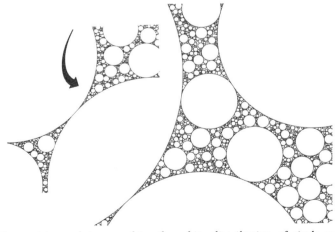

Figure B.9. *Tangent-1 osculatory packing for white distribution of circle centers.* The
embedded figure, pointed to by the arrow, is actually a magnification of a tiny section of
the packing plot.

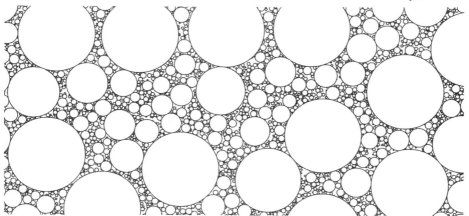

Figure B.10. *Osculatory packing for white distribution of circle centers.* In this figure, an upper bound for allowed circle radii is used.

Circle center distributions were chosen in three ways in order to generate artistic patterns. In Figure B.9 the circle centers were selected using a uniform white nose generator. To the right is is a magnification of a tiny area in the left picture. In Figure B.10, an upper bound was used for the largest allowed circle size. Figure B.11 is created from Brownian (random walk) noise. To create this figure, the center positions of the newly placed circles were computed from:

$$x_i = x_{i-1} + \lambda_1 + r_{i-1} \cos(2\pi\lambda_2)$$
$$y_i = y_{i-1} + \lambda_3 + r_{i-1} \sin(2\pi\lambda_2)$$

$$(B.4)$$

where λ is a random number. Color plate 3 shows tangent-1 spheres with a Gaussian-white center distribution. The Gaussian noise was produced by

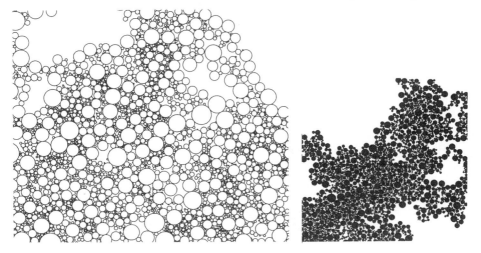

Figure B.11. *Brownian distribution of circle centers.* Also shown is a plot in which the total covering area is visually accented by filling these regions.

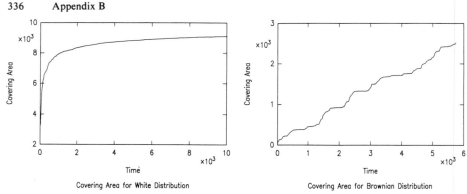

Figure B.12. *Covering-area functions for white and brown tangent-1 packing.*

$$G = (1/n) \sum_{k=1}^{n} \lambda_k \qquad\qquad (B.5)$$

where λ_k are random numbers on $(0,1)$, and $n = 5$. Note that n can have different values for the x and y directions. Color Plate 3 shows a simple, easy-to-implement model of soap bubbles produced by ray-tracing a Gaussian osculatory distribution of spherical shells (Equation (B.3) is extended to three dimensions). Two light sources were used to produce the figure, and the picture resolution is 1024x1024. Figure B.12 shows covering-area-vs.-time plots for circles placed on a 100x100-unit plane. "Time" indicates the number of attempts to place a circle. For a white distribution of circles, the value for the covering area rapidly achieves a plateau as available voids are filled. For the Brownian distribution, the covering area function has a very different shape. The various intermediate plateaus indicate packed domains in which the wandering circles temporarily get trapped (because surrounding voids are scarce). Since the circle sizes are not constrained to some minimum radius, the wandering circle can always "squeeze" its way out of a tightly packed area.

The fractal dimensions D for these pictures can be computed from the mass-radius power law relationship $m \sim r^D$. $m(r)$ is the combined area of all circles contained within a measuring circle of radius r. By observing the change in mass as a function of r, the dimension can be empirically computed. For the white osculatory tangent-1 packing, $D \sim 2$. Statistical self-similarity of the packing in Figure B.9 indicates that successive magnifications will have a similar appearance. For the Brownian distributions in Figure B.11 $D \sim 1.8$. Interestingly, recent research has used similar circle placement techniques to model thin-film growth and the kinetics of droplet formation (Family, 1988; Family and Meakin, 1988). Thin films play an increasingly important role in a variety of applications, from microelectronics to biochemical sensors. (Pick89, *Comput. Graph.*)

B.8 Markov Aggregation on a Sticky Circle

"Aggregation" describes growth arising from the agglomeration of diffusing particles. In 1981, Witten and Sander developed a computer model for aggregation starting with a single seed particle at the center of a space. Their computer program introduces a new particle which moves randomly until it approaches another particle and sticks to it. The first particles attach to the seed, but soon a branched, fractal structure evolves with a dimension of about 1.7. This process is called *diffusion limited aggregation* (DLA). Since the introduction of the Witten-Sander model in 1981, considerable research has been devoted to the properties of DLA (e.g., see Family and Landau (1984), Feder (1988)).

It is possible to place a little twist on the usual DLA experiments. Instead of using the single sticky seed particle, a sticky circle of particles is placed on a square (1024 x1024) lattice. Particles are introduced at the center of the circle and allowed to diffuse outward. They stick to the circle's edge when they are directly adjacent to it (thereby producing an "inverted DLA"). Rather than use random -1's and +1's to control the path of the diffusing particles in the x and y directions of the lattice, Markov random numbers are used to direct the walk (see "Picturing Randomness with Truchet Tiles" on page 329 to learn how to generate these random numbers). Figure B.13 shows an example structure. (For details: Pick89, *Comput. in Phys.*)

Figure B.13. *Markov aggregation on a sticky circle.* The upper right arrow shows the source of the diffusing particles at the circle's center. At the bottom is a small part of the sticky circle to which the particles adhere.

Appendix C

Suggestions for Future Experiments

This section provides some exercises and mathematical recreations for students, teachers, and other imaginative readers. References to the relevant chapters in this book are given.

1. Draw bifurcation plots for the following equations: a) $aX_t(1 - X_t)$, b) $X_t e^{r(1 - X_t)}$, and c) aX_t if $X_t < 0.5$, $a(1 - X_t)$ if $X_t > 0.5$. For what a value (x-axis of plot) does the fixed point become unstable? At what point does the chaotic region begin? See "Graphics, Bifurcation, Order and Chaos" on page 151 for background material.

2. Draw Julia set diagrams for $z \to z^2 + \mu$ where a) $\mu = -0.194 + 0.6557i$ or b) $\mu = 0.27334 + 0.00742i$. How do these shapes differ? See "Feedback" on page 96 for background material.

3. As demonstrated in "Physics: Charged Curves" on page 83, 3-D plots are useful in portraying complicated functions. Draw a 3-D plot for the following equation which describes a surface with one local minimum:

$$f(x,y) = \frac{-1}{1 + x^2} + (2y^2 - y^4) \left(e^x + \frac{1}{1 + x^2} \right) \tag{C.1}$$

By various scalings of the axes of the plot, this function takes on many different looks, and interesting behavior is revealed. See Ash and Sexton (1985) for more information on this function.

4. Even simple formulas have interesting behavior. Draw a graph of the *Devil's curve* (also known as the *Devil on two sticks*), which is the locus of

$$y^4 - a^2y^2 = x^4 - b^2x^2 \tag{C.2}$$

The polar equation is

$$r^2(\sin^2\theta - \cos^2\theta) = a^2 \sin^2\theta - b^2 \cos^2\theta. \tag{C.3}$$

Notice that the intercepts are at: $(0, \pm a)$, $(\pm b, 0)$, $(0,0)$. The asymptote is $x \pm y = 0$. See Lawrence (1972) for more information on this curve.

5. In "Number Theory" on page 173 we saw that integer equations have fascinating properties. For this problem, consider the number 153. One hundred fifty three is interesting because $153 = 1^3 + 5^3 + 3^3$. Numbers such as this are called Armstrong numbers. Any N digit number is an Armstrong number if the sum of the N-th power of the digits is equal to the original number. Another example is 370 ($370 = 27 + 343 + 0$). As an interesting number theory experiment, write a program to generate all 3-digit Armstrong numbers. See Spencer (1982) for additional information.

6. "Numerical Approximation Methods" on page 275 demonstrates intricate Halley map graphics for polynomial equations. For this exercise, try a new equation. Draw a Halley map for a Hermite polynomial, H. For example, $H_4 = 16x^4 - 48x^2 + 12$. Where do the roots of the equation lie? Where is the region of chaotic fragmentation between roots?

7. Extend the hailstone number graphs in "Patterns in Hailstone (3n+1) Numbers" on page 185 to related sequences. For example, consider $4n+1$ numbers. Start with a number, and divide by 3. If there is no remainder, the quotient is the next number in the series. For a remainder of 1, multiply by 4 and subtract 1. For a remainder of 2, multiply by 4 and add one. Repeat. To the author's knowledge, no graphs of this sequence have been published. See Wiggin (1988) for more information on $4n+1$ numbers.

8. "Fourier Analysis: A Digression and Review" on page 21 describes how complicated waveforms can be created by adding sinusoids. The exotic *Prasad* function, below, is described in a chapter on oscillations of non-differentiable functions in Hobson's book *Squaring the Circle*. The reader may wish to plot the first few terms of the summation and read more about this curve's properties:

$$W(x) = \sum_n \frac{\cos(13^n \pi x)}{2^n} \tag{C.4}$$

Another relatively obscure curve which the reader may wish to plot is the Faber function. Consider $\psi(x)$, a polygonal function of period 1, such that in $(0,1)$ $\psi(x) = x$ for $0 \le x \le 0.5$, and $\psi(x) = 1 - x$ for $0.5 \le x \le 1$. The Faber function is

$$\sum_1^\infty \frac{1}{10^n} \psi(2^{n!}x). \tag{C.5}$$

Appendix D

Descriptions for Chapter Frontpiece Figures

The large illustrations preceding the chapters in this book are briefly described in this section.

1. The frontpiece for the dedication page of the book is a Halley map for a polynomial. See "Numerical Approximation Methods" on page 275 for more information on Halley maps.

2. The figure preceding *Part I: Introduction* is a magnification of a Halley map for $\zeta^7 - 1 = 0$. Here level sets of $\beta(\zeta)$ are indicated. $\beta(\zeta) = \sup\{|H_{\zeta_0}^n|: n = 1, 2, \ldots\}$. The figure indicates contours, or levels, of β. (The term "sup" stands for supremum and indicates the least upper bound of a set. For example, $\sup\{1, 5, 9, 2\}$ is simply 9.) This figure is a magnification of a small region of the frontpiece for Chapter 13.

3. The frontpiece for Chapter 1 is the same as the preceding frontpiece, except a Chebyshev polynomial is used $(T_7(\zeta) = 0)$. Picture boundaries are: $-1 < \mathrm{Re}(\zeta) < 1$, $-1 < \mathrm{Im}(\zeta) < 1$.

4. The frontpiece for Chapter 2 is a modified Halley nodule for $\zeta^7 - 1 = 0$.

5. The frontpiece for *Part II: Representing Nature* shows a cross section of pin oak wood (Harlow, 1976).

6. The frontpiece for Chapter 3 shows a Halley nodule for $\zeta^7 + \zeta^2 - 1 = 0$. (See Pick88q, *Commun. ACM* for color version.)

7. The frontpiece for Chapter 4 shows a region inside the traditional Mandelbrot set. The method used to create the contours comes from Peitgen and Richter (1986). (See Pick89, *Algorithm* for details.)

8. The frontpiece for Chapter 5 is *The Holy Trinity* by Albrecht Durer.

9. The frontpiece for Chapter 6 shows stalks within the traditional Mandelbrot set. This is a magnification of a small region in the frontpiece for Chapter 15. Here is a hint on how to create the figure. As the trajectory of a starting point meanders around the complex plane, occasionally it is can be trapped in a cross-shaped aperture. Those starting points which lead to trajectories that

land inside the cross are then colored black, forming beautiful and eerie stalks within the M-set. (See Pick89, *Algorithm* for details.)

10. The frontpiece for Chapter 7 shows a shield-fern (*Polystichum munitum*) (Blossfeldt, 1985).

11. The frontpiece for *Part III: Pattern, Symmetry, Beauty* shows an upright birthwort (*Arsitolochia Clematitis*).

12. The frontpiece for Chapter 8 is an overrelaxed Halley map for a seventh order Chebyshev polynomial ($T_7(\zeta) = 0$). Overrelaxation can "shatter" the contours in artistically interesting ways (see section 15.1.1 and Pick89, *Comput. in Phys.*).

13. The frontpiece for Chapter 9 is a modified Halley map for $\zeta^7 - 1 = 0$. (Pick89, *Physica Scripta*.)

14. The frontpiece for Chapter 10 is a modified Halley map for $\zeta^7 - 1 = 0$.

15. The frontpiece for Chapter 11 is a Halley map for a seventh order Chebyshev polynomial ($T_7(\zeta) = 0$).

16. The frontpiece for Chapter 12 shows the posterior primary division of spinal nerves in a human, drawn by A. Vesalius (1514-1564).

17. The frontpiece for Chapter 13 is a modified Halley map for $\zeta^7 - 1 = 0$.

18. The frontpiece for Chapter 14 shows a dynamical system. An initial point at the origin creates this complicated trajectory after iterating a few million times.

19. The frontpiece for Chapter 15 shows stalks within the traditional Mandelbrot set. (Also see the frontpiece for Chapter 6).

20. The frontpiece for Chapter 16 is a magnification of a region Halley map for $\zeta^7 - 1 = 0$.

21. The frontpiece for Chapter 17 is a magnification of a region Halley map for $\zeta^7 - 1 = 0$. (Pick88, *Phys. Lett. A*.)

22. The frontpiece after Chapter 17 shows a 3-D dynamical system produced by iterating a point at the origin 5 million times.

23. The frontpiece for Appendix A is a Julia set biomorph for $z \to \sin(z) + z^2 + \mu$ ($\mu = 0.1 + 0.1i$). For more information on how to create this image, see "Genesis Equations" on page 104.

24. The frontpiece for Appendix B is a Julia set representation for $z \to z^2 + \mu$.

25. The frontpiece for Appendix C shows stalks within the inside-out Mandelbrot set defined by $z \to z^p + (1/\mu)^p$ where $p = 3$.

26. The frontpiece for Appendix D shows stalks within the traditional Mandelbrot set.

27. The frontpiece for the Reference Section shows a self-decorating egg, as defined in Chapter 13.

28. The frontpiece for Credits shows an inside-out Mandelbrot set for the mapping $z \to z^p + (1/\mu)^p$ where $p = 2$.

29. The frontpiece for the *About the Author* page represents a Julia set for $z \to \sin(z) + \mu$. ($\mu = 0.1 + 0.1i$.)

The seashell on the cover of the book is based upon a logarithmic spiral and rendered on a graphics supercomputer. The background is a digitized image of a leaf vein pattern. For more details see "Seashells" on page 218. Also see (Pick89, *IEEE Comput. Graph. Appl.*).

The tile pattern on the last page of Appendix A reveals the behavior of a geometrical process known as *inversion* acting upon a square lattice of incomplete hexagons.

The image on this page is quartic variant of a Phoenix Julia set $z = f(z^4, z^3, y)$. For a lower order Phoenix curve, see (Ushiki, 1988). The frontpiece for the Glossary section is another Phoenix variant. Arrows indicate interesting self-similar regions showing a wealth of detail when magnified.

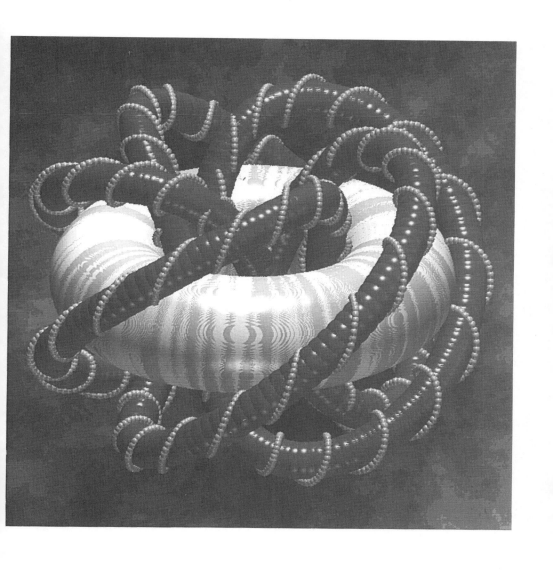

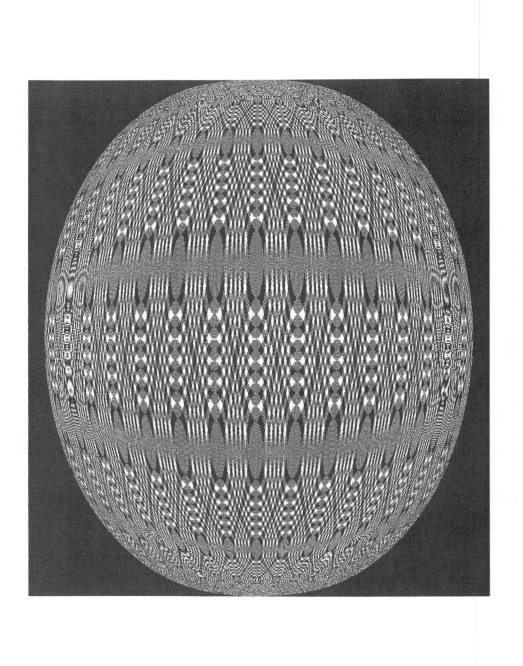

References (General)

Recommended Reading

These works are among the author's favorite references and are highly recommended. These are "the best of the best."

Barratt, K. (1980) *Logic and Design in Art, Science, and Mathematics*. Design Press: New York. (The pictures alone will stimulate readers to experiment further.)

Beiler, A. (1964) *Recreations in the Theory of Numbers*. Dover: New York.

Chen, S. (1987) *The IBM Programmer's Challenge*. TAB Books: Pennsylvania.

Davis, P., Hersh, R. (1981) *The Mathematical Experience*. Houghton Mifflin Company: Boston.

Dewdney, A.K. (1988) *The Armchair Universe*. Freeman: New York.

Devlin, K. (1988) *Mathematics: The New Golden Age*. Penguin Books: New York.

Eigen, M., Winkler, R. (1983) *Laws of the Game: How the Principles of Nature Govern Chance*. Harper Colophon: New York.

Ellis, K. (1978) Is God a Number? In *Number Power In Nature, Art, and Everyday Life*. St. Martin's Press: New York.

Gleick, J. (1987) *Chaos: Making a New Science*. Viking: New York.

Hargittai, I. (1986) Special Issue on Symmetry. In *Comput. and Math. with Appl.* Vol 12B (May-August). Pergamon Press: New York. (An entire issue devoted to symmetry in art, science, music, and literature). Also see Hargittai, I., ed. (1989) *Symmetry 2, Unifying Human Understanding*. Pergamon Press: Oxford.

Hoffman, P. (1987) The Man Who Loves Only Numbers. The Atlantic Magazine. November Issue. pp. 60-74.

James, G., James, R. (1976) *Mathematics Dictionary*, 4th Ed., Van Nostrand Reinhold Co.: New York.

Moon, F. (1987) *Chaotic Vibrations*. John Wiley and Sons, New York.

Ouspensky, P. (1970) *Tertium Organum, A Third Canon of Thought: A Key to the Enigmas of the World.* Vintage Books: New York. (This book, translated from the Russian original, may be a bit too mystical for some readers. Topics include: 4-dimensional space, art, and transfinite numbers).

Peterson, I. (1988) *The Mathematical Tourist.* Freeman: New York.

Pierce, J. (1983) *The Science of Musical Sound.* Scien. Amer. Library: New York.

Peitgen, H., Richter, P. (1986) *The Beauty of Fractals.* Springer: Berlin.

Postle, D. (1976) *Fabric of the Universe.* Crown: New York.

Press, W., Flannery, B., Teukolsky, S., Vetterling, W. (1986) *Numerical Recipes.* Cambridge Univ. Press: New York.

Reitman, E. (1989) *Exploring the Geometry of Nature.* Windcrest Books: Pennsylvania.

Reichardt, J. (1969) *Cybernetic Serendipity: The Computer and the Arts.* Prager: New York.

Rucker, R. (1982) *Infinity and the Mind.* Bantam: New York.

Shaw, A. (1984) *The Dripping Faucet as a Model Chaotic System.* Aerial Press: California.

Stevens, C. (1989) *Fractal Programming in C.* M and T Books: Redwood City, California. (This book is a dream come true for computer programmers interested in fractals.)

Stewart, I. (1987) The nature of stability. Speculations in Science and Tech. 10(4): 310-324.

Stewart, I. (1989) *Does God Play Dice? (The Mathematics of Chaos).* Basil Blackwell: New York.

Spencer, D. (1982) *Computers in Number Theory.* Computer Science Press: Maryland. (An easy-to-read book with computational recipes.)

Steinhaus, H. (1983) *Mathematical Snapshots,* 3rd ed. Oxford Univ. Press: New York. (Topics include tesselations, soap-bubbles, maps, screws, spiders, honeycombs, and platonic solids.)

"Symmetries and Asymmetries" (1985) *Mosaic* Volume 16, Number 1, January/February. (An entire issue on the subject of fractals, symmetry and chaos. *Mosaic* is published six times a year as a source of information for scientific and educational communities served by the National Science Foundation, Washington DC 20550).

Tufte, E. (1983) *The Visual Display of Quantitative Information.* Graphics Press: Connecticut.

Waisman, F. (1959) *Introduction to Mathematical Thinking.* Harper Torchbooks: New York. (Topics include remarkable curves, unreal numbers and hypercomplex numbers).

Young, L. (1965) *The Mystery of Matter.* Oxford University Press: New York.

Wainer, H., Thissen, D. (1981) Graphical Data Analysis. Ann. Rev. Psychol. 32: 191-241.

Wolff, R. (1988) The visualization challenge in the physical sciences. Computers in Science. Jan./Feb. 2(1): 16-31.

Interesting and Unusual Newsletters, Distributors, Columns, Misc.

AMYGDALA, a fascinating newsletter on fractals. Write to AMYGDALA, Box 219, San Cristobal, New Mexico 87564 for more information.

MEDIA MAGIC: The Fractal Universe Catalog, PO Box 507, Nicasio, California 94946. This fine company distributes books, videos, prints, and calendars.

ART MATRIX, creator of postcards and videotapes of exciting mathematical shapes. Write to ART MATRIX, PO Box 880, Ithaca, New York 14851 for more information.

Fractal Report, a newsletter on fractals. Published by J. de Rivaz, Reeves Telecommunications Lab. West Towan House, Porthtowan, Cornwall TR4 8AX, United Kingdom.

Celluar Automata Laboratory, by Dr. Rudy Rucker. This set of software allows the user to produce stunning animated computer graphics with ease, and simulate physical and biological phenomena. Write Autodesk, Inc., 2320 Marinship Way. Sausalito, CA 94965.

Computer Recreations column, by A. K. Dewdney, in *Scientific American.*

Algorithm - The Personal Computer Newsletter. P.O. Box 29237, Westmount Postal Outlet, 785 Wonderland Road S., London, Ontario, Canada, N6K, 1M6. Topics include fractals and recreational mathematics.

The Journal of Chaos and Graphics, an informal newsletter on aesthetic and unusual graphics derived from mathematics (see the "Works of the Author" section for more information).

I. Peterson's interesting columns, frequently on topics in mathematics and graphics, in *Science News.*

Recreational and Educational Computing Newsletter. Write to Dr. M. Ecker, 129 Carol Drive, Clarks Summit, PA 18411, for more information on this interesting newsletter.

Quantum Quarterly. This newsletter lists scientific books on fractals, mathematical recreations, etc. Contact Quantum Books, One Kendall Square, Cambridge, MA 02139.

YLEM – Artists using science and technology. This newsletter is published by an organization of artists who work with video, ionized gases, computers, lasers, holograms, robotics, and other nontraditional media. It also includes artists who use traditional media but who are inspired by images of electromagnetic phenomena, biological self-replication, and fractals. Contact: YLEM, Box 749, Orinda, CA 94563.

The Yates Collection. Softbound books, with titles such as *Repunits and Reptends*, dealing with mathematical curiosities. The books are not for the beginner. Write to Samuel Yates, 157 Capri-D, Kings Point, Delray Beach, Florida 33445.

Fractal Calendar. Address inquiries to J. Loyless, 5185 Ashford Court, Lilburn, Georgia 30247.

Creative Publications, Inc. Posters on mathematics showing, for example, the first few thousand prime numbers, huge prime numbers, etc. Address inquiries to P.O. Box 10328, Palo Alto, CA 94303.

Fractals, and the Cat in the Hat. This is actually a scholarly paper to be published in *The Journal of Recreational Mathematics.* Describes scaling laws and the recursive structure of the infinitely nested cats in a book by Dr. Seuss. Preprint available from: Dr. A. Lakhtakia, Pennsylvania State University, 227 Hammond Bldg, University Park, PA 16802.

John's Picks. A great 30-page publication which describes and markets books, and a range of products, on the subjects of: fractals, chaos, neural networks, mathematical puzzles, computer graphics, cellular automata, Escher, computer physics, games, curiosities, etc. This is published three times a year. Contact Microcomputer Applications, P.O. Box E, Suisun City, California 94585-1050.

Recommended Journals

Leonardo, published by Pergamon Press, Headington Hill Hall, Oxford OX3 0BW, UK. This fascinating interdisciplinary journal combines arts, science and technology.

Computer Music Journal, published by MIT Press, 28 Carleton Street, Cambridge, MA 02142.

Complex Systems, published by Complex Systems Press, P.O. Box 6149, Champain, IL 61821-8149. This mathematically sophisticated journal is primarily devoted to cellular automata.

"Chaos and Graphics Section" of *Computers and Graphics*, published by Pergamon Press, Headington Hill Hall, Oxford OX3 0BW, UK.

Journal of Recreational Mathematics, published by Baywood Publishing Co., 26 Austin Ave, P.O. Box 337, Amityville, NY 11701. This journal is a must for readers interested in mathematical curiosities.

Symmetry, published by VCH Publishers, Suite 909, 220 East 23rd Street, New York, New York 10160-0425. A fascinating interdisciplinary journal concerning symmetry in all areas of human endeavor.

Computer Language, published by Miller Freeman Publications, 500 Howard St, San Francisco, CA 94105. This magazine gives computer recipes for a wide range of computer applications.

References by Topic and Section

Part I - Introduction

De Bono, E. (1970) *Lateral Thinking: Creativity Step by Step*. Harper and Row: New York.

Franke, H. (1985) *Computer Graphics - Computer Art*. Springer-Verlag: Berlin.

Gardner, M. (1986) *Knotted Doughnuts and Other Mathematical Entertainments*. Freeman: New York.

Kirsh, J., Kirsh, R. (1988) The anatomy of painting style: description with computer rules. Leonardo. 21(4): 437-444.

Kluger, J. (1987) Computer Art. Discover Magazine. October Issue. pp. 57-62.

Mackintosh, A. (1988) Dr. Atanasoff's computer. Scien. Amer. August 259(2): 90-95.

Pirsig, R. (1975) *Zen and the Art of Motorcycle Maintenance*. Bantam: New York.

Rose, S. (1976) *The Conscious Brain*. Vintage: New York.

Part II - Representing Nature

Fourier Transforms, Autocorrelation Theory, Phase

Bendat, J., Piersol, R. (1966) *Measurement and Analysis of Random Data*. John Wiley and Sons: New York.

Koopmans, L. (1974) *The Spectral Analysis of Time Series*. New York: Academic Press, pp. 165-189, 279, 306-209.

MacDonald, D. (1962) *Noise and Fluctuations: An Introduction*. John Wiley and Sons: New York.

Otnes, R. K., Enochson, L. (1978) *Applied Time Series Analysis, Vol I: Basic Techniques*. Wiley: N.Y.

Pfeiffer, J. (1983) *The importance of phase in word recognition*. Thesis at the Naval Postgraduate School, Montery, California.

Visual Perception, Moire patterns

Allman, W. (1983) Are no two snowflakes alike? Science 83, 4: 24.

Glass, L. (1969) Moire effect from random dots. Nature 223: 578.

Glass, L., Perez, R. (1973) Perception of random dot interference patterns. Nature 246: 360.

Julesz, B. (1975) Experiments in the visual perception of texture. Scien. Amer. 232: 34.

Madore, B., W. Freedman (1983) Computer simulations of the Belousov-Zhabotinsky reaction. Science 222: 615.

Walker, J. (1980) The Amateur Scientist. Scien. Amer. 243: 198.

Speech Synthesis, Traditional Sound Representations

Borden, G., Harris, K. (1983) *Speech Science Primer, 2nd. ed.* Williams & Wilkins: Baltimore.

Dixon, N., Maxey, H. (1968) Terminal analog synthesis of continuous speech using the diphone method of segment assembly. AU-16: 40-50.

Greene, B., Pisoni, D., Carrell, T. (1984) Recognition of speech spectrograms. J. Acoust. Soc. of Am., in press.

Kuhn, G. (1984) Description of a color spectrogram. J. Acoust. Soc. Am. 76: 682-685.

Ladefoged, P. (1982) *A Course in Phonetics, 2nd. ed.* Harcourt Brace Jovanovich: N.Y.

Liberman, A.M., Cooper, F.S., Shankweiler, D.P., Studdert-Kennedy, M. (1968) Why are speech spectrograms hard to read? Am. Ann. Deaf. 113: 127-133.

McDermott, J. (1983) The solid-state parrot. Science 83. 4: 59-69.

Morgan, N. (1984) *Talking Chips*. McGraw-Hill: New York.

Oppenheim, A., Schafer, R. (1975) *Digital Signal Processing*. Prentice-Hall: N.J.

PROSE 2020 Text-to-speech Converter User's Manual (1982) Issue 1, Part Number S57401, Palo Alto, California.

Rayleigh, J. (1945) *The Theory of Sound, Vol. I.* Dover Publications: N.Y. p. 11.

Skekey, A (1983) The wondrous signal: speech. IEEE Commun. December: 4-5.

Stark, R.E. (1974) *Sensory Capabilities of Hearing-impaired Children*. University Park: Baltimore.

Sundberg, J. (1977) Acoustics of the Singing Voice. Scien. Amer. March: 82-88.

Thomas, J., J. Klavans, J. Nartey, C. Pickover, D. Reich, and M.B. Rosson (1984) Walrus: A developmental System for Speech Synthesis. IBM Res. Rep. (RC 10626)

Witten, I. (1982) *Principals of Computer Speech*. Academic Press: N.Y.

Music

Clarke, J., Voss, R. (1975) 1/f noise in music and speech. Nature 258: 317-318.

Chowning, J. (1973) The synthesis of complex audio spectra by means of frequency modulation. J. Audio Eng. Soc. 21(7): 46-54.

Cogan, R. (1984) *New Images of Musical Sound.* Harvard University Press: Massachusetts.

Creitz, W. (1984) Synthetic singing. *Voice News* 4: 6.

Dillon, M., Hunter, M. (1982) Automated identification of melodic variants in folk music. Computers and the Humanities. 16: 107-117.

Hofstadter, D. (1982) Metamagical Themas. Scien. Amer. 246: 16-28.

Koopmans, L. (1974) *The Spectral Analysis of Time Series.* New York: Academic Press, pp. 165-189, 279, 306-209.

Minsky, M. (1981) Music, mind and meaning. Computer Music J. 5:28-44.

Mitroo, J., Herman, N., and Badler, N. (1979) Movies from music: visualizing musical compositions. Computer Graphics (Siggraph). 13: 218-225.

Starr, D. (1984) Computer chorus. Omni Magazine. 6: 41.

Roades, C. (1985) Research in music and artificial intelligence. ACM Computing Surveys. 17:163-190.

Voss, R., Clarke, J. (1978) $1/f$ noise in music: music from $1/f$ noise. J. Acoust. Soc. of Amer. 63: 258-263.

Voss, R. (1979) $1/f$ (flicker) noise: a brief review. Proc. 33rd Annual Symp. on Freq. Control. Atlantic City. pp. 40-46.

Faces, Education

Caron, R., Caron, A., Myers, R. (1982) Abstraction of invariant face expressions in infancy. Child Development. 53: 1008-1015.

Chernoff, H. (1973) The use of faces to represent points in k-dimensional space graphically. J. Amer. Statist. Assoc. 68: 361-367.

Chernoff, H., Rizvi, M. (1975) Effect on classification error of random permutations of features in representing multivariate data by faces. J. Amer. Statistical Assoc. 70: 548-554.

Edwards, B. (1979) *Drawing on the Right Side of the Brain.* J. P. Tarcher: Los Angeles.

Gillenson, M., Chandrasekaran, B. (1975) WHATSISFACE: Human facial composition by computer graphics. In Quarterly Report of SIGGRAPH ACM (Lucido, A., ed.). Assoc. for Computing Machinery: Ohio. 9: 212-221.

Flury, B., Riedwyl, H. (1981) Graphical representation of multivariate data by means of asymmetrical faces. J. Amer. Statistical Assoc. 76: 757-765.

Jacob, R., Egeth, H., Bevan, W. (1976) The face as a data display. Human Factors. 18: 189-200.

Johnson, L., Perlmutter, M., Trabasso, T. (1979) The leg bone is connected to the knee bone: children's representation of body parts in memory, drawing, and language. Child Develop. 50: 1192-1202.

Mahler, J., Sullivan, H. (1982) Effects of mental imagery and oral and print stimuli on prose learning of intermediate grade children. Educat. Commun. and Tech. J. 30: 175-183.

Maurer, D., Barrera, M. (1981) Infant's perception of natural and distorted arrangements of a schematic face. Child Develop. 52: 196-202.

Maurer, D., Barrera, M. (1981) The perception of facial expressions by the three-month-old. Child Develop. 52: 203-206.

Nugent, G. (1982) Pictures, audio, and print: symbolic representation and effect on learning. Educational Commun. and Tech. J. 30: 163-174.

Peterson, I. (1987) Picture This. Science News 131(25): 392-395 (and cover picture).

Sakai, T., Nagao, M., and Kanade, T. (1972) Computer analysis and classification of photographs of human faces. In First USA-Japan Computer Conference Proc. Amer. Fed. Info. Process. Soc.: New Jersey. pp. 55-62.

Samuels, M. (1982) *Seeing with the Mind's Eye: The History, Techniques, and Uses of Visualization.* Random House: New York.

Winn, W. (1982) Visualization in learning and instruction: a cognitive approach. Educat. Commun. and Tech. J. 30: 3-25.

Spinnaker Software Corp. (1984) Easy Learning Series Pamphlet. (Cambridge, Massachusetts)

Taylor, M., Bacharach, V. (1981)   The development of drawing rules: Metaknowledge about drawing influences performance on nondrawing tasks. Child Develop. 52: 373-375.

Vasta, R., Green, P. (1982) Differential cue utilization by males and females in pattern copying. Child Develop. 53: 1102-1105.

Wilkinson, L. (1982) An experimental evaluation of multivariate graphical point representations. In Proc. of Human Factors in Computer Syst. 202-209.

Biology (Proteins, DNA, Cardiology, etc.)

Bishop, J. (1982) Oncogenes. Scien. Amer. March. 81-92.

Cantor, C., Schimmel, P. (1980) *Biophysical Chemistry, Part III.* W. H. Freeman and Company: San Francisco.

Eukaryotes, prokaryotes: Who's first? (1986) Science News. 129: 280.

Friedland, P. and Kedes, L. (1985) Discovering the secrets of DNA. Communications of the ACM 28: 1164-1186.

Gamow, G. (1947) *One, Two, Three...Infinity.* Viking Press: New York. (This provided some useful background for random walks as they relate to DNA vectorgrams).

Green, D.H. (1968) Shift-register derived patterns. In *Cybernetic Serendipity.* J. Reichardt, ed. Prager: New York. p. 99 (This 1-page article stimulated the DNA vectorgram work).

Hamori, E. (1985) Novel DNA sequence representations. Nature. 314: 585-586.

Holden, C. (1987) Oncogene linked to fruit-fly development. Science. 238: 160-161.

Karplus M., J. McCammon. (1979) Nature. 277, 5697.

Koshland, D. (1970) In *The Enzymes, Vol. 1.* P. Boyer, ed. Academic Press: New York.

Lewin, R. (1986) Computer genome is full of junk DNA. Science. 232: 577-578.

Lewin, R. (1986) Proposal to sequence the human genome stirs debate. Science 232: 1598-1599.

Miyahara, H., Endou, K. Domae, A., Satao, T. (1980) Arrhythmia diagnosis by the IBM electrocardiogram analysis program. J. Electrocardiology 13: 17-24.

Miyahra, H., Domae, A., Satao, T. (1984) The reproducibility of interpretation of 10 computer ECG systems by means of a microprocessor-based ECG signal generator. Computers & Biomedical Res. 17: 311-325.

Postle, D. (1976) Fabric of the Universe. Crown: New York.

Reddy, E. (1983) Nucleotide sequence analysis of the T24 human bladder carcinoma oncogene. Science 220: 1061.

Rose, S. (1976) *The Conscious Brain.* Vintage: New York.

Silverman, B.D., Linsker, R. (1986) A measure of DNA periodicity. J. Theor. Biol. 118: 295-300.

Vainshtein, B. (1986) Symmetry of biological macromoelcules and their associations Comp. and Maths. with Appls. 12B: 237-269.

Wasserman, S., Cozzarelli, N. (1986) Biochemical topology: applications to DNA recombination and replication. Science. 232: 951-956.

Image processing, Shroud of Turin, Visualization, Graphics

Avis, C., Lynn, D., Lorre, J., Lavoie, S., Clark, J., Armstrong, E., and Addington, J. (1982) Image processing of the Shroud of Turin. IEEE Proc. Int. Conf. on Cybernetics and Society. Seattle, Washington, pp. 554-558.

Damon, P. et al. (1989) Radiocarbon dating of the Shroud of Turin. Nature. February. 337: 611-615.

Foley, J., van Dam, A. (1984) Fundamentals of Interactive Computer Graphics. Addison-Wesley: Massachusetts.

Gonzalez, R., Wintz, P. (1977) *Digital Image Processing.* Addison-Wesley Publishing Co.: Massachusetts.

Jackson, J., Jumper, E., and Ercoline, W. (1982) Three dimensional characteristic of the shroud image. IEEE Proc. Int. Conf. on Cybernetics and Society. Seattle, Washington, pp. 574-575.

Jumper, E. (1982) An overview of the testing performed by the Shroud of Turin research project with a summary of results. IEEE Proc. Int. Conf. on Cybernetics and Society. Seattle, Washington, pp. 535-537.

Mueller, M. (1982) The Shroud of Turin: A critical appraisal. Skeptical Inquirer. 6(3): 15-35.

Newman, W. and Sproull, R. (1979) *Principles of Interactive Computer Graphics.* McGraw-Hill: New York.

Nickell, J. (1979) The Turin Shroud: Fake? Fact? Photograph? Popular Photography. November, pp 97-147.

Pratt, W. (1978) *Digital Image Processing.* Wiley: New York.

Ratcliff, F. (1972) Contour and Contrast. Scien. Amer. 226: 91-101.

Rosenfeld, A. (1969) *Picture Processing by Computer.* Academic Press: New York.

Stevenson, K., Habermas, G. (1982) *Verdict on the Shroud.* Dell Publishing: Pennsylvania.

Waldrop, M. (1988) The Shroud of Turin: An answer is at hand. Science. 241: 1750-1751.

Wilson, I. (1979) *The Shroud of Turin: The Burial Cloth of Jesus Christ?* (Revised Edition) Doubleday and Co.: New York

Wolff, R. (1988) The visualization challenge in the physical sciences. Computers in Science. Jan./Feb. 2(1): 16-31.

Charged Curves

Cole, R. (1986) Graphics as a learning aid. IEEE Potentials. 5(4): 26-30.

Salvadori, M., Baron, M. (1952) *Numerical methods in Engineering*. Prentice-Hall: New York.

Part III - Pattern, Symmetry, and Beauty

General Reading, General Mathematics, Graphics of Mathematics

Ash, J., Sexton, H. (1985) A surface with one local minimum. Math. Magazine. 58: 147-149.

Computer Graphics World (1989) Simple Beauty. Nov. 12(11): 78-81. (Describes author's work.)

Dawkins, R. (1986) *The Blind Watchmaker*. W.W. Norton: New York. (Dawkins also uses the term "biomorph" to describe his interesting computer-generated biological shapes.)

Dewdney, A. K. (1989) Computer recreations. Catch of the day: biomorphs on Truchet tiles, served with popcorn and snails. Scien. Amer. July 261(1): 110-113.

Fadman, C. (1958) *Fantasia Mathematica*. Simon and Schuster: New York (A book of stories and diversions all drawn from the universe of mathematics).

Flanigan, F. (1983) *Complex Variables*. Dover: New York. (A good introduction to complex variables.)

Gardner, M. (1986) *Knotted Doughnuts and Other Mathematical Entertainments*. Freeman: New York.

Hardy, G. *A Mathematician's Apology*. Cambridge Univ. Press: New York.

Hobson, E. (1965) *Squaring the Circle*. Chelsea Publishing Co.: New York.

Lawrence, J. (1972) *A Catalog of Special Plane Curves*. Dover: New York.

Peterson, I. (1987) Pictures worth a thousand numbers. Washington Post, July 19th (Sunday), section C3, first page.

Peterson, I. (1987) Portraits of Equations. Science News 132(12): 184-186 (and cover picture).

Rivlin, R. (1986) Computer graphics: the arts. Omni Magazine. 8: 30.

Rivlin, R. (1986) *The Algorithmic Image*. Microsoft Press: Redmond, WA. (also see excerpt in Computer Graphics World, August 1986).

Rucker, R. (1988) *Mind Tools: The Five Levels of Mathematical Reality*. Houghton Mifflin Co.: Boston.

Sorenson, P. (1989) Pickover's strange attractor. Special Effects Business. December/ January 1(3): 6-7; 53.

Voelcker, J. (1988) Picturing randomness. IEEE Spectrum. August 25(8): 13.

Fractals and Related

Anderson, B. (1988) Graphics high end: war of words. Computer Graphics Today. July Issue. pg. 1. (This article is not about fractals, but rather it describes the new class of graphics supercomputers which can be used to create fractals with startling speed.)

The Beauty of Fractals (1987 photo essay) Computers in Physics. Nov/Dec. pp 26-31.

Aqvist, J., Tapia, O. (1987) Surface fractality as a guide for studying protein-protein interactions. J. Molec. Graph. 5(1): 30-34.

Barnsley, M. (1988) *Fractals Everywhere.* Academic Press: New York.

Briggs, J., Peat, D. (1989) *The Turbulent Mirror.* Harper and Row: New York. (Good for beginners.)

Boyd, D. (1973) The residual set dimensions of the Apollonian packing. Mathematika 20: 170-174. (Very technical reading).

Brooks, R., Matelski, J. P. (1981) The dynamics of 2-generator subgroups of PSL(2,C). In *Riemann Surfaces and Related Topics: Proceedings of the 1978 Stony Brook Conference.* Kyra, I. and Maskit, B. (eds.) Princeton University Press: New Jersey. (Note: this 1978 paper contains computer graphics and mathematical descriptions of both Julia and Mandelbrot sets).

Devaney, R., Krych, M. (1984) Dynamics of exp(z). Ergod. Th. & Dynam. Sys. 4: 35-52.

Dewdney, A. K. (1985) Computer Recreations. Scien. Amer. 253: 16-24.

Denning, P. (1985) Computing in the frontiers of science and engineering, cover page description. Commun. ACM. Vol 28.

Douady, A., Hubbard, J. (1982) Iteration des polynomes quadratiques complexes. Comptes Rendus (Paris) 2941: 123-126.

Foley, J., and van Dam, A. (1984) Fundamentals of Interactive Computer Graphics. Addison-Wesley: Massachusetts.

Family, F. (1988) Introduction to droplet growth processes: simulation theory and experiments. In *Random Fluctuations and Pattern Growth: Experiments and Models.* Stanley, H., Ostrowsky, N. (eds.) Kluwer: Boston.

Family, F., Meakin, P. (1988) Droplet growth. Phys Rev. Lett. 61:428.

Family, F., Landau, D., eds. (1984) *Kinetics of Aggregation and Gelation.* North-Holland: Amsterdam.

Feder, J. (1988) *Fractals.* Plenum: New York.

Fatou, P. (1919/1920) Sur les equations fonctionelles. Bull. Soc. Math. Fr. 47: 161-271.

Gardner, M. (1968) Packing of circles and spheres. Scien. Amer. 218: 130-125.

Hamilton, W. R. (1969) *Elements of Quaternions, Vol. I and II,* reprinted by Chelsea Publishing Co.: New York.

Hirsch, M. (1989) Chaos, Rigor, and Hype. Mathematical Intelligencer. 11(3):6-9. (Pages 8 and 9 include James Gleick's response to the article.)

Hubbard, J. (1986) Order in chaos. Engineering: Cornell Quarterly. 20(3): 20-26 (Winter Issue).

Julia, G. (1918) Memoire sur l'iteration des fonctions rationnelles, J. Math. Pure Appl. 4: 47-245.

Kadanoff, L. (1986) Fractals: where's the physics? Physics Today February, 6-7.

Kausch-Blecken, H. Schmeling, V., Tschoegl, N. (1970) Osculatory packing of finite areas with circles. Nature. March 225: 1119-1121.

Kaye, B. (1989) *A Randomwalk Through Fractal Dimensions*. VCH Publishers: New York.

La Brecque, M (1985) Fractal Symmetry. Mosaic 16: 10-23.

Lakhtakia, A., Vasundara, V., Messier, R., Varadan, V. (1987) On the symmetries of the Julia sets for the process $z \rightarrow z^p + c$. J. Phys. A: Math. Gen. 20: 3533-3535.

Lakhtakia, A., Vasundara, V., Messier, R., Varadan, V. (1987) The generalized Koch Curve. J. Phys. A: Math. Gen. 20: 3537-3541.

Lakhtakia, A., Vasundara, V., Messier, R., Varadan, V. (1986) Self-similarity versus self-affinity: the Sierpiński gasket revisited. J. Phys. A: Math. Gen. 19: L985-L989.

Mandelbrot, B. (1983) *The Fractal Geometry of Nature*, Freeman, San Francisco.

Mandelbrot, B. (1983) On the quadratic mapping $z \rightarrow z^2 - \mu$ for complex μ and z: The fractal structure of its M set, and scaling. Physica 17D: 224-239.

Musgrave, K. (1989) The synthesis and rendering of eroded fractal terrains. Computer Graphics (ACM-SIGGRAPH). July 23(3): 41-50.

Norton, A. (1982) Generation and display of geometric fractals in 3-D, Computer Graphics (ACM-SIGGRAPH) 16: 61-67.

Peitgen, H., Richter, P. (1984) Die Unendliche Reise. Geo (German Edition) 6:100-124.

Peitgen, H., Richter, P. (1986) *The Beauty of Fractals*. Springer: Berlin.

Peitgen, H., Saupe, D. (editors) (1988) *The Science of Fractal Images*. Springer: Berlin.

Peterson, I. (1984) Ants in the labyrinth and other fractal excursions, Science News. 125: 42-43.

Richardson, L. (1960) The problem of contiguity. In *Statistics of Deadly Quarrels*. (Wright, Q.,, Lienau, C., eds.) Boxwood Press: Pittsburgh.

Robinson, A. (1985) Fractal fingers in viscous fluids. Science 228: 1077-1080.

Roux, S., Guyon, E., Sornette, D. (1988) Hull percolation. J. Phys. Math. Gen. 21:L475-L482.

Schroeder, P. (1986) Plotting the Mandelbrot Set. Byte December 207-211.

Sorenson, P. (1984) Fractals. Byte. Sept. 9: 157-172 (a fascinating introduction to the subject).

Thomsen, D. (1982) A place in the sun for fractals. Science News. 121: 28-32.

Ushiki, S. (1988) Phoenix. IEEE Trans. Circuits and Syst. July 35(7): 788-789.

Voss, R. (1985) Random fractal forgeries. In *Fundamental Algorithms in Computer Graphics*. R. Earnshaw, ed. Springer-Verlag: Berlin.

Voss, R. (1988) Fractals in nature: from characterization to simulation. In *The Science of Fractal Images*, Peitgen, H., Saupe, D. (editors).

West, S. (1984) The new realism. Science 84, 5: 31-39.

West, B., Goldberger, A. (1987) Physiology in fractal dimensions. Amer. Scien. 75: 354-365. (This article describes the fractal characterization of the lungs's bronchial tree, the Weierstrass function, the fractal geometry of the heart, and "fractal time").

Witten, T., Sander, L. (1981) Phys. Rev. Lett. 47: 1400.

Synthesizing Nature

Aono, M., Kunii, L. (1984) Botanical Tree Image Generation. IEEE Computer Graphics and Appl. 4: 10-34.

Bloomenthal, J. (1985) Modeling the mighty maple. Computer Graphics (ACM SIGGRAPH). San Francisco. 19(3) 305-311.

Braun, S. (1986) Botany with a twist. Science 86. 7: 63-64.

Cohen, L. (1964) Random walk with transition probabilities that depend on the direction of motion. Math. Magazine 37(4): 248-250. (This work was used for designing plants).

Dixon, R. (1983) The mathematics and computer graphics of spirals in plants. Leonardo 16: 86-90.

Jena, R. (1984) *Mathematical Approach to Pattern and Form in Plant Growth.* John Wiley and Sons: New York.

Kappraff, J. (1986) The geometry of coastlines. Comp. and Maths. with Appls. 12B: 655-671.

Kappraff, J. (1986) A course in the mathematics of design. Comp. and Maths. with Appls. 12B: 913-948.

Kawaguchi, Y. 1982. A morphological study of the form of nature. SIGGRAPH July '82 Proc.: Boston. 16(3): 223.

Kolata, G. (1984) Esoteric math has practical result. Science 225: 494-495.

Prusinkiewicz, P., Lindenmayer, A, Hanan, J. (1988) Developmental models of herbaceous plants for computer imagery purposes. Computer Graphics (ACM-SIGGRAPH) August 22(4): 141-150.

Reeves, W., Blau, R. (1985) Approximate and probabilistic algorithms for shading and rendering structured particle systems. Computer Graphics (ACM SIGGRAPH) 19(3): 313-322.

Rivlin, R. (1986) *The Algorithmic Image.* Microsoft Press, WA.

Thompson, D. (1961) *On Growth and Form.* Cambridge: Cambridge, UK.

Viennot, X., Eyrolles, G. Janey, N., Arques, D. (1989) Combinatorial analysis of ramified patterns and computer imagery of trees. Computer Graphics (ACM-SIGGRAPH) July 23(3): 31-40.

Yessios, C. (1979) Computer drafting of stones, wood, plant and ground materials. Computer Graphics (ACM-SIGGRAPH) August '79 Proc., Chicago 13(2): 190.

Cellular Automata

Brown, D. (1987) Competition of cellular automata rules. Complex Systems. 1: 169-180.

Conway, J., Berlekamp, E., Guy, R. (1982) *Winning Ways for Your Mathematical Plays.* Academic Press: New York.

Levy, S. (1985) The portable universe: getting to the heart of the matter with cellular automata. The Whole Earth Review Magazine. Winter issue, 42-48.

Maeder, D. (1987) The free energy concept in cellular automaton models of solid-solid phase transitions. Complex Systems 1: 131-144.

Peterson, I. (1987) Forest fires, barnacles, and trickling oil. Science News. 132: 220-221.

Poundstone, W. (1985) The Recursive Universe. William Morrow and Company: New York.

Schrandt, R., S. Ulam (1970) On recursively defined geometrical objects and patterns of growth. In *Essays on Cellular Automata*, A. Burks, ed. Univ. of Illinois Press, Chicago.

Wolfram, S. (1983) Statistical mechanics of cellular automata. Rev. Modern Physics. 55, 601-644.

Chaos, Bifurcations, Dynamical Systems

Abraham, R., Shaw, C. (1985) *Dynamics – The Geometry of Behavior, Part 3: Global Behavior*. Aerial Press: California. (Actually, the entire book collection of Aerial Press, including the Visual Math Series, is an educational wonderland).

Abraham, R., Shaw, C. (1983) *Dynamics – The Geometry of Behavior, Part 2: Chaotic Behavior*. Aerial Press: California.

Aronson, D., Chory, M., Hall, G. and McGehee, R. (1980) A discrete dynamical system with subtly wild behavior. In *New Approaches to Nonlinear Problems in Dynamics*, P.J. Holmes, ed. Soc. for Industry and Appl. Math.

Berge, P., Pomeau, Y., Vidal, C. (1984) *Order Within Chaos* Wiley: New York.

Campbell, D., Crutchfield, J., Farmer, D., Jen, E. (1985) Experimental mathematics: the role of computation in nonlinear science. Commun. ACM. 28: 374-389.

Crutchfield, J., Farmer, J., Packard, N. (1986) Chaos. Scien. Amer. 255: 46-57;

Devaney, R. (1986) Chaotic bursts in nonlinear dynamical systems. Science 235: 342-345.

Dewdney, A. K. (1987) Probing the strange attractions of chaos. Scien. Amer. July Issue, 108-111.

Collet, P., J.P. Eckmann. (1980) *Iterated Maps on the Interval as Dynamical Systems*. Birkhauser: Boston.

Feigenbaum, M. (1979) The universal metric properties of nonlinear transformations. J. Statistical Physics. 21: 669-706.

Feigenbaum, M. (1981) Universal behavior in nonlinear systems. Los Alamos Science. 1: 4-27.

Finney R., D. Ostberg (1976) *Elementary Differential Equations with Linear Algebra*. Mass: Addison-Wesley.

Fisher, A. (1985) Chaos: The Ultimate Asymmetry. Mosaic 16: 24-30.

Fischer, P., Smith, W. (1985) *Chaos, Fractals, and Dynamics*. Marcel Dekker, Inc.: New York.

Glass, L., Mackey, M. (1988) *From Clocks to Chaos: The Rhythms of Life* Princeton Univ. Press: New Jersey.

Hassell, M. (1974) Insect Populations. J. Anim. Ecol. 44: 283-296.

Hofstadter, D. (1981) Strange Attractors. Scien. Amer. 245: 16-29.

Hofstadter, D. (1986) *Metamagical Themas: Question for the Essence of Mind and Pattern*. Bantam: New York.

Kudrewicz, J., Grudniewicz, J. and Swidzinske, B. (1986) Chaotic oscillation as a consequence of the phase slipping phenomenon in a discrete phase-locked loop. Proc. of the IEEE Int. Symp. on Circuits and Syst. 1: 74-78.

Levi, B. (1981) Period-doubling route to chaos shows universality. Physics Today. March, pp. 17-19.

Lorenz, E. (1963) Deterministic nonperiodic flow. J. Atmos. Sci. 20: 130.

May, R. (1976) Simple mathematical models with very complicated dynamics. Nature. 261: 459-467.

Moon, F. (1987) *Chaotic Vibrations*. John Wiley and Sons, New York.

Nussbaum, R., Peitgen, O. (1984) Special and spurious solutions of $\dot{x}(t) = -\alpha f(x(t-1))$. Memoirs of the American Mathematical Society. 51: 1- 129.

Peterson, I. (1986) Toying with a touch of chaos. Science News. 129: 277-278.

Schwenk, T. (1976) *Sensitive Chaos*. Schocken Books: New York.

Shaw, A. (1984) *The Dripping Faucet as a Model Chaotic System*. Aerial Press: California.

Sinanoglu, O. (1975) Theory of chemical reaction networks. J. Am. Chem. Soc. 97:2309-2320. (The Sinanoglu references are included here because they are helpful for "Pattern Formation and Chaos in Networks" on page 142.)

Sinanoglu, O. (1981) 1- and 2-topology of reaction networks. J. Math. Phys. 22:1504-1512.

Stoker, J. (1953) Mathematical methods in nonlinear vibration theory, In Proc. Symp. Nonlinear Circuit Analysis, Vol. 2. Interscience Publishers: New York. 28-55.

Taubes, G. (1984) The mathematics of chaos. Discover Magazine. September Issue, 30-45.

Number Theory

Bidwell, J. (1973) Pascal's triangle revisited. Mathematics Teacher. 66: 448-452.

Crandall, R. (1978) On the "3x+1" problem. Math. of Computation 32: 1281-1292.

Crypton, D. (1985), Prime numbers and the national security. Science Digest. Oct. 86-88.

Dodge, C. (1969) *Numbers and Mathematics*. Prindle, Weber, and Schmidt: Boston (easy reading).

Gardner, M. (1977) Pascal's triangle. In Mathematical Carnival. Vintage Books: New York.

Garner, L. (1981) On the Collatz 3n+1 problem. Proc. Amer. Math. Soc. 82: 19-22.

Gordon, J., Goldman, A., Maps, J. (1986) Superconducting-normal phase boundary of a fractal network in a magnetic field. Phys. Rev. Let. 56: 2280-2283.

Hayes, B. (1984) Computer recreations: on the ups and downs of hailstone numbers. Scien. Amer. 250: 10-16.

Holter, N., Lakhtakia, A., Varadan, V., Vasundara, V. Messier, R. (1986). On a new class of planar fractals: the Pascal-Sierpiński gaskets. J. Phys. A: Math. Gen. 19: 1753-1759.

Jansson, L. (1973) Spaces, functions, polygons, and Pascal's triangle. Mathematics Teacher, 66: 71-77.

Lakhtakia, A., Vasundara, V., Messier, R., Varadan, V. (1988) Fractal sequences derived from the self-similar extensions of the Sierpiński gasket. J. Phys. A: Math. Gen. 21: 1925-1928.

Legarias, J. (1985) The $3x+1$ problem and its generalizations. Amer. Math. Monthly, January 3-23.

Schröder, M. (1984) *Number Theory in Science and Communication.* Springer: New York (This book is recommended highly. An interesting book, by a fascinating author).

Schröder, M. (1982) A simple function. Math. Intelligencer. 4: 158-161.

Stein, M., Ulam, S., Wells, M. (1964) A visual display of the distribution of primes. Math. Monthly 71: 516-520.

System Product Interpreter User's Guide, Release 4 (1984) IBM manual (SC24-5238-2).

Trigg, C. (1982-83) Palindromic octagonal numerals. J. Recr. Math. 15(1): 41-46.

Usiskin, Z. (1973) Perfect square patterns in the Pascal triangle. Math. Magazine Sept.-Oct. 203-208.

Wagon, S. (1985) The Colatz problem. Math. Intelligencer 7: 72-76.

Wiggin, B. (1988) Wonderous numbers – conjecture about the $3n+1$ family. J. Recr. Math. 20(1): 52-56.

Zhiqing, L. (1985) Pascal's pyramid. Math. Spectrum 17(1):1-3.

Numerical Methods

Benzinger, H., Burns, S., Palmore, J. (1987) Chaotic complex dynamics and Newton's method. Physics Letters A. 119: 441-445.

Grove, W. (1966) *Brief Numerical Methods.* Prentice-Hall: New Jersey (Has an excellent section on root-finding methods).

Hamming, R. (1973) *Numerical Methods for Scientists and Engineers.* Dover Publications, New York.

May, R. (1976) Simple mathematical models with very complicated dynamics. Nature. 261: 459-467.

Peterson, I. (1987) Zeroing in on chaos. Science News 131:137-139;

Press, W. Flannery, B. Teukolsky, S., Vetterling, W. (1986) *Numerical Recipes.* Cambridge University Press: New York.

Tritton, D. (1986) Chaos in the swing of a pendulum. New Scient. July Issue: 37-40.

Wimp J. (1984) *Computation with Recurrence Relations.* Pitman Publishing: Boston.

Ornaments, Artistic Textures, Symmetry

Audsley, W. (1968) *Designs and Patterns from Historic Ornament.* Dover: New York.

Blossfeldt, K. (1985) *Art Forms in the Plant World.* Dover: New York.

Boivin, J. (1978) *The Heart Single Field Theory* (available for $2.50 from J. Boivin, 4531 Bordeaux, Montreal, Canada H2H 1Z9); reprinted in Speculations in Science and Technology 3, 185-204 (1980).

Doczi, G. (1986) Seen and unseen symmetries. Comp. and Maths. with Appls. 12B: 39-62.

Dowlatshahi, A. (1979) *Persian Designs and Motifs.* Dover: New York.

Gardner, M. (1969) Spirals, In *The Unexpected Hanging.* Simon and Schuster: N.Y.

Grunbaum, B., Grunbaum, Z., Shephard, G. (1986) Symmetry in Moorish and other ornaments. Comp. and Maths. with Appls. 12B: 641-653.

Haas, M. (1956) *The Thai System of Writing* Graphic Arts Press: NY.

Harlow, W. (1976) *Art forms from Plant Life.* Dover: New York.

Hayes, B. (1986) On the bathtub algorithm for dot-matrix holograms, Computer Language, 3: 21-25;

Dewdney, A. K. (1986) Computer Recreations. Scien. Amer. Sept. pp. 14-23.

Jacobson, J. (1982) Analytic computer art. Proc. 2nd Symp. on Small Computers in the Arts, pp 47-60.

Lockwood, E., Macmillan, R. (1978) *Geometric Symmetry.* Cambridge University Press: N.Y.

Makovicky, E. (1986) Symmetrology of art: coloured and generalized symmetries. Comp. and Maths. with Appls. 12B: 949-980.

Mamedov, K. (1986) Crystallographic patterns. Comp. and Maths. with Appls. 12B: 511-529.

Niman, J. Norman, J., Stahl, S. (1978) The teaching of mathematics through art (a report on the conference March 20-21, 1978) Metropolitan Museum of Art and Hunter College of the City University of New York. pp. 1-55.

O'Brien, J. (1968) *How to Design by Accident.* Dover: New York.

Peachey, D. (1985) Solid texturing of complex surfaces. Computer Graphics (ACM SIGGRAPH). 19(3): 279-286.

Perlin, K. (1985) An image synthesizer. Computer Graphics (ACM SIG-GRAPH). 19(3): 287-296.

Postle, D. (1976) *The Fabric of the Universe.* Crown Publishers Inc., N.Y.

Polya, G. (1924) Uber die analogie der kristallsymmetrie in der ebene. Z. Kristallographie. 60: 278-282.

Rowe, W. (1976) *Flora and Fauna Design Fantasies.* Dover: New York.

Rozsa, E. (1986) Symmetry in Muslim arts. Comp. and Maths. with Appls. 12B, 725-750.

Zvilna, J. (1986) Colored symmetries in space-time. Comp. and Maths. with Appls. 12B: 895-911.

Additional Reading

– a potpourri of enjoyable, curious, or unusual topics.

Barnsley, M., Sloan, A. (1987) Chaotic compression (a new twist on fractal theory speeds complex image transmission to video rates). Computer Graphics World. November. 107-108.

Batty, M. (1985) Fractals – geometry between dimensions. New Scientist. April. 31-40.

Berezin, A. (1987) Super super large numbers. J. Recr. Math. 19(2): 142-143.

Braden, B. (1985) Design of an oscillating sprinkler. Mathematics Magazine 58: 29-33.

Casey, S. (1987) Formulating fractals. Computer Lang. 4(4): 28-38.

Dunham, D., Lindgram, J., Witte, D. (1981) Creating repeating hyperbolic patterns. ACM SIGGRAPH Computer Graphics 15(3): 215-220.

Donnini, R. (1986) The visualization of music: symmetry and asymmetry. Comp. and Maths. with Appls. 12B: 435-463.

Eigen, M., Winkler, R. (1983) *Laws of the Game: How the Principles of Nature Govern Chance.* Harper Colophon: New York.

Entsminger, G. (1989) Stochastic fiction – Fiction from fractals. Micro Cornucopia. Sept-Oct. 49: 96.

Fairfield, J. (1983) Segmenting blobs into subregions. IEEE Trans. Sys. Man and Cyber. SMC-13: 363-367.

Feldman, W. (1931) Rabbinical mathematics and astronomy. 2nd American edition. Hermon Press, New York.

Fogg, L. (1989) PostScriptals: Ultimate fractals via postscript. Micro Cornucopia. Sept-Oct. 49: 16-22. (Discusses the "ultimate" fractal at a resolution of 2540 dots per inch. Also challenges the reader to beat this "world's highest resolution fractal.")

Fournier, A., Fussel, D., Carpenter, L. (1982) Computer rendering of stochastic models. Commun. ACM. 25: 371-378. (How to create natural irregular objects).

Gardner, M. (1973) Fantastic patterns traced by programmed worms. Scien. Amer. November 116-123.

Gardner, M. (1978) White and brown music, fractal curves, and 1/f fluctuations, Scien. Amer. April 16-31.

Gardner, M. (1976) In which monster curves force redefinition of the word curve, Scien. Amer. December 235:124-133.

Grebogi, C., Ott, E. Yorke, J. (1985) Chaos, strange attractors, and fractal basin boundaries in nonlinear dynamics. Science 238: 632-637. (A great overview, with definitions of terms used in the chaos literature).

Grebogi, C., Ott, E. Yorke, J. (1985) Attractors on an N-Torus: quasiperiodicity versus chaos. Physica 15D: 354-373. (Contains some gorgeous diagrams of dynamical systems).

Hayes, B. (1983) A progress report on the fine art of turning literature into drivel. 249: 18-26.

Hofstadter, D. (1980) *Gödel, Escher, Bach.* Vintage: New York.

Jensen, R. (1987) Classical chaos. Amer. Scien. 75:168-181.

Kahlert, C. (1986) Analogues to a Julia boundary away from analyticity. Z. Naturforsch. 42A: 324-328.

Kawaguchi, Y. (1985) *Growth Morphogenesis – A Journey to the Origins of Form* JICC Publishing, Inc.: Tokyo.

Knuth, D. (1984) The complexity of songs. Commun. ACM. 27(4): 344-346.

Koch, A., Tarnia, T. (1988) The aesthetics of viruses. Leonardo. 21(2): 161-165.

Koenig, S., Williams, G. (1983) Modeling lowland Maya settlement patterns. IBM Res. Rep. (RC 10018). (Describes novel application of Monte Carlo methods).

Kolata, G. (1986) Shakespeare's new poem: an ode to statistics. Science. 231: 335-336 (Describes how statistical techniques are used to authenticate Shakespeare's writings).

Lehtihet, H. and Miller, B. (1986) Numerical simulation of a billiard in a gravitational field. Physica 21D: 93-104.

Lewin, R. (1988) Mathematics at 100. Science. 240: 721.

McKean, K. (1987) The orderly pursuit of disorder. Discover. January 72-81.

McKean, K. (1982) Computers, fiction, and poetry. Byte. July. 50-53.

Meinhardt, H. (1986) Formation of symmetric and asymmetric structures during the development of higher organisms. Comp. and Maths. with Appls. 12B: 419-433.

Millington, T., Millington, W. (1961) *Dictionary of Mathematics.* Barnes and Noble: New York.

Ogden, J., Adelson, E., Bergen, J., Burt, P. (1985) Pyramid-based computer graphics. RCA Engineer, Sept./Oct. 30(5): 4-15. (Describes the synthesis of clouds, galaxies, waves, and woodgrains).

Pathria, R. (1962) A statistical study of randomness among the first 10,000 digits of pi. Math. of Computation. (April) 16(78): 188-197.

Pavlovic, B., Trinajstic, N. (1986) On symmetry and asymmetry in literature. Comp. and Maths. with Appls. 12B: 197-227.

Peitgen, H., Saupe, D., Haeseler F. (1984) Cayley's problem and Julia sets. Math. Intelligencer. 6(2): 11-20 (Fascinating material and beautiful graphics).

Peterson, I. (1985) The sound of data. Science News 127: 348-350. (Describes the transformation of data to sound).

Phipps, T. (1985) Enhanced fractals. Byte. March 21-23.

Prusinkiewicz, P. Applications of L-systems to computer imagery. Proc. of the 3rd Int. Workshop on Graph Grammars and their Appl. to Computer Science, Springer (in press).

Raimi, R. (1969) The peculiar distribution of first digits. Scien. Amer. 221: 109-120. (Explains why the number "1" appears so often in various tables).

Rosato, A., Prinz, F., Swendsen, R. Why the Brazil nuts are on top: size segregation of particulate matter by shaking. Phys. Rev. Let. 58(10): 1028-1040. (Describes Monte Carlo methods).

Rudnick, J., Gaspari, G. (1987) The shapes of random walks. Science 237: 384-388. (For technical reading).

Schröder, M. (1983) Where is the next Mersenne prime hiding? Math. Intelligencer. 5(3): 31-33.

Sinnot, R. (1986) Making your own globular cluster. Sky and Telescope. 71(4): 398-399. (Gives pseudocode for graphical display of star clusters).

Sizer, W. (1986) Continued Roots. Mathematics Magazine. 59(1): 23-27.

Skilling, J. (1984) The maximum entropy method. Nature 309: 748-749. (Describes a method for sharpening blurred images).

Smith, C. (1987) The tiling patterns of Sebastien Truchet and the topology of structural hierarchy. Leonardo. 20(4): 373-385.

Stanley, D.W., Petersen, F.J. (1979) Fast Fourier transforms on your home computer. Morgan, C.P. (ed.) *The Byte Book of Computer Music*. Peterborough, NH. pgs 97-103.

Steen, L. (1988) The science of pattern. Science. 240: 611-616.

Strogatz, S. (1988) Love affairs and differential equations. Mathematics Magazine. 61(1): 35. (This is an analysis of the time-evolution of the love affair between Romeo and Juliet).

Thomsen, D. (1980) Making music – fractally. Science News. March 117:189-190.

Yuen, S., Taylor, J. (1987) Enhancements of small peaks using the moire technique. Computers and Graphics 11(1): 33-34. (Describes how to enhance peaks in 3-D line drawings).

Voelcker, J. (1988) Picturing randomness. IEEE Spectrum. August 25(8): 13;

Voss, R. (1987) Enhanced surface displays. IBM Tech. Discl. Bul. 29(9): 3840-3841. (Describes how to enhance scanned images).

Weisburd, S. (1987) The spark: personal testimony of creativity. Science News. 132: 298-300.

Works of the Author

Many sections in this book contain references to the author's work. These references can be found in the list below.

Because the papers referenced in this book belong to different disciplines, journal names are sometimes less abbreviated than is customary. Letters are sometimes placed after publication dates to help avoid ambiguity, e.g. three 1988 papers by the author might be labeled "1988a," "1988b," and "1988c" etc.

Biology, Medicine

Pickover, C. (1989) On genes and graphics. *Speculations in Science and Tech.* 12(1): 5-15.

Pickover, C. (1989) A note on the visualization of heart sounds. *Leonardo*, in press. *IBM Res. Rep. (RC 14196)*.

Pickover, C. (1987a) DNA Vectorgrams: representation of cancer gene sequences as movements along a 2-D cellular lattice. *IBM J. Res. Dev.* 31: 111-119.

Pickover, C., Evangelisti, C. (1986a) The use of symmetrized dot-patterns in the characterization and detection of cardiac abnormalities. *IBM Tech. Discl. Bull.* 29(6): 2726-2731.

Pickover, C. (1984a) Spectrographic representations of globular protein breathing motions. *Science* 223: 181.

Pickover, C. (1984b) Frequency representations of DNA sequences: Application to a bladder cancer gene. *J. Molec. Graphics* 2: 50.

Pickover, C. (1984c) The use of random-dot displays in the study of biomolecular conformation. *J. Molec. Graphics* 2: 34.

Pickover, C. (1984d) Computer-drawn faces characterizing nucleic acid sequences. *J. Molec. Graphics* 2: 107-110.

Levinson, B., Pickover, C., F. Richards (1983) Dimerization of colicin E3* in the absence of immunity protein. *J. Biological Chemistry* 258: 10967.

Pickover, C. A. (1982) X-ray scattering from biomolecules in solution: application to the study of molecular conformation. Ph.D. Thesis, Dept. Molecular Biophysics and Biochemistry, Yale University, New Haven, Ct. (243 pages).

Pickover, C., D. Engelman (1982) X-ray scattering from biomolecules in solution: application to the study of molecular conformation and dynamics. *Biophysics J.* 37(2): 381.

Pickover, C., D. Engelman (1982) On the interpretation and prediction of x-ray scattering profiles from biomolecules in solution. *Biopolymers* 21: 817.

McKay, D. B., Pickover, C. A., T. A. Steitz (1982) The *E. coli lac* repressor is elongated with its operator DNA binding domains located at both ends. *J. Molec. Biology* 156: 175.

McKay, D., Weber, I., Pickover, C., T. Steitz (1981) Control of the lac operon expression: structural studies of E. coli lac repressor and CAP binding proteins. In *Structural Aspects of Recognition and Assembly in Biological Macromolecules* Balaban ISS: Rehovot and Philadelphia.

Pickover, C. A., McKay, D.B., Engelman, D. M., T. A. Steitz (1979) Substrate binding closes the cleft between the domains of yeast phosphoglycerate kinase. *J. Biol. Chem.* 254: 11323.

Pickover, C. (1978) The influence of ions on cellular differentiation in the cellular slime mold, *Dictyostelium Discoideum*, Honors Thesis, Biology Dept., Franklin and Marshall College. Lancaster, Pa.

Login, G.A. and C.A. Pickover (1977) Sticky traps and spider prey. *Carolina Tips* 50: 25.

Education

Pickover, C. (1985a) On the educational uses of computer-generated cartoon faces. *J. Educat. Tech. Syst.* 13: 185-198.

Pickover, C. (1985b) A computer-graphics system useful in military and commercial air traffic safety. *IBM Tech. Discl. Bull.* 28: 390-391.

Pickover, C. (1984e) The use of computer-drawn faces as an educational aid in the presentation of statistical concepts. *Computers and Graphics* 8: 163-166.

General

Pickover, C. (1990) Unusual graphic representations of complex data. In *Frontiers in Computing Systems Research*. Tewksbury, S., ed. Plenum: New York. (Chapter 1) pgs. 1-33, in press.

Music

Pickover, C. (1988b) Synthetic singing voices: a speech synthesizer generates an excerpt from Handel's Messiah. *Computer Tech. Rev.* (Winter Issue). 7(16): 79-89.

Pickover, C. (1986b) Representation of melody patterns using topographic spectral distribution functions. *Computer Music J.* 10(3), 72-78.

Speech Analysis

Pickover, C., Dixon, N., Evangelisti, C. (1987b) Simulated spectrogram for speech synthesis development. *IBM Tech. Discl. Bull.* (March). 29(10): 4394-4396.

Pickover, C. (1987c) Acoustic Bar Code, *IBM Tech. Discl. Bull.* 30(5) : 334.

Pickover, C., Evangelisti, C. (1987d) Speech synthesis by FM digital addition. *IBM Tech. Discl. Bull.* 29(9) 3761-3764.

Cohen, L., Pickover, C. (1986c) A comparison of joint time frequency distribution for speech signals, *invited talk. IEEE Int. Conf. on Circuits & Systems*, 1: 42-45.

Pickover, C. (1986d) On the use of computer generated symmetrized dot-patterns for the visual characterization of speech waveforms and other sampled data. *J. Acoust. Soc. Am.* 80(3): 955-960.

Pickover, C., Khorasani, A. (1986e) Fractal characterization of speech waveform graphs. *Computers and Graphics* 10: 51-61.

Pickover, C. (1986f) A Monte Carlo approach for ε placement in waveform fractal-dimension calculation. *Computer Graphics Forum*, 5(3), 203-209.

Pickover, C., Evangelisti, C. (1986g) Autocorrelation-faces: an aid to deaf children learning to speak. *IBM Tech. Discl. Bull.* 28: 3412-3416.

Nartey, J., Pickover, C. (1986) Generation of "H" sounds in text-to-speech synthesis. *IBM Tech. Discl. Bull.* 28(12): 5427-5428.

Nartey, J., Pickover, C. (1986) Generation of nasalized vowels in text-to-speech synthesis. *IBM Tech. Discl. Bull.* 28(12) 5462-5463.

Pickover, C., Martin, M. (1985c) Short-term phase characterization in dynamic signal analysis. *IBM Tech. Discl. Bull.* 27: 6769-6771.

Pickover, C., Kubovy, M. (1985d) Speech vectorgram. *IBM Tech. Discl. Bull.* 27: 6774-6775.

Pickover, C. (1985e) The use of the grid search technique for improving synthetic speech control-data. *IBM Tech. Discl. Bull.* 28: 1248-1249.

Pickover, C. (1985f) Tusk: a versatile graphics workstation for speech research. *IBM Res. Rep.* (RC 11497).

Klavans, J., Nartey, J., Pickover, C. Reich, D., Rosson, M., and Thomas, J. (1984) The Walrus speaks: a developmental system for speech synthesis. *Proc., Voice I/O Systems Applications Conference '84.*

Klavans, J., Nartey, J., Pickover, C. Reich, D., Rosson, M., and Thomas, J. (1984) WALRUS: High-quality text-to-speech research system. *Proc. of IEEE Speech Synthesis and Recognition* p. 19-28.

Miscellaneous, and New Topics

(Note: The articles in this section are recent and are either not discussed, or only briefly discussed, in the present book. Perhaps a forthcoming book will include the following topics.)

Pickover, C. (1990) Is there a double smoothly undulating integer? *J. Recr. Math.* 22(1): 77-78.

Pickover, C. (1990) A vacation on Mars (An artist's journey in a computer graphics world), submitted to *Commun. ACM.*

Pickover, C. (1990) On the aesthetics of inversion and osculation, submitted to *Commun. ACM.*

Pickover, C., Angelo, M. (1990). On the existence of cakemorphic integers. *J. Recr. Math.*, in press.

Pickover, C. (1990) All known replicating Fibonacci-digits less than one billion, *J. Recr. Math*, 22(3): 202-204.

Pickover, C. (1990) DNA Tetragrams: Representation of genetic sequences as tetrahedral movements, submitted to *J. Molec. Graphics.*

Pickover, C., McCarty, K. (1990) Visualizing Cantor cheese construction. *Computers and Graphics*, 14(2), in press.

Pickover, C. (1990) Inverted Mandelbrot sets, *The Visual Computer.* 5: 377.

Pickover, C. (1989) Inside the Mandelbrot set. *Algorithm*, Nov/Dec 1(1): 9-13. *Algorithm - The Personal Computer Newsletter* can be ordered from P.O. Box 29237, Westmount Postal Outlet, 785 Wonderland Road S, London, Ontario, Canada, N6K, 1M6.

Pickover, C. (1990) Close encounters with strange attractors. *Algorithm*, Jan/Feb 1(2), 8-11.

Lakhtakia, A., Pickover. C. (1990) Some observations on palindromic numbers, *J. Recr. Math.* 22(1):55-60.

Pickover, C. (1990) Pentagonal chaos. In *Five-Fold Symmetry* I. Hargittai, ed., in press.

Pickover, C. (1990) The $n^{(3/2)}$ problem, submitted to *J. Recr. Math.*

Pickover, C. (1990) Partition graphs for consecutive integer sums, *J. Recr. Math.*, in press.

Pickover, C. (1990) Visualizing chaos: Lyapunov surfaces and volumes. *IEEE Computer Graphics and Appl.*, March 10(2): 15-19.

Pickover, C. (1990) Some experiments with a leaning tower of books. *Computer Language*, May 7(5) 169-160.

Pickover, C. (1990) Some observations on reversed numbers and palindromes. *J. Recr. Math.*, in press. (A palindromic number reads the same backwards or forwards, e.g. 12321.)

Pickover, C. (1990) The Moire effect: practical and pictorial patterns. *Algorithm*, 1(6).

Pickover, C. (1990) Computer experiments in molecular evolution. *Speculations in Science and Tech.*, in press. IBM Res. Rep. (RC 14467).

Pickover, C. (1989) A short recipe for seashell synthesis. *IEEE Comput. Graph. and Appl.*, November 9(6): 8-11.

Pickover, C., Khorasani E. (1989) Infinite triangular arrays. *J. Recr. Math.*, in press.

Lakhtakia, A., Pickover, C. (1989) The Connell number sequence, *J. Recr. Math.*, in press.

Pickover, C. (1989) Results of the very-large-number contest, *J. Recr. Math.*, 22(3):166-169.

Pickover, C., Khorasani, E. (1990) Visualization of the Gleichniszahlen-Reihe, an unusual number theory sequence. *Math. Spectrum*, in press.

Pickover, C. (1989) Growing your own font. *Algorithm* July/ August 1(5):11-12.

Pickover, C. (1990) Picturing spherical Lissajous figures. *Leonardo*, in press.

Pickover, C., Gursky, M. (1990) Pair square numbers. *J. Recr. Math.*, in press.

Pickover, C., Runger, G. (1990) The 2N problem. *J. Recr. Math.*, submitted.

Pickover, C. (1990) Computer renditions of polyhedral models, *Symmetry*, 1(1), 41-44.

Pickover, C., Segall, M. (1990) Pentagonal symmetry in historic ornament. Submitted to *Five-Fold Symmetry* I. Hargittai, ed. VCH: New York.

Pickover, C. (1989) Book review for Ian Stewart's book *Does God Play Dice? Leonardo*, in press.

Pickover, C. (1990) From math comes beauty: spirals, monkey curves, and saddles, submitted to *Commun. Acm.*

Pickover, C. (1990) Who are the ten most influential scientists in history? *The History and Social Science Teacher*, 25(3): 158-161.

Pickover, C., Biyani, S. (1988) Surface acoustic wave joystick. *IBM Tech. Discl. Bull.* June 31(1): 457-459.

Fisher, J., Grossman, B., Pickover, C., Reed, A., Schloss, R. (1989) Liquid crystal display super-cube for 3D display applications. *IBM Technical Disclosure Bulletin* July 32(2): 287-290. (For a list of other inventions by the author, contact the author).

MATHEMATICS AND BEAUTY SERIES

Complex Variable Theory

Pickover, C., Lakhtakia, A. (1990) Continued roots in the complex plane. *J. Recr. Math.*, 22(3), in press.

Pickover, C. (1989) How to design using recursive composite functions. *Leonardo*, 22(2): 219-222.

Pickover, C. (1988e) Chaotic behavior of the transcendental mapping $(z \to \cosh(z) + \mu)$, *The Visual Computer, An International Journal of Computer Graphics*. 4: 243-246.

Pickover, C. (1987e) Mathematics and Beauty V: Turbulent complex curls. *Computers and Graphics*, 11(4): 499-508.

Pickover, C., Khorasani, E. (1985g) Computer graphics generated from the iteration of algebraic transformations in the complex plane. *Computers and Graphics* 9: 147-151.

General

Pickover, C. (1989) Picturing randomness on a graphics supercomputer. IBM Res. Rep. (RC 14468), IBM J. Res. Dev., in press.

Pickover, C. (1989) Markov aggregation on a sticky circle. *Computers in Physics*, Jul/Aug 3(4):79-80.

Pickover, C. (1989) Beauty in strange proportions. Structure of Symmetry Symposium, Budapest, Hungary. IBM Res. Rep. (RC 14173).

Pickover, C. (1989) Symmetrized random-dot patterns. *Recreational and Educational Computing Newsletter* Sept./Oct. 4(7): 3. (For information on this informal journal, write to Dr. M. Ecker, 129 Carol Drive, Clarks Summit, PA 18411.)

Chaos and Related

Pickover, C. (1989) Picturing randomness with Truchet Tiles. *J. Recr. Math.* 21(4): 256-259.

Pickover, C. (1990) Pentagonal Chaos. In *Five-Fold Symmetry* I. Hargittai, ed. VCH: New York.

Pickover, C. (1989) The new "Chaos and Graphics" section of *Computers and Graphics. Comput. Graph.* 13(1), 55-56.

Pickover C. (Assoc. Editor) (1989) *Computers and Graphics, An International Journal.* Of particular interest is the newly formed "Chaos and Graphics Section". Write to Pergamon Press, Fairview Park, Elmsford, New York, 10523, USA, or Pergamon Press, Headington Hill Hall, Oxford OX3 OBW, England, for more information.

Pickover, C. (Editor) (1988) *J. Chaos and Graphics, Vol. 3.* IBM Res. Rep. (RA 198) (17 different authors; this is an informal, irregularly published newsletter which is favorably reviewed in the 1987 Winter *Whole Earth Review*, No. 57, pg. 36, and also in *Computer Pict.*, January/February (1988) pg. 88. Write to the author for a free copy).

Pickover C. (1988) Mathematics and Beauty: Video Tape. Contains colorful, animated computer graphics. Can be seen, for example, at the Japanese Phenomena Art Gallery, Saibu Gas Museum (Asian Pacific Exposition Fukuoka '89, Japan).

Pickover, C. (1989) Circles which kiss: a note on osculatory packing. *Computers and Graphics* 13(1): 63-67.

Pickover, C. (1988g) Pattern formation and chaos in networks, *Commun. ACM.* February 31(2): 136-151.

Pickover, C. (1988h) A note on rendering chaotic "repeller distance-towers." *Computers in Physics*, May/June 2(3): 75-76.

Pickover, C. (1987f) Graphics, bifurcation, order and chaos. *Computer Graphics Forum*, 6: 26-33.

Pickover, C. (editor) (1987) *J. Chaos and Graphics, Vol. 2*. IBM Res. Rep. (RA 192) (13 different authors).

Pickover, C. (editor) (1987) *J. Chaos and Graphics, Vol. 1*. IBM Res. Rep. (RA 186) (10 different authors).

Number Theory

Pickover, C. (1990) On the aesthetics of Sierpiński gaskets formed from large Pascal's triangles. *Leonardo*. 23(3), in press.

Pickover C., Lakhtakia, A. (1989) Diophantine equation graphs for $x^2y = c$. *J. Recr. Math.*, 21(3), 167-170.

Pickover, C. (1989) Hailstone $(3n+1)$ number graphs. *J. Recr. Math.* 21(2): 112-115.

Pickover, C. (1987g) Blooming Integers: An elegantly simple algorithm generates complex patterns (Mathematics and Beauty III). *Computer Graphics World* (March), 10(3): 54-57.

Pickover, C. (1987h) A recipe for self-decorating eggs. *Comput. Lang.* 4(11): 55-58.

Dynamical Systems

Pickover, C. (1987i) Mathematics and beauty: time-discrete phase planes associated with the cyclic system, $\{\dot{x}(t) = -f(y(t)), \ \dot{y}(t) = f(x(t))\}$. *Computers and Graphics*. 11(2), 217-226.

Pickover, C. (1988j) A note on rendering 3-D strange attractors. *Computers and Graphics*, 12(2), 263-267.

Pickover, C. (1989) Visualization of time-discrete dynamical systems. *Visual Computer*. 5: 375-377.

Synthesizing Nature

Pickover, C. (1989) The fractal simulation of biological shapes. *Proc. Fifth Intl. Meet. Biosteriometrics*. Basel, Switzerland.

Pickover, C. (1988k) Mathematics and Beauty II: A sampling of spirals and "strange" spirals in nature, science, and art. *Leonardo* (May) 21(2): 173-181.

Pickover, C. (1988l) From noise comes beauty: textures reminiscent of rug weavings and wood grains spring from simple formulas (Mathematics and Beauty X). *Computer Graphics World*, March, 11(3): 115-116.

Pickover, C. (1989) How to Design Using Random Walks With Transition Probabilities That Depend on Direction of Motion. *Computer Language*, in press. IBM Res. Rep. (RC 13153).

Pickover, C. (1987j) Mathematics and Beauty IV: Computer graphics and wild monopodial tendril plant growth. *Computer Graphics World*, 10(7): 143-145.

Pickover, C. (1987k) Biomorphs: computer displays of biological forms generated from mathematical feed back loops. *Computer Graphics Forum* 5(4): 313-316.

Image Processing, Turin Shroud

Pickover, C. (1988c) Rendering of the Shroud of Turin using sinusoidal pseudocolor and other image processing techniques, *Computers and Graphics* 12(1): 81-90.

Pickover, C. (1988n) Mathematics and Beauty VII: Visualization of quaternion slices. *Image and Vision Comp.*, November, 6(4): 235-237. (This paper has several color figures).

Pickover, C. (1988o) The use of image processing techniques in rendering maps with deterministic chaos. *The Visual Computer, An Intl. J.* 4: 271-276.

Cellular Automata

Pickover, C. (1989) Mathematics and Beauty VIII: Tesselation automata derived from a single defect. *Comp. and Math. with Appl.* 17: 321-336. Also appears in: Hargittai, I., ed. (1989) *Symmetry 2, Unifying Human Understanding.* Pergamon Press: Oxford.

Numerical Approximation and Physics

Pickover, C. (1989) Chaotic fragmentation in Halley's paradise. *Physica Scripta.* 39: 193-195.

Pickover, C. (1989) Halley maps for a trigonometric and rational function *Comp. and Math. with Appl.*, 17: 125-132. Also appears in: Hargittai, I., ed. (1989) *Symmetry 2, Unifying Human Understanding.* Pergamon Press: Oxford. IBM Res. Rep. (RC 12804).

Pickover, C. (1988p) Symmetry, beauty and chaos in Chebyshev's paradise. *The Visual Computer, An Intl. J.*, 4: 142-147.

Pickover, C. (1988q) A note on Chaos and Halley's method. *Commun. ACM*, November, 31(11) 1326-1329.

Pickover, C. (1988r) Aesthetics and iterative approximation. *Comp. Lang.* November 5(11):53-57.

Pickover, C. (1988s) Overrelaxation and chaos. *Phys. Lett. A.* July 130(3): 125-128.

Pickover, C. (1989) A note on computer experiments with chaotic shattering of level sets. *Computers in Phys.*, Nov/Dec 3(6): 69-73.

Glossary

This is an informal and brief reminder of the meanings of terms (for more detailed descriptions, see the relevant references in the bibliography). Some of the special symbols used in this book are listed within the glossary entry *Symbol*.

Abacus   Instrument for performing calculations by sliding beads along rods or grooves.

Abscissa   The horizontal coordinate of a point in a plane rectangular coordinate system (the x-axis).

Acoustics   The study of sound.

Affine transformation   Loosely speaking, an affine transformation acts by shrinking, enlarging, shifting, rotating or skewing an original pattern, set of points, or object.

Altaic   Belonging to the Altai mountains of central Asia.

Algebraic function   A function containing or using only algebraic symbols and operations such as $2x + x^2 + \sqrt{2}$.

Algebraic operations   Operations of addition, subtraction, multiplication, division, extraction of roots, and raising to integral or fractional powers.

Amplitude   (of a wave) The absolute value of the maximum displacement from zero value during one period of an oscillation.

Analog-to-digital converter   Electronic device that transforms continuous signals into signals with discrete values.

Analytic function   An analytic function is differentiable throughout a neighborhood of each point. It can be shown that an analytic function has continuous derivatives of all orders and can be expanded as a Taylor series. Functions with a power series expansion are analytic.

Angstrom   A unit of measure corresponding to one ten-billionth of a meter.

Amino acid   Basic building blocks of proteins.

Articulation   Movements of the vocal tract to produce speech sounds.

Aspiration   A sound with friction produced at the glottis.

Attack   The initial rise of a waveform.

Attractor   *Predictable attractors* correspond to the behavior to which a system settles down or is "attracted" (for example, a point or a looping closed cycle). The structure of these attractors is simple and well understood. A *strange attractor* is represented by an unpredictable trajectory where a minute difference in starting positions of 2 initially adjacent points leads to totally uncorrelated positions later in time or in the mathematical iteration. The structure of these attractors is very complicated and often not well understood.

Autism   A syndrome characterized by difficulty in forming interpersonal relationships and in developing language.

Autocorrelation   For the acoustic applications in this book, the autocorrelation function for data describes the general dependance of the values of the data at one time on the values at another time.

Autonomous   The behavior of an autonomous dynamical system is expressed by an equation which is independent of time. If a time-dependent term is added, this represents an "external influence" which drives the system away from this equilibrium, for example, by adding or subtracting energy. Systems with a time-dependent term are non-autonomous (an unsteady fluid flow is such a system).

Bifurcation   Any value of a parameter at which the number and/or stability of steady states and cycles changes is called a bifurcation point, and the system is said to undergo a bifurcation.

Bilateral symmetry   The property of having two similar sides. Each side is a "mirror image" of the other.

Binomial coefficients   The coefficients in the expansion of $(x + y)^n$. For example, $(x + y)^2 = x^2 + 2xy + y^2$ so that the binomial coefficients of order 2 are 1, 2 and 1.

Catenary   The curve assumed by a uniform, flexible chain hanging freely from its extremities. Its equation is $f(z) = \cosh(z) = (e^z + e^{-z})/2$.

Cellular automata   A class of simple mathematical systems that are becoming important as models for a variety of physical processes. Though the rules governing the creation of cellular automata are simple, the patterns they produce are complicated and sometimes seem almost random, like a turbulent fluid flow or the output of a cryptographic system. Cellular automata are characterized by the fact that they act on a discrete space or grid as opposed to a continuous medium.

Center   See *limit*.

Chernoff face   A representation of multidimensional data where data parameters are mapped to facial coordinates of a computer-drawn face. These faces were first discussed by Harvard statistician Herman Chernoff, in 1973.

Chaos   Irregular behavior displaying sensitive dependence on initial conditions. Chaos has been referred to by some physicists as the seemingly paradoxical combination of randomness and structure in certain nonperiodic solutions of dynamical systems. Chaotic behavior can sometimes be defined by a simple formula. Some researchers believe that chaos theory offers a mathematical framework for understanding much of the noise and turbulence that is seen in experimental science.

Chaotic trajectory   A chaotic trajectory exhibits three features. 1) The motion stays within a bounded region – it does not get larger and larger without limit. 2) The trajectory never settles into a periodic pattern. 3) The motion exhibits a sensitivity to initial conditions. See also *Chaos*.

Cilia   Minute hair-like processes.

Complex number   A number containing a real and imaginary part, and of the form $a + bi$ where $i = \sqrt{-1}$.

Conservative dynamical systems   In mechanics, conservative dynamical systems, also known as Hamiltonian dynamical systems, are frictionless. These systems do not entail a continual decrease of energy. See also *dissipative dynamical systems*.

Converge   To draw near to. A variable is sometimes said to converge to its limit.

Cycle   The cycle describes predictable periodic motions, like circular orbits. In phase plane portraits, the behavior often appears as smooth closed curves.

Dalton   The mass of one hydrogen atom (1.67×10^{-24} grams).

Damp   To diminish progressively in amplitude of oscillation.

Dichotomous   branching   Dividing into two parts. With dichotomous (or polychotomous) branching, a branch divided into two (or many) directions,

and each branch goes in a different direction from the original. See also *monopodial branching*.

Differential   equations   Equations often of the form $dx_i/dt = f_i(x)$ where $x_i(t)$ represents the ith variable and the function $f_i(x)$ gives the time, or spatial, evolution of $x_i(t)$. Mathematical models in the physical and biological sciences are often formulated as differential equations.

Dissipative dynamical systems   These are systems typical of the macroscopic engineering world in which some resisting source causes energy loss. In dissipative dynamical systems the volume of phase space occupied by an ensemble of starting points decreases with time. See also *conservative dynamical systems*.

Disulfide bond   A strong sulfur-to-sulfur chemical bond

Dynamical   systems   Models containing the rules describing the way a given quantity undergoes a change through time or iteration steps. For example, the motion of planets about the sun can be modelled as a dynamical system in which the planets move according to Newton's laws. A discrete dynamical system can be represented mathematically as $x_{t+1} = f(x_t)$. A continuous dynamical system can be expressed as $dx/dt = f(x,t)$.

Feedback   The return to the input of a part of the output of a system.

Fibonacci   sequence   The sequence $1,1,2,3,5,8,13 \ldots$, ($F_n = F_{n-2} + F_{n-1}$), which governs many patterns in the plant world.

Finite difference equations   Equations often of the form $x_i(t + 1) = f_i(x(t))$ where $x_i(t)$ represents the value of the *i*th component at a time, or other coordinate, *t*.

Fixed point A point which is invariant under the mapping (i.e., $x_t = x_{t+1}$ for discrete systems, or $x = f(x)$ for continuous systems). A particular kind of fixed point is a *center*. For a center, nearby trajectories neither approach nor diverge from the fixed point. In contrast to the center, for a *hyperbolic fixed point*, some nearby trajectories approach and some diverge from the fixed point. A *saddle point* is an example of a hyperbolic fixed point. An *unstable fixed point* (or repulsive fixed point or repelling fixed point) *x* of a function occurs when $f'(x) > 0$. A *stable fixed point* (or attractive fixed point) *x* of a function occurs when $f'(x) < 0$. For cases where $f'(x) = 0$ higher derivatives need to be considered.

Focus (of a conic section) A conic section is a set of points for which the distances of each from a fixed point called the *focus* and from a fixed line called the directrix are in constant ratio.

Folium of Descartes A plane curve represented in rectangular coordinates by $x^3 + y^3 = 3axy$.

Fourier analysis The separation of a complex wave into its sinusoidal components.

Fractals Objects (or sets of points, or curves, or patterns) which exhibit increasing detail ("bumpiness") with increasing magnification. Many interesting fractals are self-similar. B. Mandelbrot informally defines fractals as "shapes that are equally complex in their details as in their overall form. That is, if a piece of a fractal is suit-ably magnified to become of the same size as the whole, it should look like the whole, either exactly, or perhaps only after slight limited deformation."

Formant A group of overtones corresponding to a resonant frequency of the air in the vocal tract. Vowels can be characterized with three to five formants. Formants are displayed in a spectrogram as broad bands of energy.

Fricative Sounds produced by turbulent air flow, such as the English "s." In general, these are high frequency sounds produced by forcing air through a narrow aperture.

Fundamental frequency The lowest frequency component of a complex tone.

Gasket A piece of material from which sections have been removed. *Mathematical gaskets*, such as Sierpiński gaskets, can be generated by removing sections of a region according to some rule. Usually the process of removal leaves pieces which are similar to the initial region, thus the gasket may be defined recursively.

Gaussian white noise White noise which is subsequently altered so that it has a bell-shaped distribution of values. In this book, Gaussian noise is often approximated by summing random numbers. The reader may also wish to use the following formula which will generate a Gaussian distribution: $r = \sqrt{-\log(r_1)} \times \cos(2\pi r_2)\sigma + \mu$, where r_1 and r_2 are two random numbers from a $(0,1]$ uniform distribution, and σ and μ are the desired standard deviation and mean of the Gaussian distribution.

Glottis The space between the vocal folds.

Invariant curve Generalization of a *fixed point* to a line (in this case, a *curve* is invariant under the map or flow).

Harmonic An oscillation whose frequency is an integral multiple of the fundamental frequency.

Helix A space curve lying on a cylinder (or sphere, or cone) which maintains a constant distance from a central line (i.e. a "spiral extended in space").

Henon map The Henon map defines the point (x_{n+1}, y_{n+1}) by the equations $x_{n+1} = 1.4 + 0.3y_n - x_n^2$, $y_{n+1} = x_n$. Note that there are various expressions for the Henon map, including $x_{n+1} = 1 + y_n - \alpha x_n^2$, $y_{n+1} = \beta x_n$.

Homeomorphism This is best explained by an example. Consider a circle inside a square. Draw a line from the circle's center out through the circle and square. The line intersects the circle at point P and the square at P'. The mapping $g:P \rightarrow P'$ assigns to each point of the circle a point of the square and vice versa. In addition, two adjacent points on one shape are mapped to two adjacent points of the other. The mapping g is a *homeomorphism*. The circle and triangle are *homeomorphic*.

Hypernasality A voice quality characterized by excessive nasal resonance.

Hyponasality A voice quality characterized by inadequate nasal resonance.

In phase Two signals with pressure waves that crest and trough at the same time.

Inf See *symbol*.

Intensity Magnitude of sound expressed in power or pressure.

Iteration Repetition of an operation or set of operations. In mathematics, composing a function with itself, such as in $f(f(x))$, can represent an iteration. The computational process of determining x_{i+1} given x_i is called an iteration.

Julia set Set of all points which do not converge to a fixed point or finite attracting orbit under repeated applications of the map. Most Julia sets are fractals, displaying an endless cascade of repeated detail. An alternate definition: repeated applications of a function f determine a trajectory of successive locations $x, f(x), f(f(x))$, $f(f(f(x)))$, ... visited by a starting point x in the complex plane. Depending on the starting point, this results in two types of trajectories, those which go to infinity and those which remain bounded by a fixed radius. The Julia set of the function f is the boundary curve which separates these regions.

Limit In general, the ultimate value towards which a variable tends.

Linear transformation A relation where the output is directly proportional to the input. A function satisfying two conditions: 1) $F(\vec{p} + \vec{q}) = F(\vec{p}) + F(\vec{q})$ and 2) $F(r\vec{p}) = rF(\vec{p})$.

Logistic equation The nonlinear equation $x_{n+1} = kx_n(1 - x_n)$ is called the logistic equation, and it has been used in ecology as a model for predicting population growth.

Lotka-Volterra equations The Hamiltonian system defined by $(dx/dt = ax - bxy$, $dy/dt = -cy + dxy)$, which was one of the first predator-prey equations which predicted cylic variations in population.

Lorenz attractor $\dot{x} = -10x + 10y$, $\dot{y} = 40x - y - xz$, $\dot{z} = -8z/3 + xy$. Initially the system starts anywhere in the three-dimensional phase space, but as transients die away the system is attracted onto a two-lobed surface. For a more general formulation, the Lorenz equations are sometimes written with variable coefficients.

Loudness The subjective, psychological sensation of sound intensity.

Lyapunov exponent

Lyapunov exponent A quantity, sometimes represented by the Greek letter Λ, used to characterize the divergence of trajectories in a chaotic flow. For a 1-D formula, such as the logistic equation, $\Lambda = \lim\limits_{N \to \infty} 1/N \sum\limits_{n=1}^{N} \ln |dx_{n+1}/dx_n|$.

Mandelbrot set For each complex number μ let $f_\mu(x)$ denote the polynomial $x^2 + \mu$. The Mandelbrot set is defined as the set of values of μ for which successive iterates of 0 under f_μ do not converge to infinity. An alternate definition: the set of complex numbers μ for which the *Julia set* of the iterated mapping $z \to z^2 + \mu$ separates disjoint regions of attraction. When μ lies outside this set, the corresponding Julia set is fragmented. The term "Mandelbrot Set" is originally associated with this quadratic formula, although the same construction gives rise to a (generalized) Mandelbrot Set for any iterated function with a complex parameter.

Markov process A stochastic process in which the "future" is determined by the "present."

Manifold Curve or surface. The classical *attractors* are manifolds (they're smooth). Strange *attractors* are not manifolds (they're rough and fractal).

Monopodial branching The formation of offshoots from a main axis. A branch divides in two at the growth point, and one follows the direction of the main axis while the other goes in a different direction to form a lateral branch. See also *dichotomous branching.*

Nasal a sound in which the soft palate is lowered so that there is no velic closure, and air may go out through the nose, as in English "m."

Nasalization Lowering of the soft palate during a sound in which air is going out through the mouth, as in the vowel between nasals in English "mom."

Newton's method A method of approximating roots of equations. Suppose the equation is $f(x) = 0$, and a_1 is an approximation to the roots. The next approximation, a_2, is found by $a_2 = a_1 - f(a_1)/f'(a_1)$, where f' is the derivative of f.

Nonlinear equation Equations where the output is not directly proportional to the input. Equations which describe the behavior of most real-world problems. The response of a nonlinear system can depend crucially upon initial conditions.

Oncogenes Genetic sequences which have been detected in tumors representative of each of the major forms of human cancer. Some oncogenes have been shown to be able to induce malignant transformations in certain cell lines.

Oral sounds Sounds which are resonated in the mouth.

Perfect numbers   An integer which is the sum of all its divisors excluding itself. For example, 6 is a perfect number since 6=1+2+3.

Period   The time taken for one cycle of vibration of a wave.

Periodic   Recurring at equal intervals of time.

Phase-locked loop   A circuit consisting of a phase detector which compares the frequency of a voltage controlled oscillator with that of an incoming signal. The output of the phase detector is fed back to the voltage-controlled oscillator in order to keep it in phase with the incoming signal.

Phase portrait   The overall picture formed by all possible initial conditions in the $(x, \dot{x})$ plane is referred to as the phase portrait. Consider a pendulum's motion which comes to rest due to air resistance. In the abstract two-dimensional *phase space* (with coordinates x, the displacement, and $\dot{x}$ the velocity) motions appear as noncrossing spirals converging asymptotically towards the resting, fixed state. This focus is called a *point attractor* which attracts all local transient motions.

Plosive   A type of consonant sound made by sudden release of air impounded behind an occlusion of the vocal tract.

Poincare map   A Poincare map is established by cutting trajectories in a region of phase space with a surface one dimension less than the dimension of the phase space.

Polychotomous   branching   See *dichotomous branching.*

Polynomial   An algebraic expression of the form $a_0x^n + a_1x^{n-1} + \cdots a_{n-1}x + a_n$ where n is the degree of the expression and $a_0 \neq 0$.

Quasiperiodicity   Informally defined as a phenomenon with multiple periodicity. One example is the astronomical position of a point on the surface of the earth, since it results from the rotation of the earth about its axis and the rotation of the earth around the sun.

Quadratic mapping   Also known as the *logistic map*, this famous discrete dynamical system is defined by $x_{t+1} = cx_t(1 - x_t)$.

Quaternion   A 4-dimensional "hyper" complex number of the form $Q = a_0 + a_1i + a_2j + a_3k$.

Pure tone   A sound with a single sine wave component.

Rational function   A function which can be expressed as the quotient of two polynomials.

Recursive   An object is said to be recursive if it partially consists of or is defined in terms of itself. A *recursive operation* invokes itself as an intermediate operation.

Resonance   Vibratory response to an applied force. A vibration of large amplitude caused by a relatively small periodic stimulus.

Sierpiński gasket   See *gasket.*

Steady state   Also called equilibrium point or *fixed point*. A set of values of the variables of a system for which the system does not change as time proceeds.

Strange attractor   See *attractor.*

Stress   In speech science, the use of extra respiratory energy during a syllable.

Sup   See *symbol*.

Symbol   A letter or mark representing quantities, relations, or operations. To aid the reader, the following lists some of the special mathematical symbols used in the book: z or ζ, a complex number; $|z|$, the modulus of z; Re z, the real part of z; Im z, the imaginary part of z; $\pi(n)$, the number of primes which are not greater than n; *cosh*, the hyperbolic cosine; *inf*, the greatest lower bound; *sup*, the least upper bound; $\dot{s}$, the derivative of s with respect to t; $f \circ g$, the composition of f and g; $p \wedge q$, p and q; $p \vee q$, p or q; $T_n(x)$, the Tchebychef polynomial of degree n; μ, a complex number constant.

Tesselation   A division of a plane into polygons, regular or irregular.

Timbre   The quality given to a sound by its overtones.

Trajectory   A seqence of points in which each point produces its suc-cessor according to some mathematical function.

Transfinite number   An infinite cardinal or ordinal number. The smallest transfinite number is called "aleph-nought" (written as $\aleph_0$) which counts the number of integers.

Tractrix   A plane curve represented in parametric equations by $x = a(\ln \cot \phi/2 - \cos \phi)$, $y = a \sin \phi$.

Transcendental functions   Functions which are not algebraic, for example, circular, exponential, and logarithmic functions.

Transformation   The operation of changing (as by rotation or mapping) one configuration or expression into another in accordance with a mathematical rule.

Velum   The soft, movable part of the palate at the back of the mouth.

Waveform   A curve that represents the condition of a wave-propagating medium at a given instant. Also called a *wave shape*.

Witch of Agnesi   A plane curve represented in rectangular coordinates by $y = 8a^3/(x^2 + 4a^2)$.

Index

Credits

All of the presented computer graphics and pseudocode were created by the author. Some of the computer graphics have appeared previously in published papers (see list below and references). The drawings and photographs of nature and ancient human cultures (plants, shells, carpets, etc.) come from the *Dover Pictorial Archive* (Mineola, New York). See the reference sections for specific titles of Dover books.

The quotations interspersed throughout the book come from a variety of sources. The quotation by Sven G. Carlson on art and science appeared in his letter to *Science News* (Vol. 132, 1987, pg. 382). Quotations by Ronald Graham and Paul Erdös were excerpted from Paul Hoffman's excellent article ("The Man Who Loves Only Numbers," Nov. 1987, *The Atlantic Magazine*, pg. 60). The Einstein quotation in the preface appeared in Martin Gardner's article "Order and Surprise," Vol. 17, The Philosophy of Science (1985) pg. 109. The French quotation in Chapter 2 comes from S. Luria's book, *Life: The Unfinished Experiment*. The cartoons "Nonlinear dynamical system" and "Creating chaos out of order" are from a large collection of drawings ©1988 by Jacques Boivin. The quotation by Peter B. Schroeder comes from his December 1986 article in *Byte Magazine* (pg. 207). Many of the statistics on computers and the human brain in Chapter 2 come from the *Guinness Book of World Records*. Dr. Padmanabhan Santhanam provided the sample of Tamil writing.

Many of the author's computer graphics images have appeared in published papers. Listed below are some sources. Figure 3.4 appeared in *Computer Music Journal* and is ©1986 by Massachusetts Institute of Technology. Figure 3.5 appeared in *Science Magazine* and is ©1984 by AAAS. Figure 3.6 appeared in *The Journal of Molecular Graphics* and is ©1984 by Butterworth & Co. Figure 4.1, and the following few figures, appeared in *J. Acoust. Soc. Amer.* Figure 4.5 appeared in *IBM Tech. Discl. Bull.* Figure 4.9 and other face figures appeared in *J. Educat. Tech. Syst.* and are ©1985 by Baywood Publishing, Inc. Figure 4.18, and other DNA-vectorgram figures, appeared in *IBM J. Res. Devel.* The distance-tower in the color plates section appeared in *Comput. in Phys.* Figure 8.7 appeared in *Comput. Graph. Forum.* Various network figures such as Figure 10.3 appeared in *Commun. ACM.* Figure 12.7, Figure 13.11, and

Figure 13.21 appeared in *Comput. Graph. World.* Figure 2.4 appeared in *Comput. Lang.* Figure 12.18 and other spiral designs appeared in *Leonardo.* Many figures appeared in *Comput. and Graph.*, including Figure 4.15, Figure 5.6, and Figure 14.2. Most of the figures in "Tesselation Automata Derived from a Single Defect" on page 295 and "Numerical Approximation Methods" on page 275 appear in *Comp. and Math. with Appl.*, and also in: Hargittai, I., ed. (1989) *Symmetry 2, Unifying Human Understanding.* Pergamon Press: Oxford.

A Final Illustration of Chaos

"Chaos in the Pit of Doublivores
(Animals that Eat at Both Ends)"
- J. Grandville (*Un Autre Monde*)

Acknowledgements

I thank M. Henderson for assistance in classifying some of the behavior of dynamical systems appearing in this book and for other mathematical suggestions. C. Bennett introduced me to tesselation automata Type 4A. Artist Jacques Boivin has been a friend for many years, and I thank him for the use of his wonderful cartoons. S. Ulrich, J. Shutt, C. Reynolds, B. Grossman, A. Lakhtakia, K. McCarty, E. Adams, P. Pattnaik, L. Cohen, Y. Epelboin, E. Khorasani, and G. Ditlow provided helpful comments over the years. B. McAuliffe and J. Dunkin provided text processing assistance. I thank Dr. Don Engelman, Dr. Ira Feit, and Dr. John Thomas for their earlier support and guidance.

I thank my family for their continued support. The attitude of family members towards each other shapes one's attitude forever towards the world.

About the Author

Clifford A. Pickover received his Ph.D. from Yale University's Department of Molecular Biophysics and Biochemistry. He graduated first in his class from Franklin and Marshall College, after completing the four-year undergraduate program in three years. Pickover is currently an associate editor for the international journal *Computers and Graphics* and is a member of the editorial board for *Computers in Physics* and *Speculations in Science and Technology*. He is also a guest editor for *Computers in Physics*, for a special issue on chaos, and a member of the Book Review panel for *Leonardo*, an international journal on topics in art and science. Dr. Pickover's primary interest is in scientific visualization.

In 1990, he received first prize in the Institute of Physics "Beauty of Physics Photographic Competition." His research has recently received considerable attention by the press – including *CNN*'s "Science and Technology Week," *Science News*, and *The Washington Post* – and also in international exhibitions and museums. *Omni* magazine recently described him as "Van Leeuwenhoek's twentieth century equivalent." The July 1989 issue of *Scientific American* featured his graphic work, calling it "strange and beautiful, stunningly realistic." Pickover has received several awards for various inventions in the areas of novel computer input devices and display methodologies. He can be reached in care of the publisher.